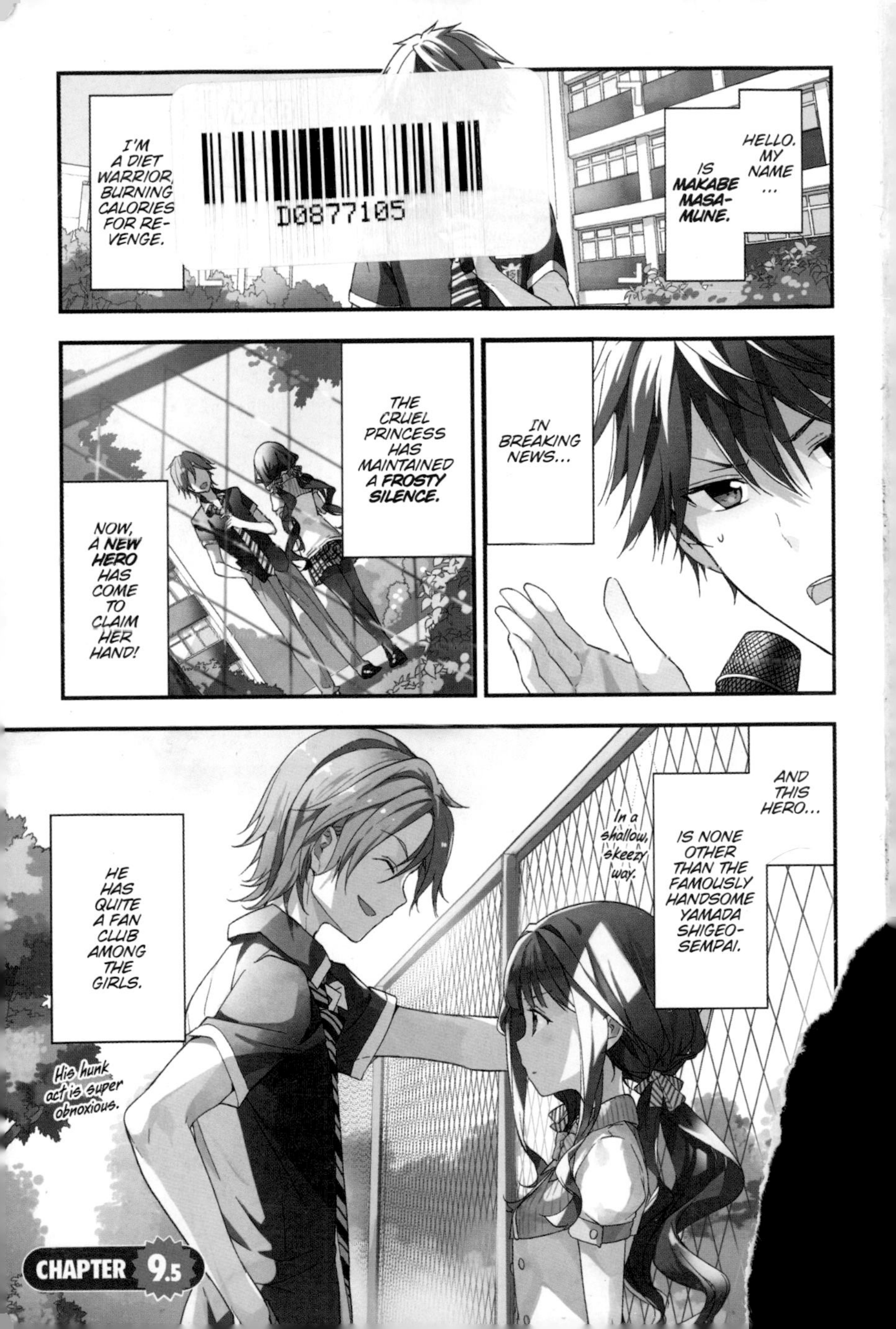
HELLO. MY NAME... IS MAKABE MASAMUNE.
I'M A DIET WARRIOR, BURNING CALORIES FOR REVENGE.
IN BREAKING NEWS...
THE CRUEL PRINCESS HAS MAINTAINED A FROSTY SILENCE.
NOW, A NEW HERO HAS COME TO CLAIM HER HAND!
AND THIS HERO...
IS NONE OTHER THAN THE FAMOUSLY HANDSOME YAMADA SHIGEO-SEMPAI.
In a shallow, skeezy way.
HE HAS QUITE A FAN CLUB AMONG THE GIRLS.
His hunk act is super obnoxious.
CHAPTER 9.5

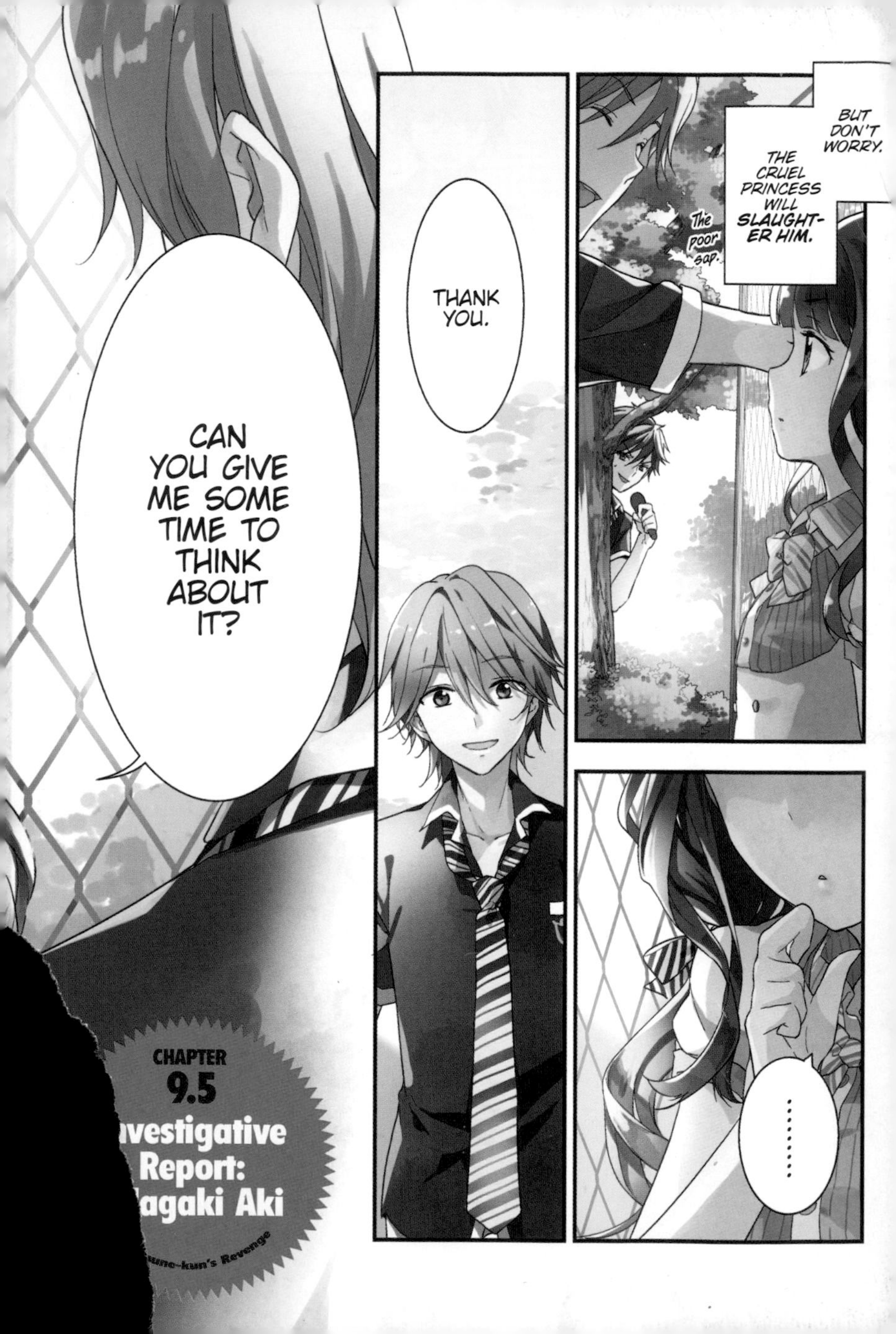

BUT DON'T WORRY.
THE CRUEL PRINCESS WILL SLAUGHTER HIM.
The poor sap.
......
THANK YOU.
CAN YOU GIVE ME SOME TIME TO THINK ABOUT IT?
CHAPTER 9.5
vestigative Report:
agaki Aki
une-kun's Revenge

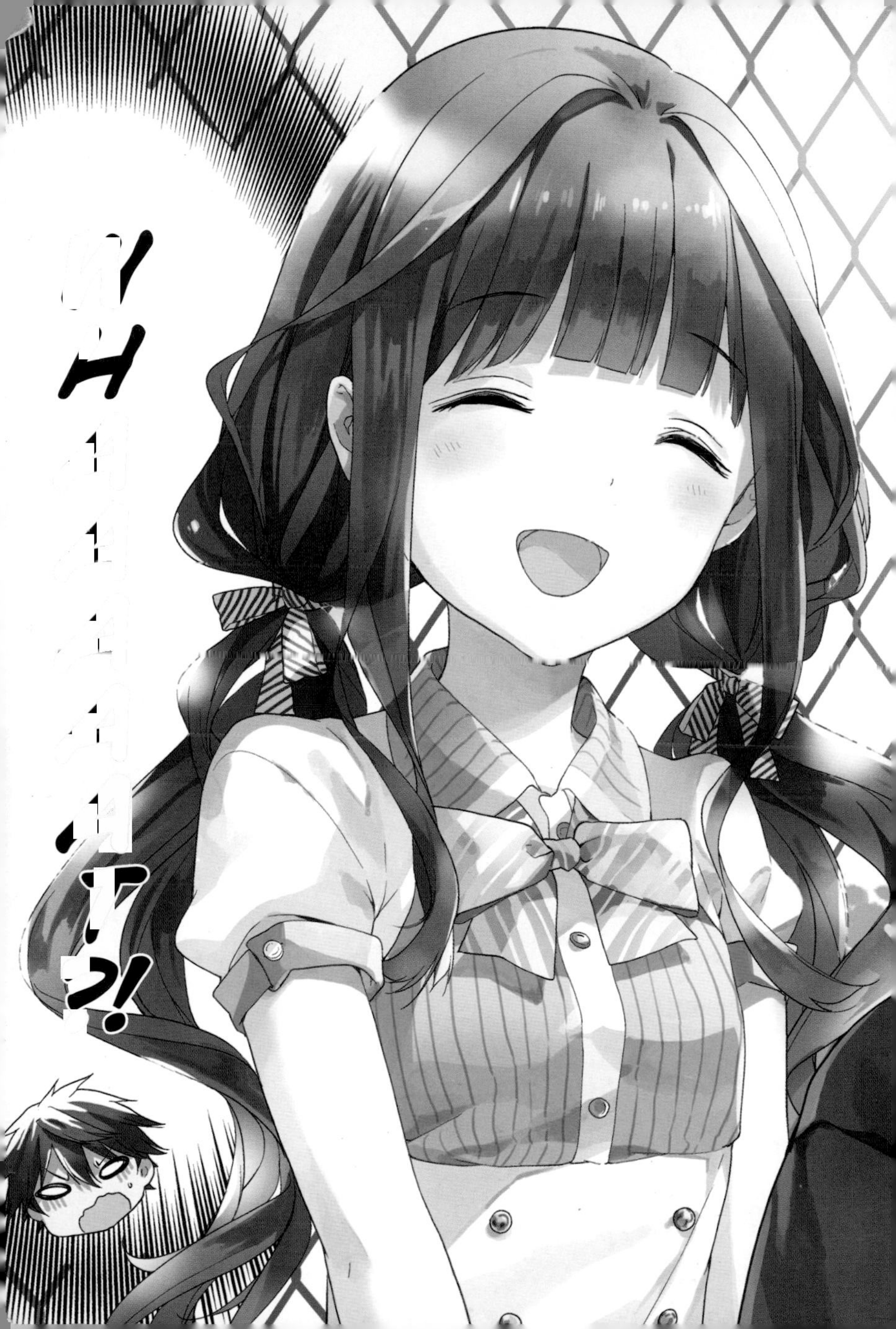

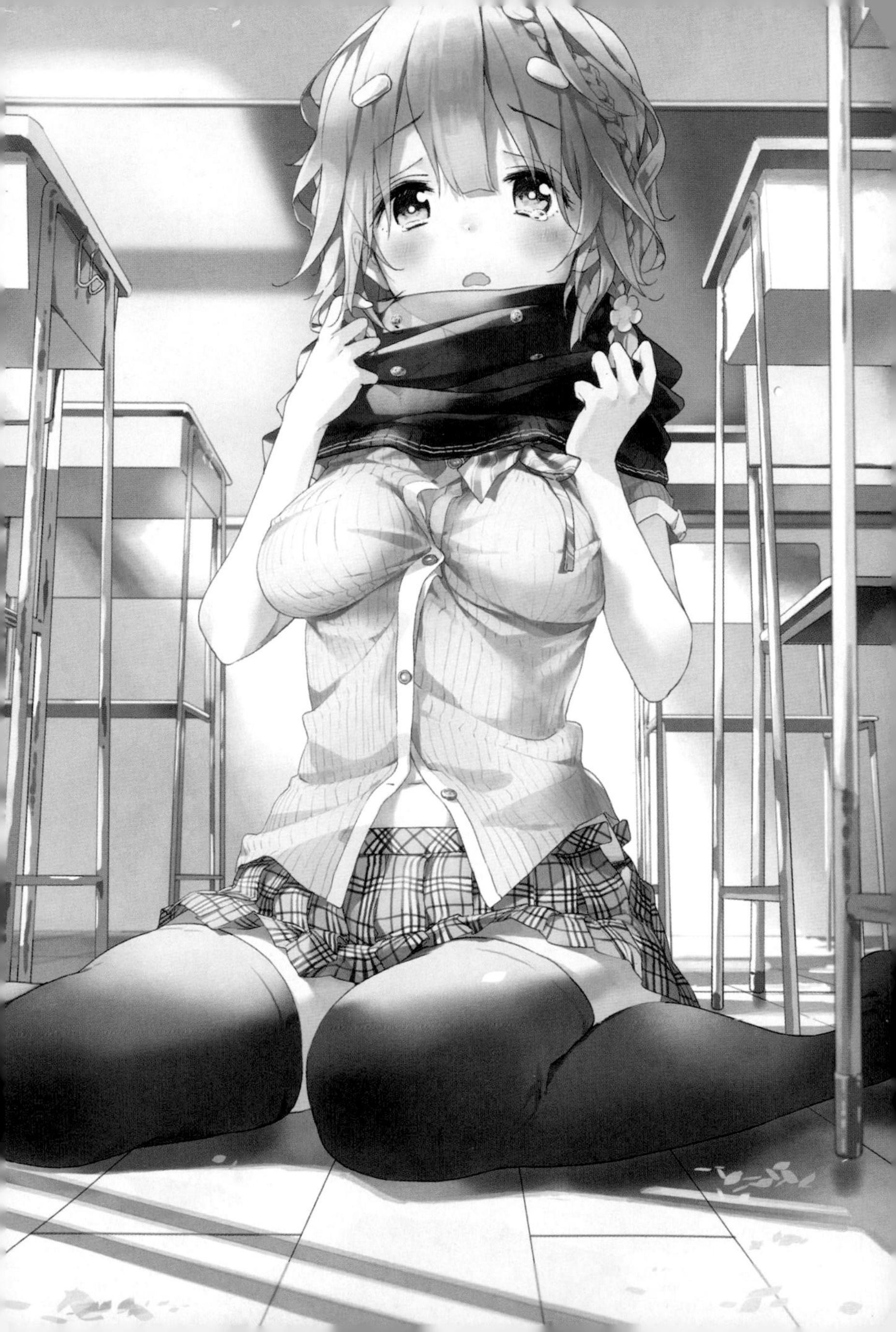

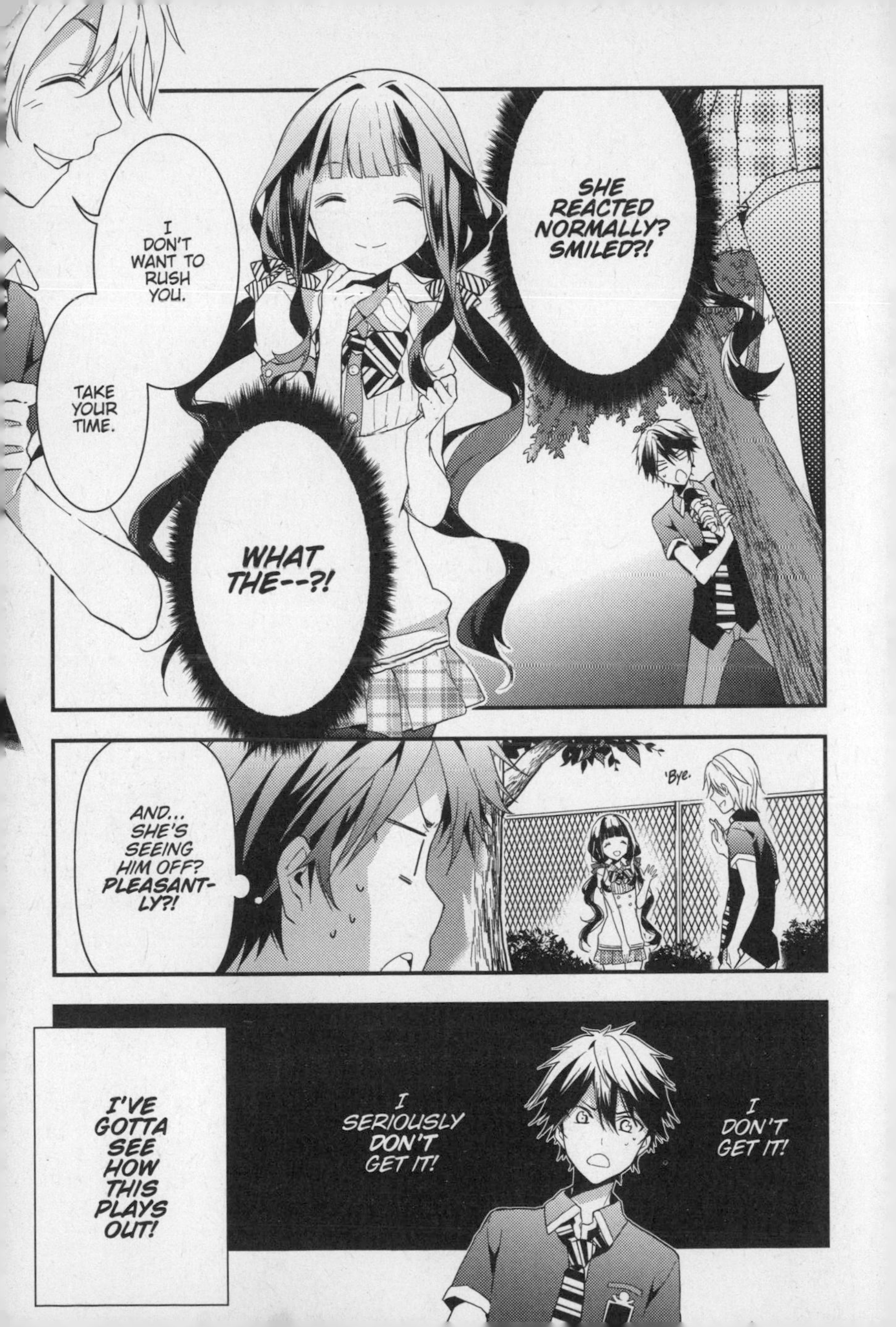
SHE REACTED NORMALLY? SMILED?!
I DON'T WANT TO RUSH YOU.
TAKE YOUR TIME.
WHAT THE--?!
'Bye.
AND... SHE'S SEEING HIM OFF? PLEASANTLY?!
I DON'T GET IT!
I SERIOUSLY DON'T GET IT!
I'VE GOTTA SEE HOW THIS PLAYS OUT!

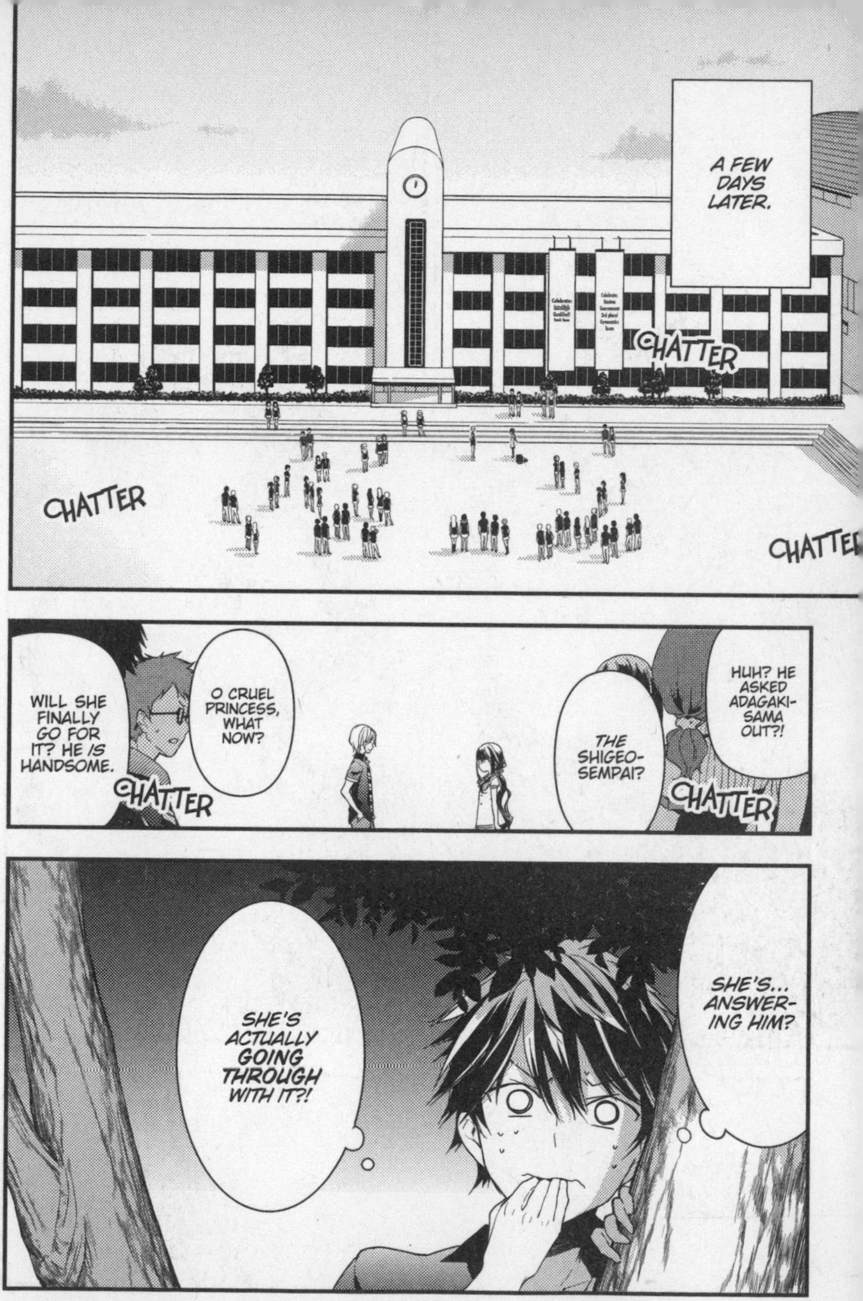
A FEW DAYS LATER.
CHATTER
CHATTER
CHATTER
HUH? HE ASKED ADAGAKI-SAMA OUT?!
THE SHIGEO-SEMPAI?
CHATTER
O CRUEL PRINCESS, WHAT NOW?
WILL SHE FINALLY GO FOR IT? HE IS HANDSOME.
CHATTER
SHE'S... ANSWERING HIM?
SHE'S ACTUALLY GOING THROUGH WITH IT?!

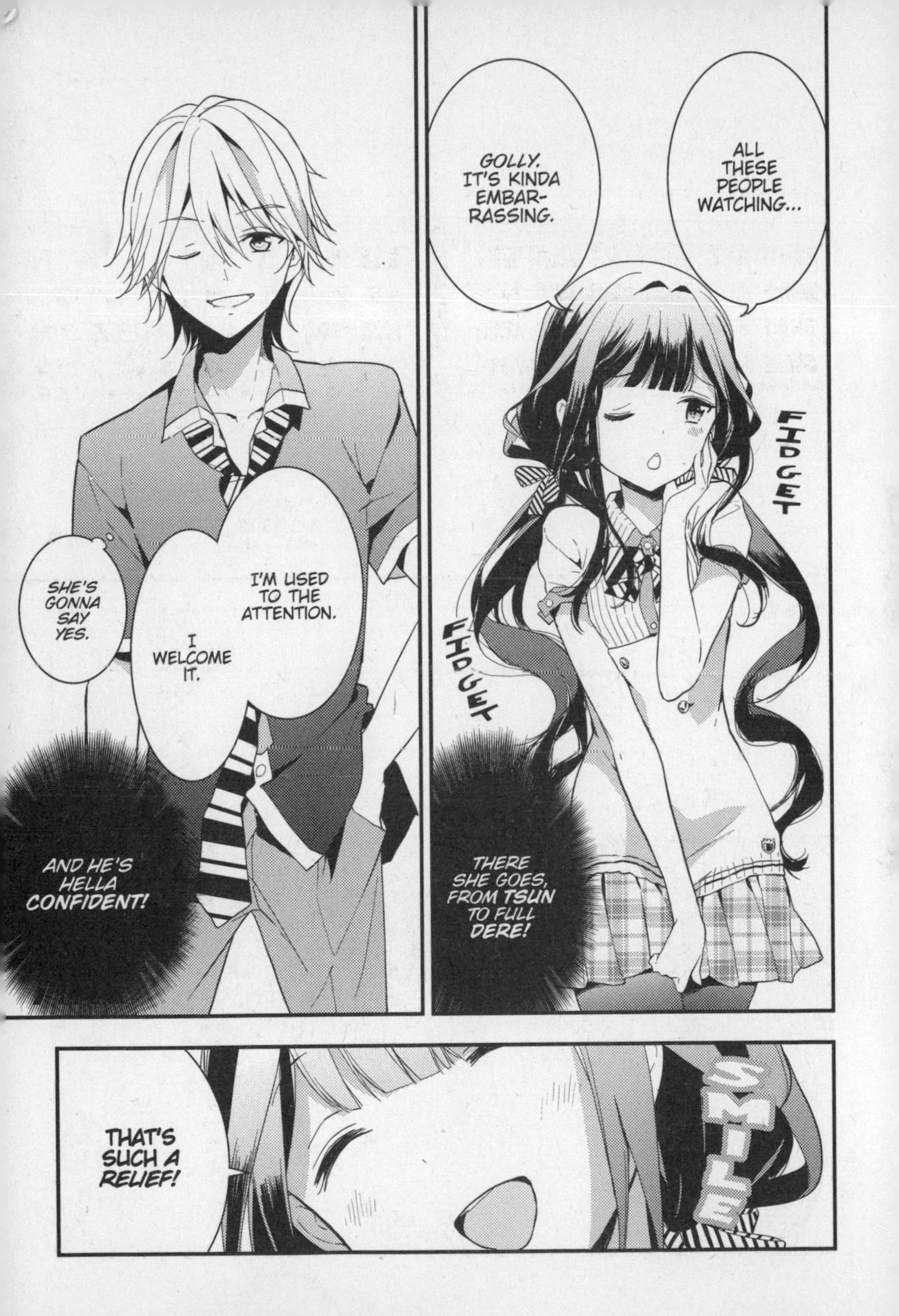
ALL THESE PEOPLE WATCHING...
GOLLY. IT'S KINDA EMBAR-RASSING.
FIDGET
FIDGET
THERE SHE GOES, FROM TSUN TO FULL DERE!
I'M USED TO THE ATTENTION.
I WELCOME IT.
SHE'S GONNA SAY YES.
AND HE'S HELLA CONFIDENT!
SMILE
THAT'S SUCH A RELIEF!

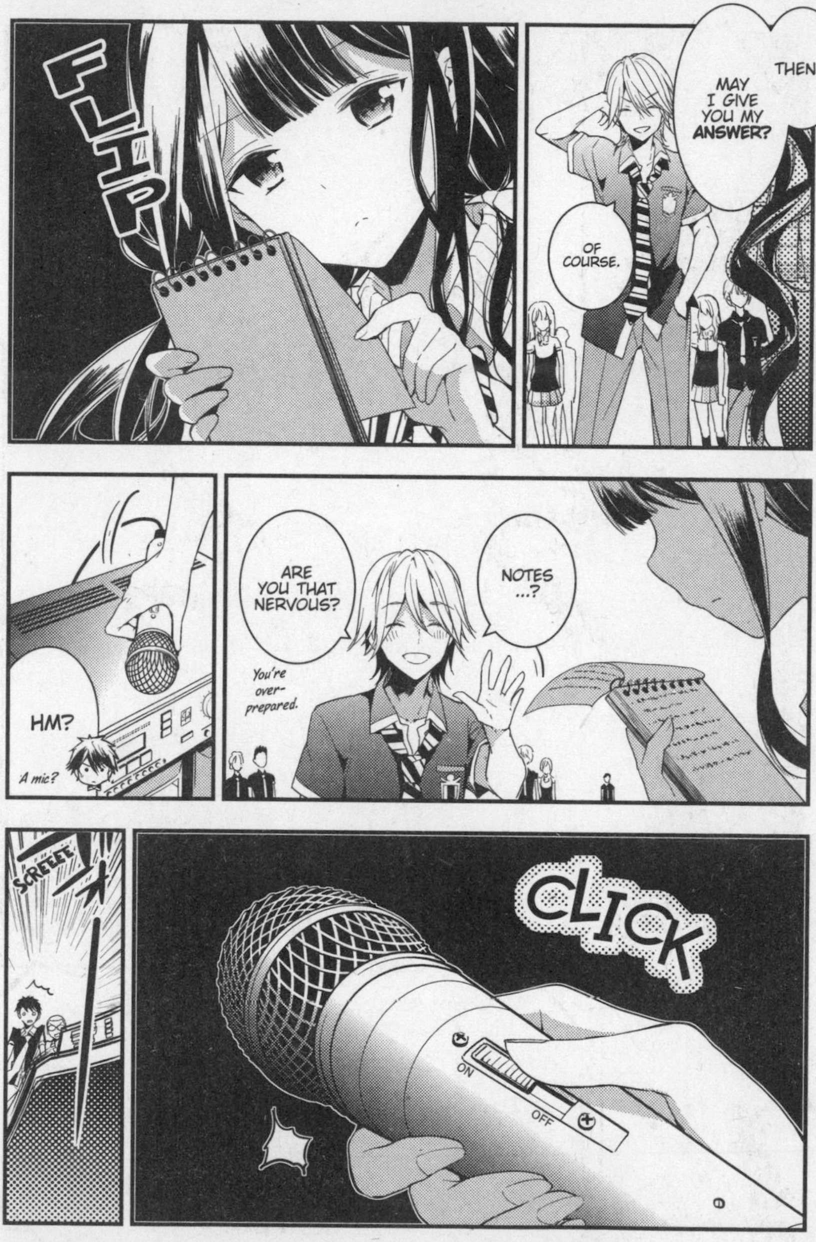
THEN... MAY I GIVE YOU MY ANSWER?
OF COURSE.
FLIP
NOTES ...?
ARE YOU THAT NERVOUS?
You're over-prepared.
HM?
A mic?
CLICK
ON
OFF
SCREEEE

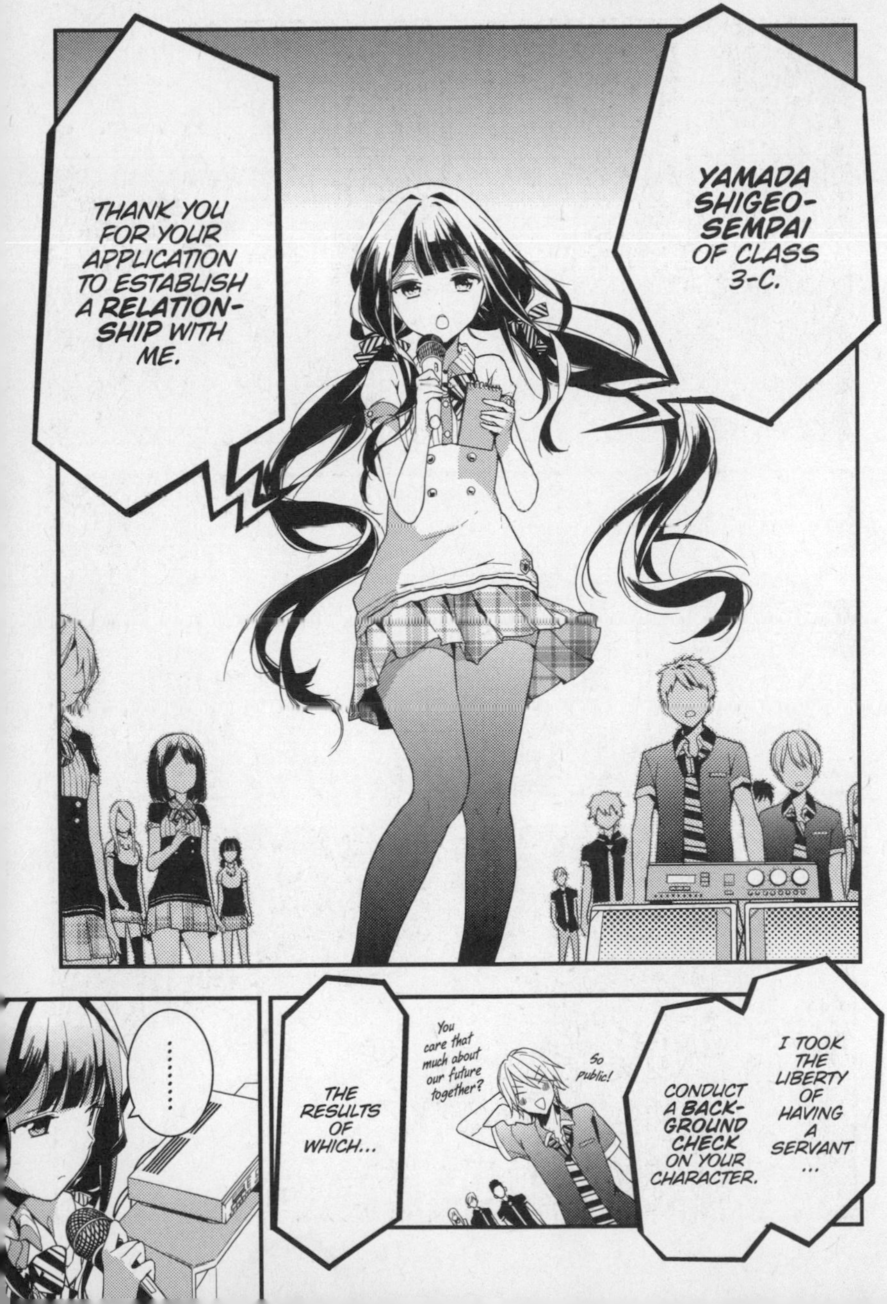
YAMADA SHIGEO-SEMPAI OF CLASS 3-C.
THANK YOU FOR YOUR APPLICATION TO ESTABLISH A RELATIONSHIP WITH ME.
I TOOK THE LIBERTY OF HAVING A SERVANT ...
CONDUCT A BACKGROUND CHECK ON YOUR CHARACTER.
So public!
You care that much about our future together?
THE RESULTS OF WHICH...
......

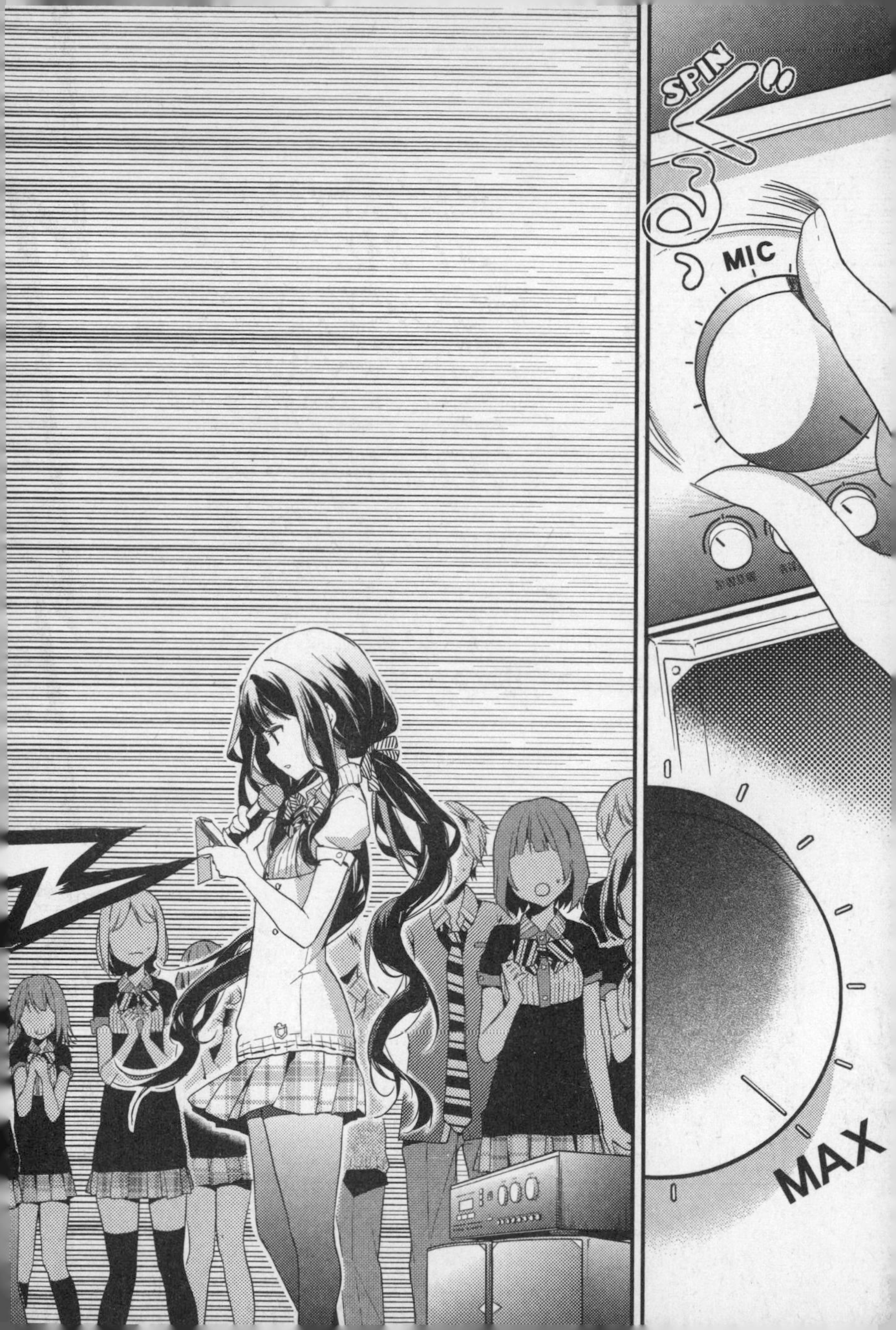
SPIN
MIC
MAX

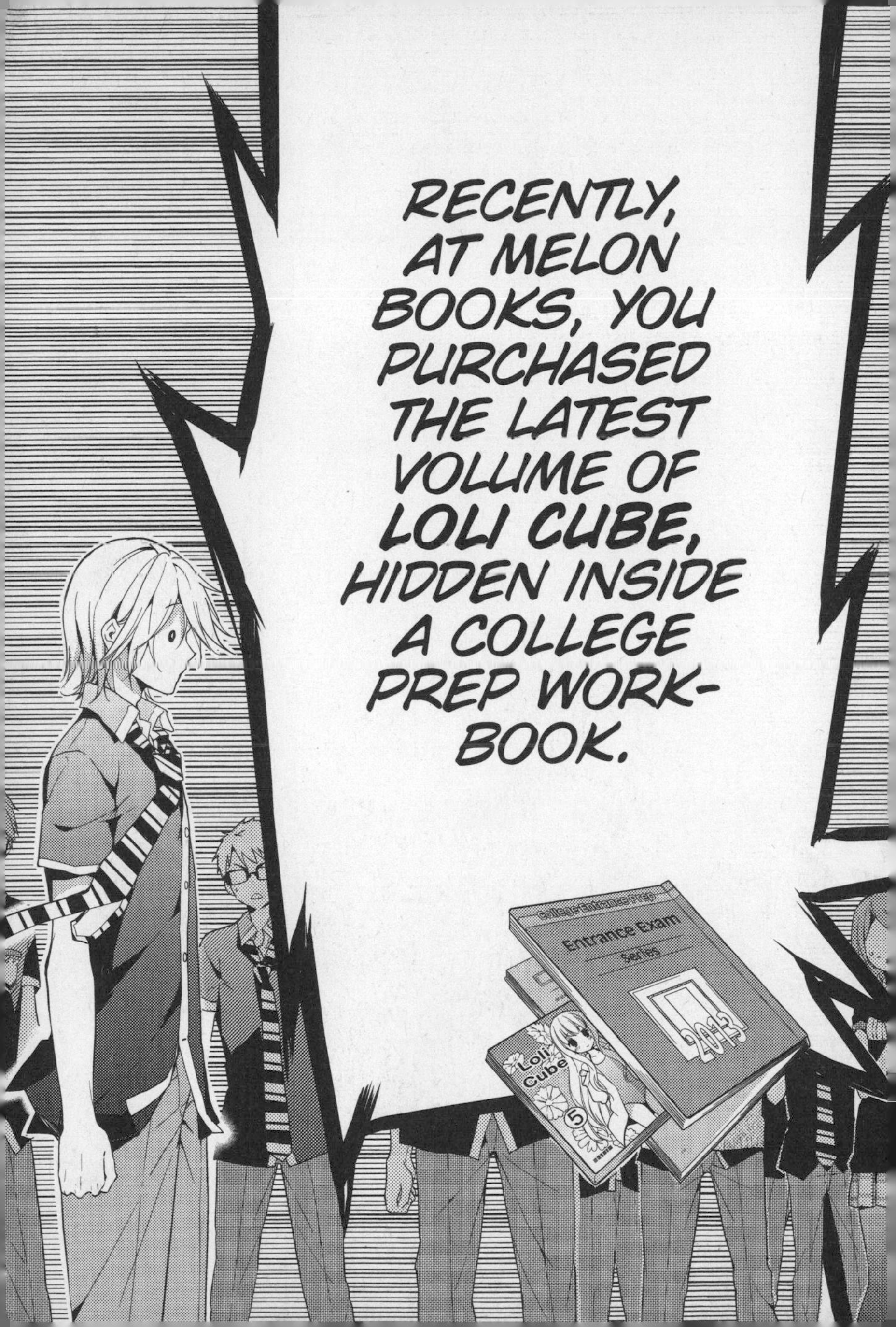
RECENTLY, AT MELON BOOKS, YOU PURCHASED THE LATEST VOLUME OF LOLI CUBE, HIDDEN INSIDE A COLLEGE PREP WORK-BOOK.
College Entrance Prep
Entrance Exam
Series
2013
Loli Cube
5

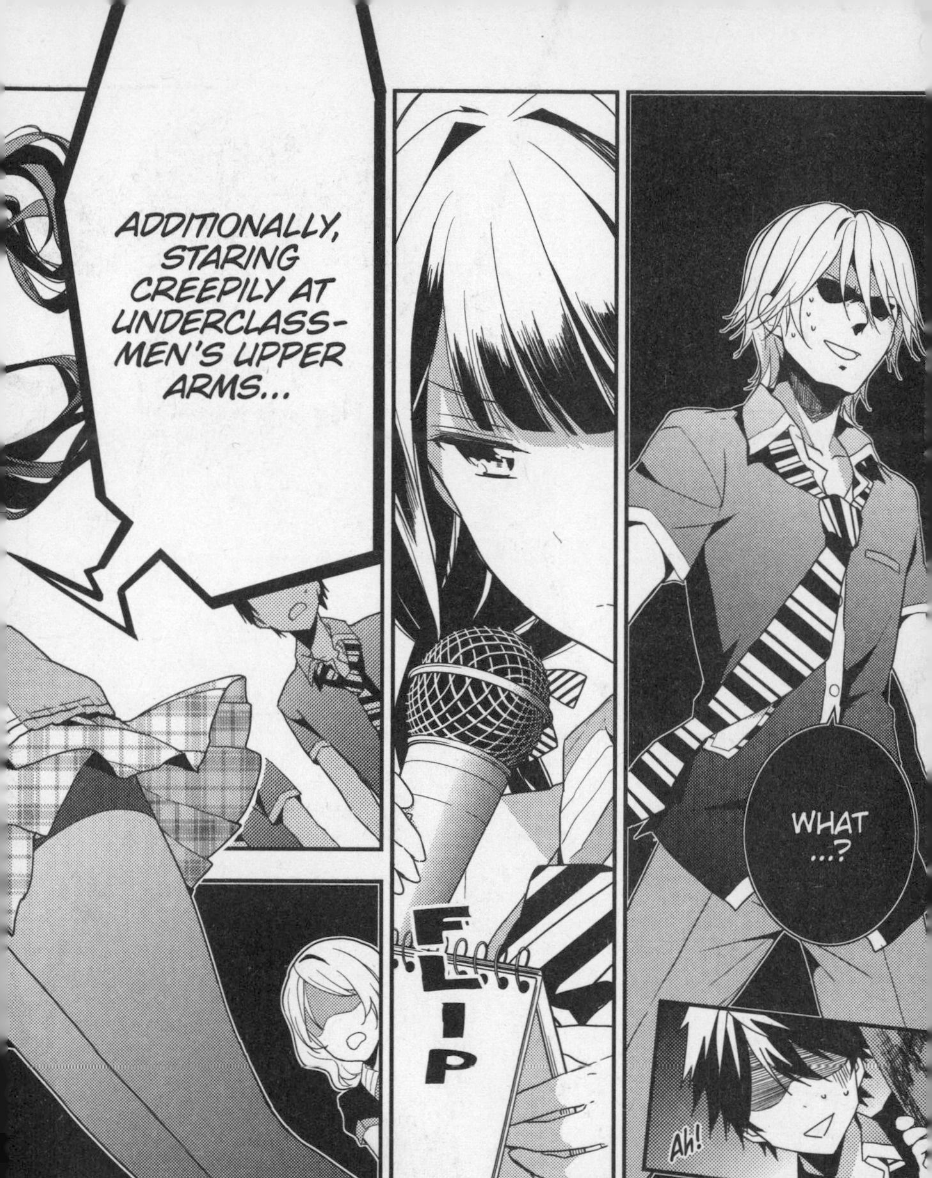
WHAT ...?
Ah!
FLIP
ADDITIONALLY, STARING CREEPILY AT UNDERCLASS-MEN'S UPPER ARMS...

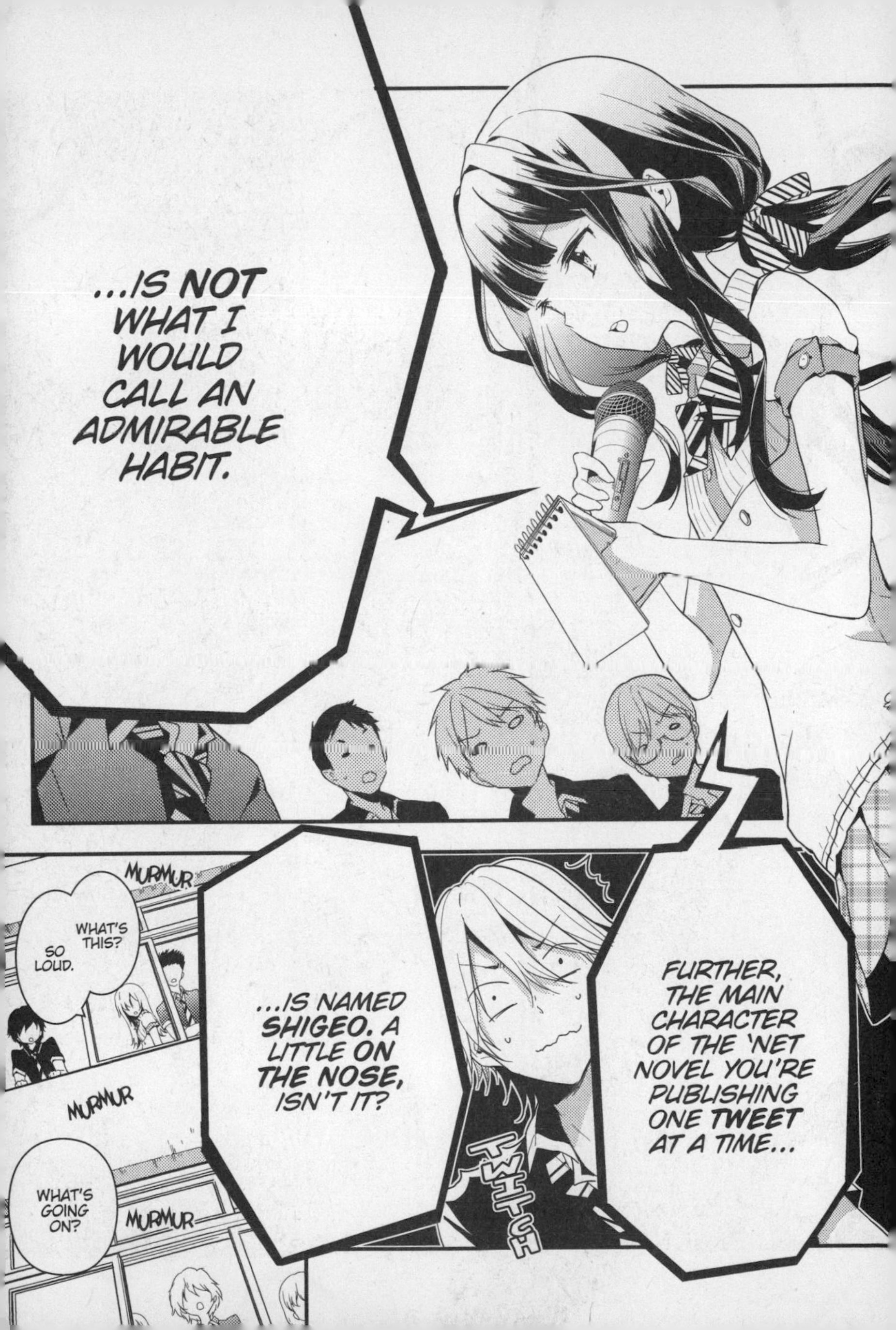
...IS NOT WHAT I WOULD CALL AN ADMIRABLE HABIT.
FURTHER, THE MAIN CHARACTER OF THE 'NET NOVEL YOU'RE PUBLISHING ONE TWEET AT A TIME...
...IS NAMED SHIGEO. A LITTLE ON THE NOSE, ISN'T IT?
TWITCH
MURMUR
WHAT'S THIS?
SO LOUD.
MURMUR
WHAT'S GOING ON?
MURMUR

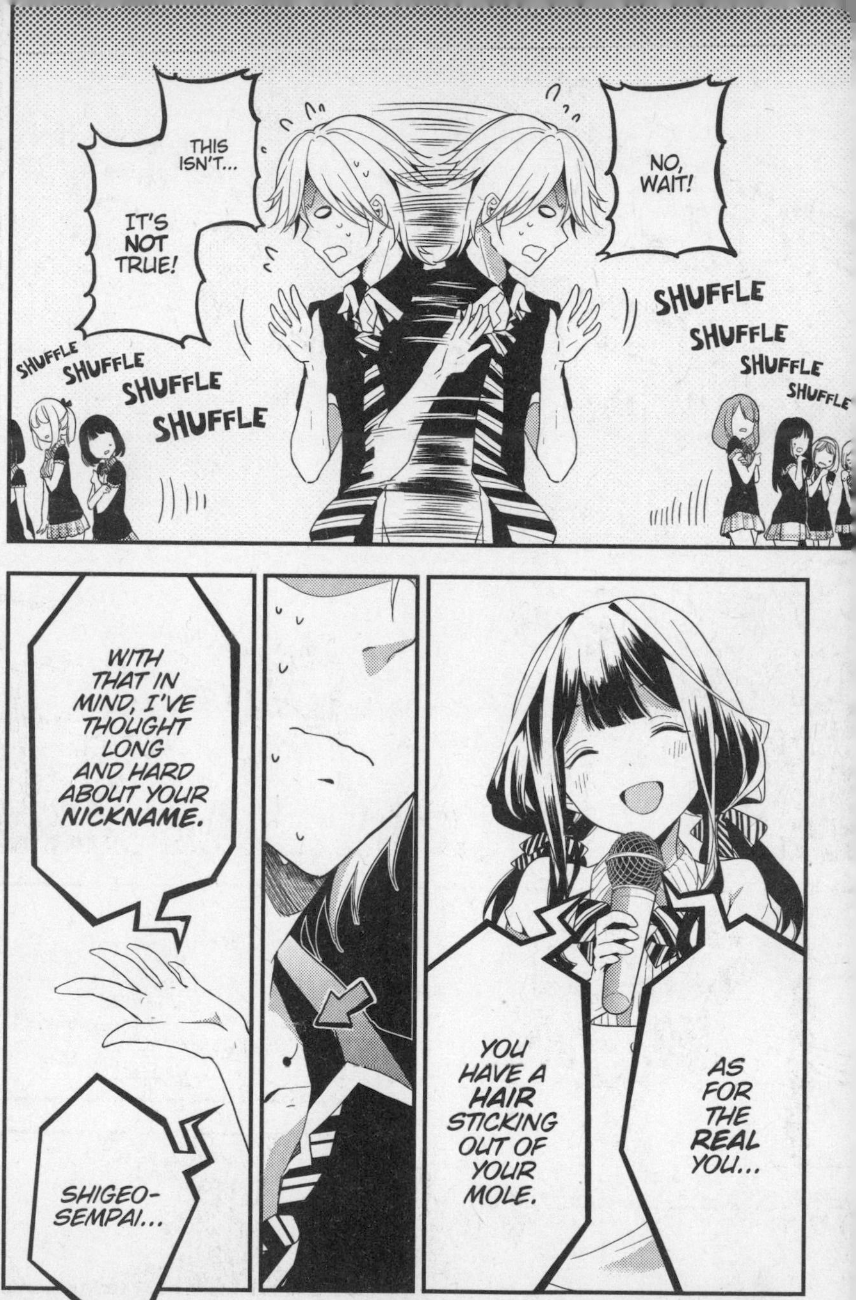
NO, WAIT!
THIS ISN'T...
IT'S NOT TRUE!
SHUFFLE SHUFFLE SHUFFLE SHUFFLE
SHUFFLE SHUFFLE SHUFFLE SHUFFLE
AS FOR THE REAL YOU...
YOU HAVE A HAIR STICKING OUT OF YOUR MOLE.
WITH THAT IN MIND, I'VE THOUGHT LONG AND HARD ABOUT YOUR NICKNAME.
SHIGEO-SEMPAI...

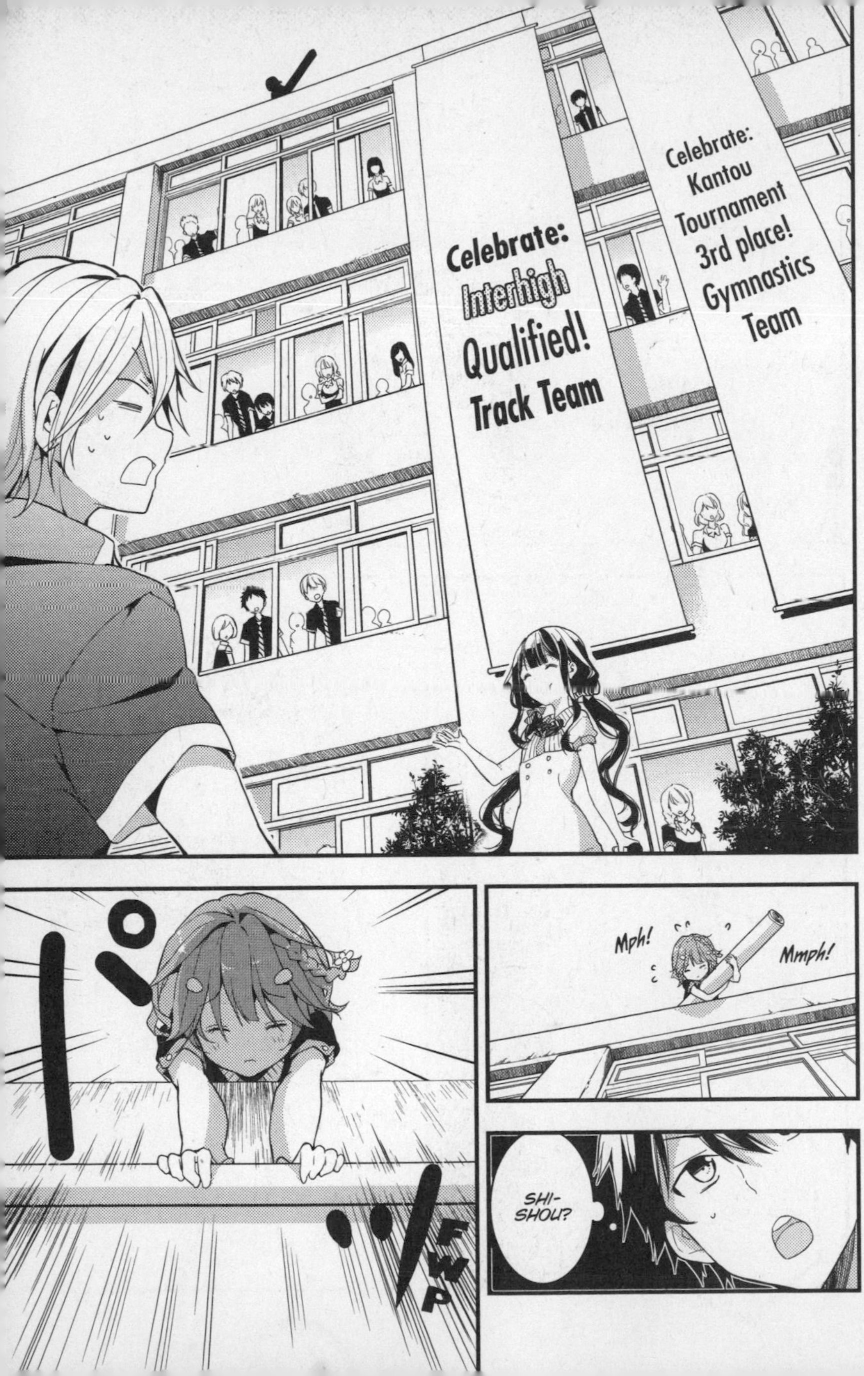

Celebrate: Kantou Tournament 3rd place! Gymnastics Team
Celebrate: Interhigh Qualified! Track Team
Mmph!
Mph!
SHI-SHOU?
パッ!
FWP

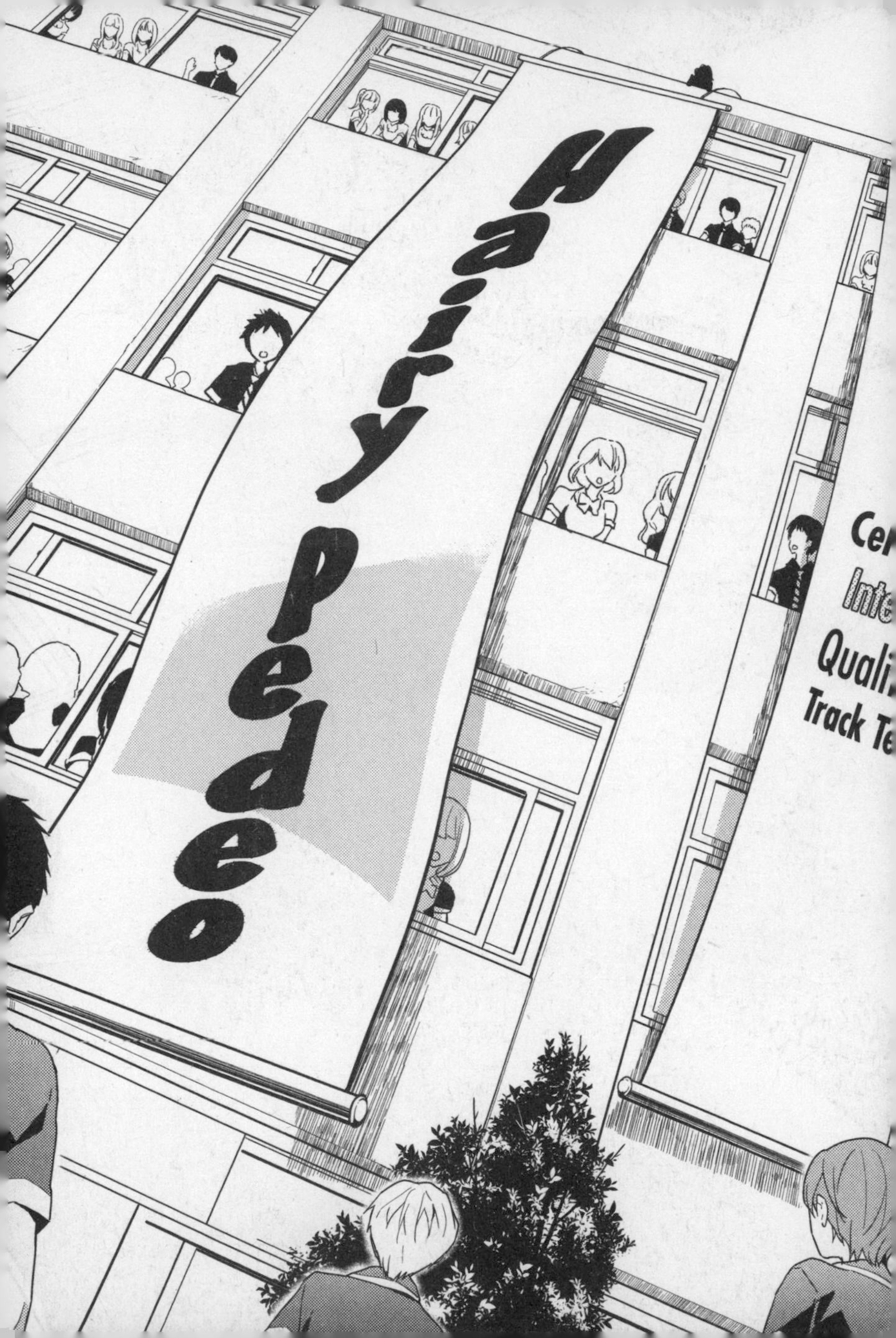
Hairy pedeo
Cer
Inte
Quali
Track Te

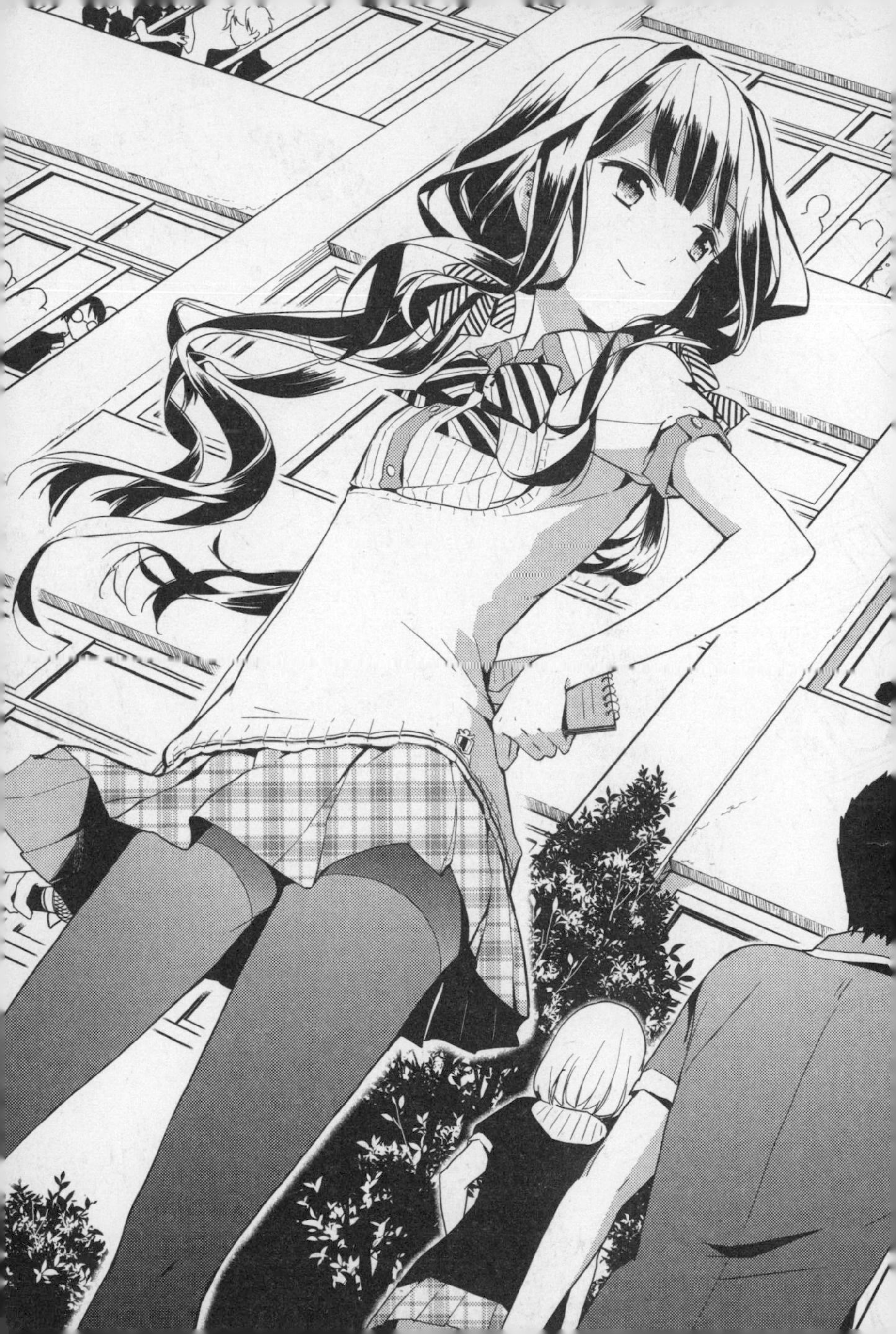

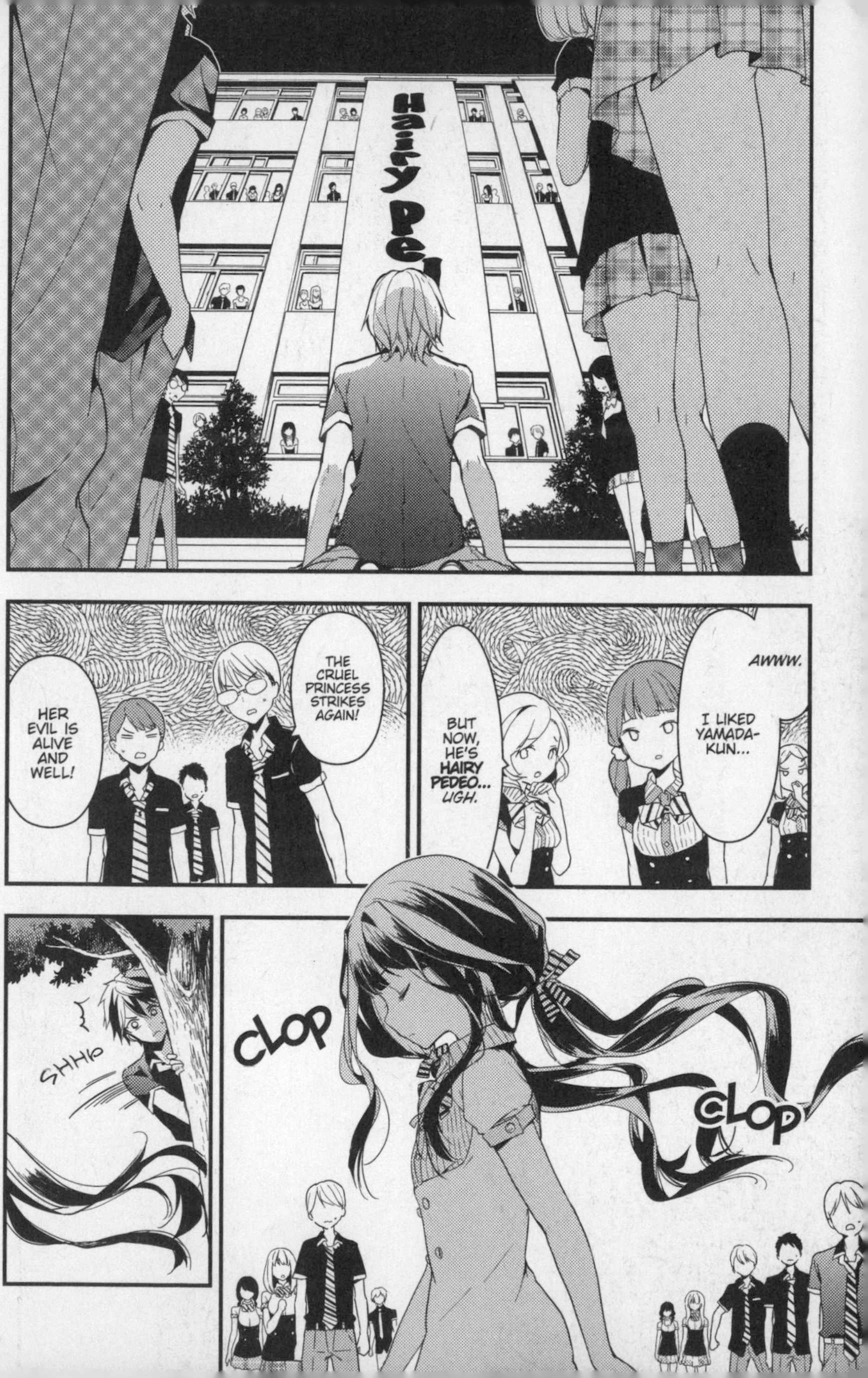
Hairy Pe
AWWW.
I LIKED YAMADA-KUN...
BUT NOW, HE'S HAIRY PEDEO... UGH.
THE CRUEL PRINCESS STRIKES AGAIN!
HER EVIL IS ALIVE AND WELL!
CLOP
CLOP
SHHK

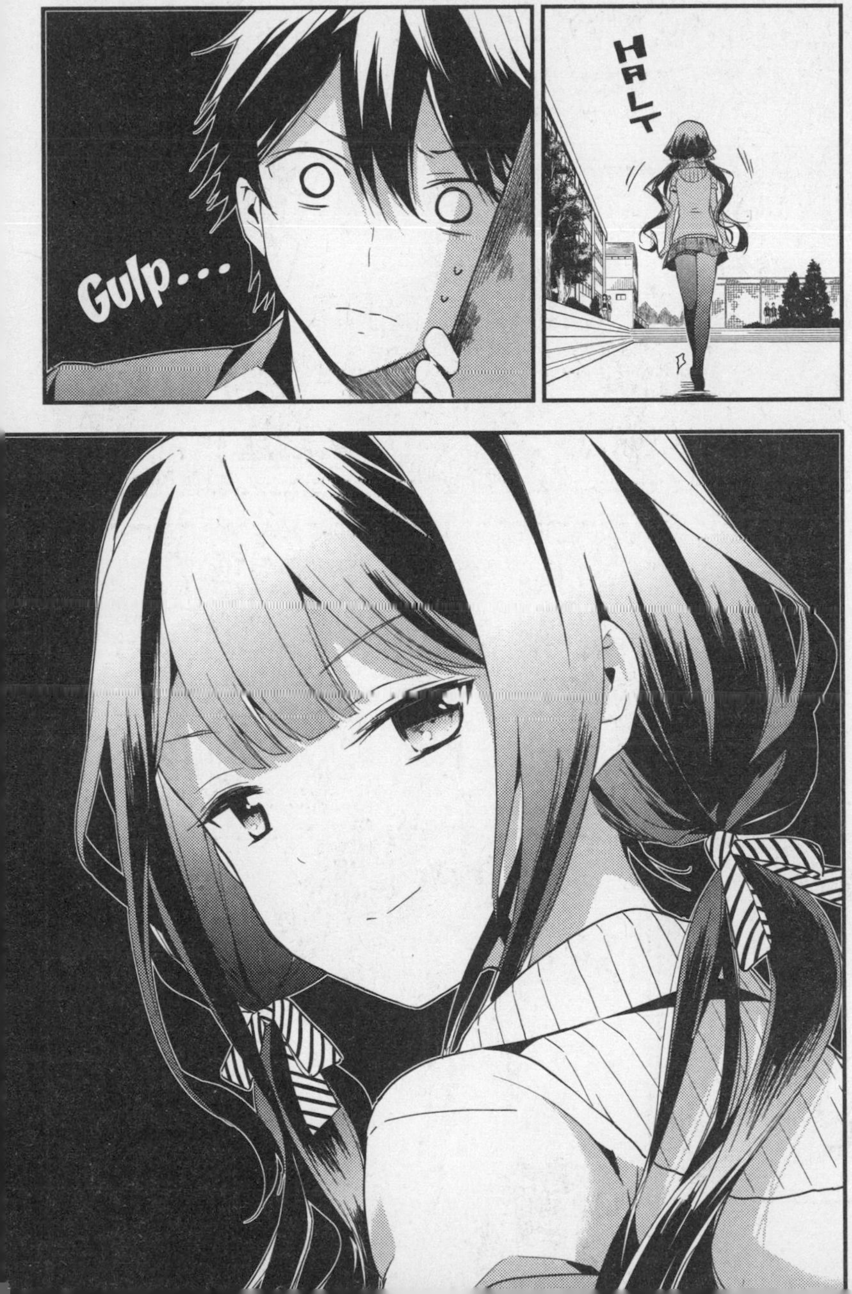
HALT
Gulp...

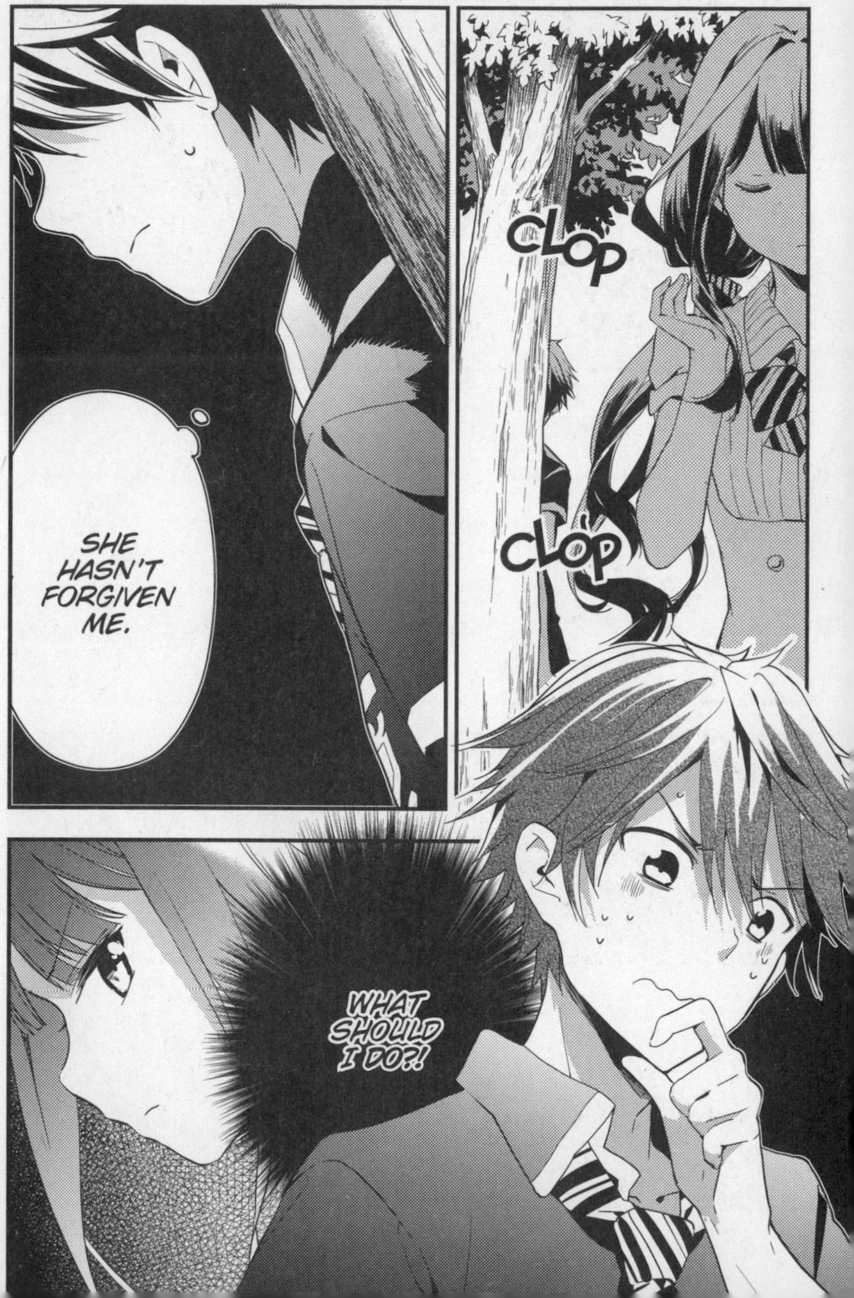
CLOP
CLOP
SHE HASN'T FORGIVEN ME.
WHAT SHOULD I DO?!

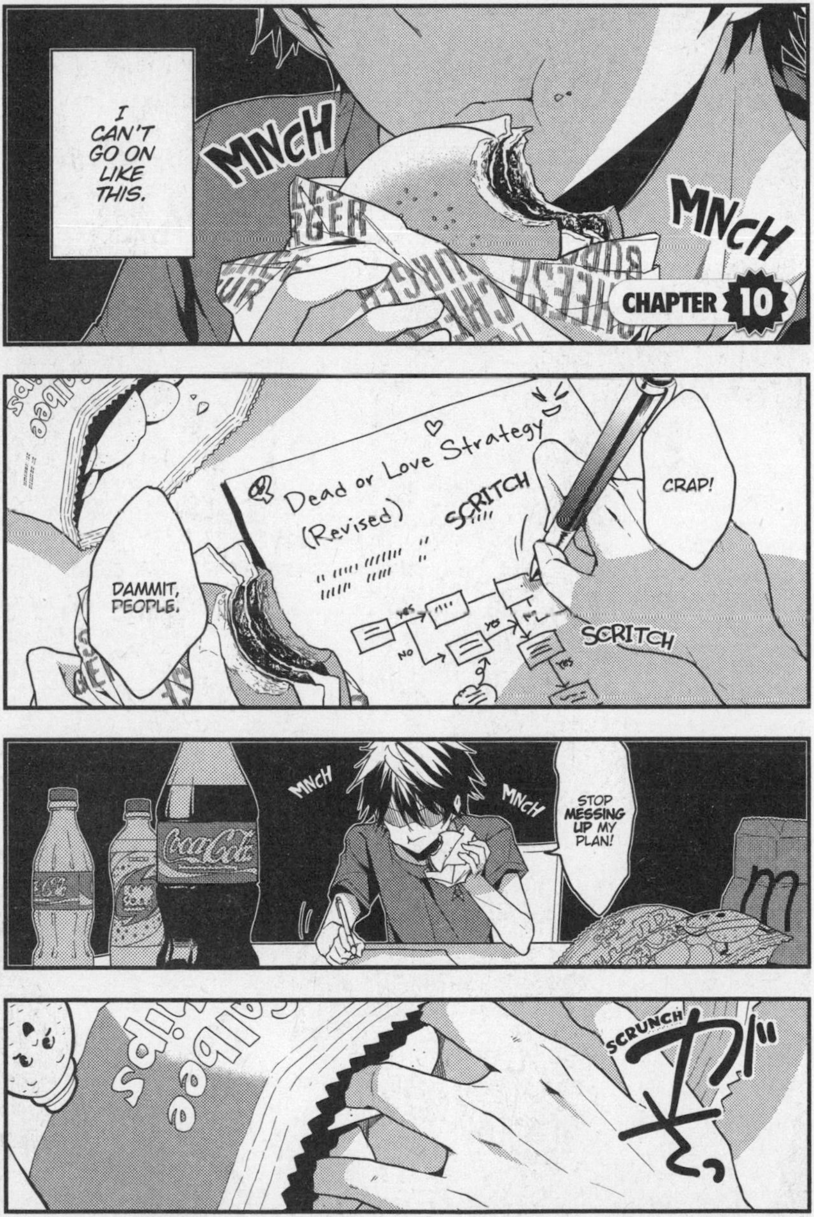
MNCH
I CAN'T GO ON LIKE THIS.
MNCH
CHAPTER 10
CRAP!
Dead or Love Strategy (Revised)
SCRITCH
SCRITCH
YES
NO
DAMMIT, PEOPLE.
STOP MESSING UP MY PLAN!
MNCH
MNCH
Coca-Cola
SCRUNCH
Calbee chips

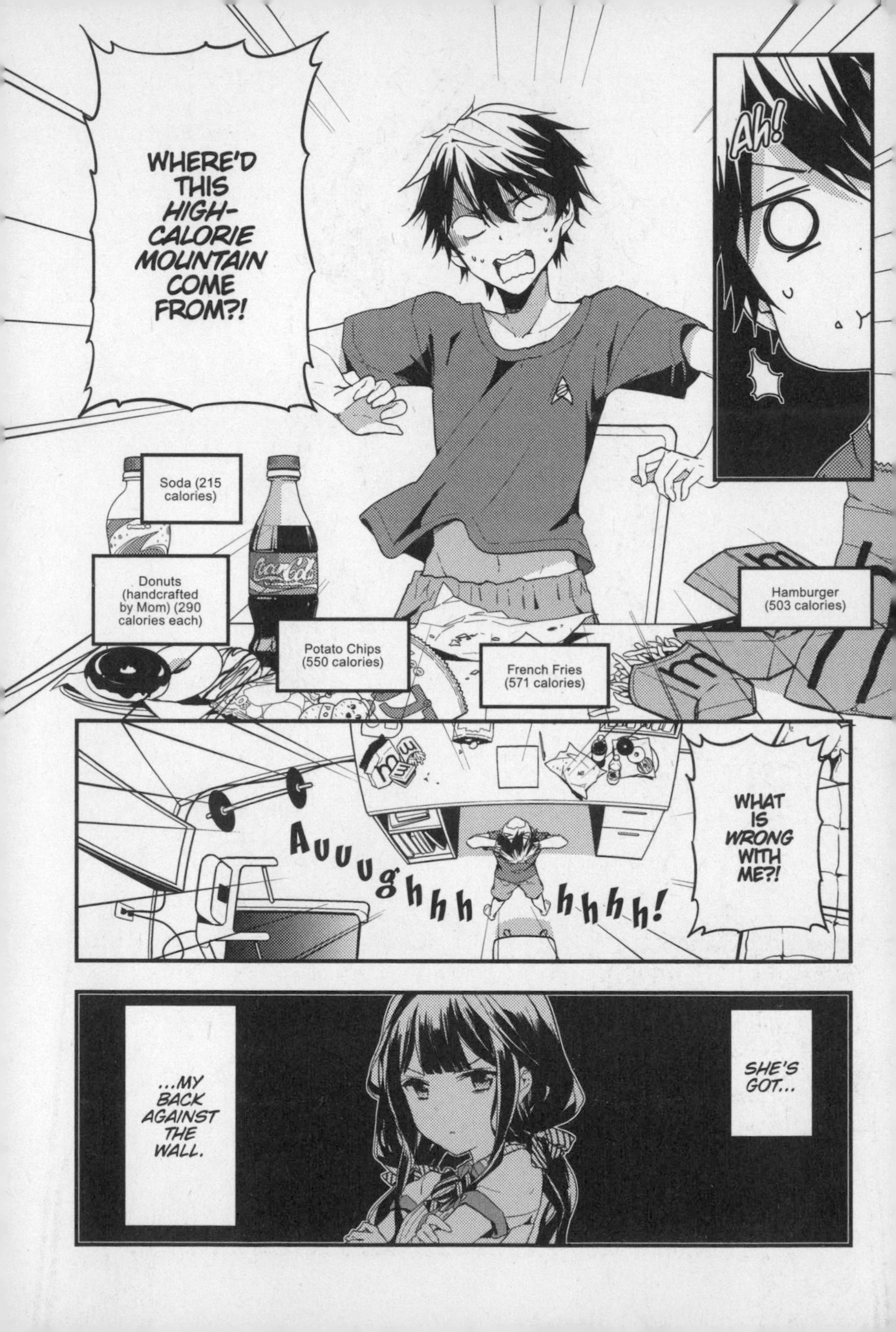
Ah!
WHERE'D THIS HIGH-CALORIE MOUNTAIN COME FROM?!
Hamburger (503 calories)
Soda (215 calories)
French Fries (571 calories)
Potato Chips (550 calories)
Donuts (handcrafted by Mom) (290 calories each)
WHAT IS WRONG WITH ME?!
Auuughhhhhhhh!
SHE'S GOT...
...MY BACK AGAINST THE WALL.

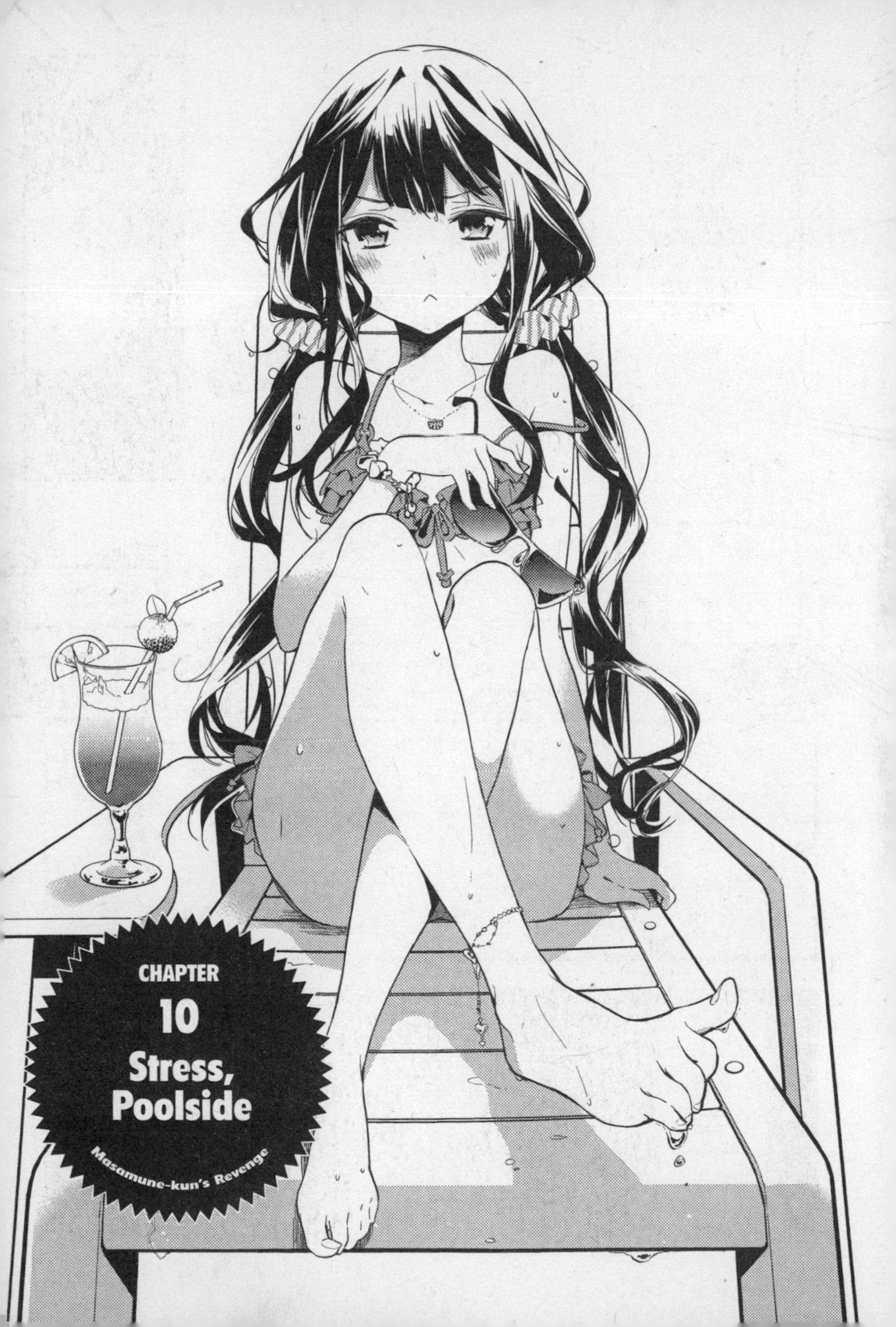
CHAPTER
10
Stress, Poolside
Masamune-kun's Revenge

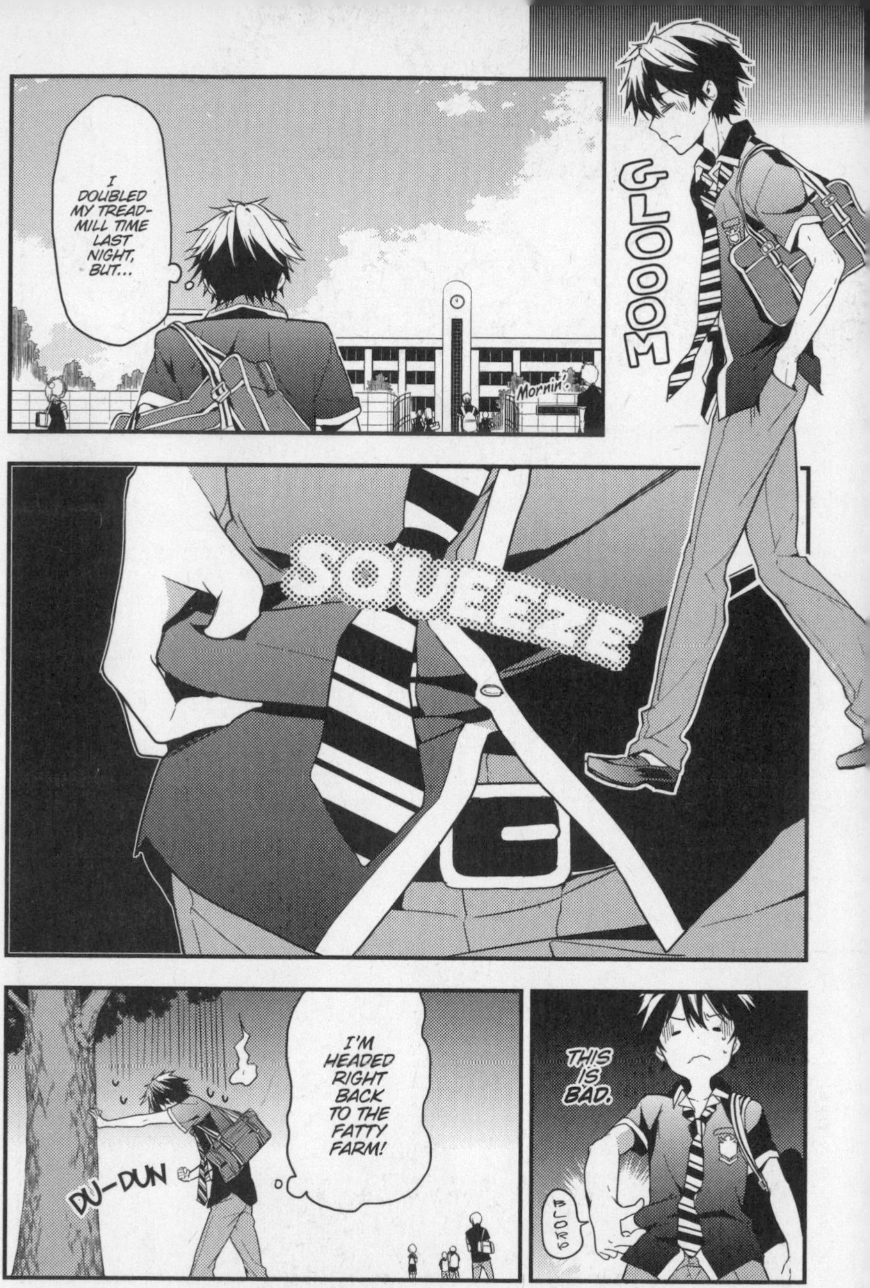
GLOOOOM
I DOUBLED MY TREAD-MILL TIME LAST NIGHT, BUT...
Mornin'!
SQUEEZE
THIS IS BAD.
I'M HEADED RIGHT BACK TO THE FATTY FARM!
DU-DUN

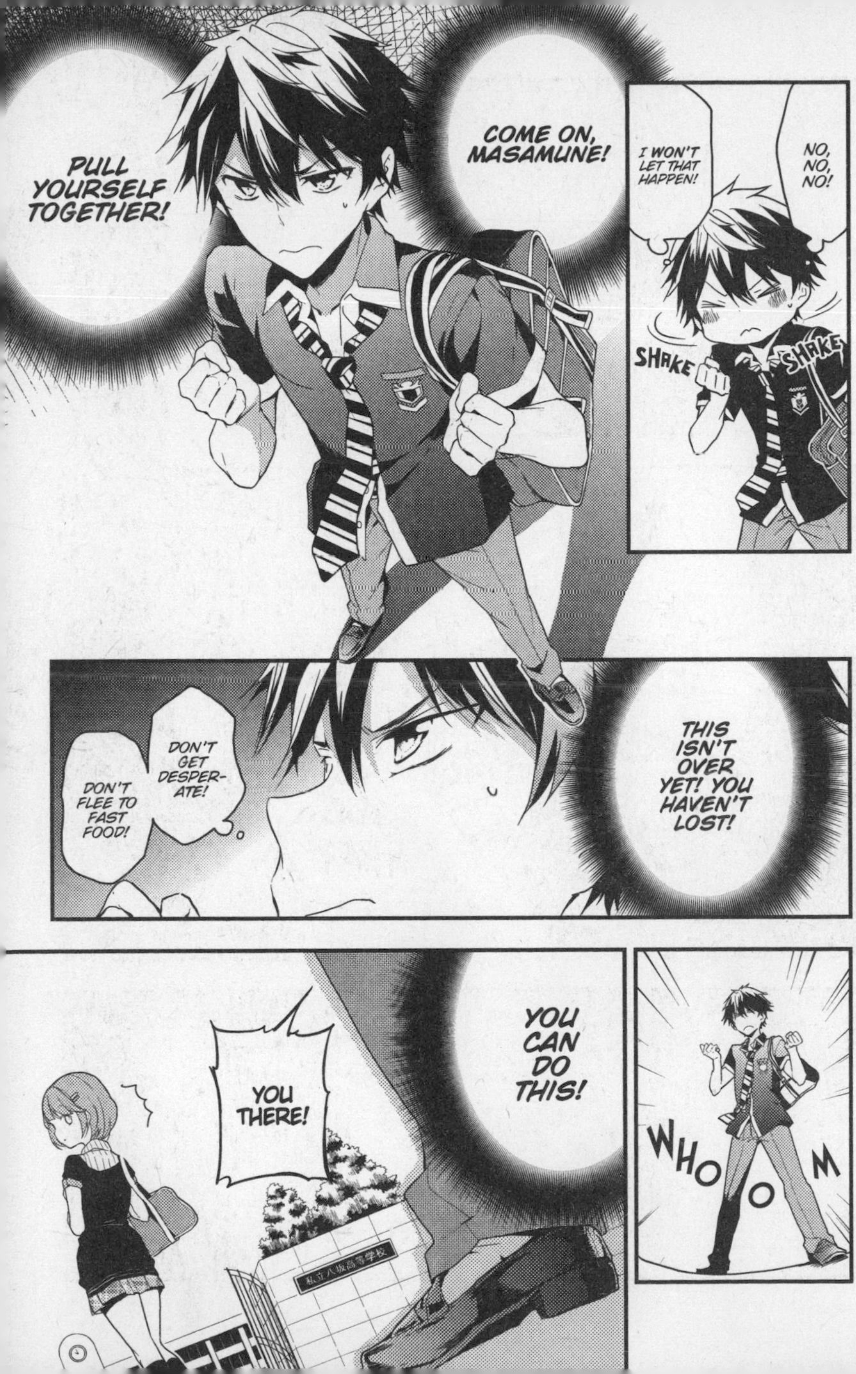
NO, NO, NO!
I WON'T LET THAT HAPPEN!
SHAKE
SHAKE
COME ON, MASAMUNE!
PULL YOURSELF TOGETHER!
THIS ISN'T OVER YET! YOU HAVEN'T LOST!
DON'T GET DESPERATE!
DON'T FLEE TO FAST FOOD!
WHOOM
YOU CAN DO THIS!
YOU THERE!

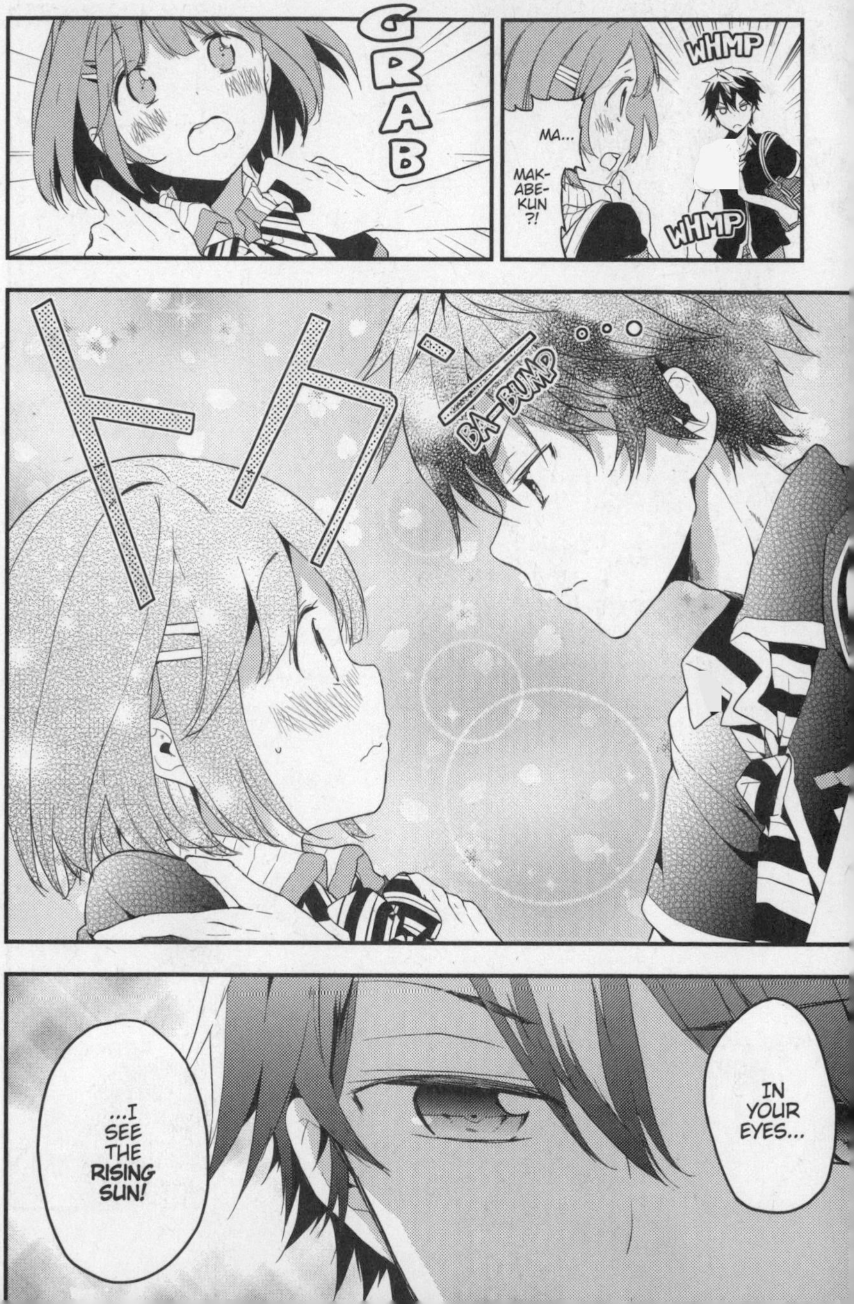
WHMP
MA...
MAKABE-KUN?!
WHMP
GRAB
BA-BUMP
IN YOUR EYES...
...I SEE THE RISING SUN!

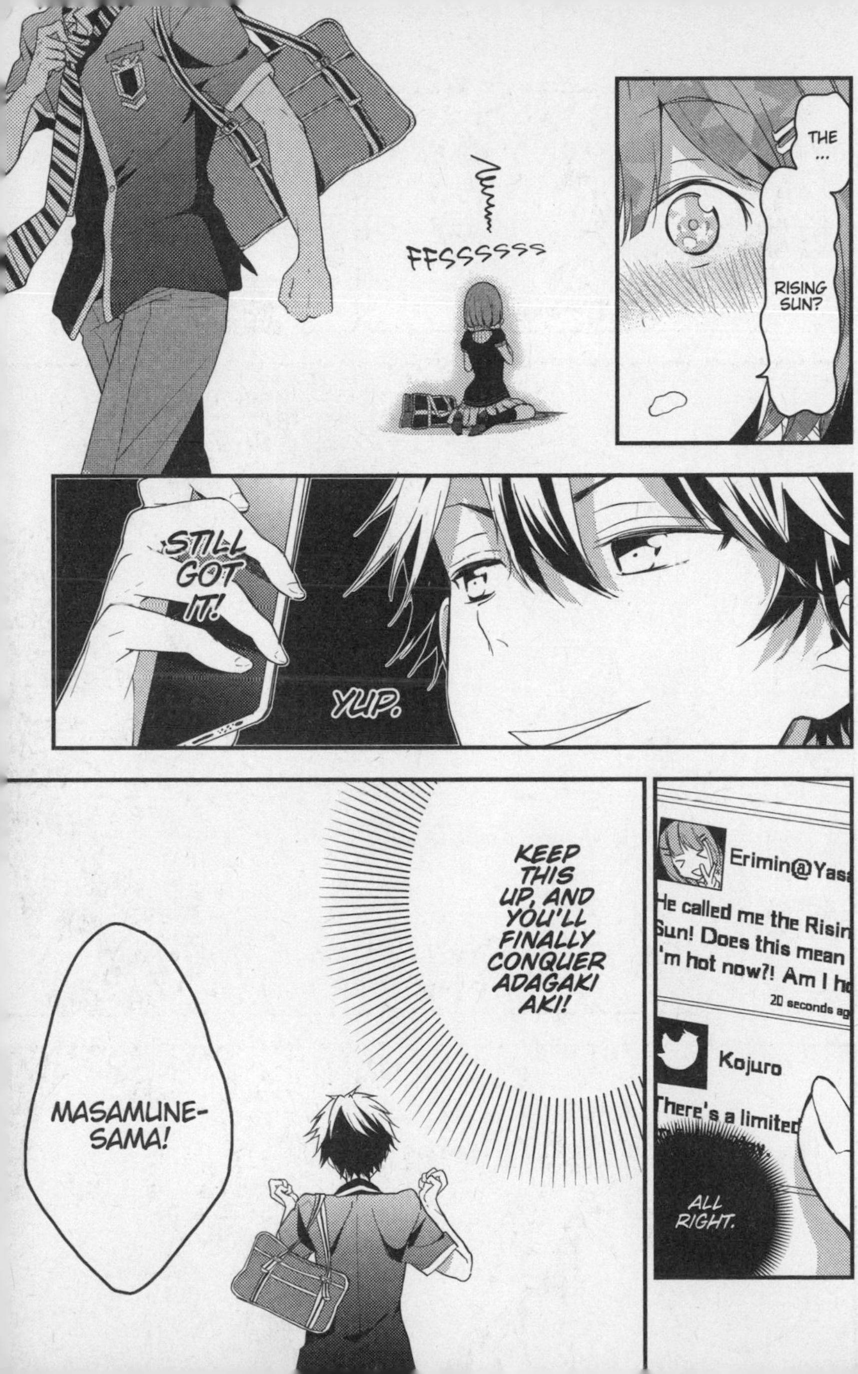
THE ...
RISING SUN?
FFSSSSSS
STILL GOT IT!
YUP.
Erimin@Yasa
He called me the Risin
Sun! Does this mean
'm hot now?! Am I h
20 seconds ag
Kojuro
There's a limited
ALL RIGHT.
KEEP THIS UP, AND YOU'LL FINALLY CONQUER ADAGAKI AKI!
MASAMUNE-SAMA!

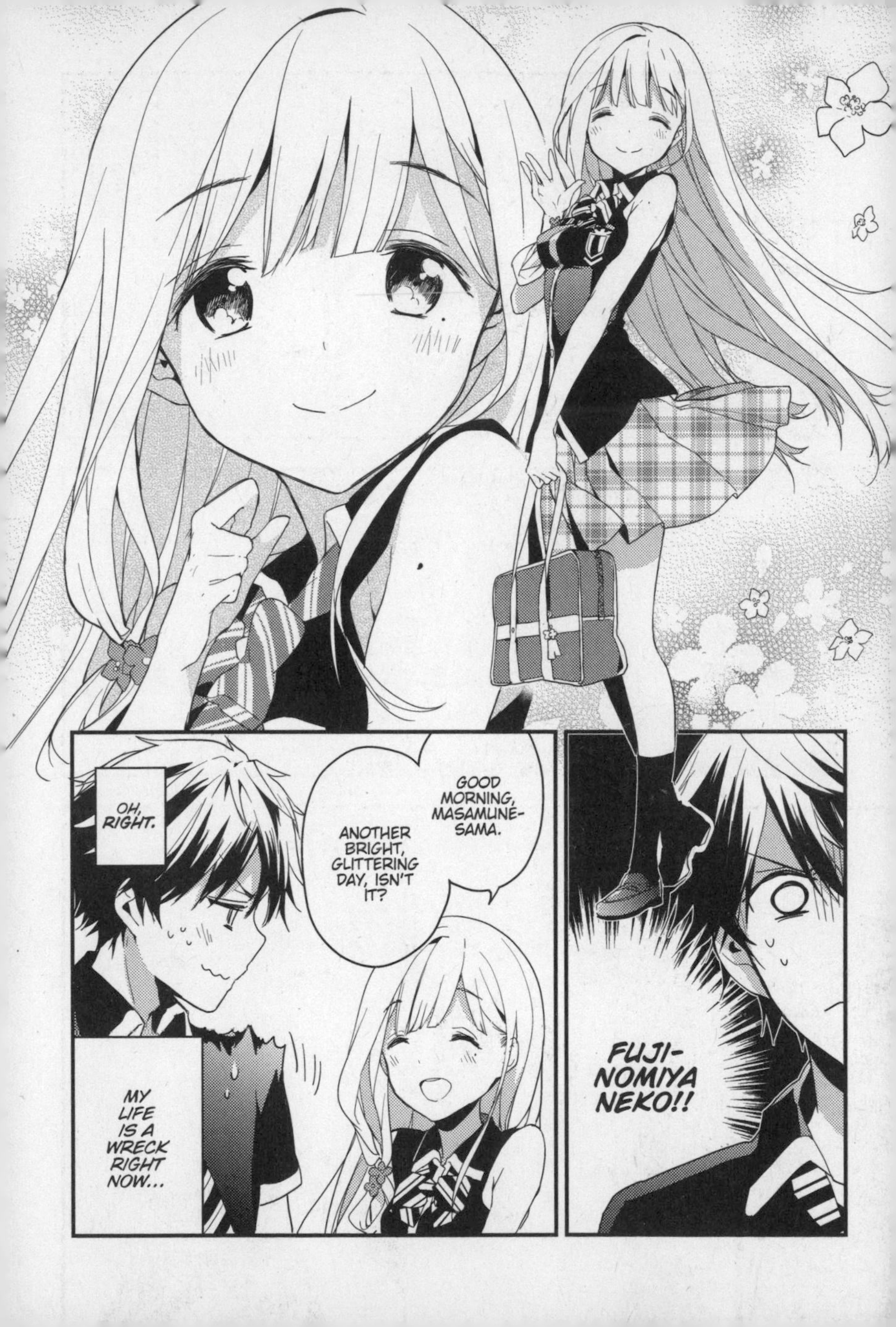
FUJI-NOMIYA NEKO!!
GOOD MORNING, MASAMUNE-SAMA. ANOTHER BRIGHT, GLITTERING DAY, ISN'T IT?
OH, RIGHT.
MY LIFE IS A WRECK RIGHT NOW...

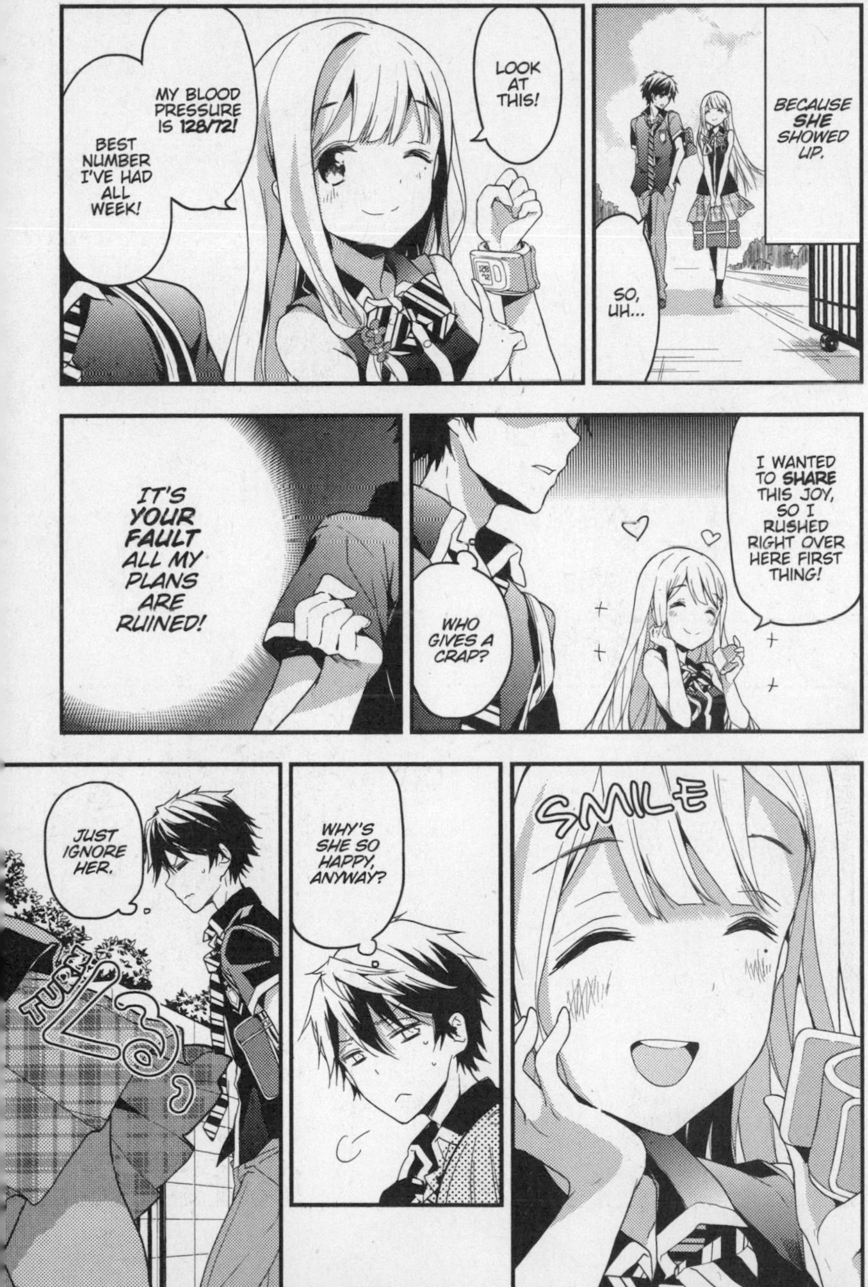
BECAUSE SHE SHOWED UP.
SO, UH...
LOOK AT THIS!
MY BLOOD PRESSURE IS 128/72!
BEST NUMBER I'VE HAD ALL WEEK!
I WANTED TO SHARE THIS JOY, SO I RUSHED RIGHT OVER HERE FIRST THING!
WHO GIVES A CRAP?
IT'S YOUR FAULT ALL MY PLANS ARE RUINED!
SMILE
WHY'S SHE SO HAPPY, ANYWAY?
JUST IGNORE HER.
TURN

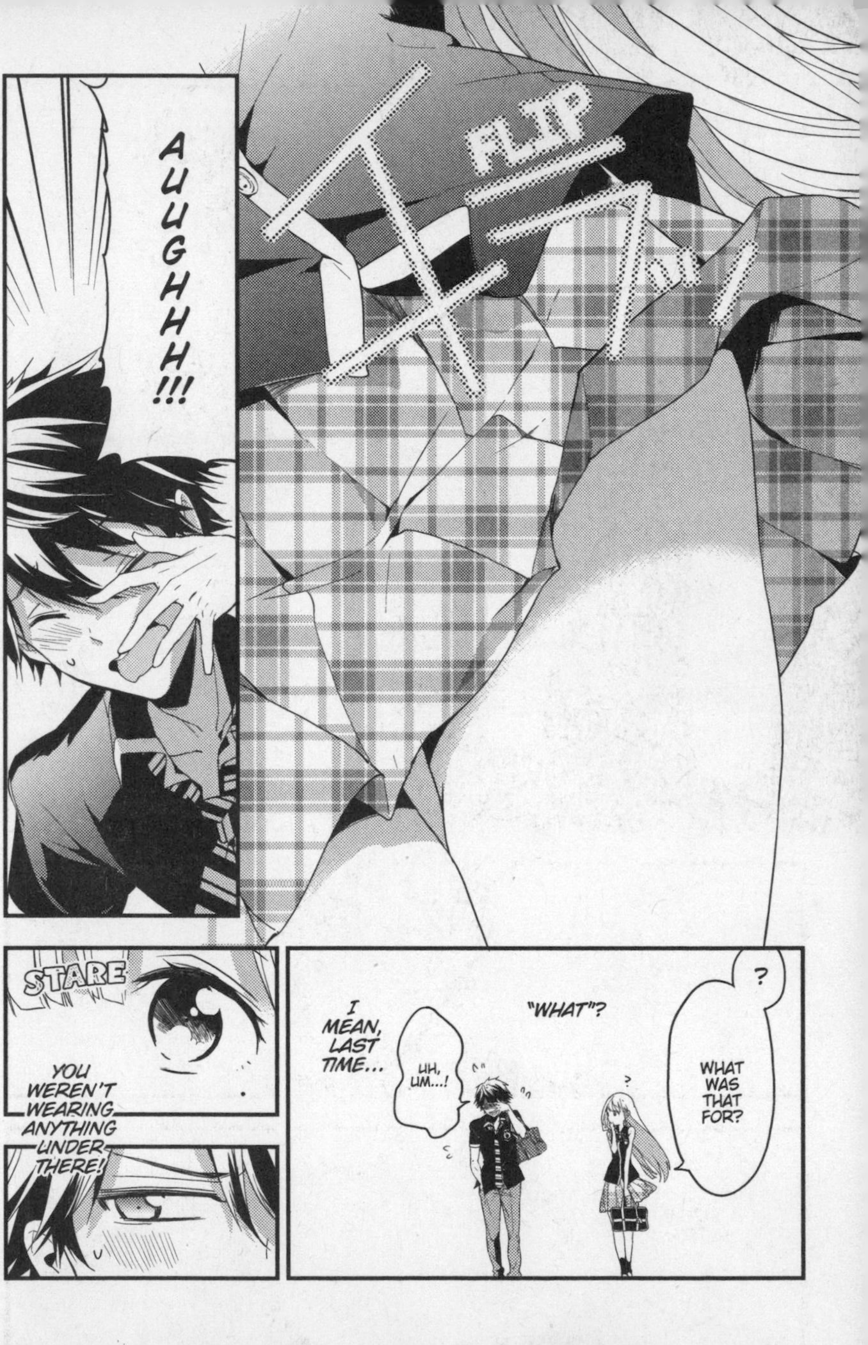
FLIP
AUUGHHH!!!
?
WHAT WAS THAT FOR?
"WHAT"?
UH, UM...!
I MEAN, LAST TIME...
STARE
YOU WEREN'T WEARING ANYTHING UNDER THERE!

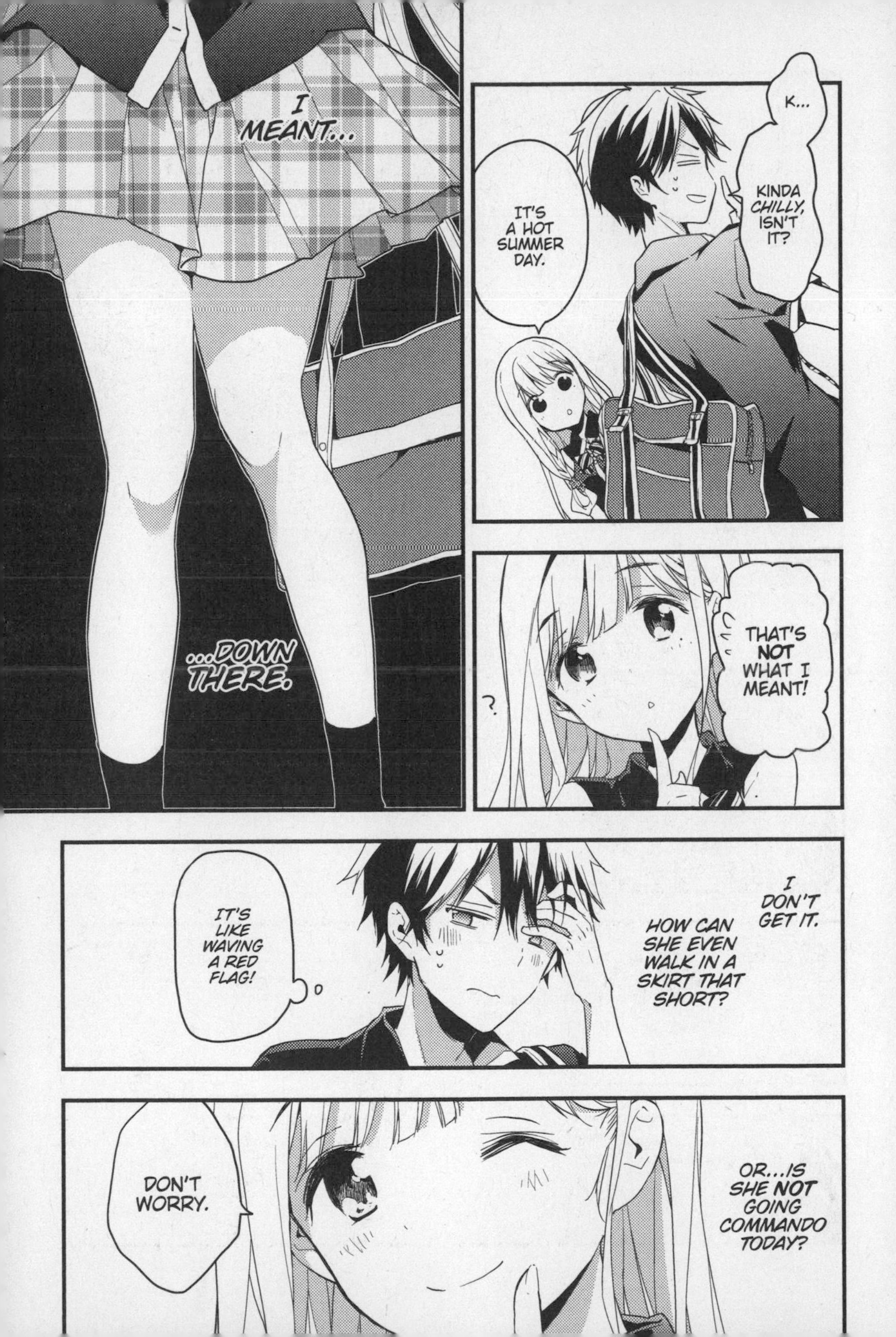
K...
KINDA CHILLY, ISN'T IT?
IT'S A HOT SUMMER DAY.
THAT'S NOT WHAT I MEANT!
?
I MEANT...
...DOWN THERE.
I DON'T GET IT.
HOW CAN SHE EVEN WALK IN A SKIRT THAT SHORT?
IT'S LIKE WAVING A RED FLAG!
OR...IS SHE NOT GOING COMMANDO TODAY?
DON'T WORRY.

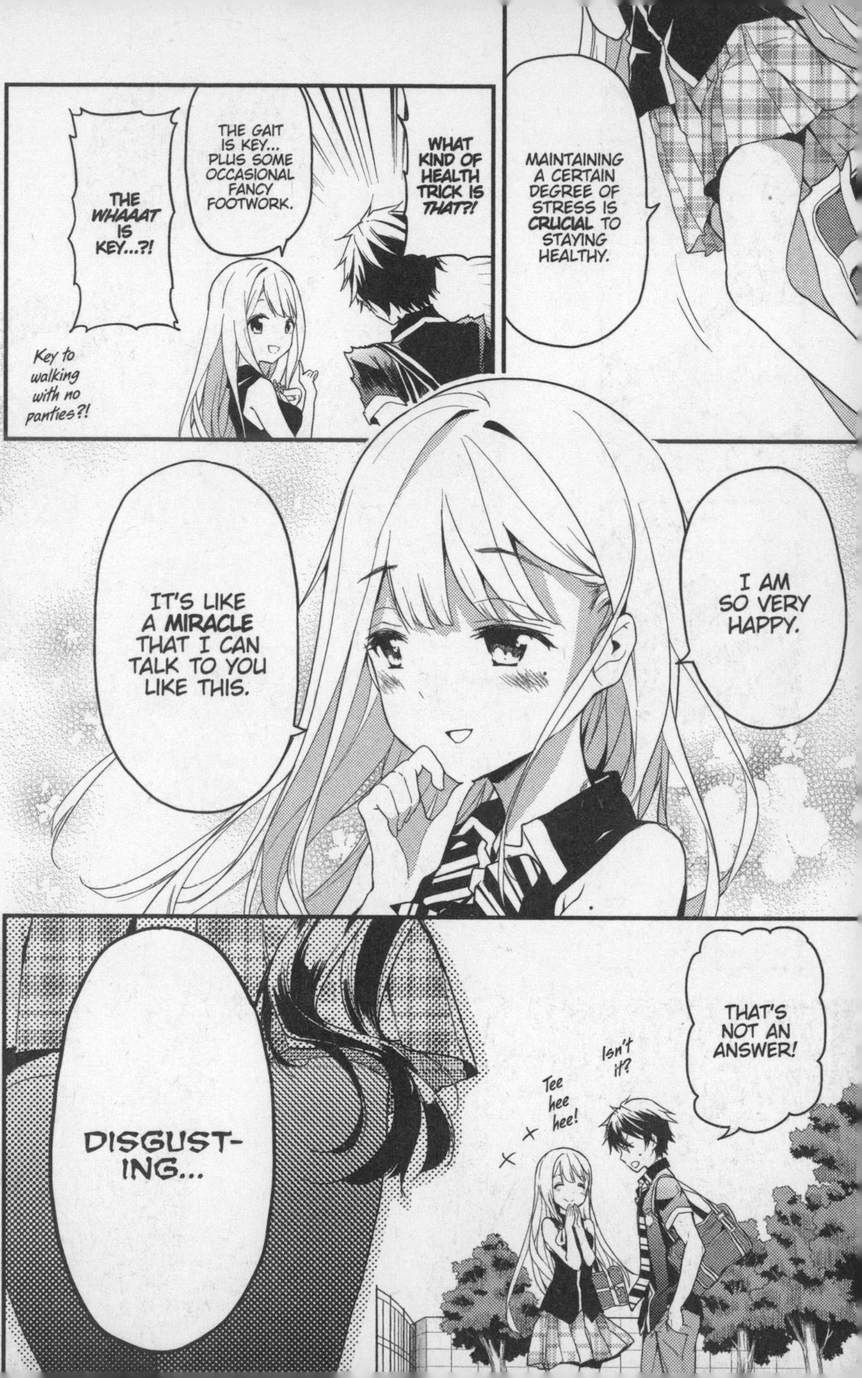
MAINTAINING A CERTAIN DEGREE OF STRESS IS CRUCIAL TO STAYING HEALTHY.
WHAT KIND OF HEALTH TRICK IS THAT?!
THE GAIT IS KEY... PLUS SOME OCCASIONAL FANCY FOOTWORK.
THE WHAAAT IS KEY...?!
Key to walking with no panties?!
I AM SO VERY HAPPY.
IT'S LIKE A MIRACLE THAT I CAN TALK TO YOU LIKE THIS.
THAT'S NOT AN ANSWER!
Isn't it?
Tee hee hee!
DISGUST-ING...

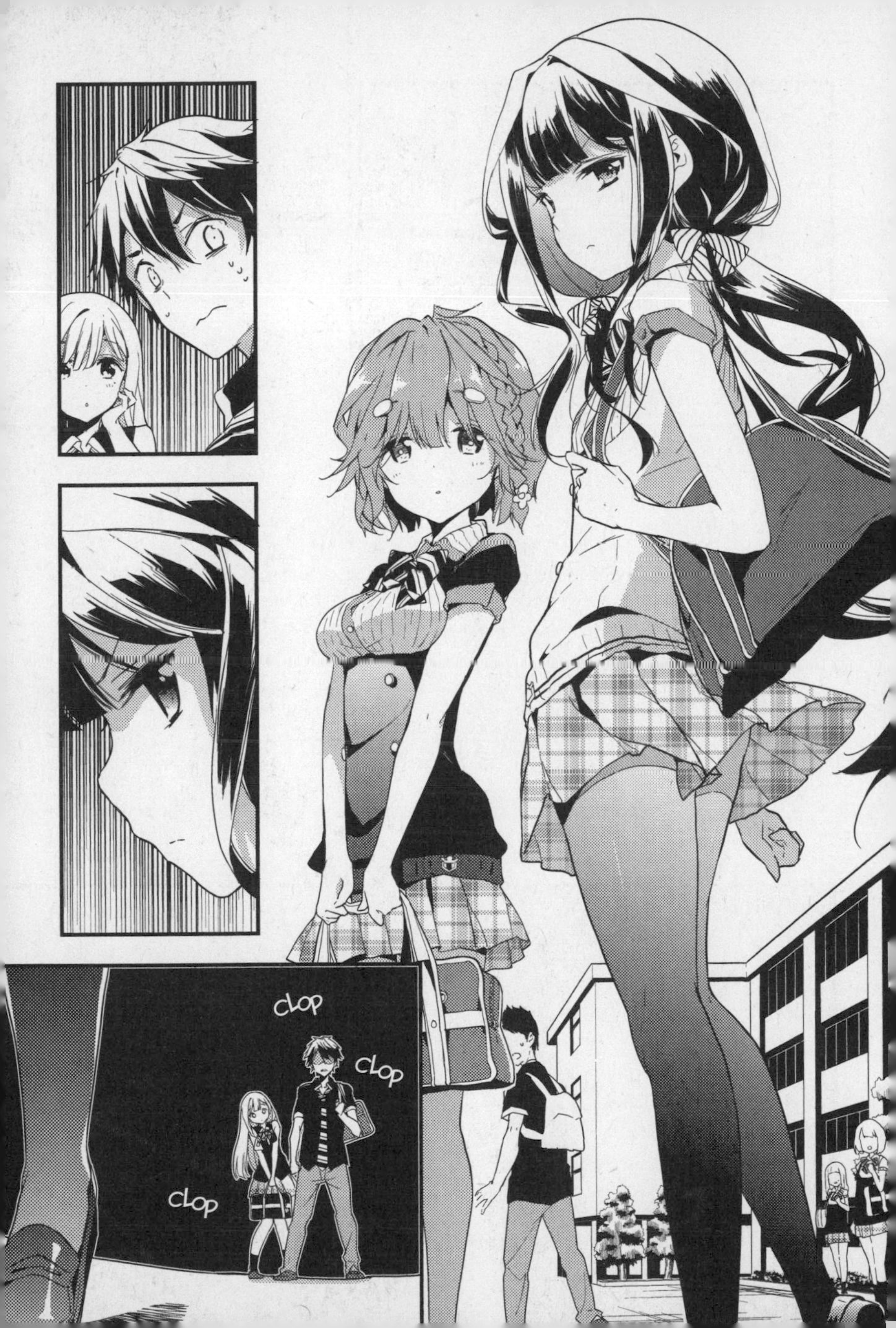
CLOP
CLOP
CLOP

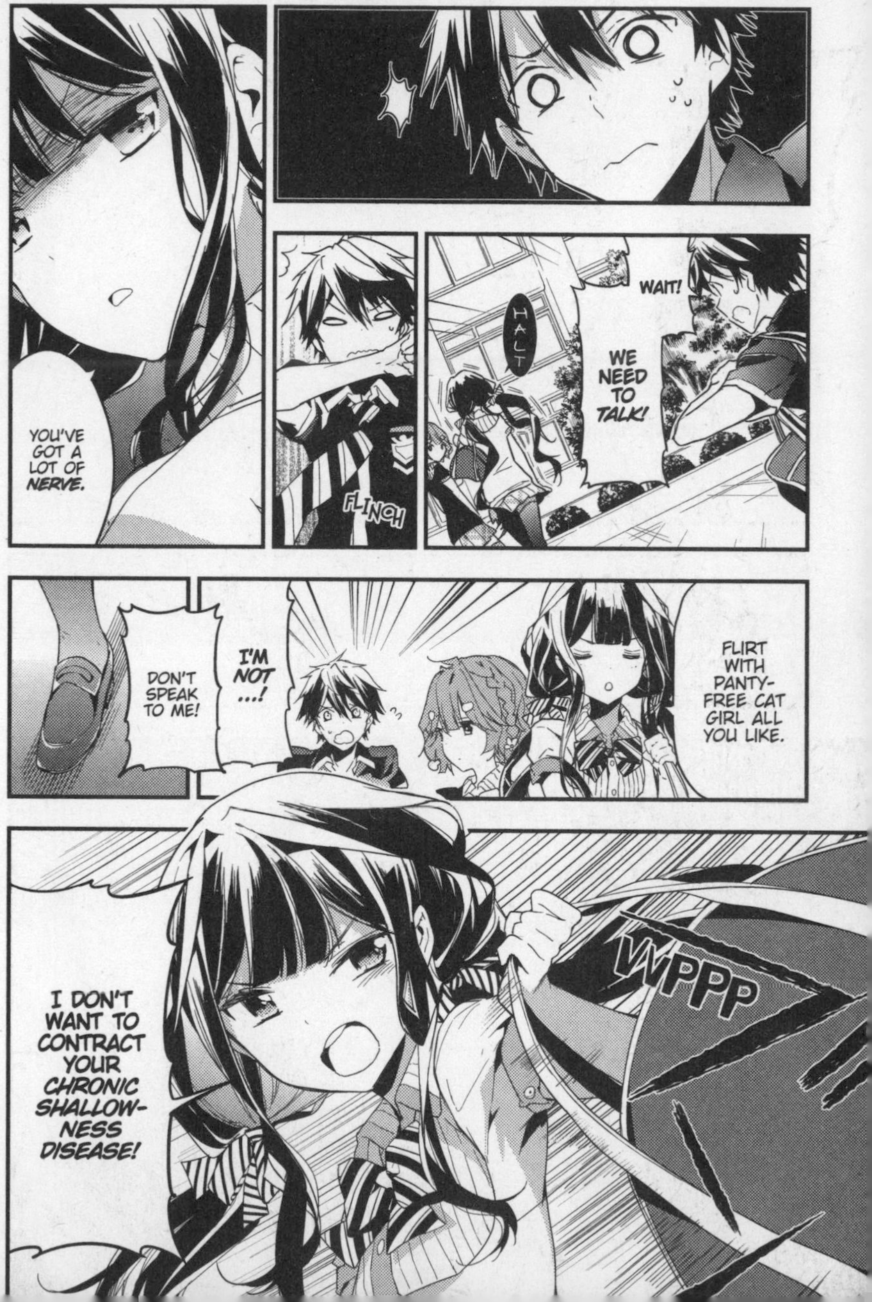
WAIT!
HALT
WE NEED TO TALK!
FLINCH
YOU'VE GOT A LOT OF NERVE.
FLIRT WITH PANTY-FREE CAT GIRL ALL YOU LIKE.
I'M NOT ...!
DON'T SPEAK TO ME!
VVPPP
I DON'T WANT TO CONTRACT YOUR CHRONIC SHALLOW-NESS DISEASE!

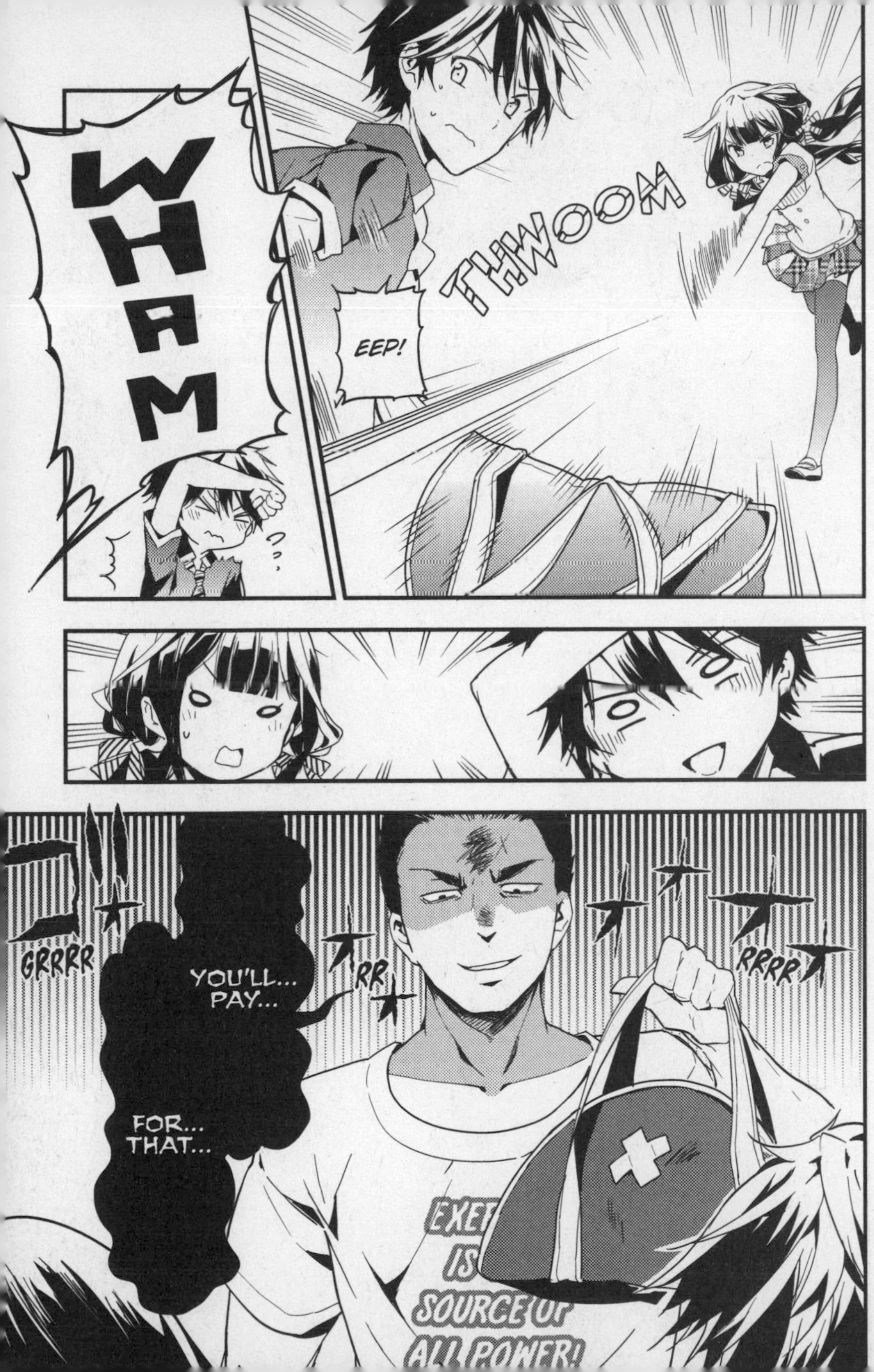
THWOOM
EEP!
WHAM
RRRR
RR
GRRRR
YOU'LL... PAY...
FOR... THAT...
SOURCE OF ALL POWER!

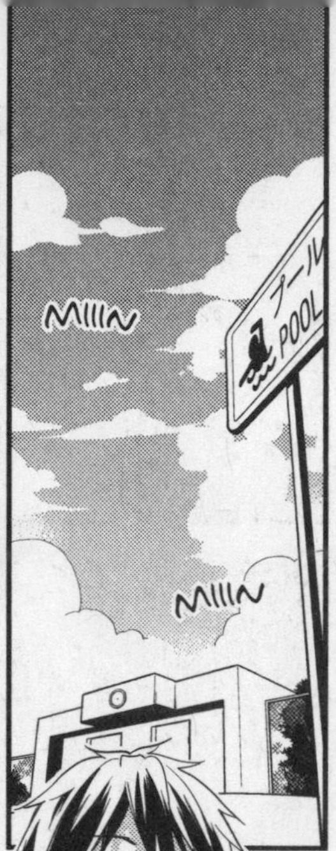
MIIIN
プール
POOL
MIIIN

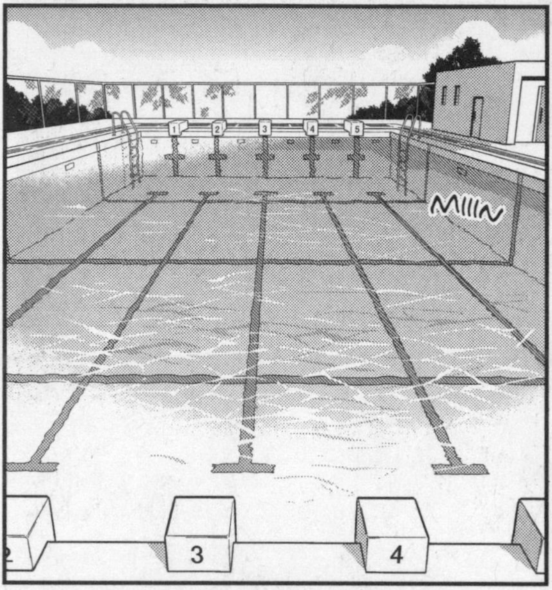
MIIIN
3
4

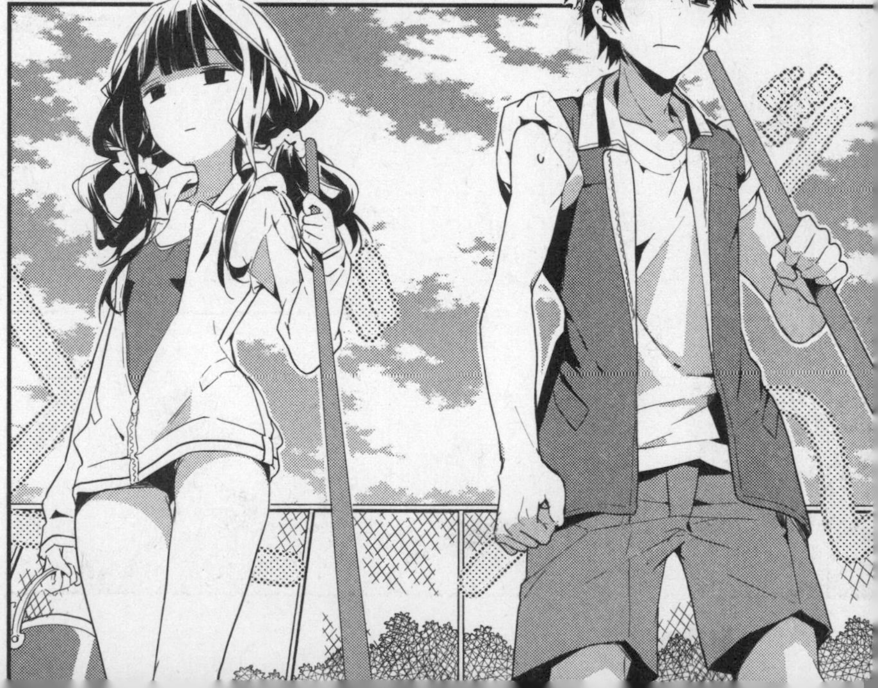

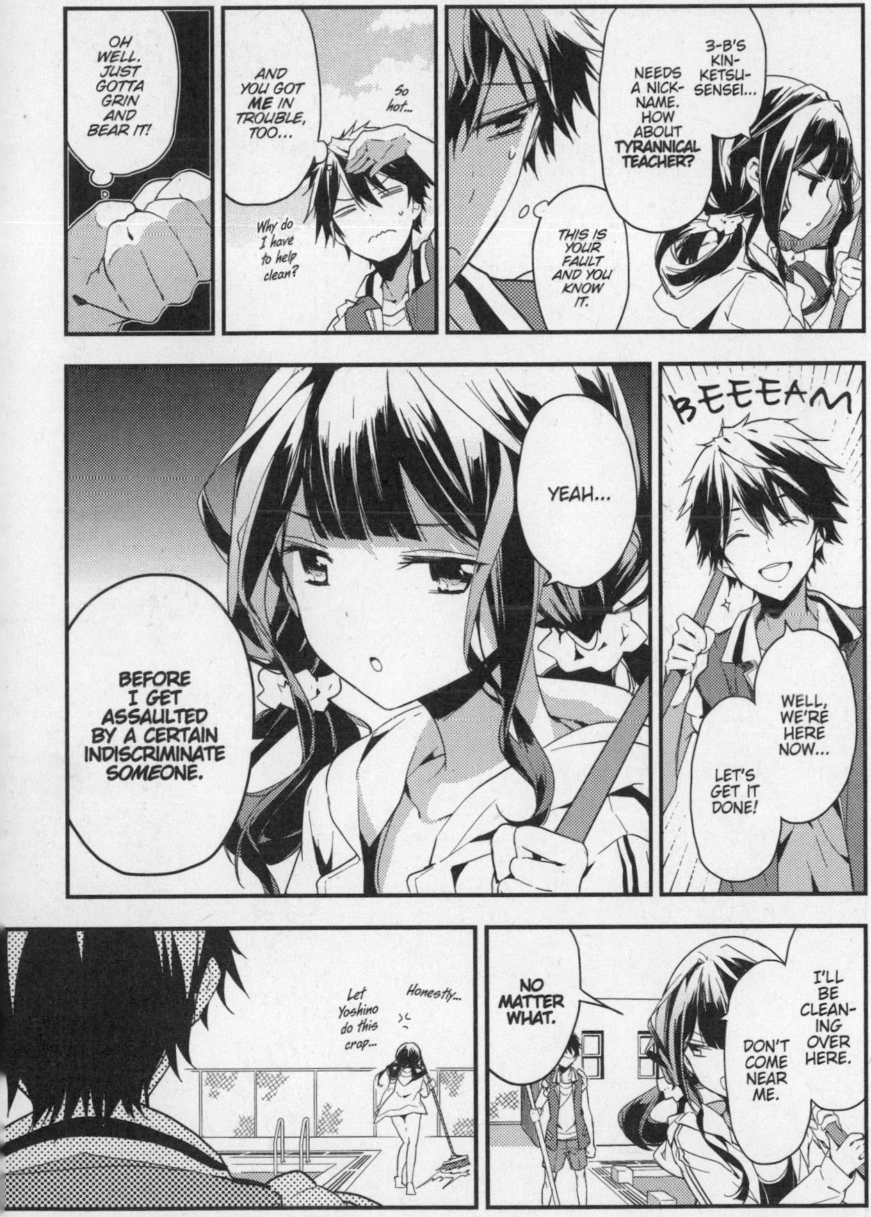
3-B'S KIN-KETSU-SENSEI...
NEEDS A NICK-NAME. HOW ABOUT TYRANNICAL TEACHER?
THIS IS YOUR FAULT AND YOU KNOW IT.
So hot...
AND YOU GOT ME IN TROUBLE, TOO...
Why do I have to help clean?
OH WELL. JUST GOTTA GRIN AND BEAR IT!
BEEEAM
WELL, WE'RE HERE NOW...
LET'S GET IT DONE!
YEAH...
BEFORE I GET ASSAULTED BY A CERTAIN INDISCRIMINATE SOMEONE.
I'LL BE CLEANING OVER HERE.
DON'T COME NEAR ME.
NO MATTER WHAT.
Honestly...
Let Yoshino do this crap...

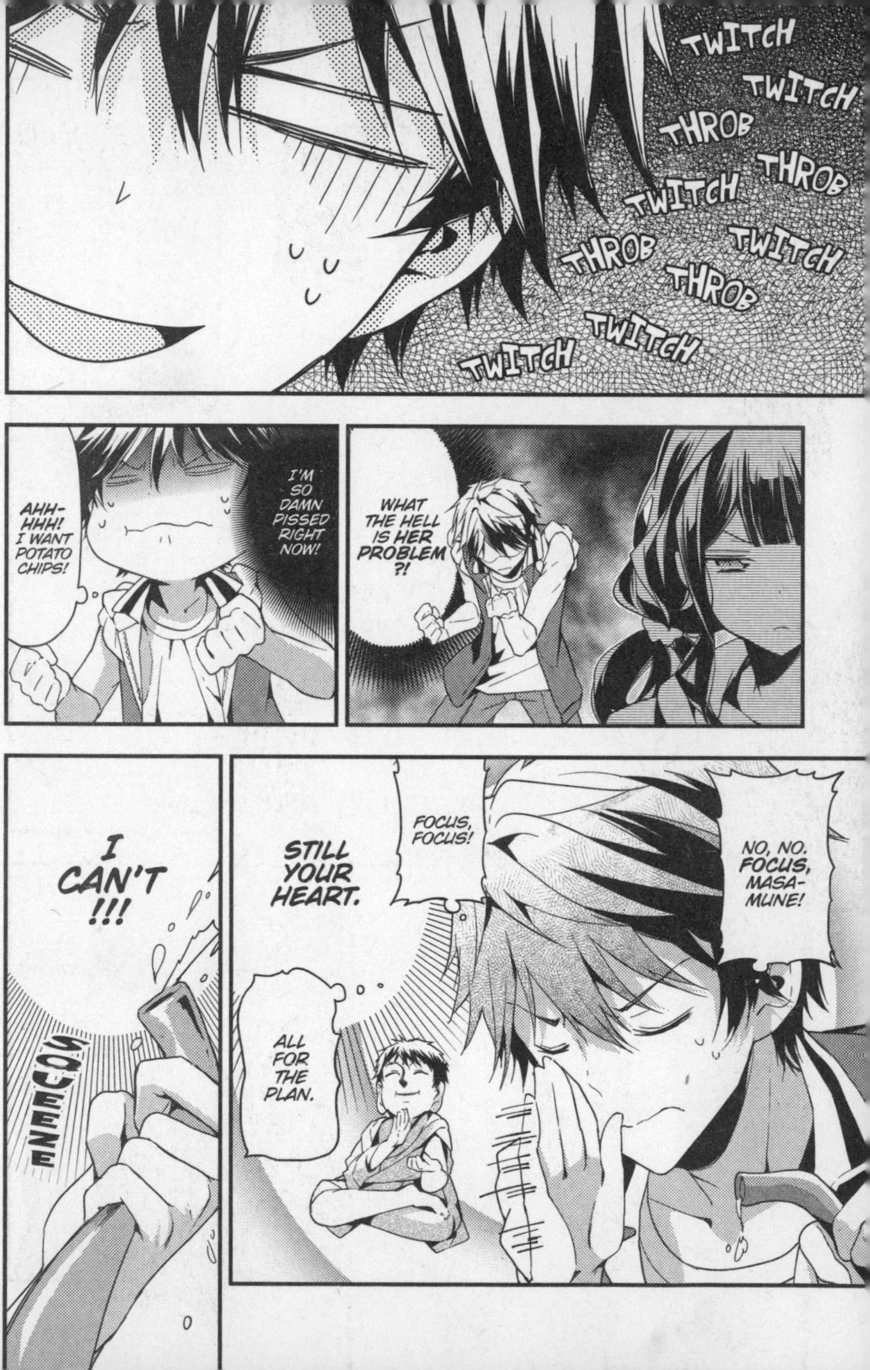
TWITCH
TWITCH
THROB
THROB
TWITCH
TWITCH
THROB
THROB
TWITCH
TWITCH
WHAT THE HELL IS HER PROBLEM ?!
I'M SO DAMN PISSED RIGHT NOW!
AHHHHH! I WANT POTATO CHIPS!
NO, NO. FOCUS, MASA-MUNE!
FOCUS, FOCUS!
STILL YOUR HEART.
ALL FOR THE PLAN.
I CAN'T !!!
SQUEEEZE

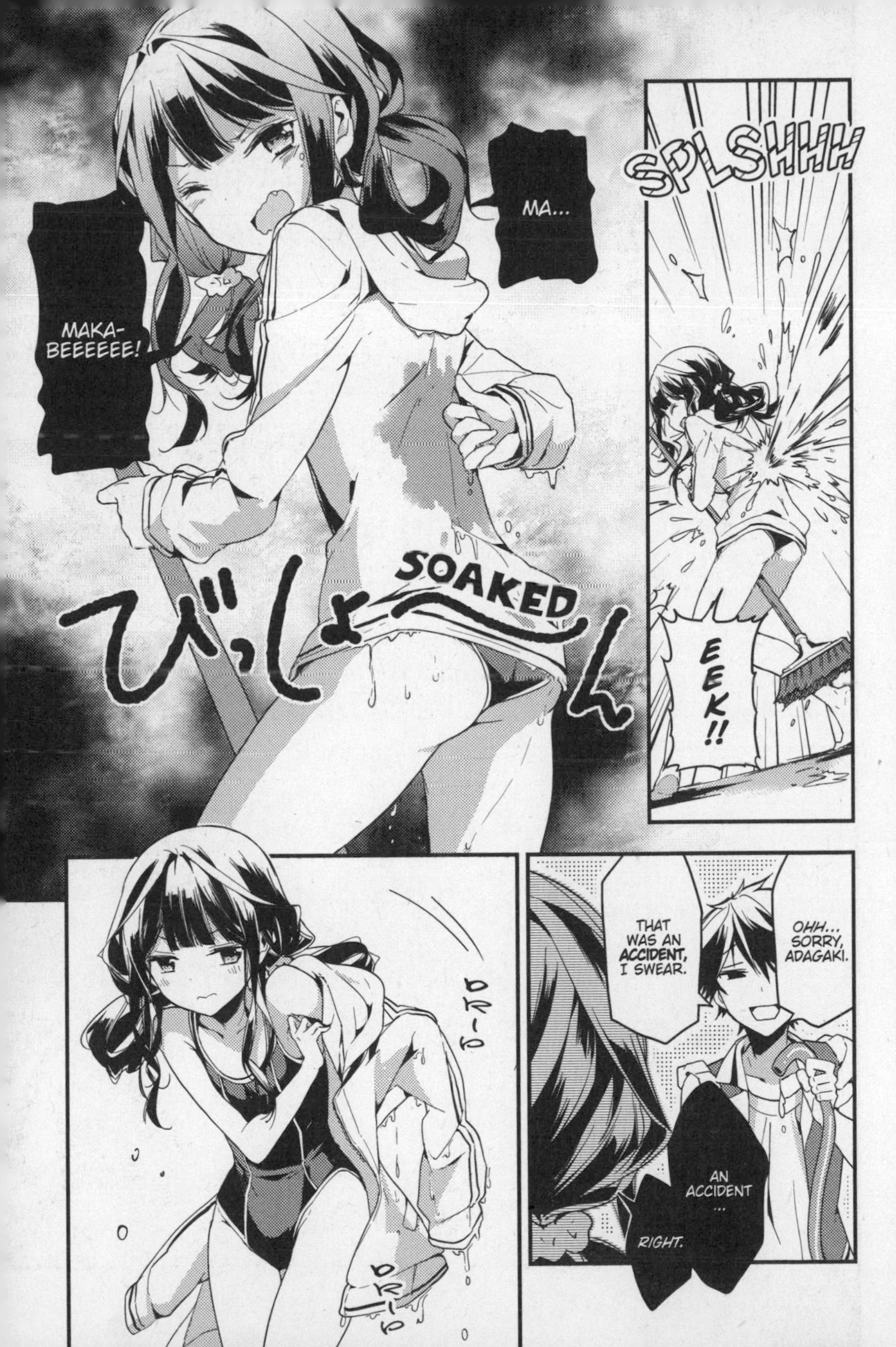
SPLSHHH
EEK!!
MA...
MAKA-BEEEEEE!
SOAKED
びしょ～ん
OHH... SORRY, ADAGAKI.
THAT WAS AN ACCIDENT, I SWEAR.
AN ACCIDENT ...
RIGHT.

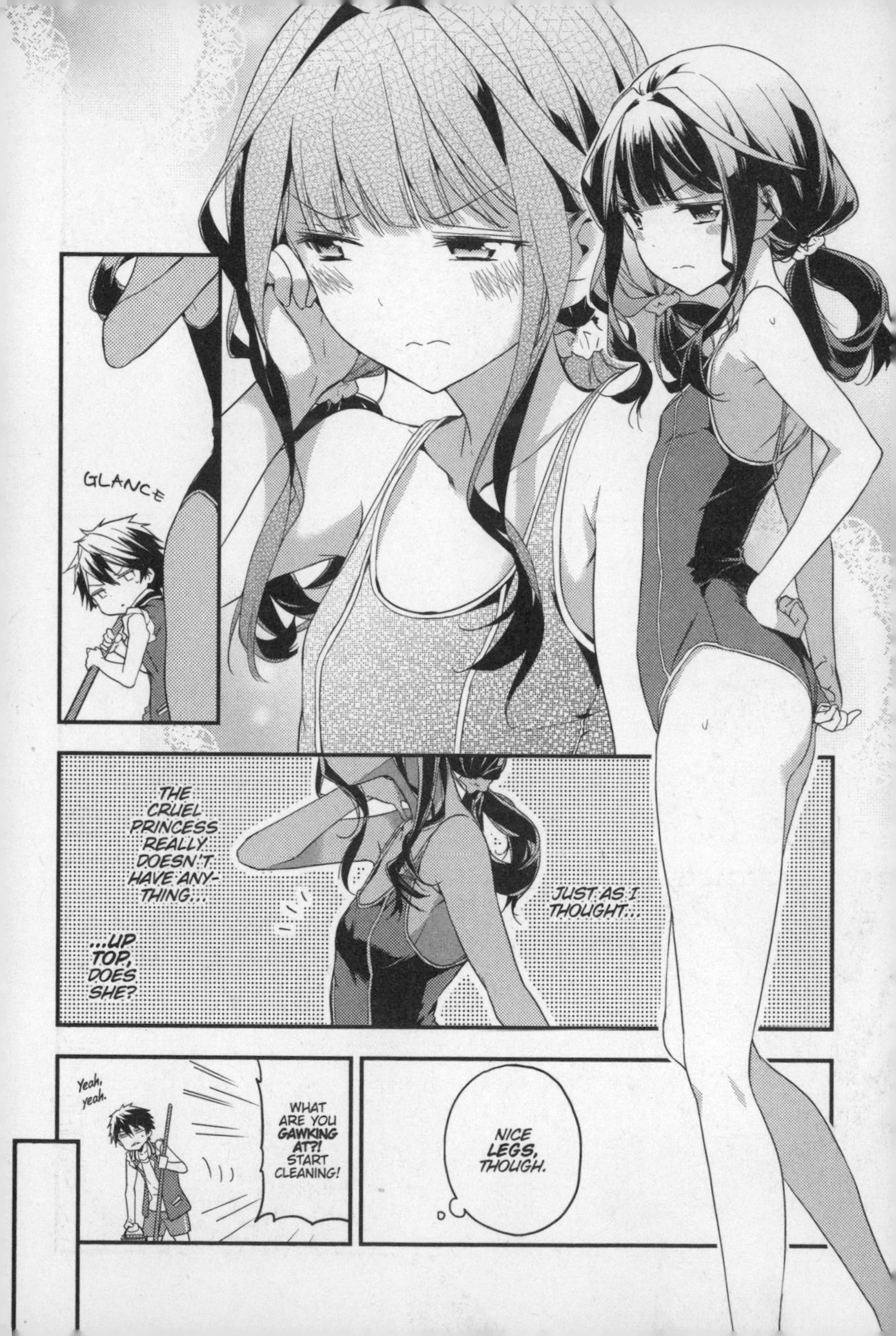
GLANCE
JUST AS I THOUGHT...
THE CRUEL PRINCESS REALLY DOESN'T HAVE ANYTHING...
...UP TOP, DOES SHE?
NICE LEGS, THOUGH.
WHAT ARE YOU GAWKING AT?! START CLEANING!
Yeah, yeah.

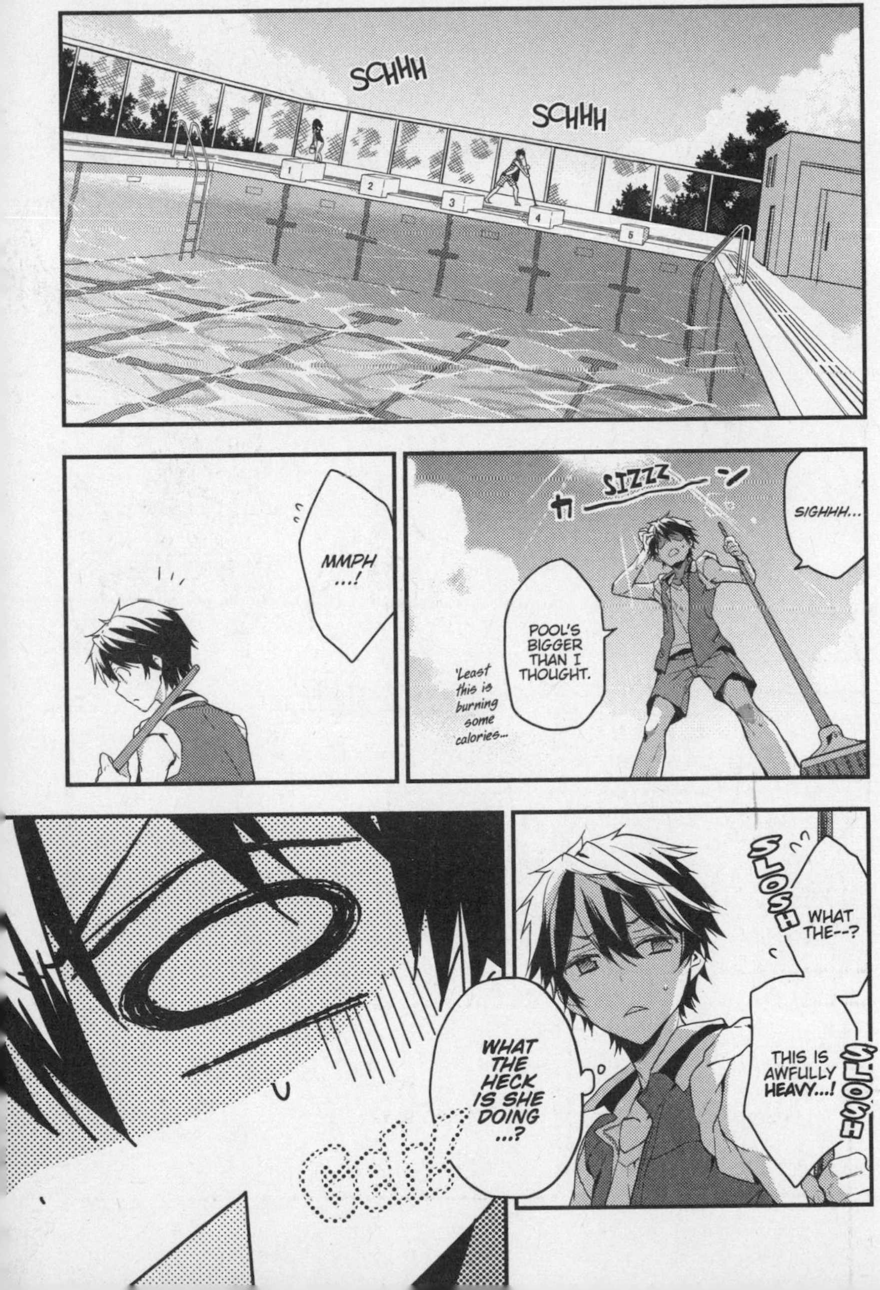
SCHHH
SCHHH
SIGHHH...
SIZZZ
POOL'S BIGGER THAN I THOUGHT.
'Least this is burning some calories...
MMPH ...!
SLOSH
WHAT THE--?
THIS IS AWFULLY HEAVY...!
SLOSH
WHAT THE HECK IS SHE DOING ...?

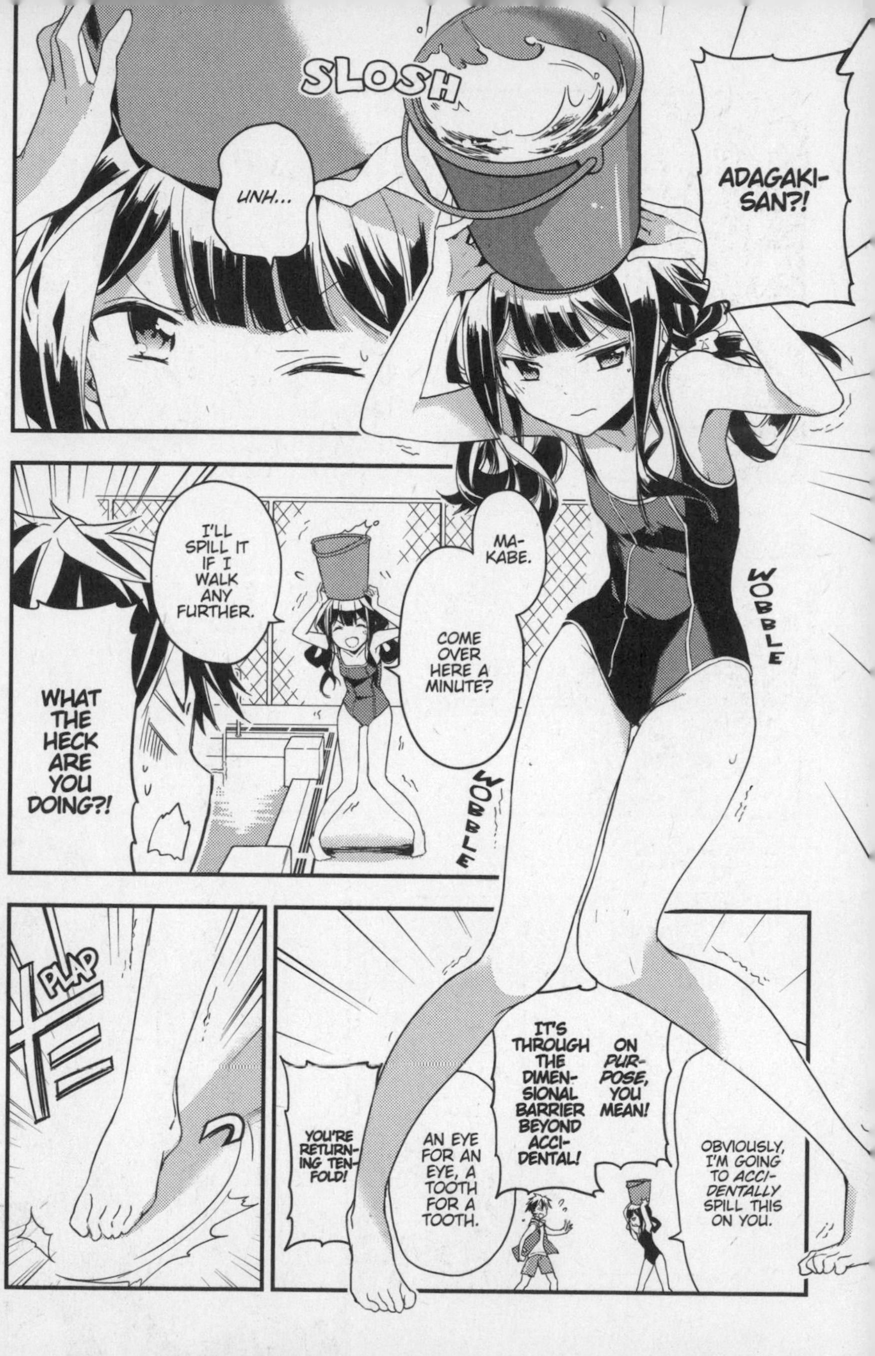
ADAGAKI-SAN?!
SLOSH
UNH...
WOBBLE
MA-KABE.
COME OVER HERE A MINUTE?
I'LL SPILL IT IF I WALK ANY FURTHER.
WHAT THE HECK ARE YOU DOING?!
WOBBLE
OBVIOUSLY, I'M GOING TO ACCIDENTALLY SPILL THIS ON YOU.
ON PURPOSE, YOU MEAN!
IT'S THROUGH THE DIMENSIONAL BARRIER BEYOND ACCIDENTAL!
AN EYE FOR AN EYE, A TOOTH FOR A TOOTH.
YOU'RE RETURNING TENFOLD!
PLAP

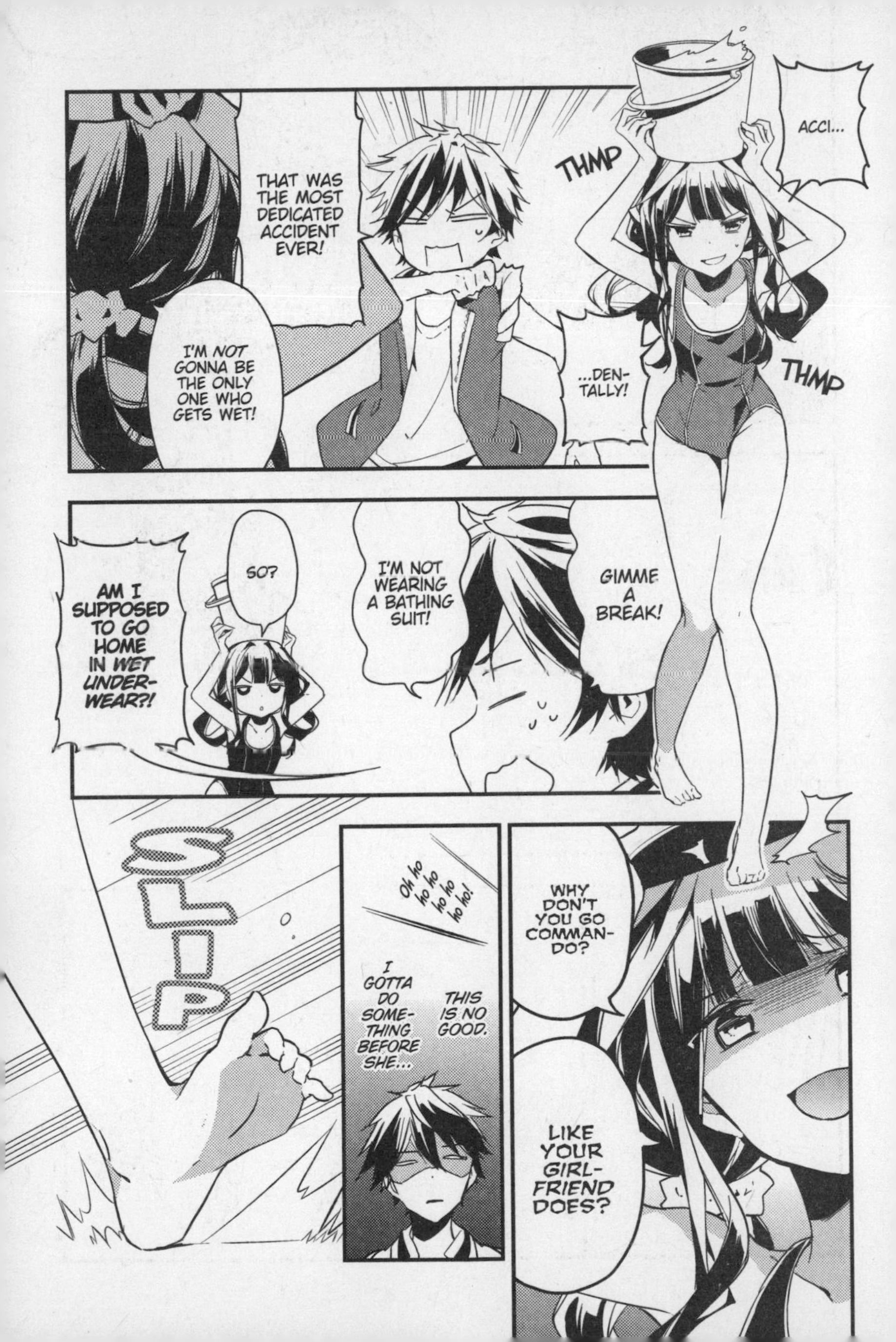
ACCI...
THMP
THMP
...DEN-TALLY!
THAT WAS THE MOST DEDICATED ACCIDENT EVER!
I'M *NOT* GONNA BE THE ONLY ONE WHO GETS WET!
GIMME A BREAK!
I'M NOT WEARING A BATHING SUIT!
SO?
AM I SUPPOSED TO GO HOME IN *WET UNDER-WEAR*?!
WHY DON'T YOU GO COMMAN-DO?
LIKE YOUR GIRL-FRIEND DOES?
Oh ho ho ho ho ho ho!
THIS IS NO GOOD.
I GOTTA DO SOME-THING BEFORE SHE...
SLIP

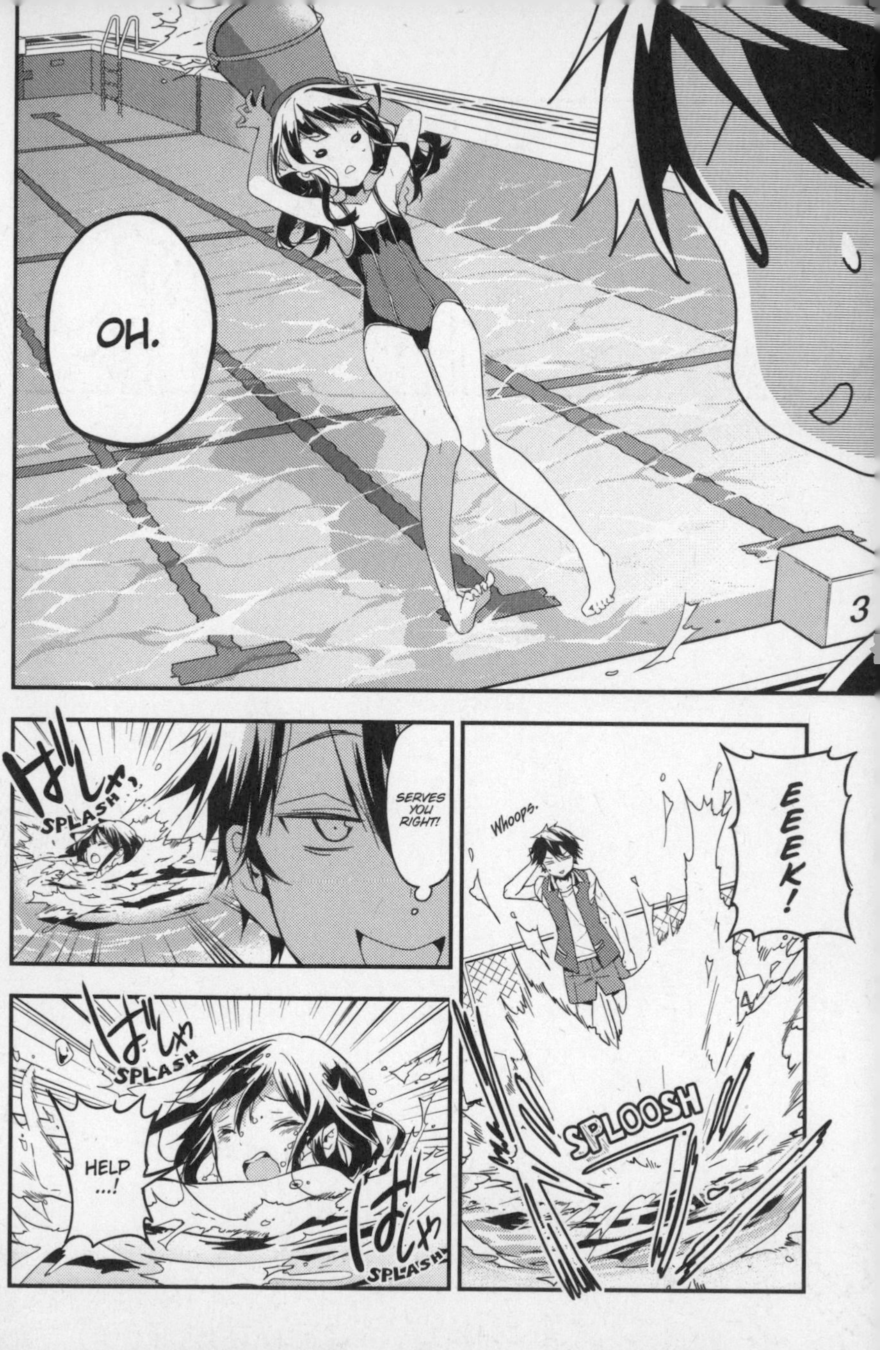
OH.
3
EEEK!
Whoops.
SPLOOSH
SPLASH
SERVES YOU RIGHT!
SPLASH
HELP ...!
SPLASH

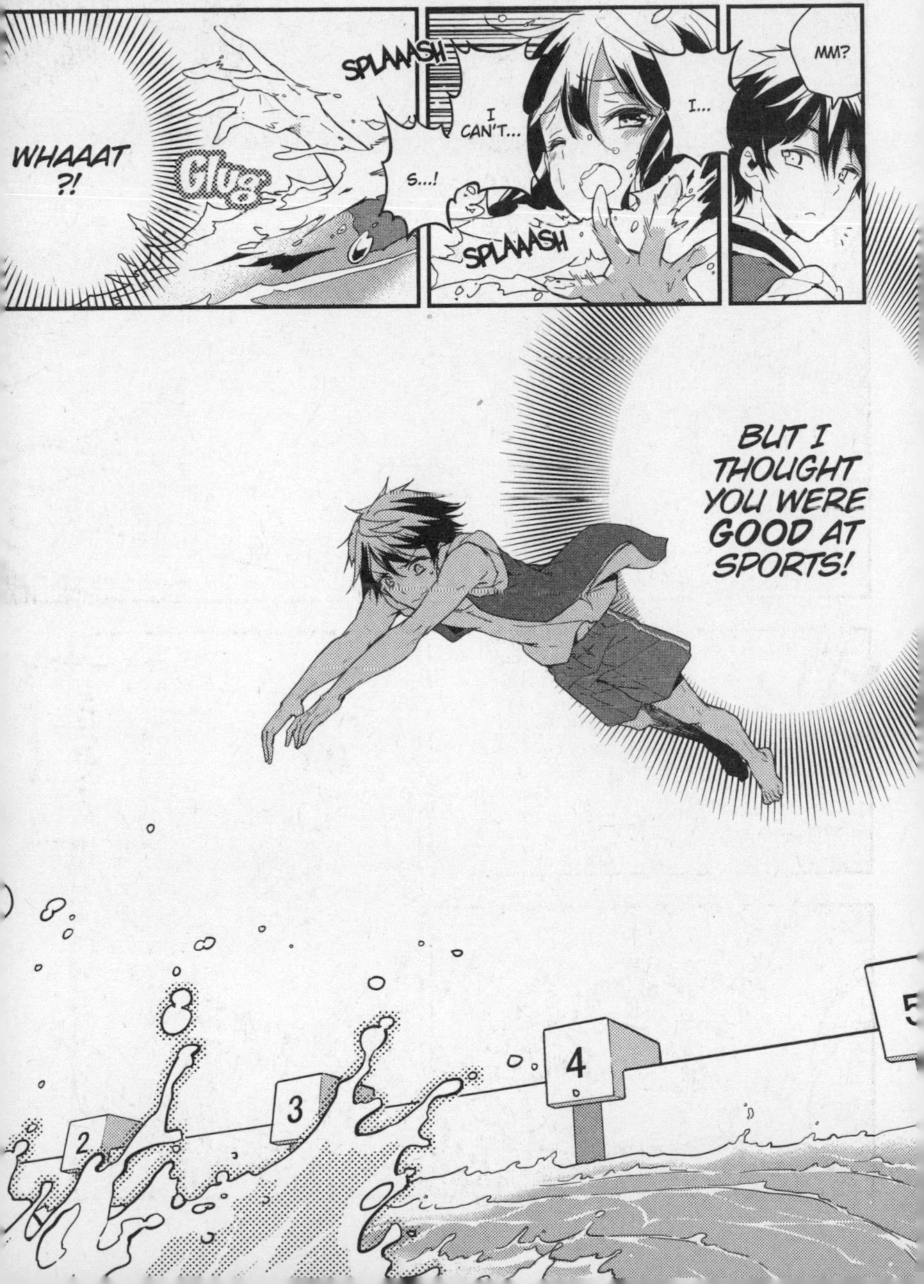
MM?
I...
I CAN'T...
SPLAAASH
S...!
SPLAAASH
Glug
WHAAAT ?!
BUT I THOUGHT YOU WERE GOOD AT SPORTS!

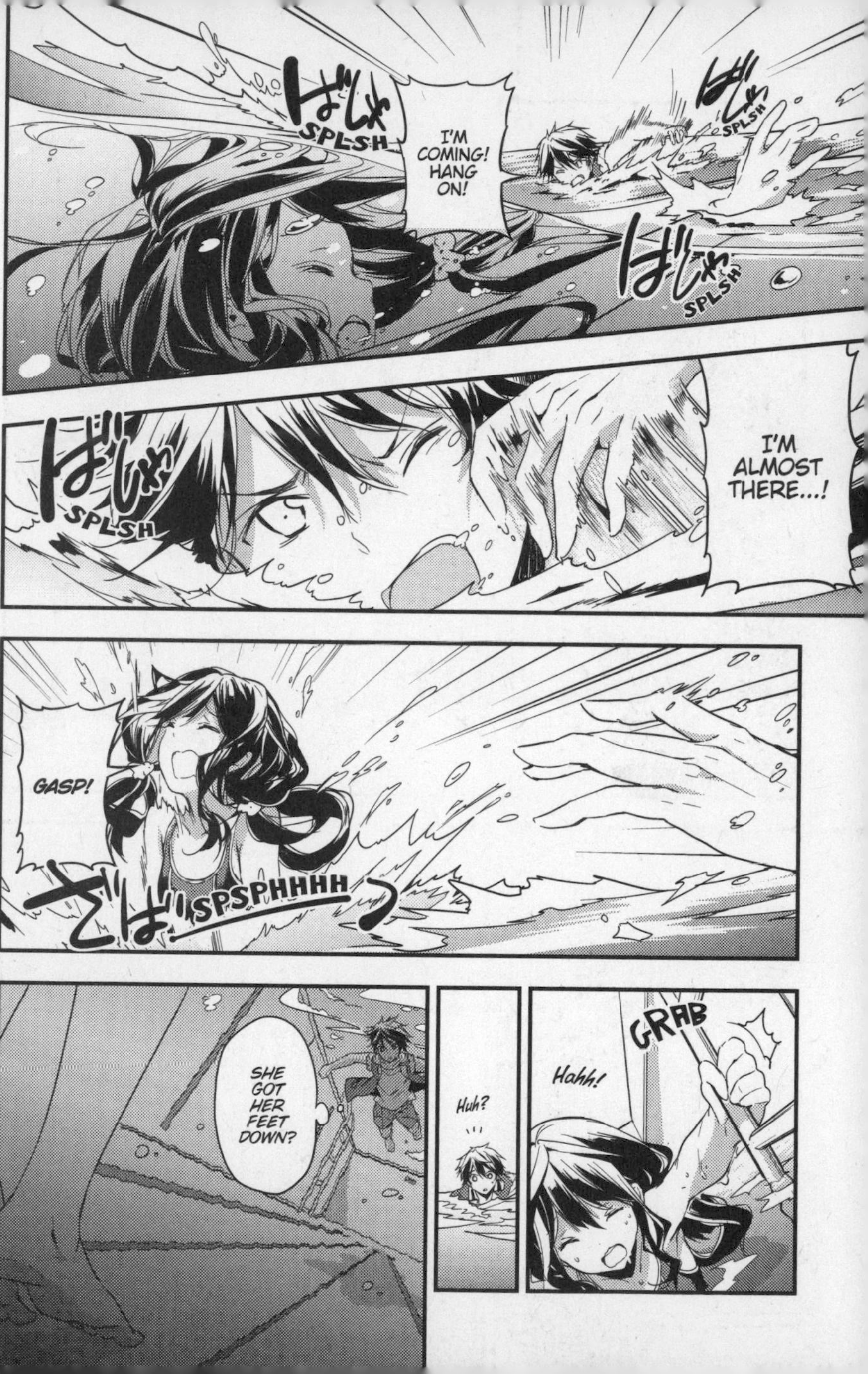
ばじゃ SPLSH
I'M COMING! HANG ON!
ばじゃ SPLSH
ばじゃ SPLSH
I'M ALMOST THERE...!
ばじゃ SPLSH
GASP!
ざばっ SPSPHHHH
GRAB
Hahh!
Huh?
SHE GOT HER FEET DOWN?

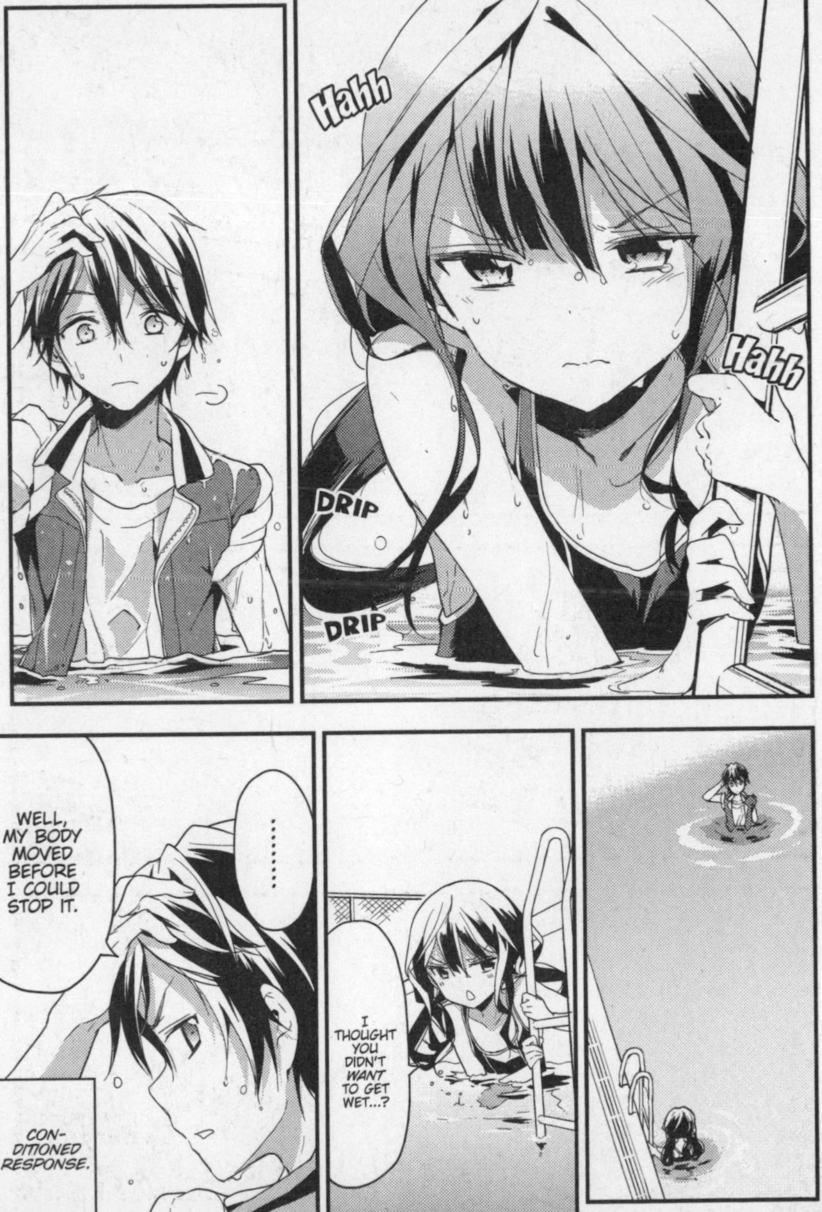
Hahh
Hahh
DRIP
DRIP
I THOUGHT YOU DIDN'T *WANT* TO GET WET...?
......
WELL, MY BODY MOVED BEFORE I COULD STOP IT.
CON-DITIONED RESPONSE.

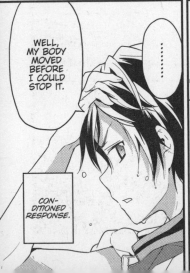

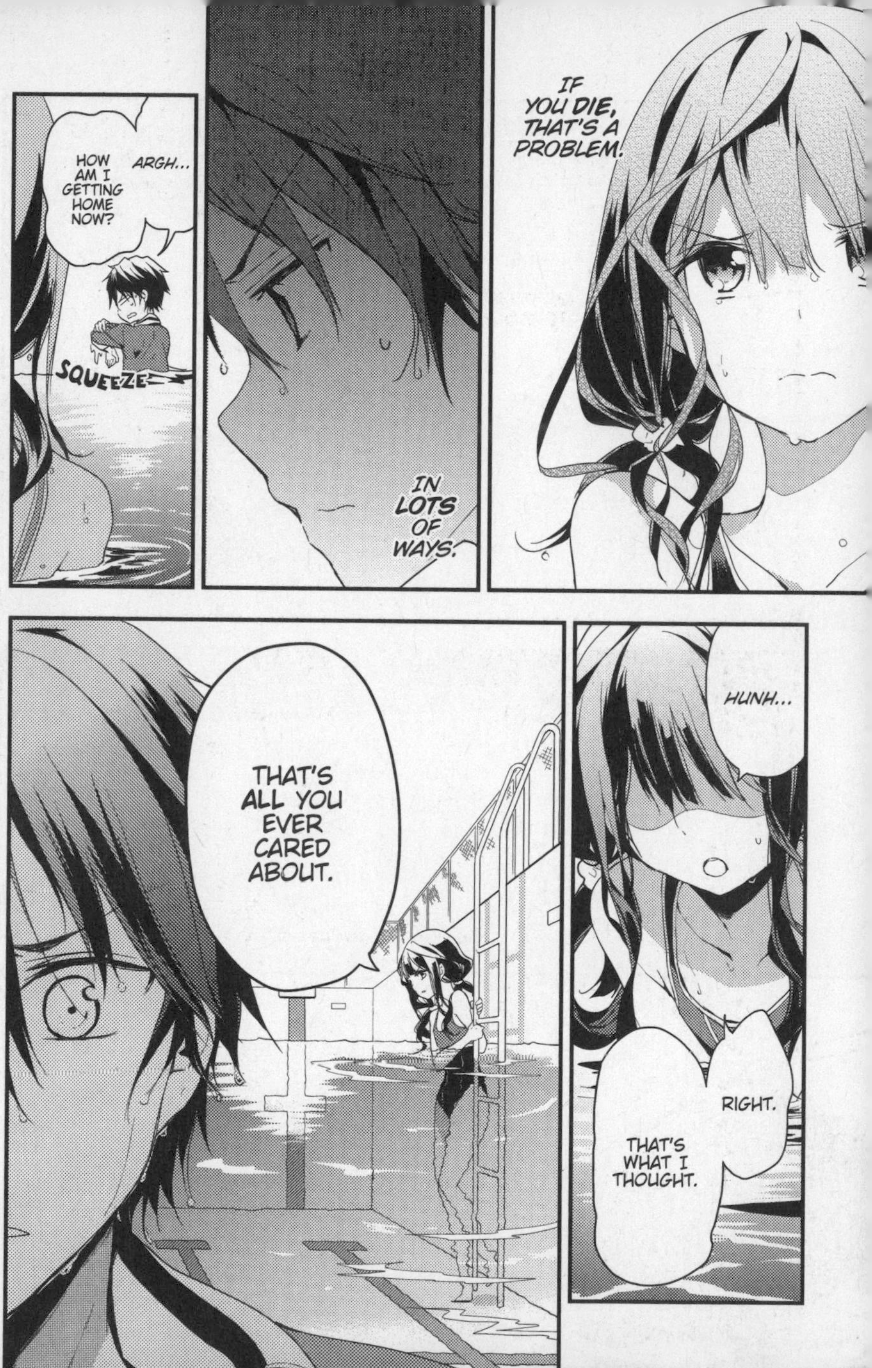
IF YOU DIE, THAT'S A PROBLEM!
IN LOTS OF WAYS.
ARGH...
HOW AM I GETTING HOME NOW?
SQUEEZE
HUNH...
RIGHT.
THAT'S WHAT I THOUGHT.
THAT'S ALL YOU EVER CARED ABOUT.

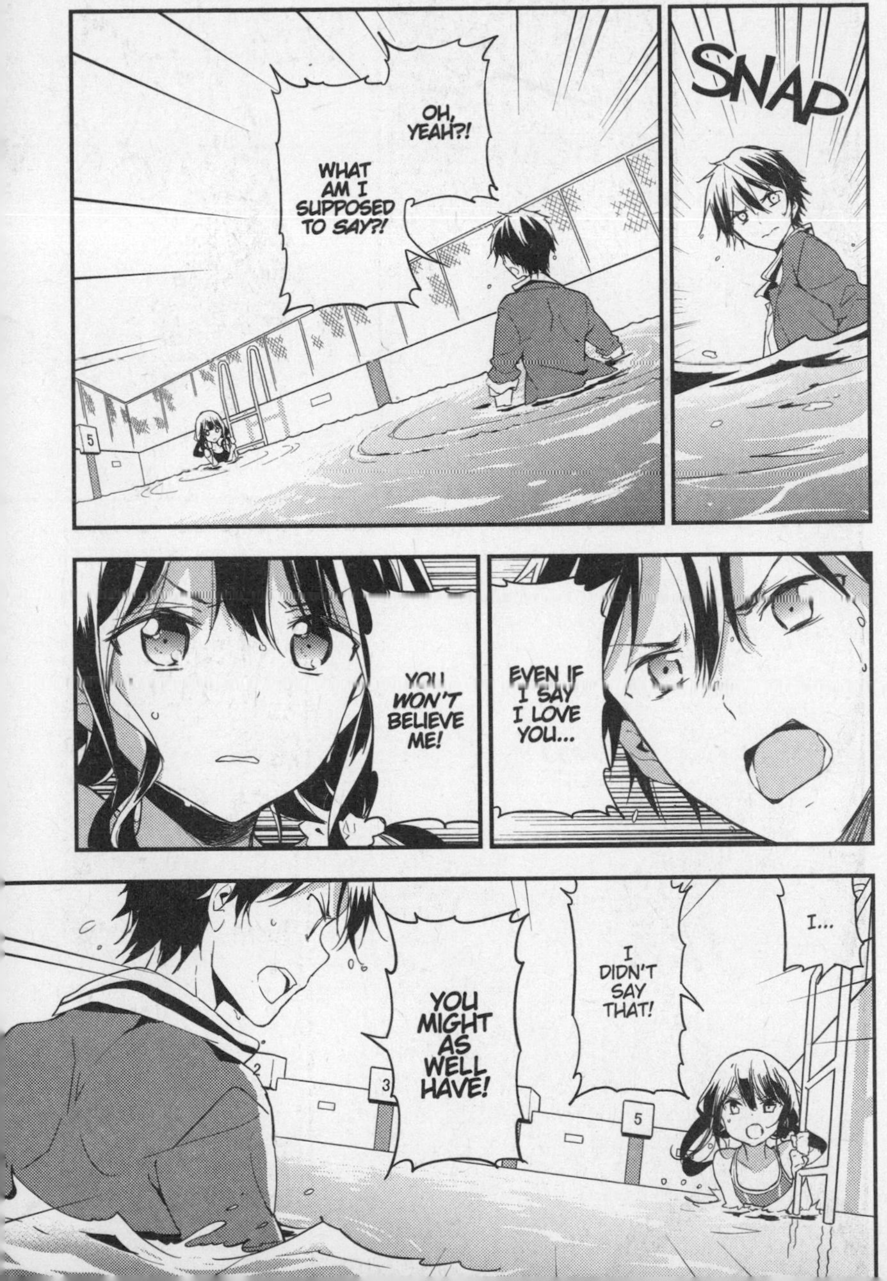
SNAP
OH, YEAH?!
WHAT AM I SUPPOSED TO SAY?!
EVEN IF I SAY I LOVE YOU...
YOU WON'T BELIEVE ME!
I...
I DIDN'T SAY THAT!
YOU MIGHT AS WELL HAVE!

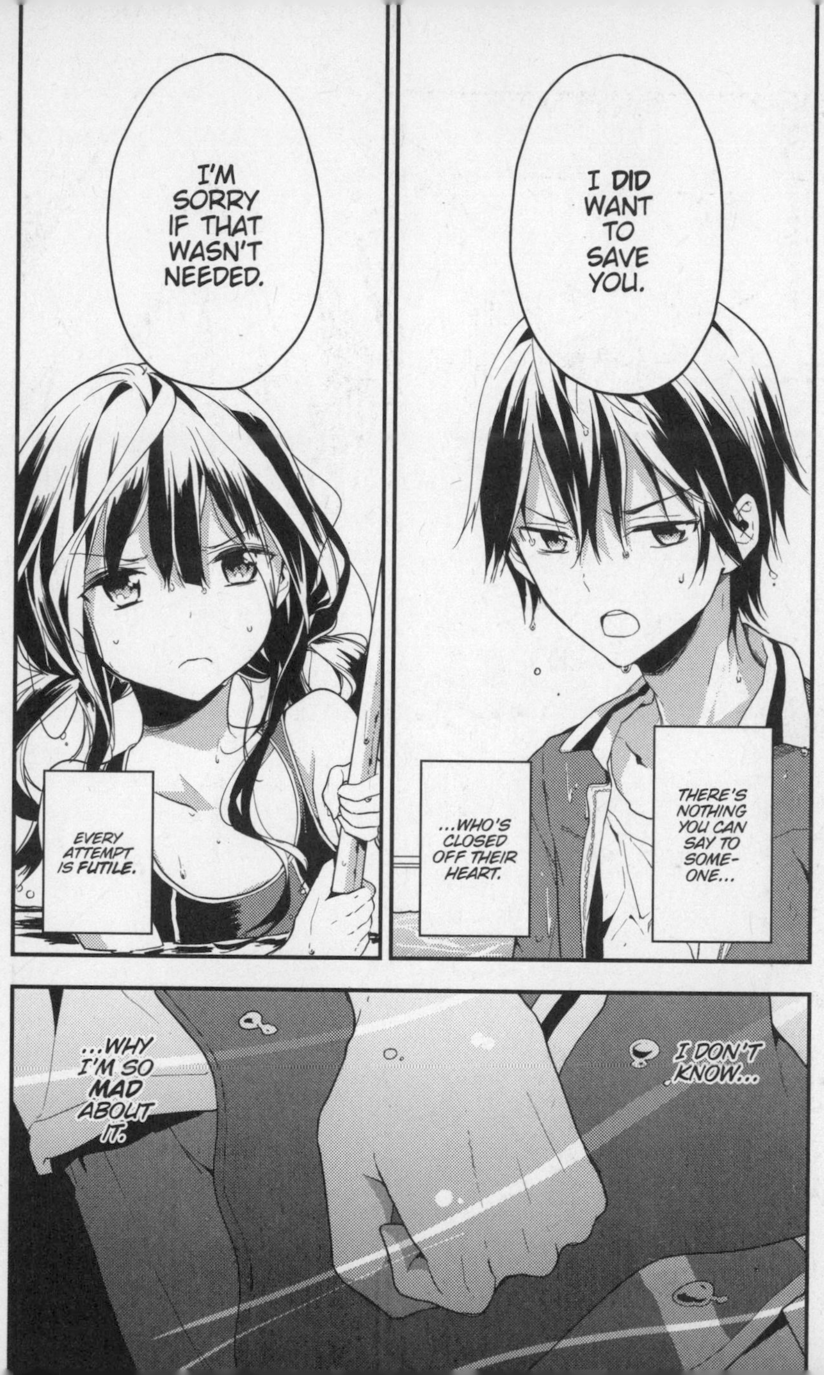
I DID WANT TO SAVE YOU.
THERE'S NOTHING YOU CAN SAY TO SOME-ONE...
...WHO'S CLOSED OFF THEIR HEART.
I'M SORRY IF THAT WASN'T NEEDED.
EVERY ATTEMPT IS FUTILE.
I DON'T KNOW...
...WHY I'M SO MAD ABOUT IT.

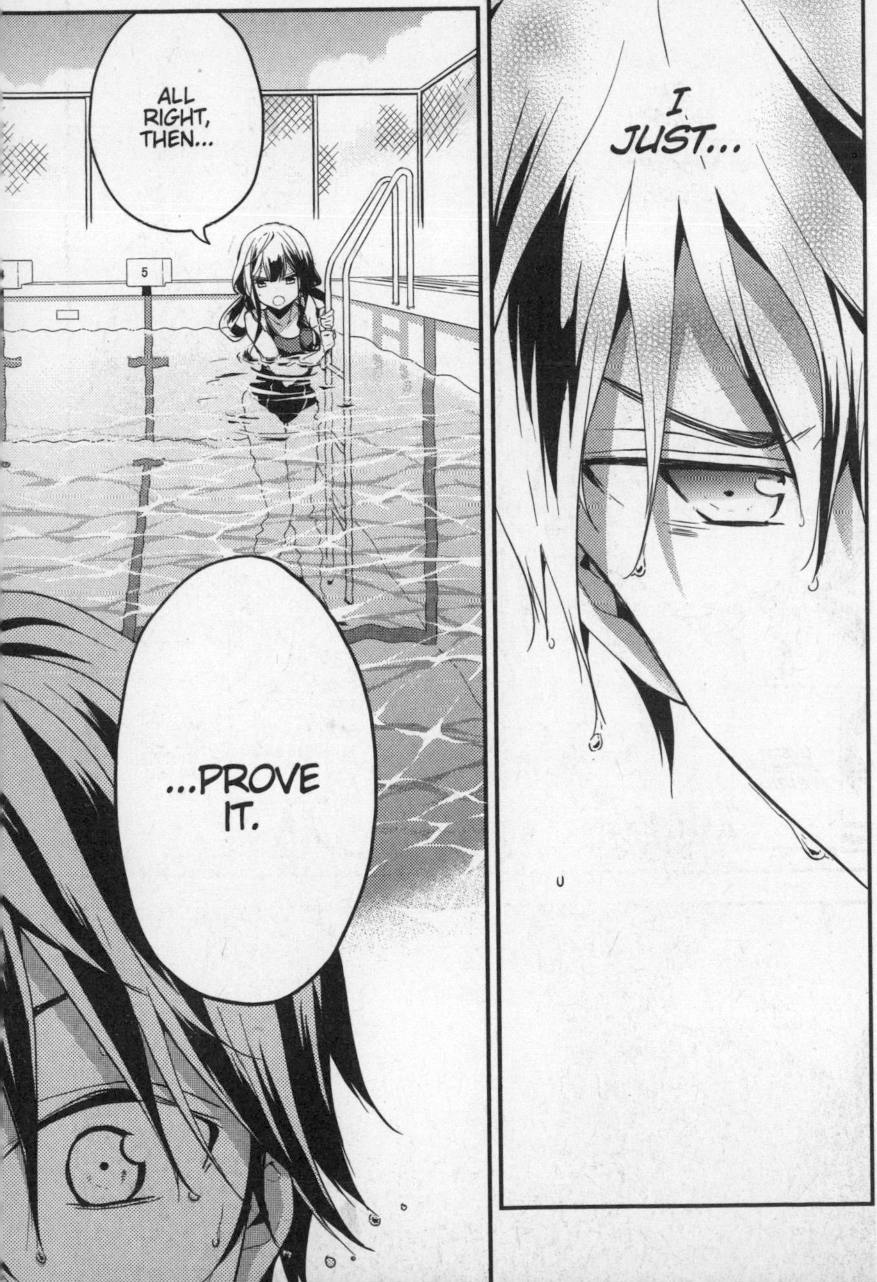
I JUST...
ALL RIGHT, THEN...
...PROVE IT.

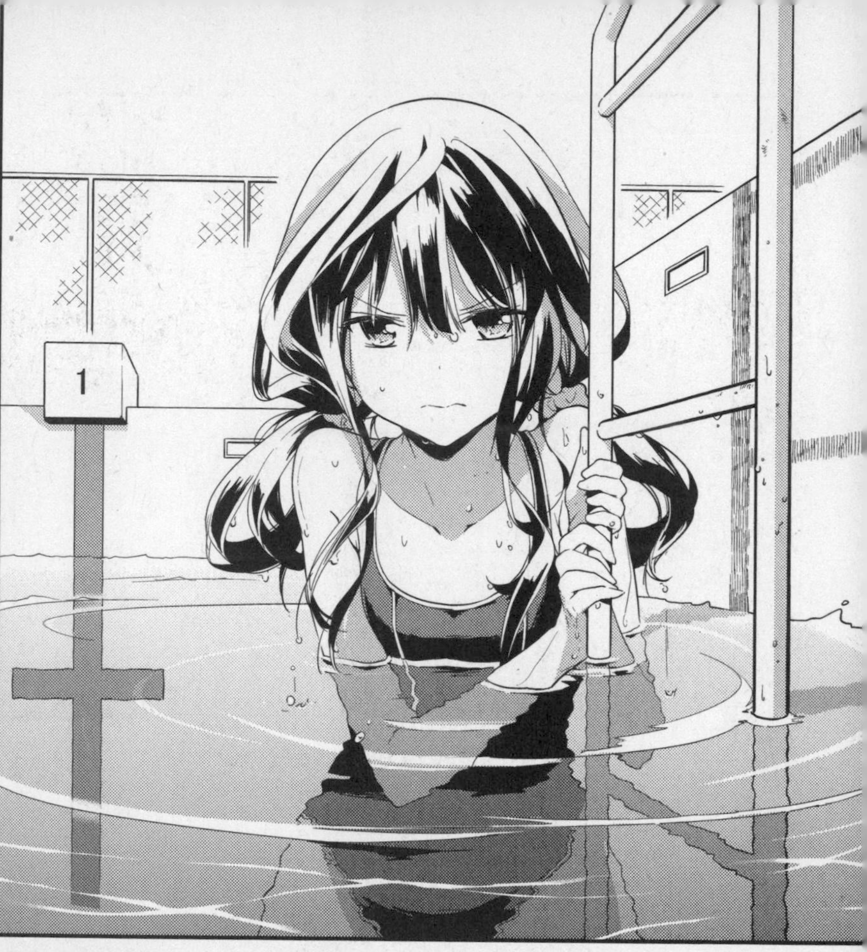
1

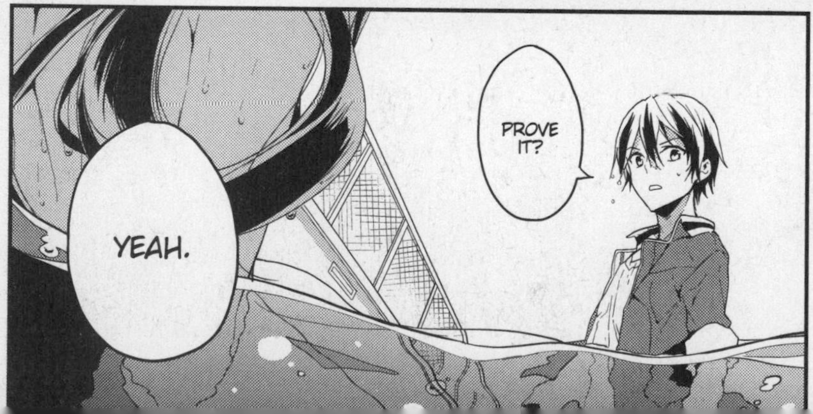
PROVE IT?
YEAH.

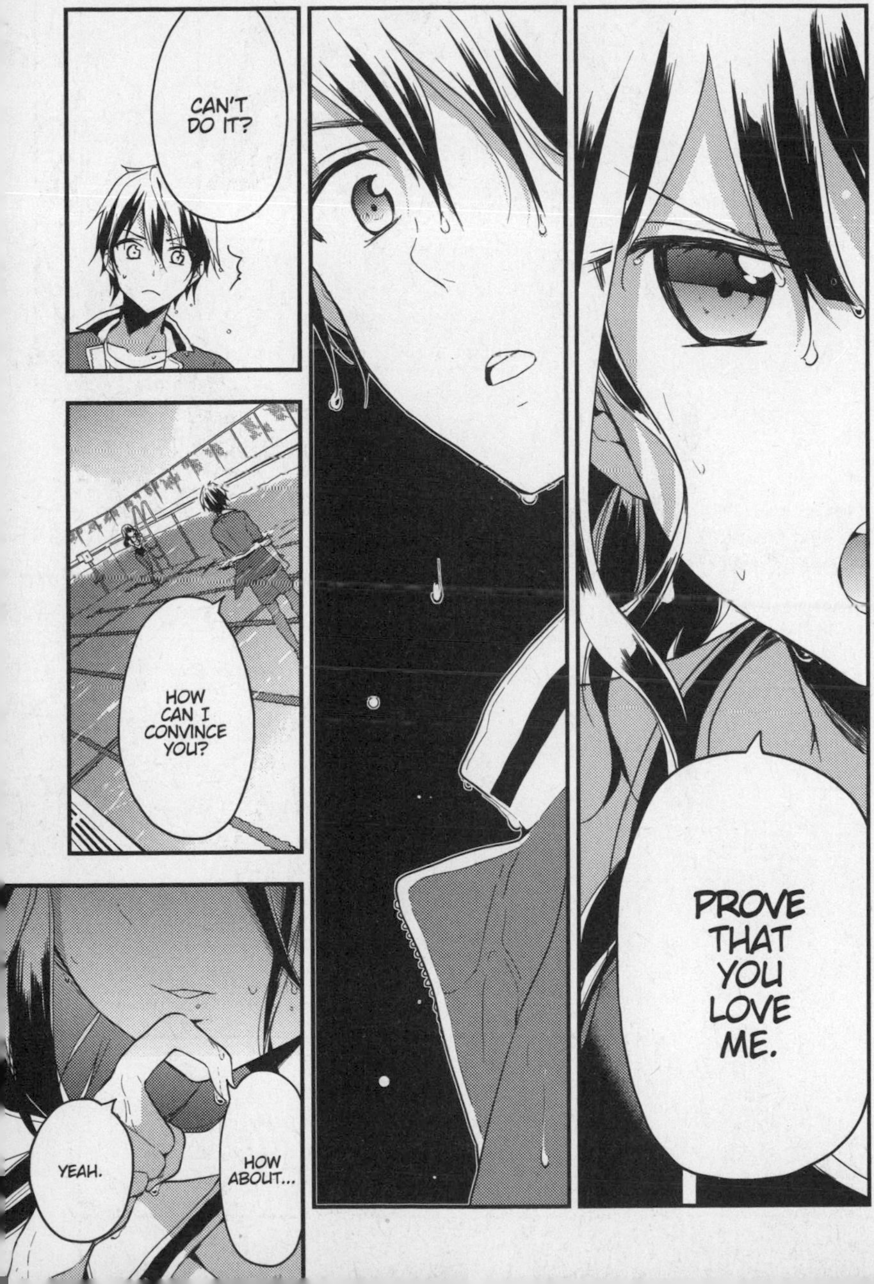
PROVE THAT YOU LOVE ME.
CAN'T DO IT?
HOW CAN I CONVINCE YOU?
HOW ABOUT...
YEAH.

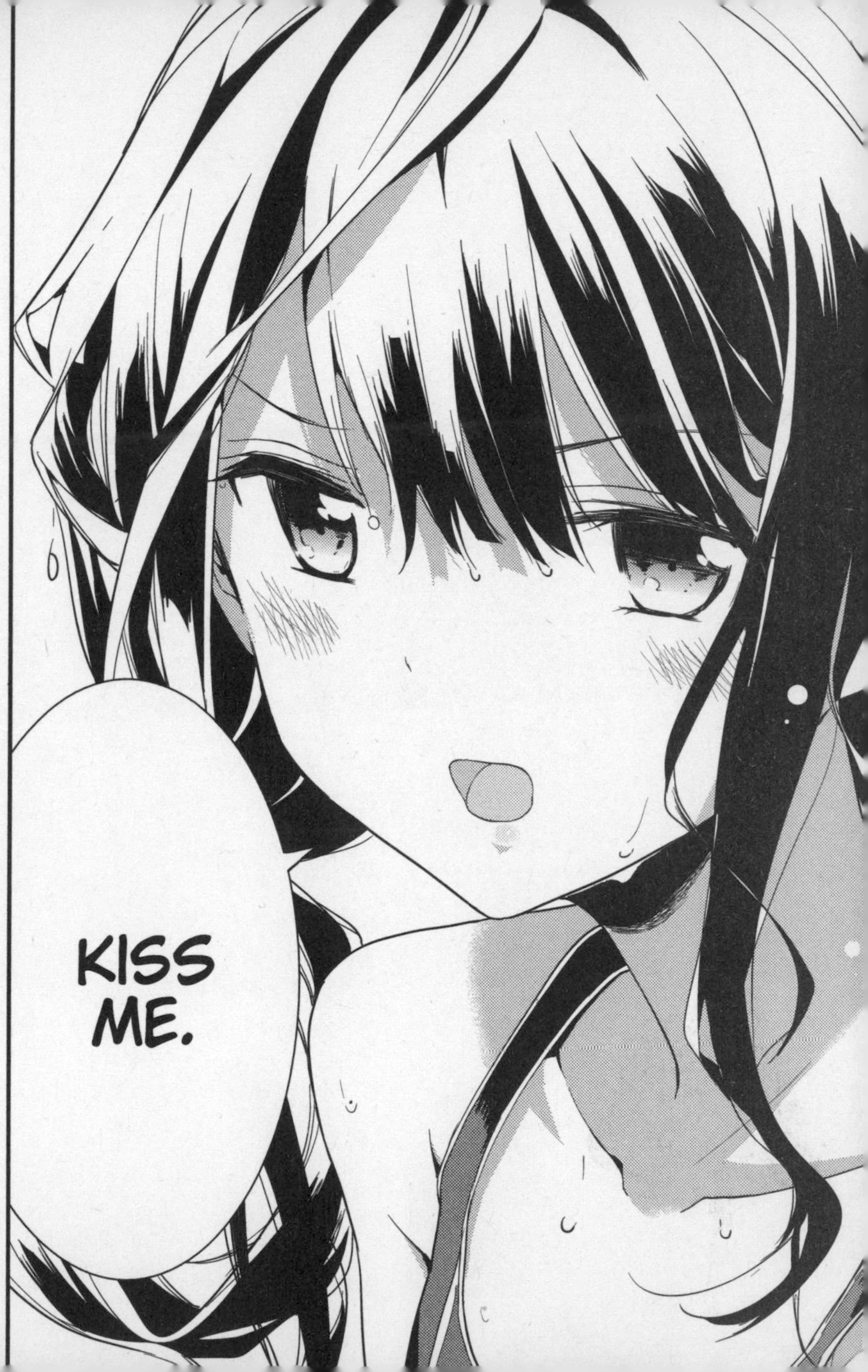
KISS ME.

3

Masamune-kun's REVENGE
Presented by Hazuki Takeoka & TIV

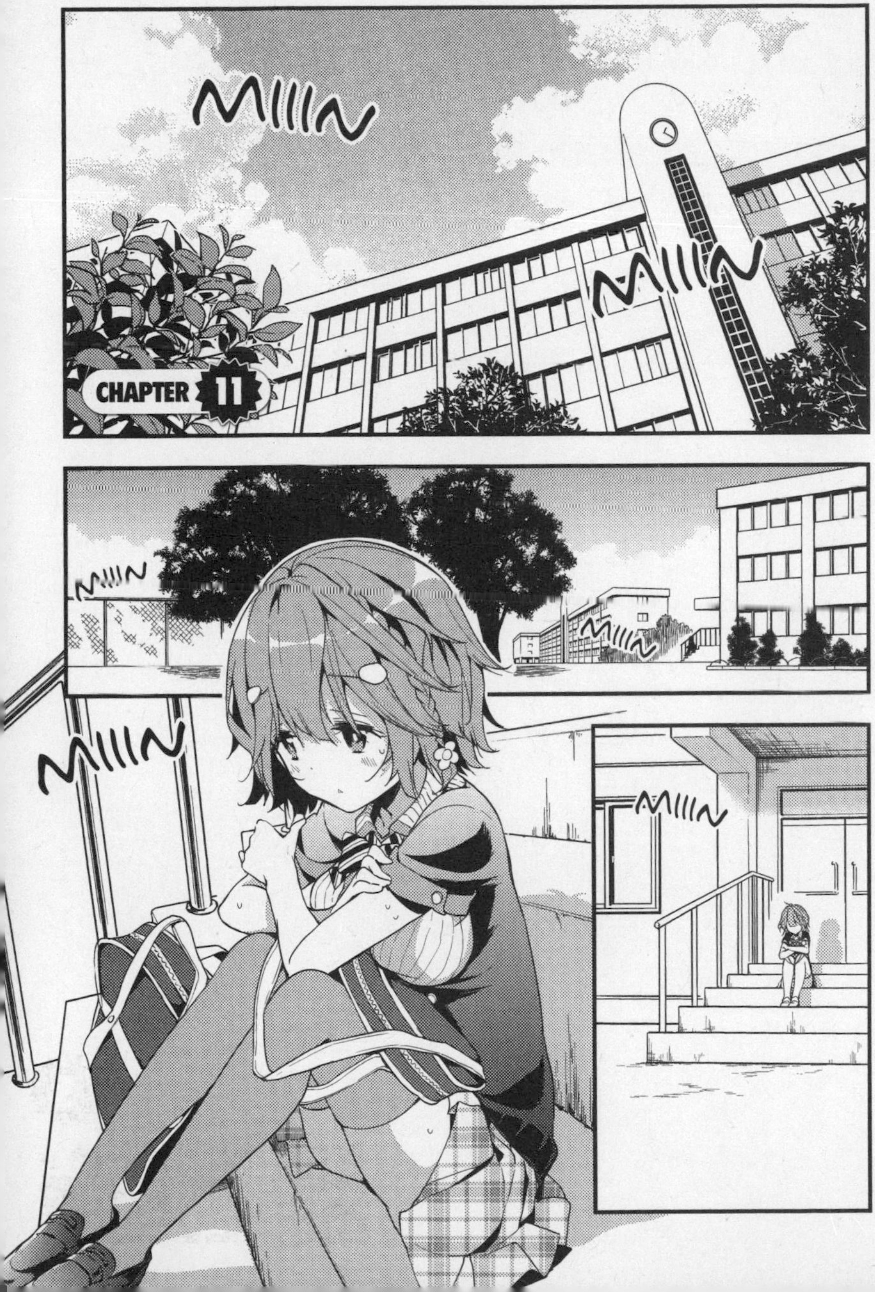
MIIIN
MIIIN
CHAPTER 11
MIIIN
MIIIN
MIIIN
MIIIN

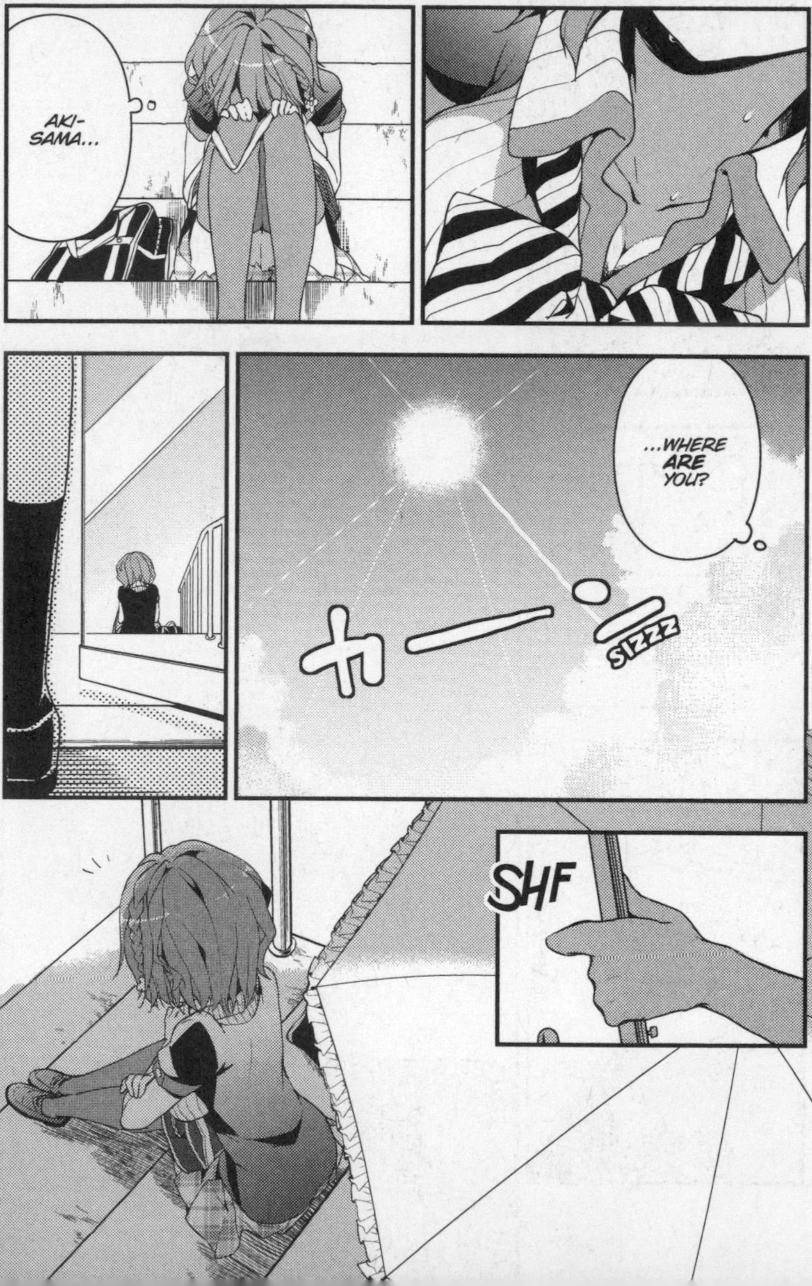
AKI-SAMA...
...WHERE ARE YOU?
カー
SIZZZ
SHF

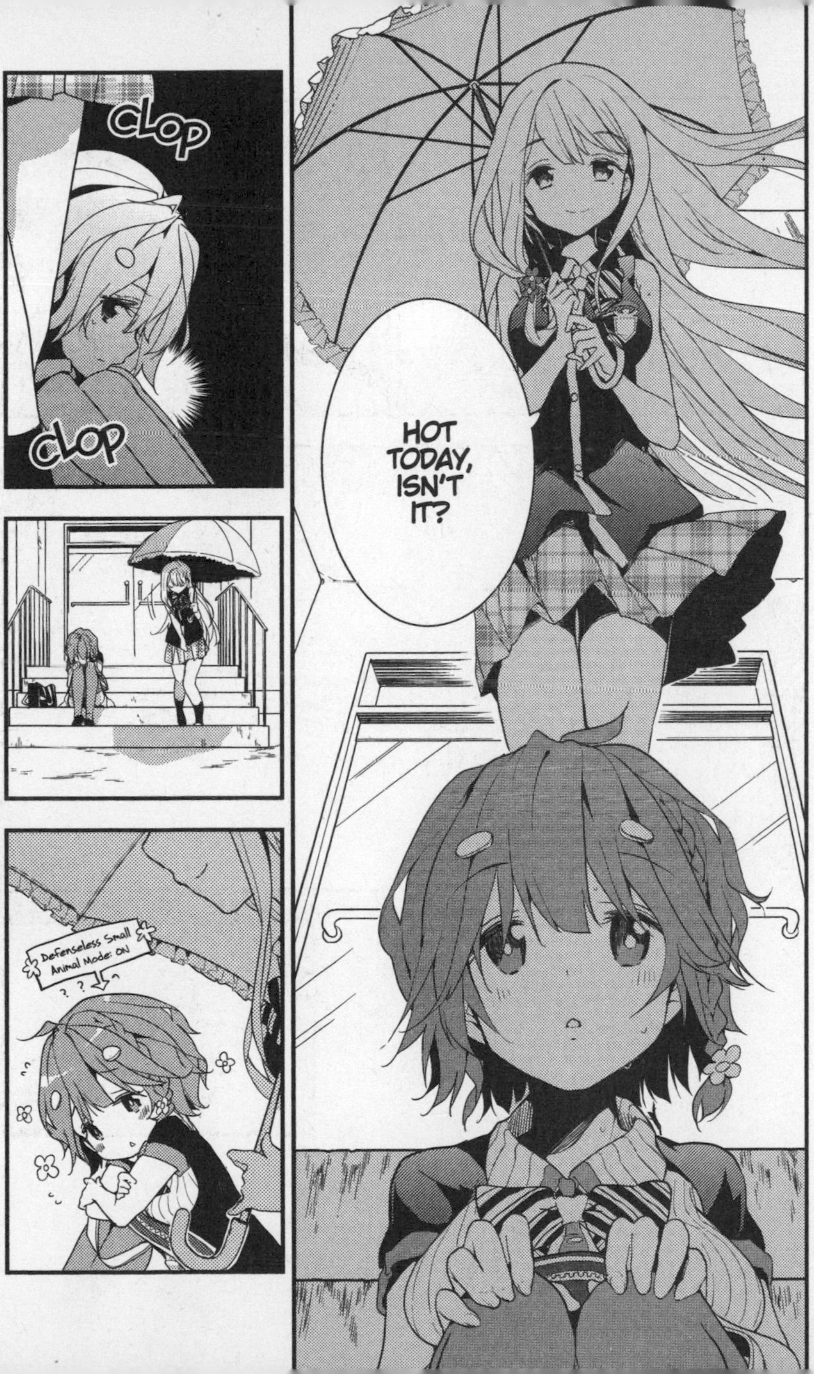
HOT TODAY, ISN'T IT?
CLOP
CLOP
Defenseless Small Animal Mode: ON

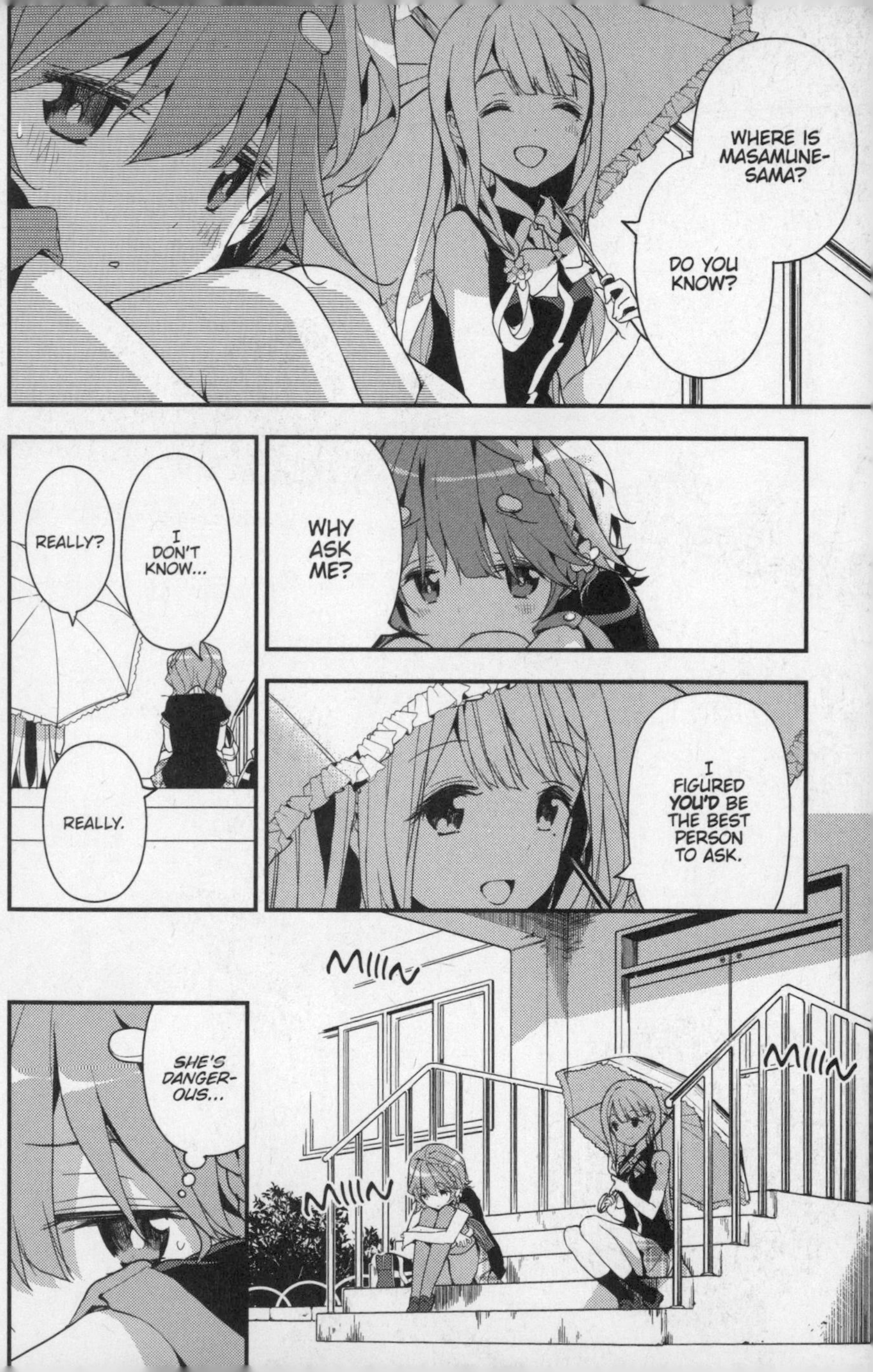
WHERE IS MASAMUNE-SAMA?
DO YOU KNOW?
WHY ASK ME?
I FIGURED YOU'D BE THE BEST PERSON TO ASK.
I DON'T KNOW...
REALLY?
REALLY.
MIIIN
MIIIN
MIIIN
SHE'S DANGER-OUS...

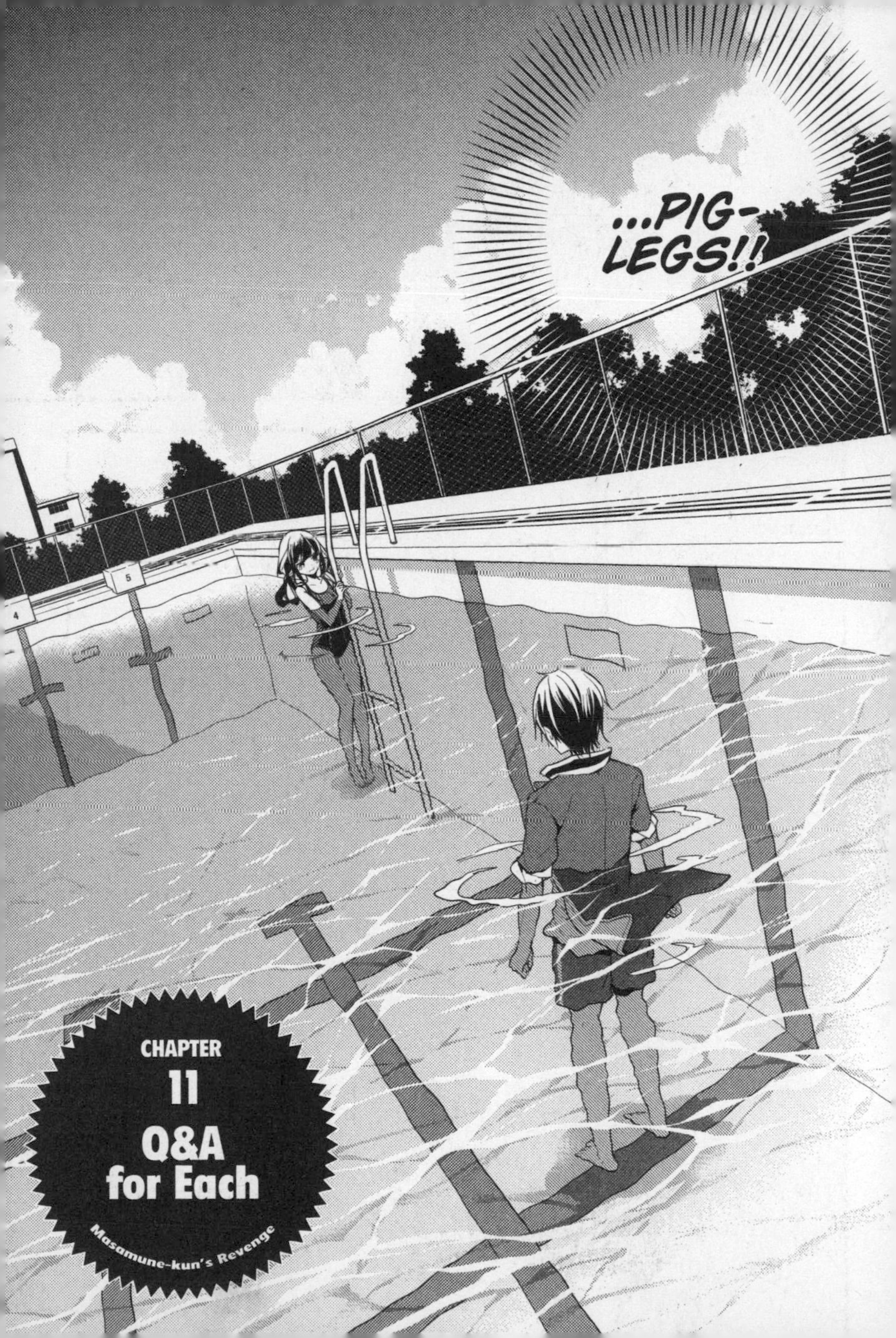
...PIG-LEGS!!
4
5
CHAPTER 11 Q&A for Each
Masamune-kun's Revenge

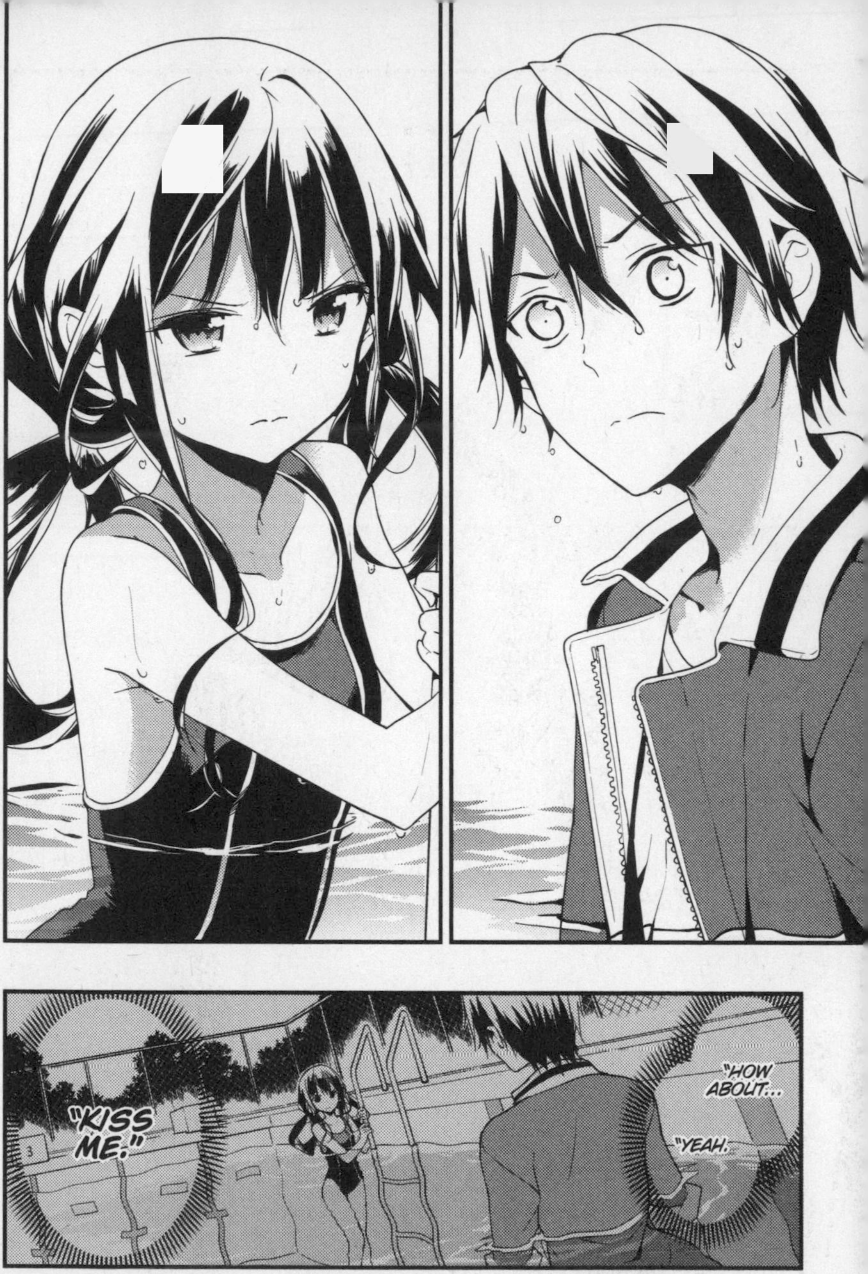
"HOW ABOUT...
"YEAH."
"KISS ME."

Kiss

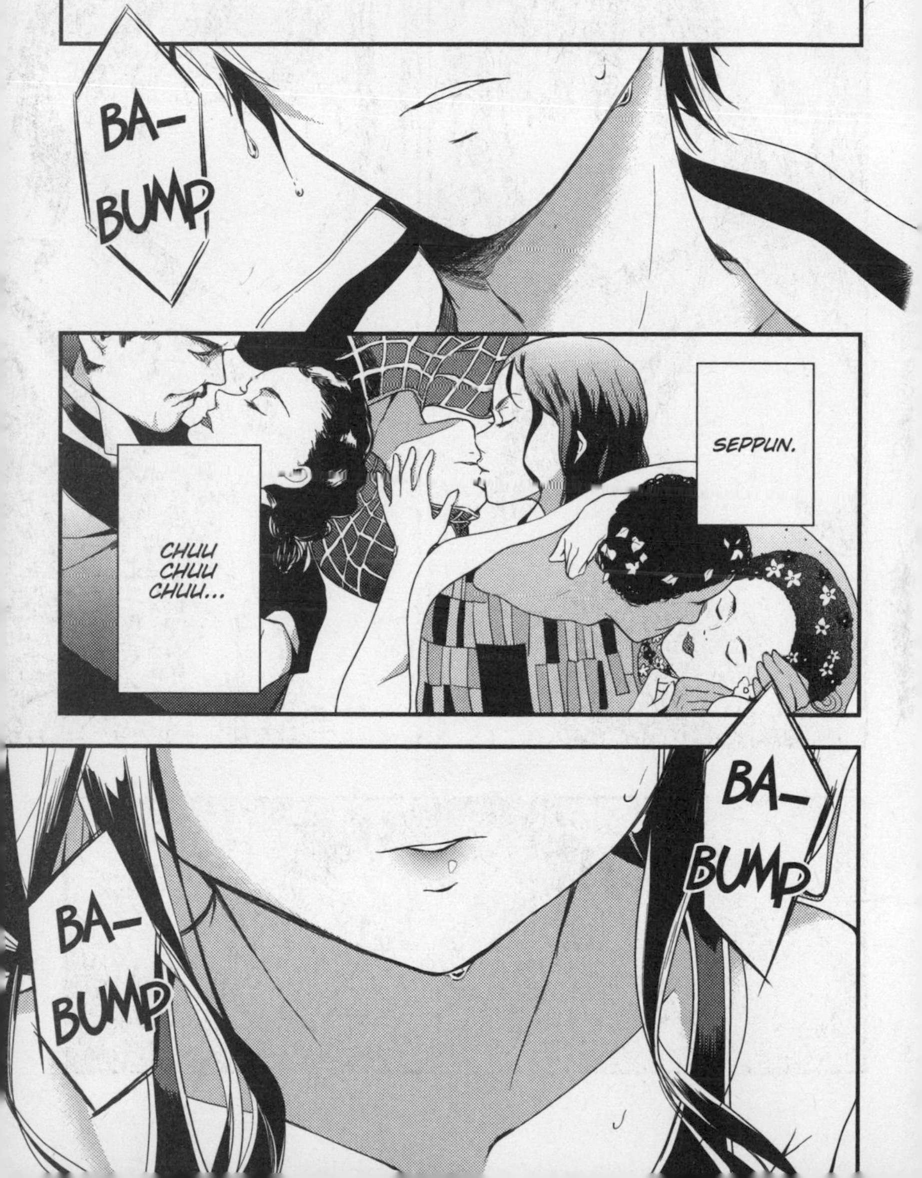
BA-BUMP
SEPPUN.
CHUU CHUU CHUU...
BA-BUMP
BA-BUMP

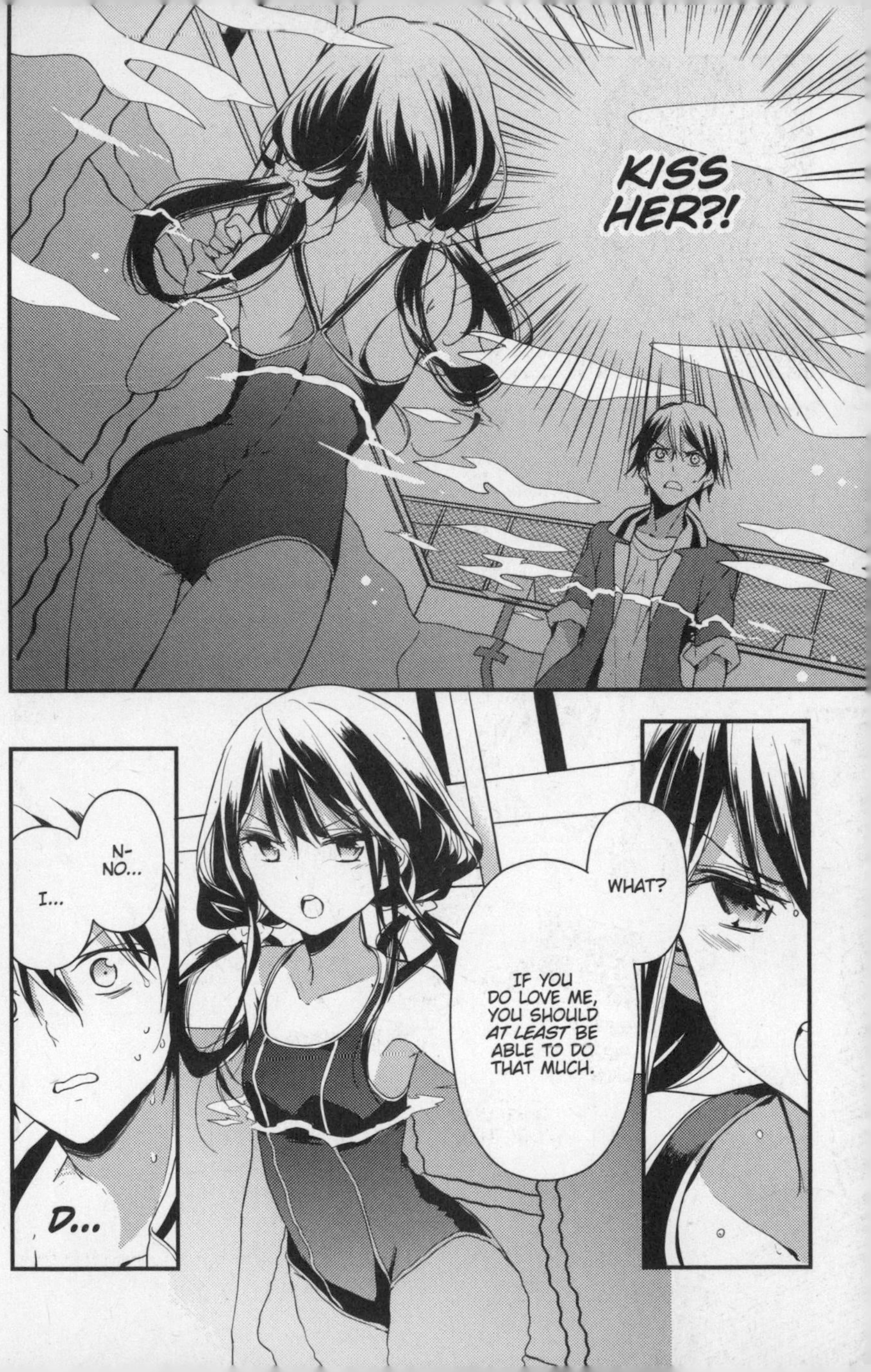
KISS HER?!
WHAT?
IF YOU DO LOVE ME, YOU SHOULD AT LEAST BE ABLE TO DO THAT MUCH.
N- NO...
I...
D...

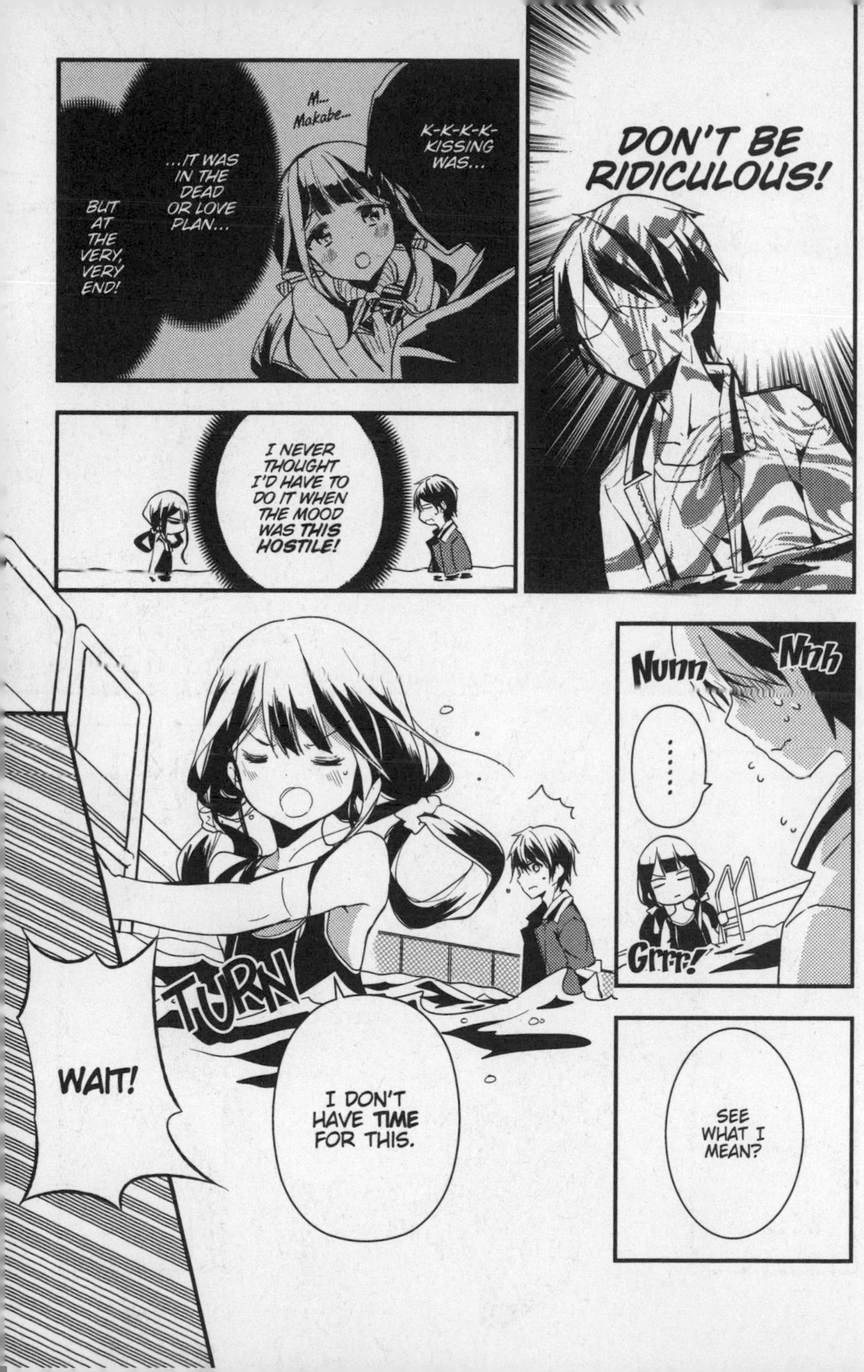
DON'T BE RIDICULOUS!
K-K-K-K-KISSING WAS...
M... Makabe...
...IT WAS IN THE DEAD OR LOVE PLAN...
BUT AT THE VERY, VERY END!
I NEVER THOUGHT I'D HAVE TO DO IT WHEN THE MOOD WAS THIS HOSTILE!
Nnh
Nunn
......
Grrr!
SEE WHAT I MEAN?
TURN
I DON'T HAVE TIME FOR THIS.
WAIT!

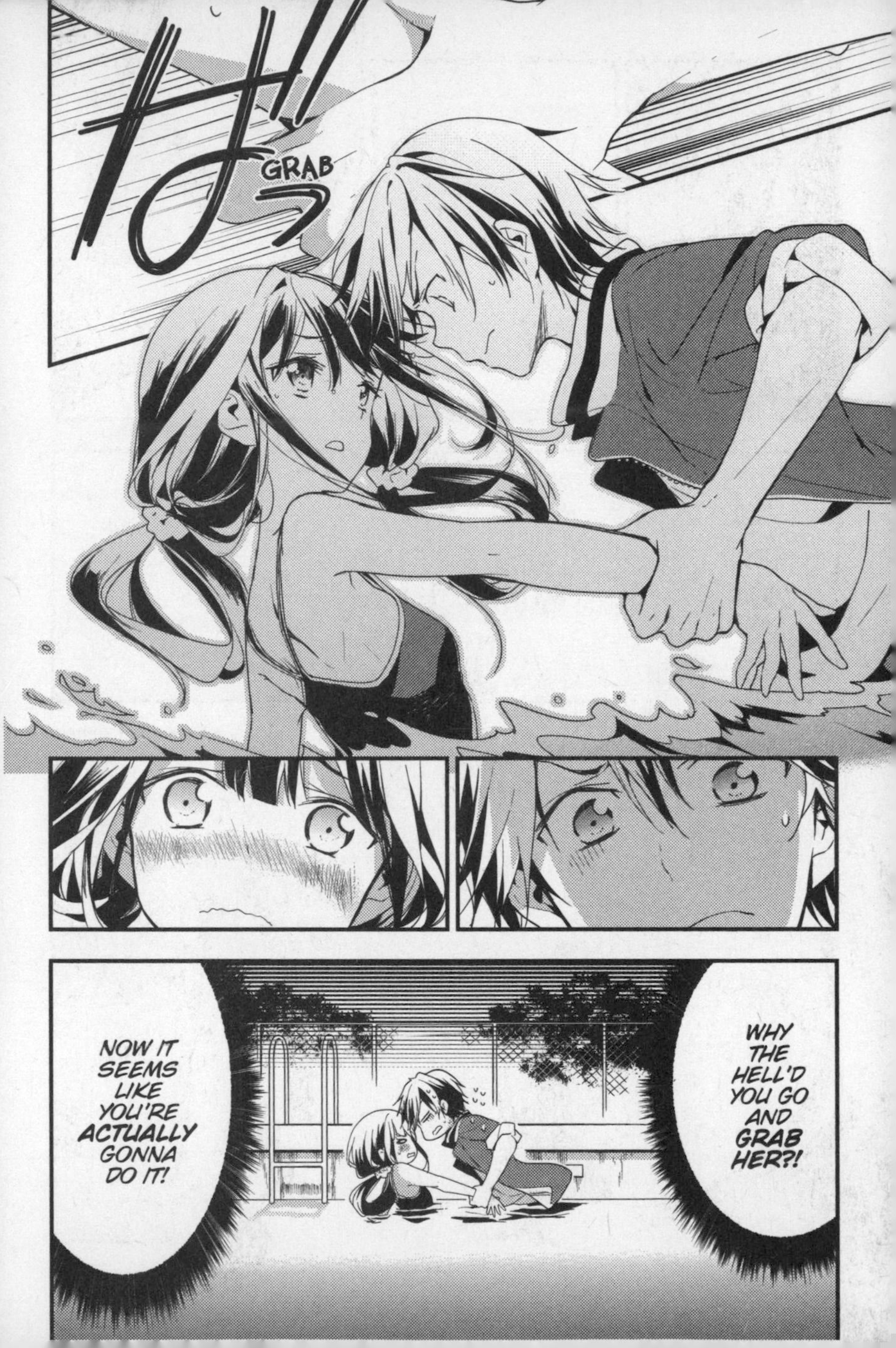
GRAB
WHY THE HELL'D YOU GO AND GRAB HER?!
NOW IT SEEMS LIKE YOU'RE ACTUALLY GONNA DO IT!

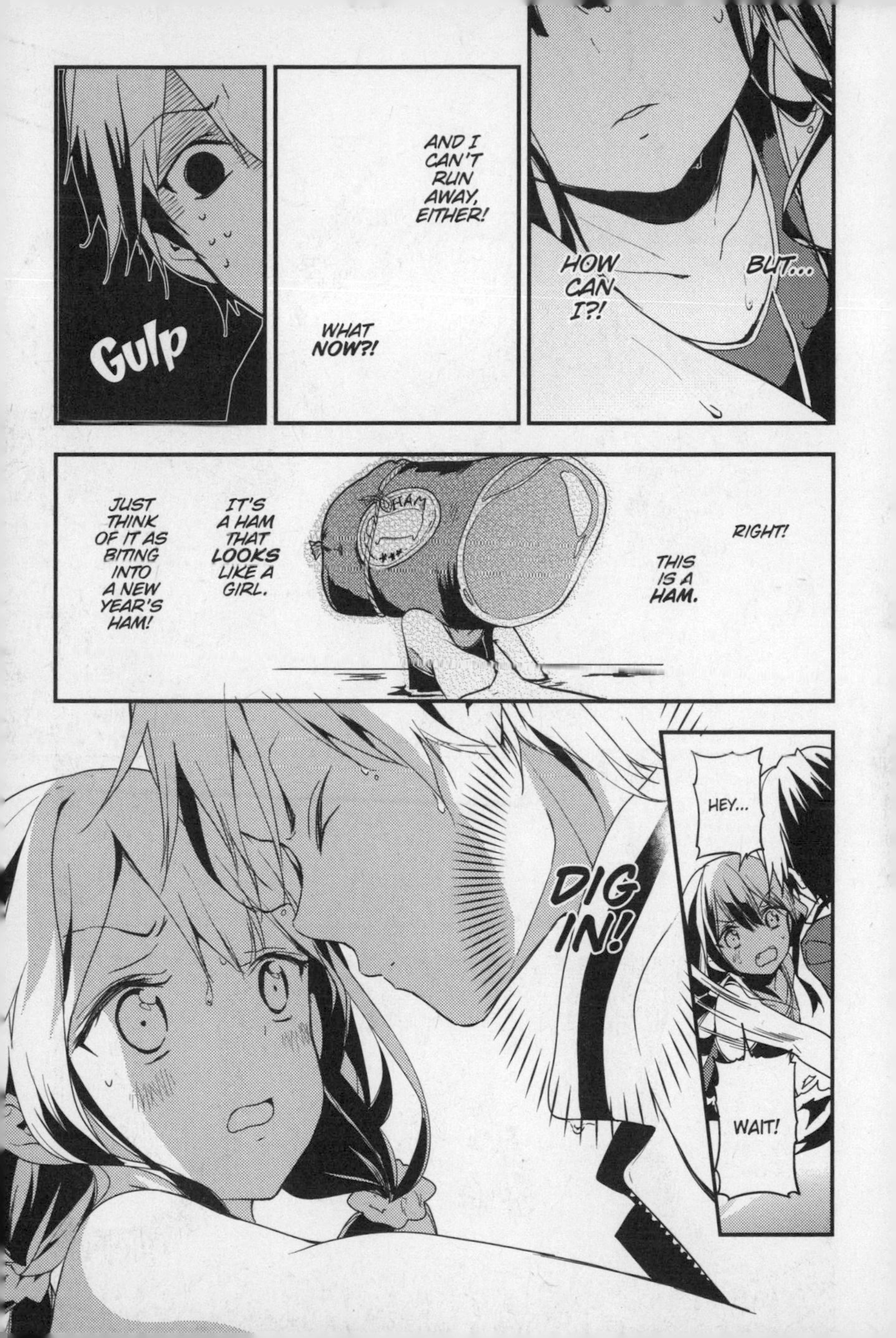
BUT...
HOW CAN I?!
AND I CAN'T RUN AWAY, EITHER!
WHAT NOW?!
Gulp
RIGHT!
THIS IS A HAM.
HAM
IT'S A HAM THAT LOOKS LIKE A GIRL.
JUST THINK OF IT AS BITING INTO A NEW YEAR'S HAM!
HEY...
WAIT!
DIG IN!

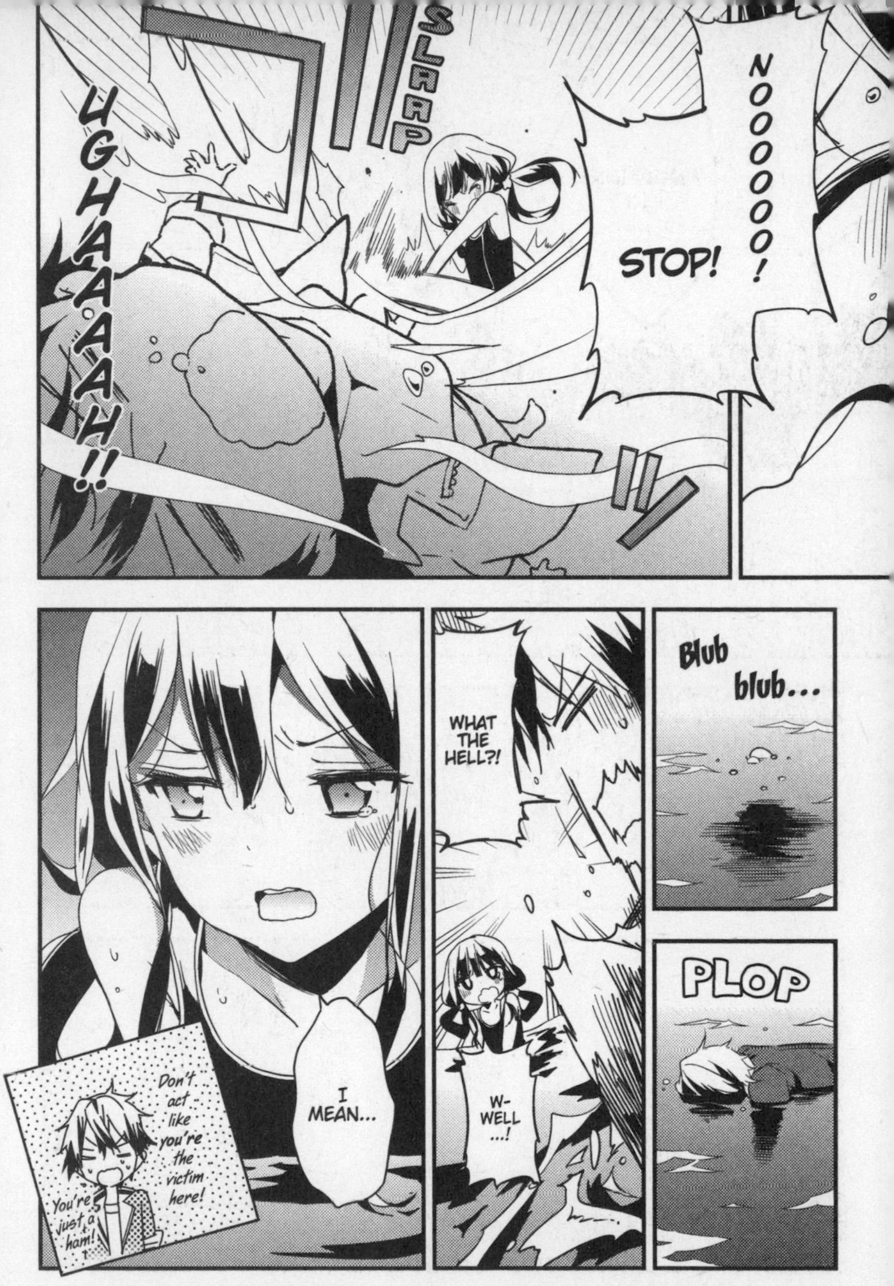
NOOOOOOO!
STOP!
SLRRP
UGHAAAAAAH!!
Blub blub...
PLOP
WHAT THE HELL?!
W-WELL ...!
I MEAN...
Don't act like you're the victim here!
You're just a ham!

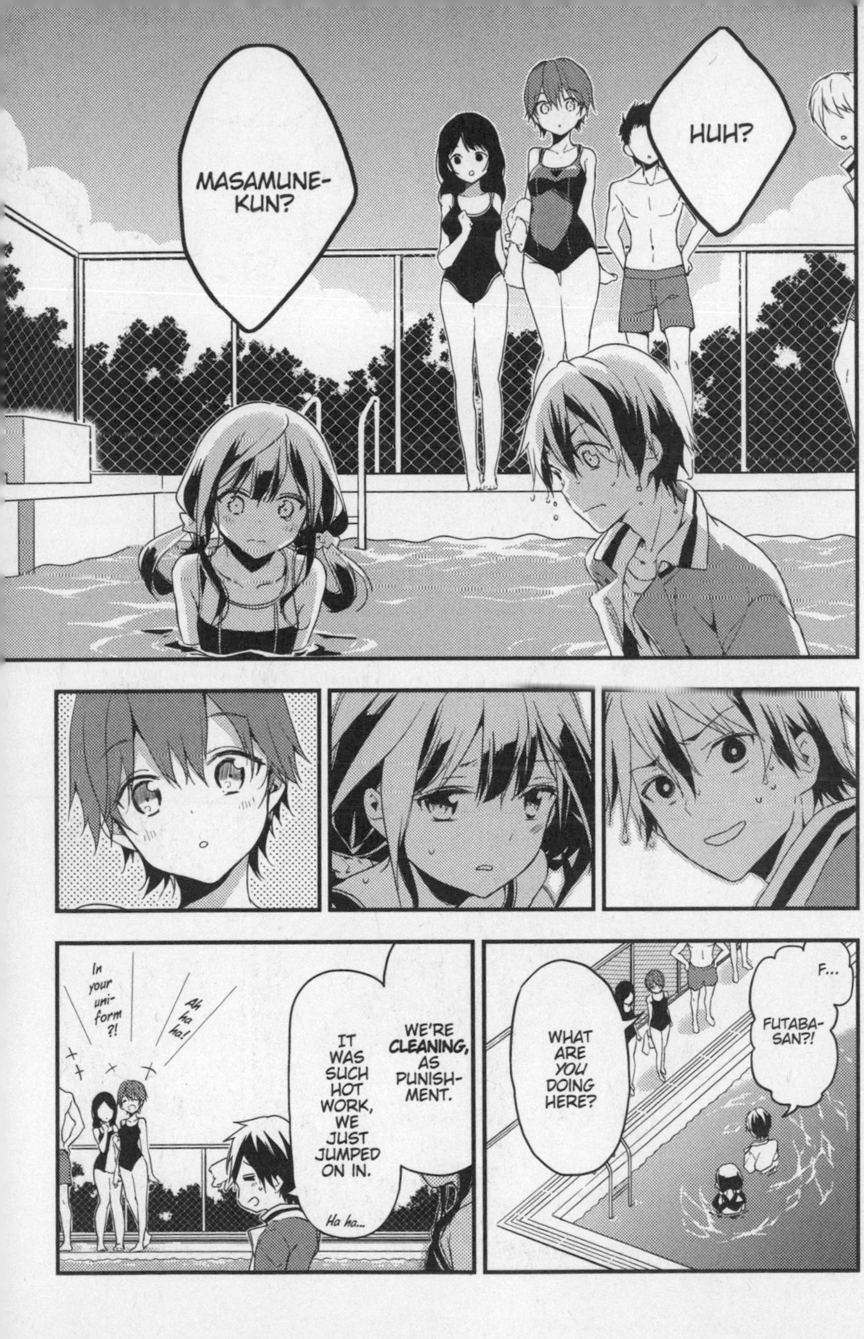
HUH?
MASAMUNE-KUN?
F...
FUTABA-SAN?!
WHAT ARE YOU DOING HERE?
WE'RE CLEANING, AS PUNISHMENT.
IT WAS SUCH HOT WORK, WE JUST JUMPED ON IN.
Ha ha...
Ah ha ha!
In your uniform?!

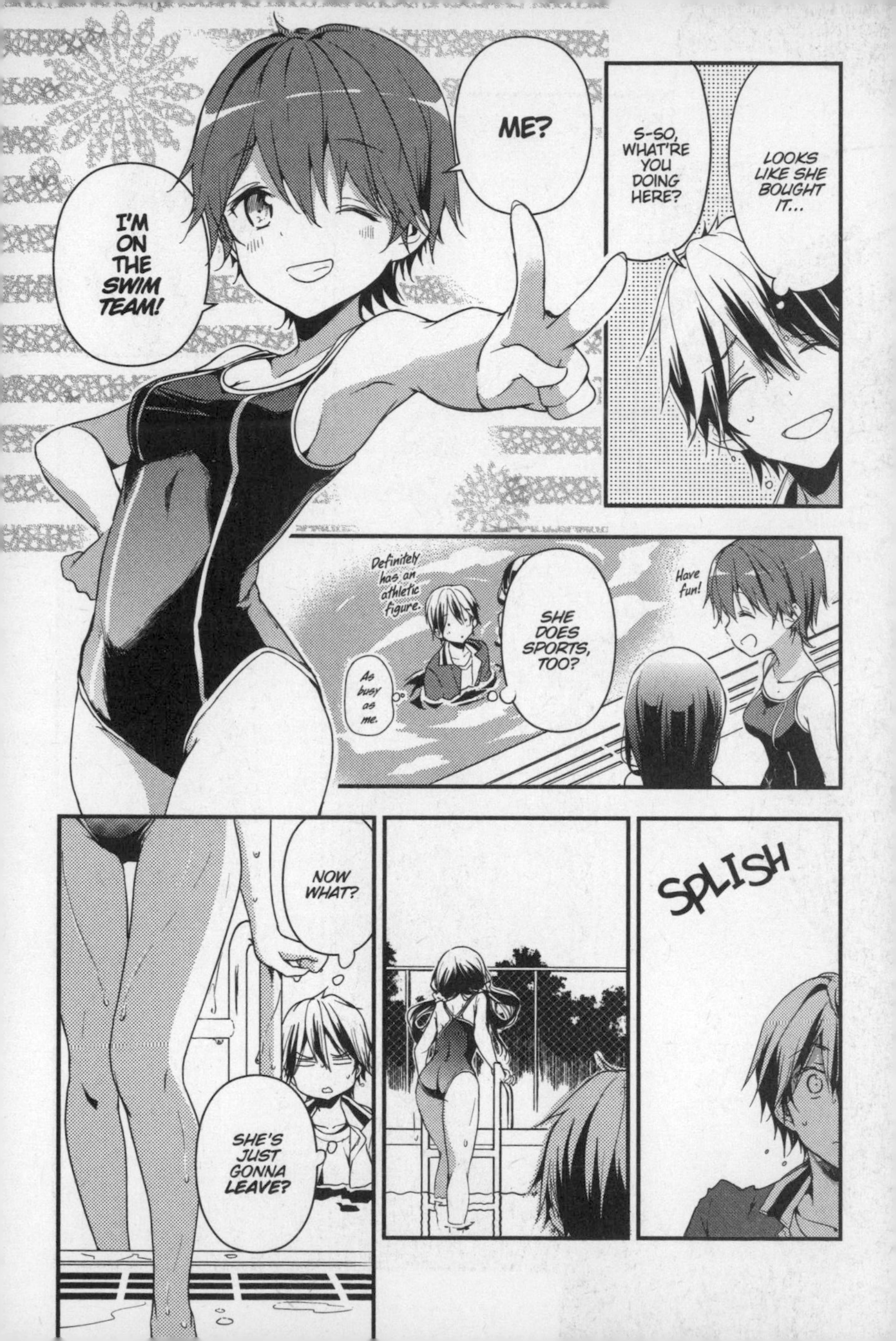
LOOKS LIKE SHE BOUGHT IT...
S-SO, WHAT'RE YOU DOING HERE?
ME?
I'M ON THE SWIM TEAM!
Have fun!
SHE DOES SPORTS, TOO?
Definitely has an athletic figure.
As busy as me.
SPLISH
NOW WHAT?
SHE'S JUST GONNA LEAVE?

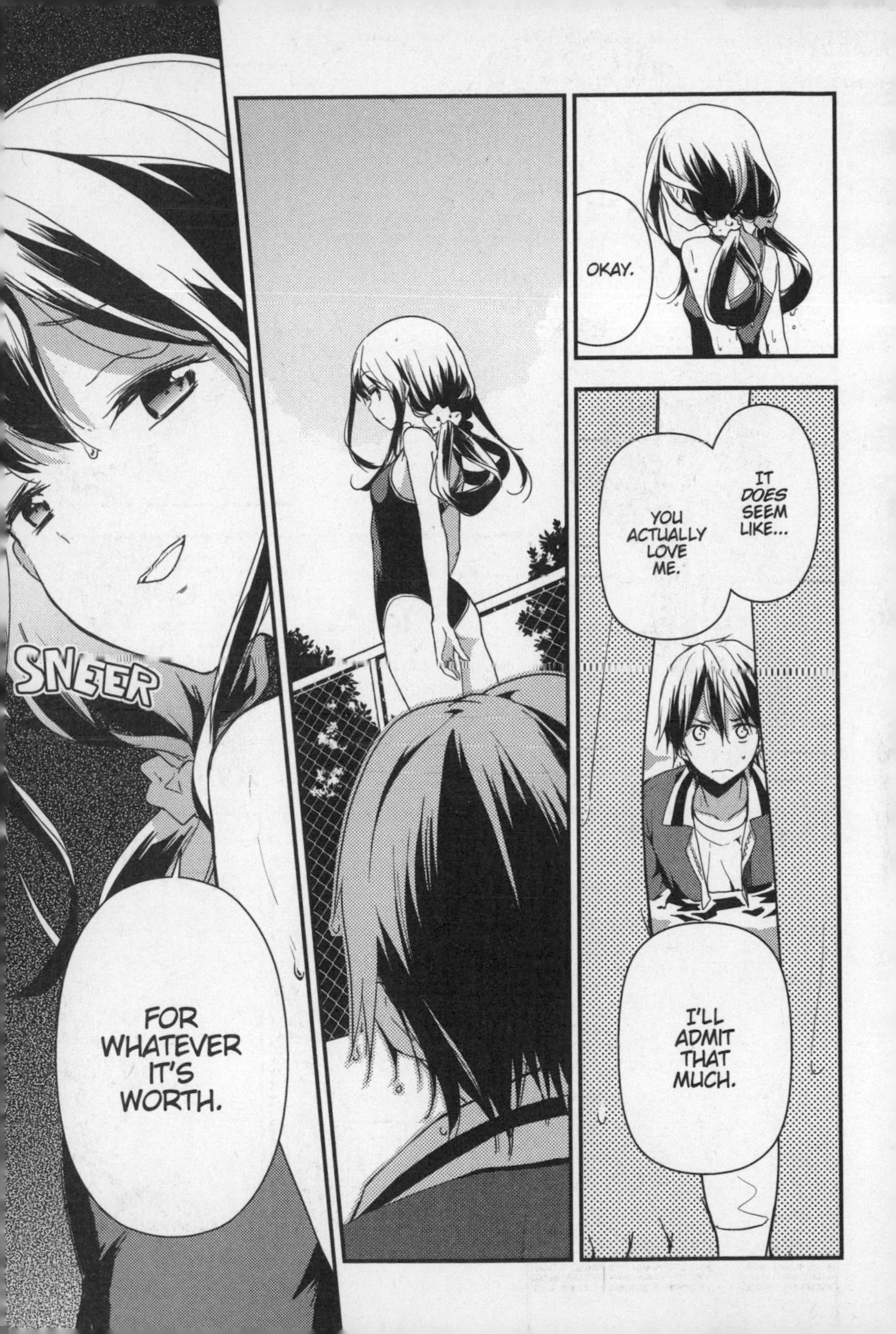
OKAY.
IT DOES SEEM LIKE... YOU ACTUALLY LOVE ME.
I'LL ADMIT THAT MUCH.
SNEER
FOR WHATEVER IT'S WORTH.

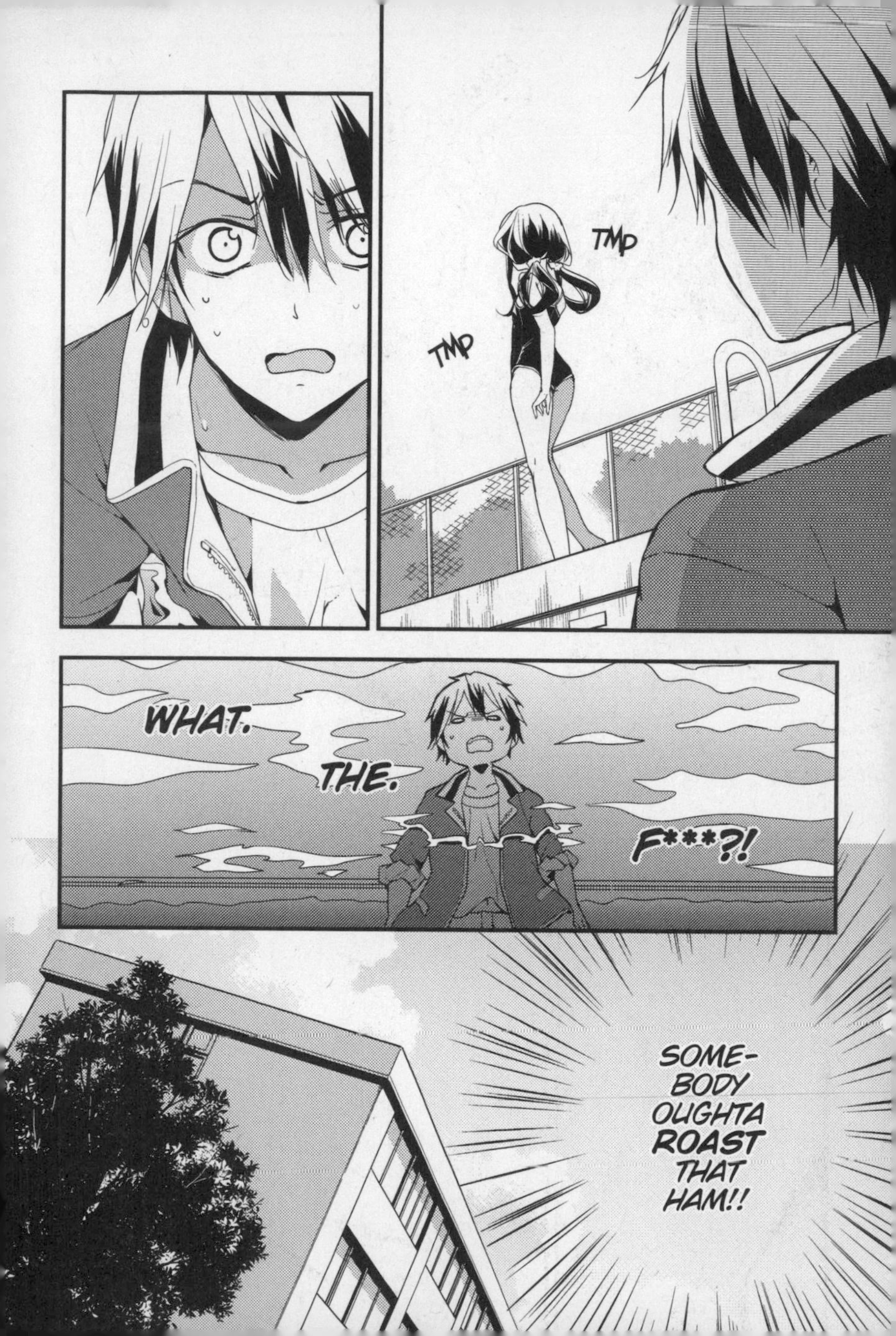
TMP
TMP
WHAT.
THE.
F***?!
SOME-
BODY
OUGHTA
ROAST
THAT
HAM!!

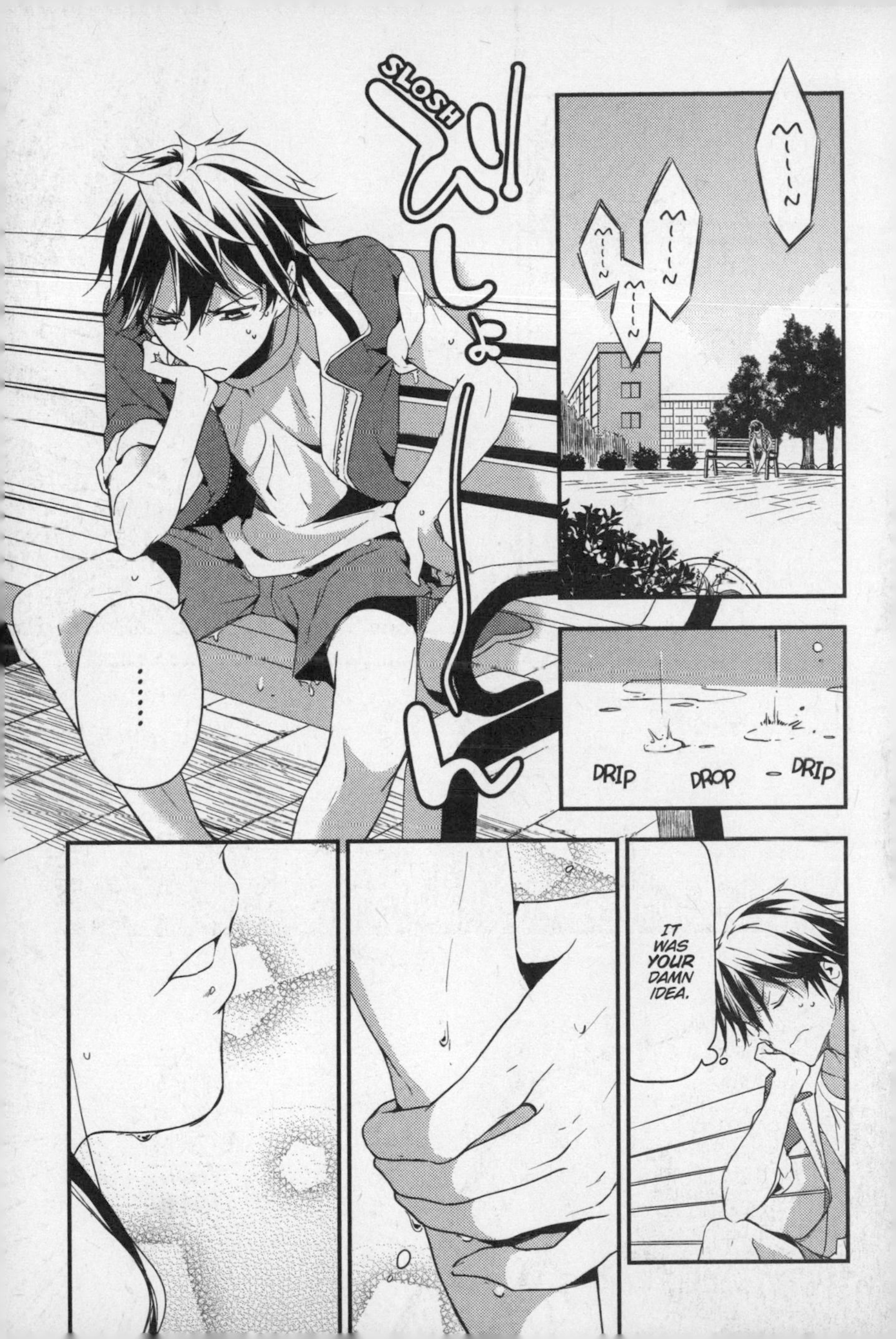
MIIN
MIIN
MIIN
MIIN
DRIP
DROP
DRIP
SLOSH
......
IT WAS YOUR DAMN IDEA.

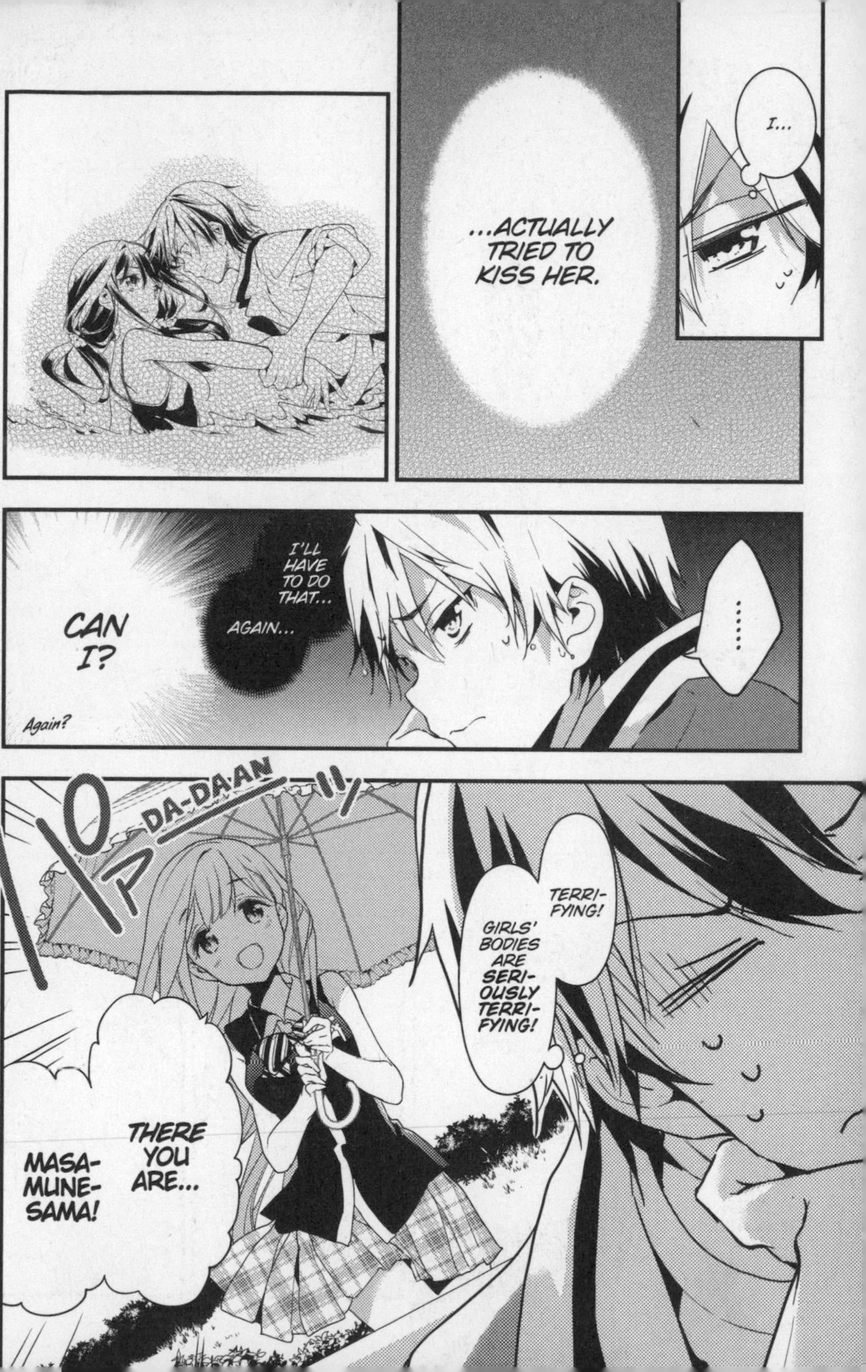
I...
...ACTUALLY TRIED TO KISS HER.
......
I'LL HAVE TO DO THAT...
AGAIN...
CAN I?
Again?
TERRI-FYING!
GIRLS' BODIES ARE SERI-OUSLY TERRI-FYING!
DA-DA-AN
THERE YOU ARE...
MASA-MUNE-SAMA!

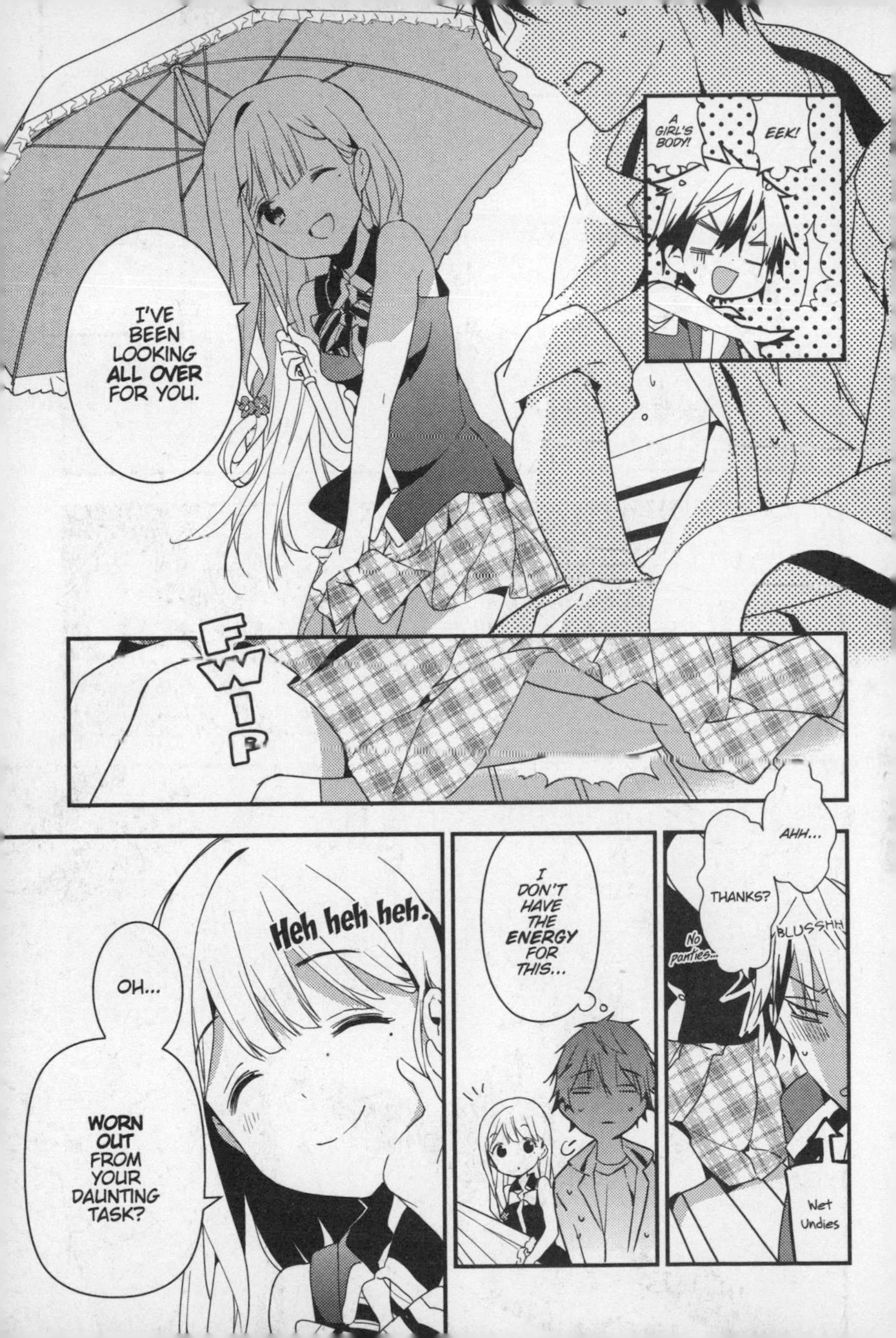
EEK!
A GIRL'S BODY!
I'VE BEEN LOOKING ALL OVER FOR YOU.
FWIP
AHH...
THANKS?
BLUSSHH
No panties...
Wet Undies
I DON'T HAVE THE ENERGY FOR THIS...
Heh heh heh.
OH...
WORN OUT FROM YOUR DAUNTING TASK?

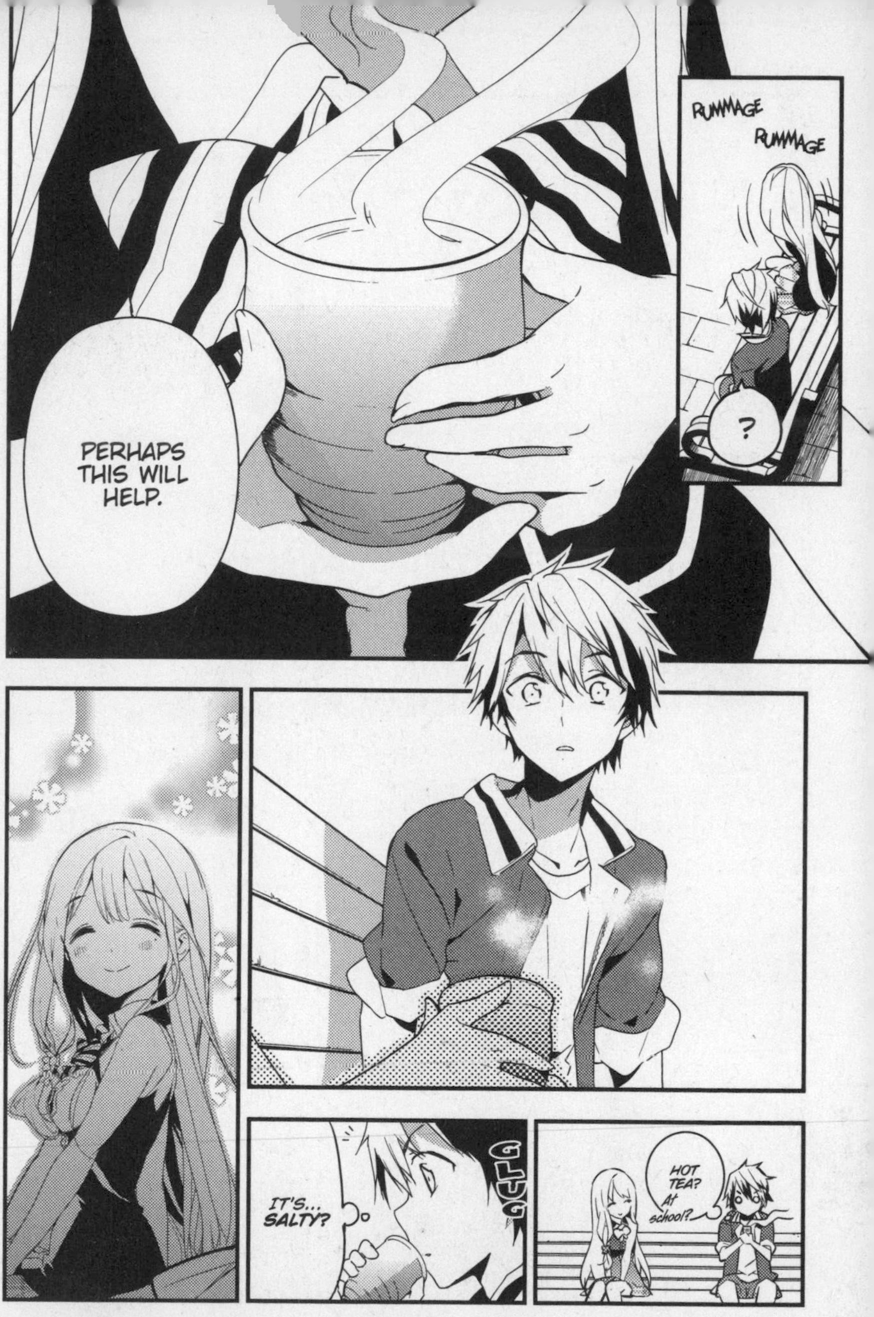
RUMMAGE
RUMMAGE
?
PERHAPS THIS WILL HELP.
HOT TEA? At school?
GLUG
IT'S... SALTY?

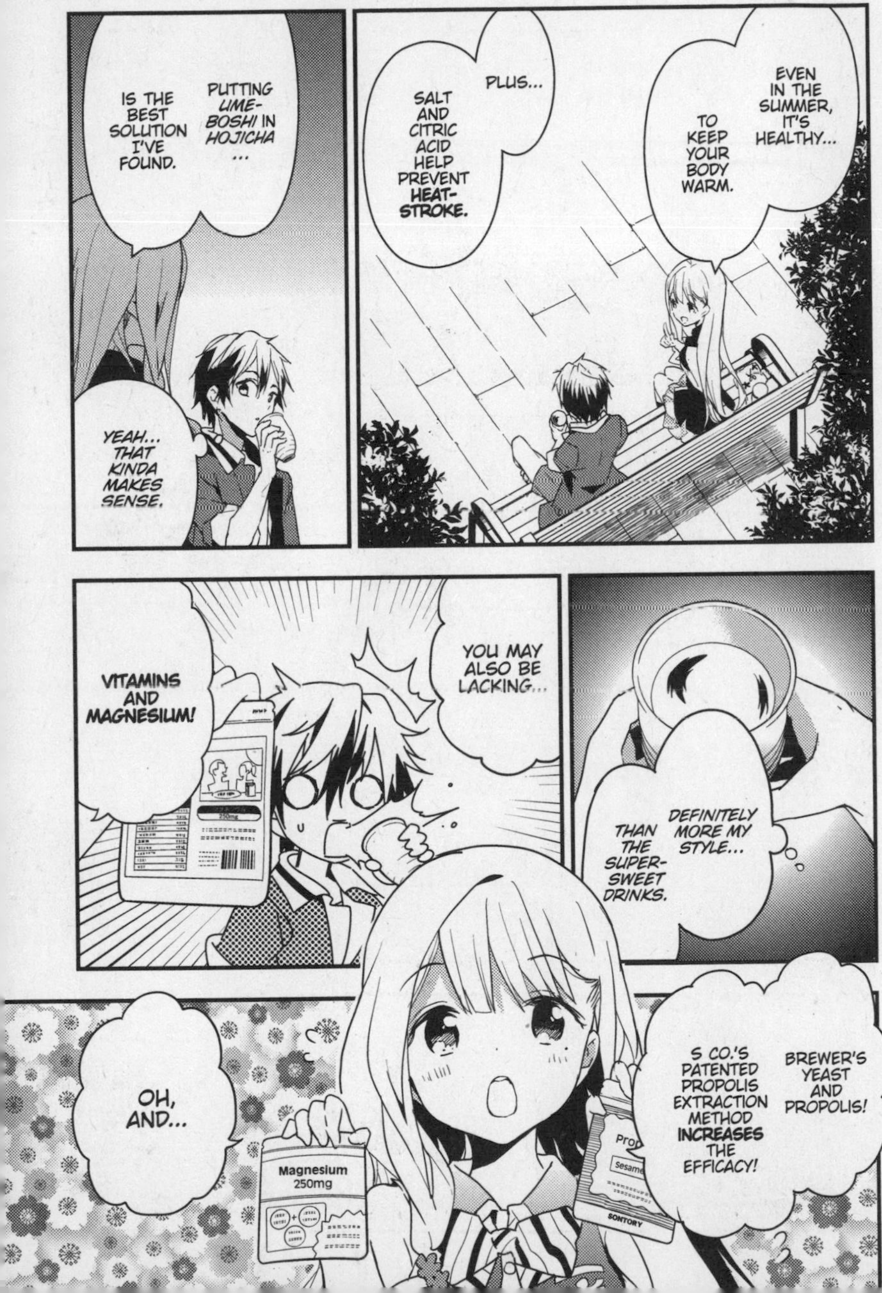
EVEN IN THE SUMMER, IT'S HEALTHY...
TO KEEP YOUR BODY WARM.
PLUS...
SALT AND CITRIC ACID HELP PREVENT **HEAT-STROKE.**
PUTTING *UME-BOSHI* IN *HOJICHA* ...
IS THE BEST SOLUTION I'VE FOUND.
YEAH... THAT KINDA MAKES SENSE.
DEFINITELY MORE MY STYLE...
THAN THE SUPER-SWEET DRINKS.
YOU MAY ALSO BE LACKING...
250mg
VITAMINS AND MAGNESIUM!
BREWER'S YEAST AND PROPOLIS!
S CO.'S PATENTED PROPOLIS EXTRACTION METHOD **INCREASES** THE EFFICACY!
SONTORY
Magnesium 250mg
OH, AND...

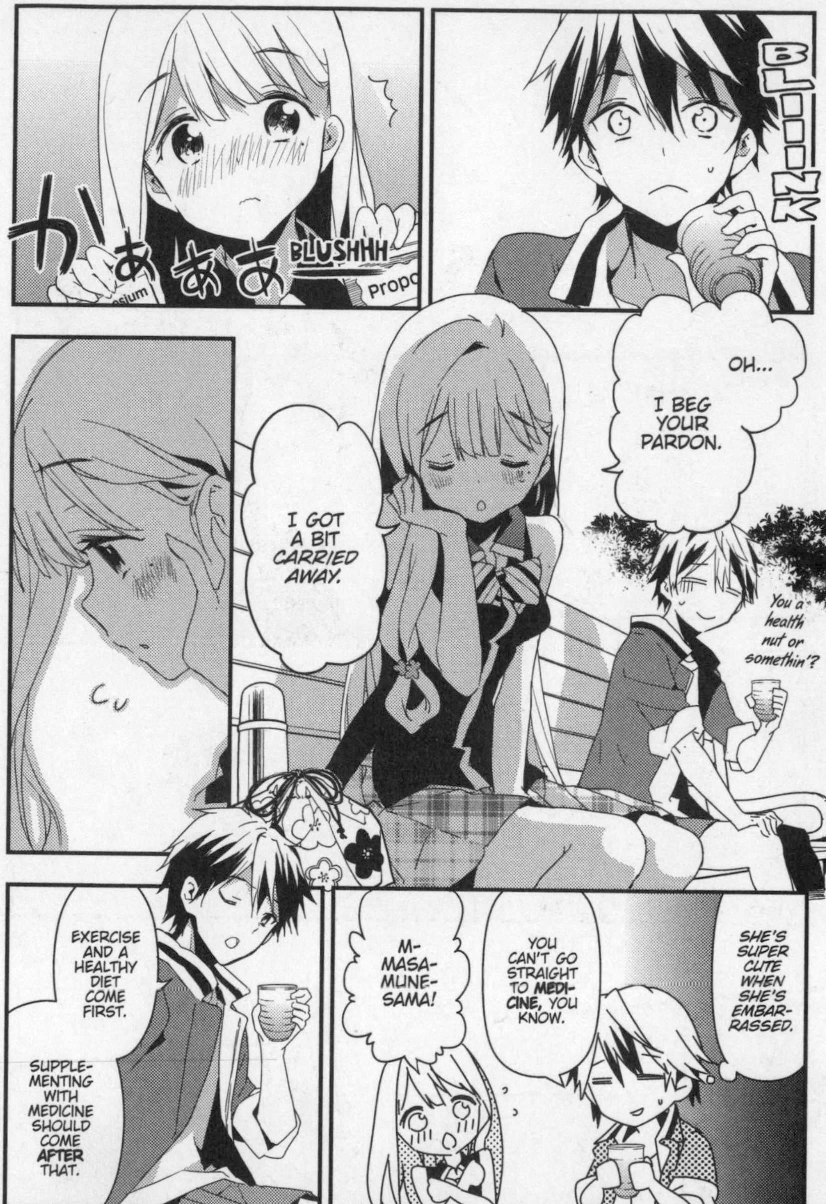
BLIIIINK
かぁぁぁ
BLUSHHH
Propo
OH... I BEG YOUR PARDON.
You a health nut or somethin'?
I GOT A BIT CARRIED AWAY.
SHE'S SUPER CUTE WHEN SHE'S EMBARRASSED.
YOU CAN'T GO STRAIGHT TO MEDICINE, YOU KNOW.
M-MASAMUNE-SAMA!
EXERCISE AND A HEALTHY DIET COME FIRST.
SUPPLEMENTING WITH MEDICINE SHOULD COME AFTER THAT.

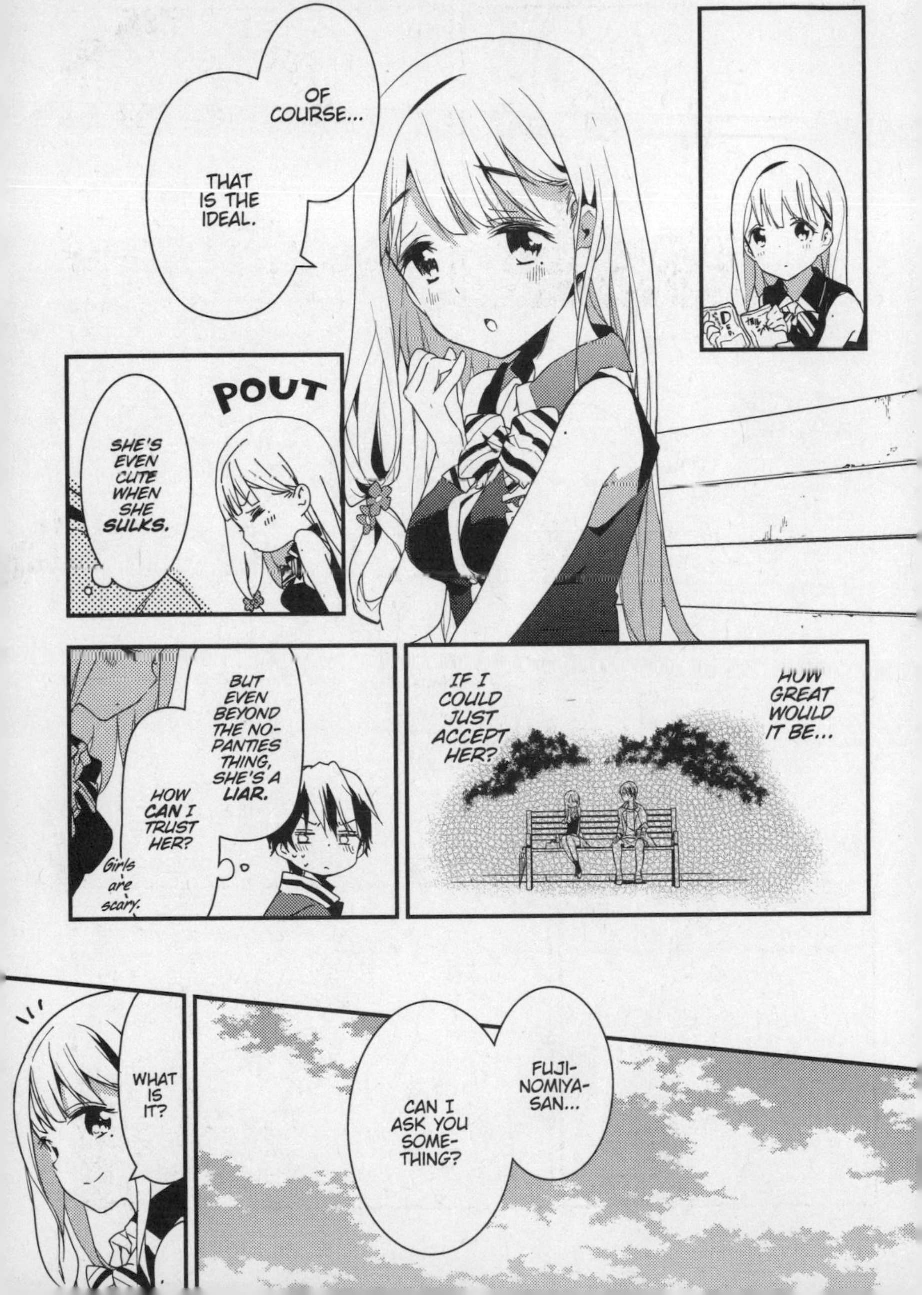
OF COURSE...
THAT IS THE IDEAL.
POUT
SHE'S EVEN CUTE WHEN SHE SULKS.
HOW GREAT WOULD IT BE...
IF I COULD JUST ACCEPT HER?
BUT EVEN BEYOND THE NO-PANTIES THING, SHE'S A LIAR.
HOW CAN I TRUST HER?
Girls are scary.
FUJI-NOMIYA-SAN...
CAN I ASK YOU SOME-THING?
WHAT IS IT?

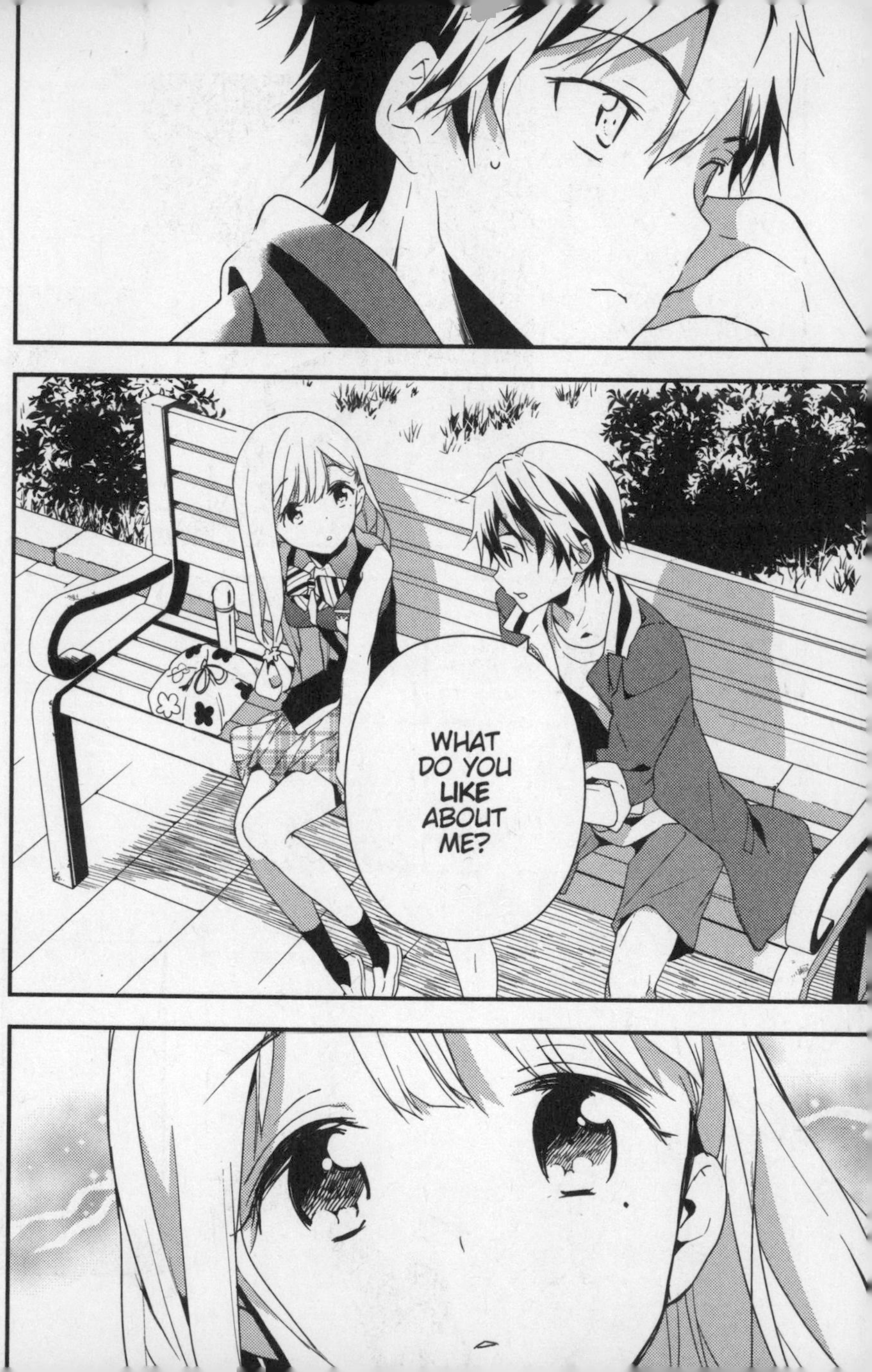
WHAT DO YOU LIKE ABOUT ME?

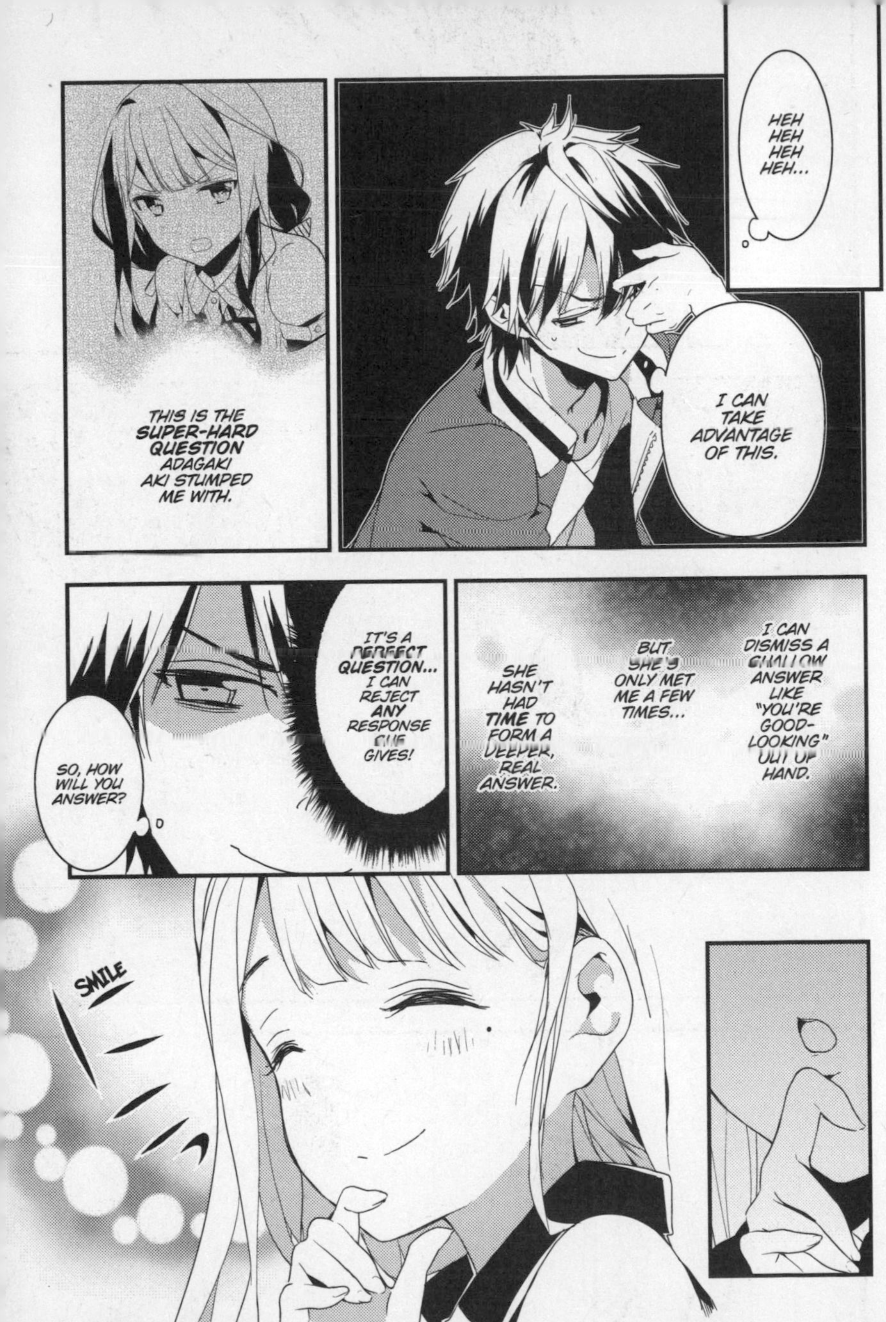
HEH HEH HEH HEH...
I CAN TAKE ADVANTAGE OF THIS.
THIS IS THE SUPER-HARD QUESTION ADAGAKI AKI STUMPED ME WITH.
I CAN DISMISS A SHALLOW ANSWER LIKE "YOU'RE GOOD-LOOKING" OUT OF HAND.
BUT SHE'S ONLY MET ME A FEW TIMES...
SHE HASN'T HAD TIME TO FORM A DEEPER, REAL ANSWER.
IT'S A PERFECT QUESTION... I CAN REJECT ANY RESPONSE SHE GIVES!
SO, HOW WILL YOU ANSWER?
SMILE

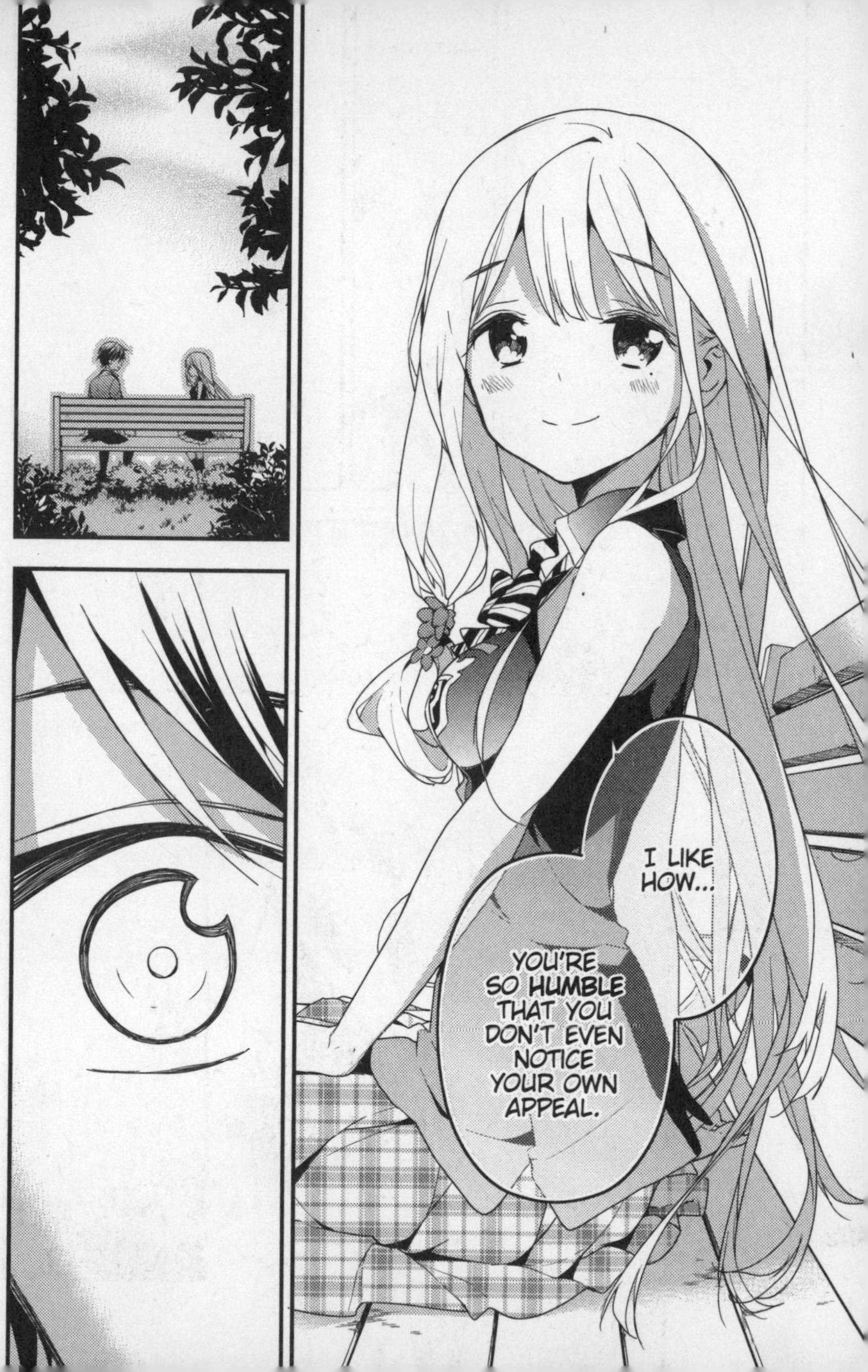
I LIKE HOW...
YOU'RE SO HUMBLE THAT YOU DON'T EVEN NOTICE YOUR OWN APPEAL.

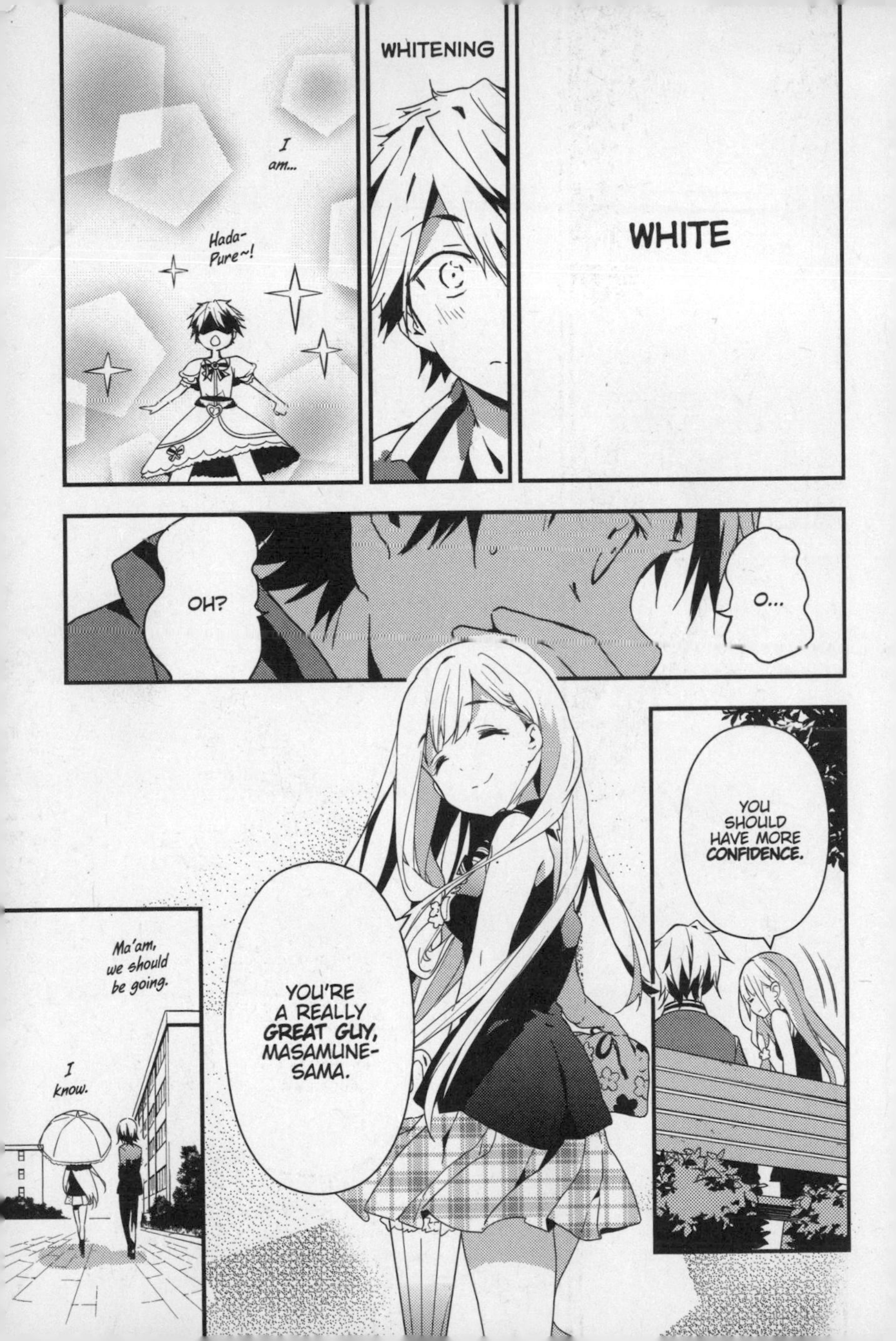
WHITE
WHITENING
I am...
Hada-Pure~!
O...
OH?
YOU SHOULD HAVE MORE CONFIDENCE.
YOU'RE A REALLY GREAT GUY, MASAMUNE-SAMA.
Ma'am, we should be going.
I know.

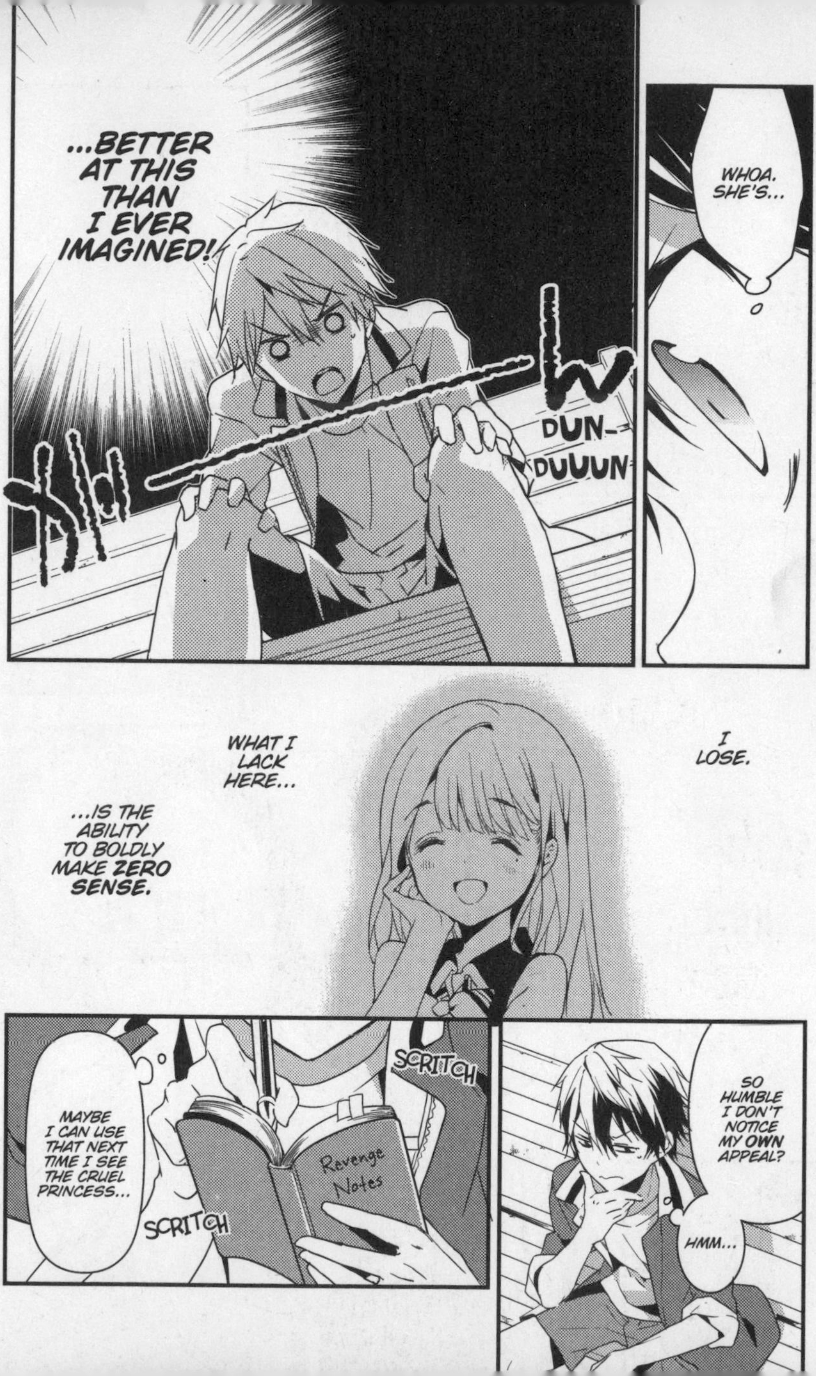
WHOA. SHE'S...
...BETTER AT THIS THAN I EVER IMAGINED!
DUN-DUUUN
I LOSE.
WHAT I LACK HERE...
...IS THE ABILITY TO BOLDLY MAKE ZERO SENSE.
SO HUMBLE I DON'T NOTICE MY OWN APPEAL?
HMM...
SCRITCH
MAYBE I CAN USE THAT NEXT TIME I SEE THE CRUEL PRINCESS...
Revenge Notes
SCRITCH

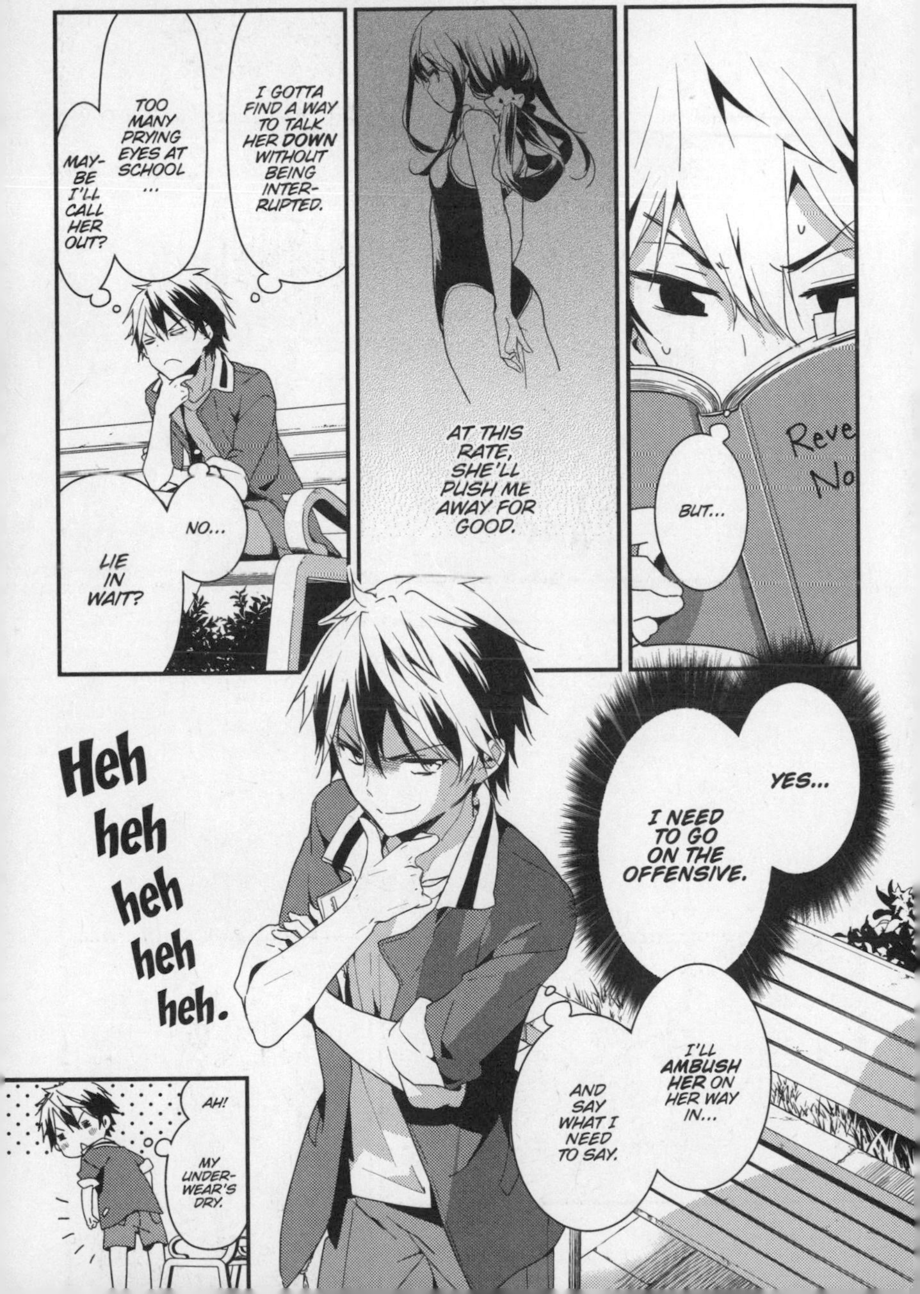
BUT...
AT THIS RATE, SHE'LL PUSH ME AWAY FOR GOOD.
I GOTTA FIND A WAY TO TALK HER DOWN WITHOUT BEING INTER-RUPTED.
TOO MANY PRYING EYES AT SCHOOL...
MAY-BE I'LL CALL HER OUT?
NO...
LIE IN WAIT?
YES...
I NEED TO GO ON THE OFFENSIVE.
I'LL AMBUSH HER ON HER WAY IN...
AND SAY WHAT I NEED TO SAY.
Heh heh heh heh heh.
AH!
MY UNDER-WEAR'S DRY.

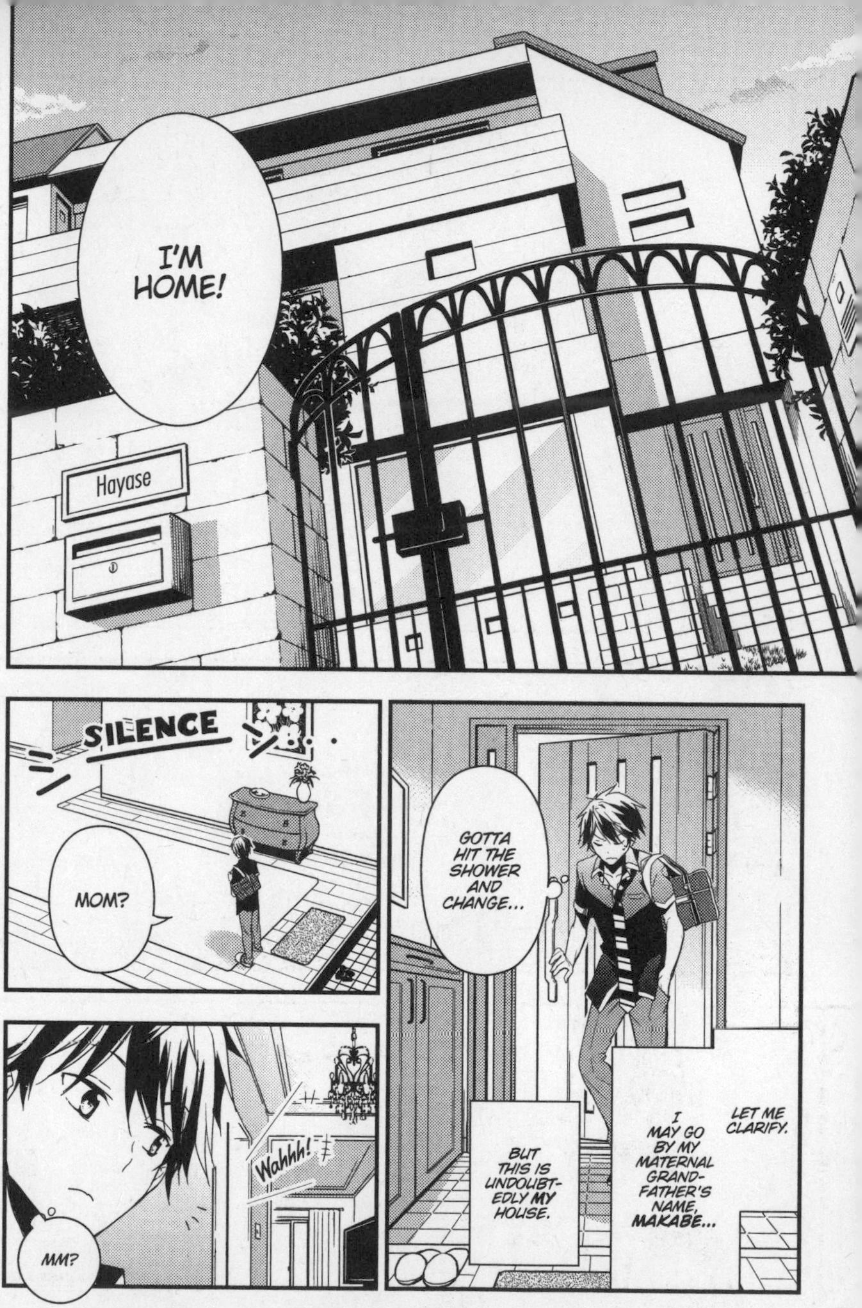
I'M HOME!
Hayase
GOTTA HIT THE SHOWER AND CHANGE...
LET ME CLARIFY.
I MAY GO BY MY MATERNAL GRAND-FATHER'S NAME, MAKABE...
BUT THIS IS UNDOUBT-EDLY MY HOUSE.
SILENCE
MOM?
Wahhh!
MM?

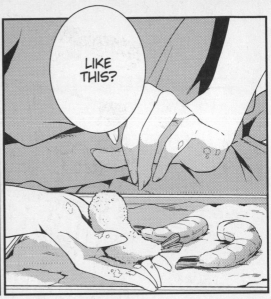

YES, YES. JUST LIKE THAT.

VERY GOOD!

LIKE THIS?

Next, eggs!

NOISY IN HERE...

Is Chinatsu home?

Flour

OH, MA-KUN!

WELCOME HOME!

Flour

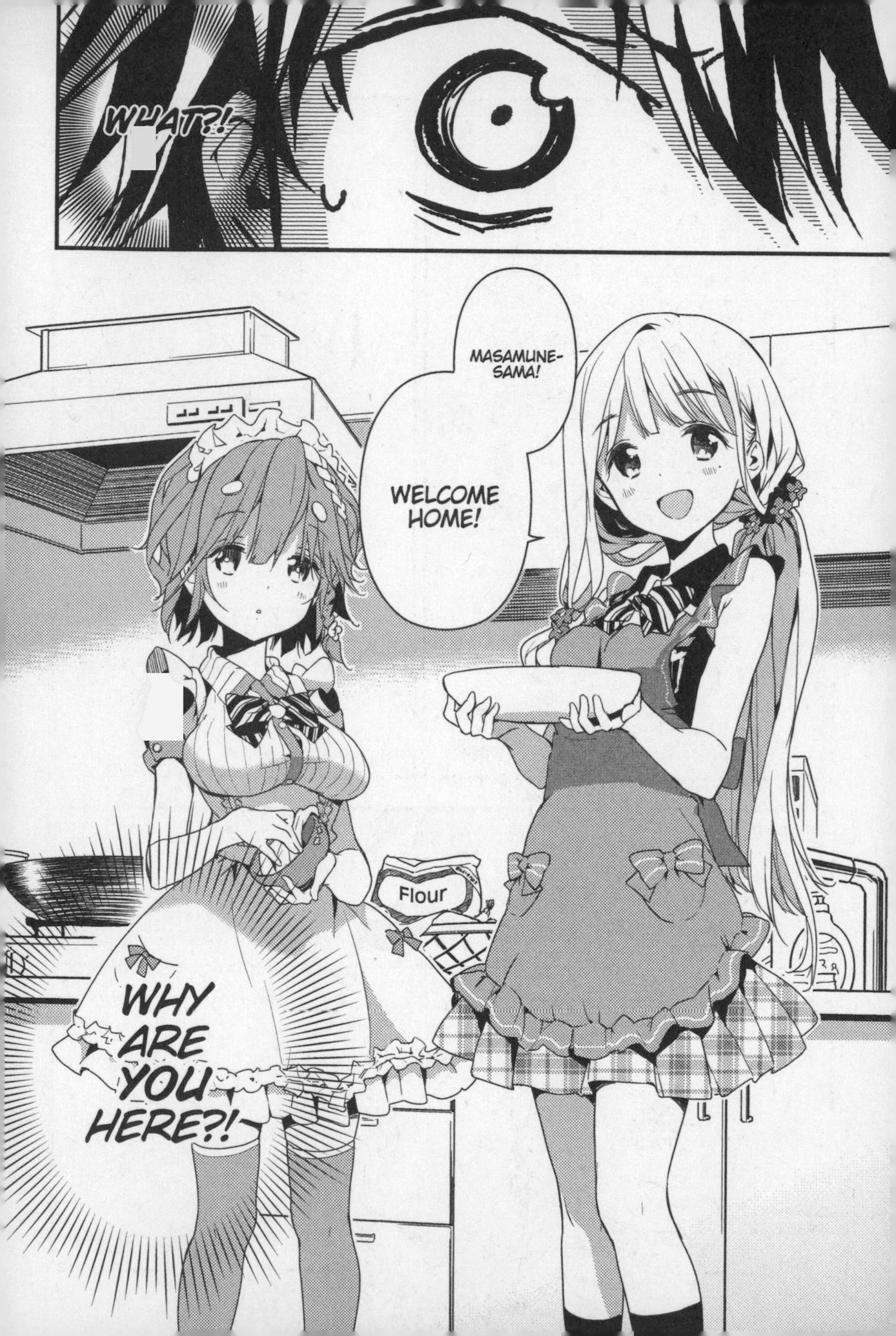
WHAT?!
MASAMUNE-SAMA!
WELCOME HOME!
Flour
WHY ARE YOU HERE?!

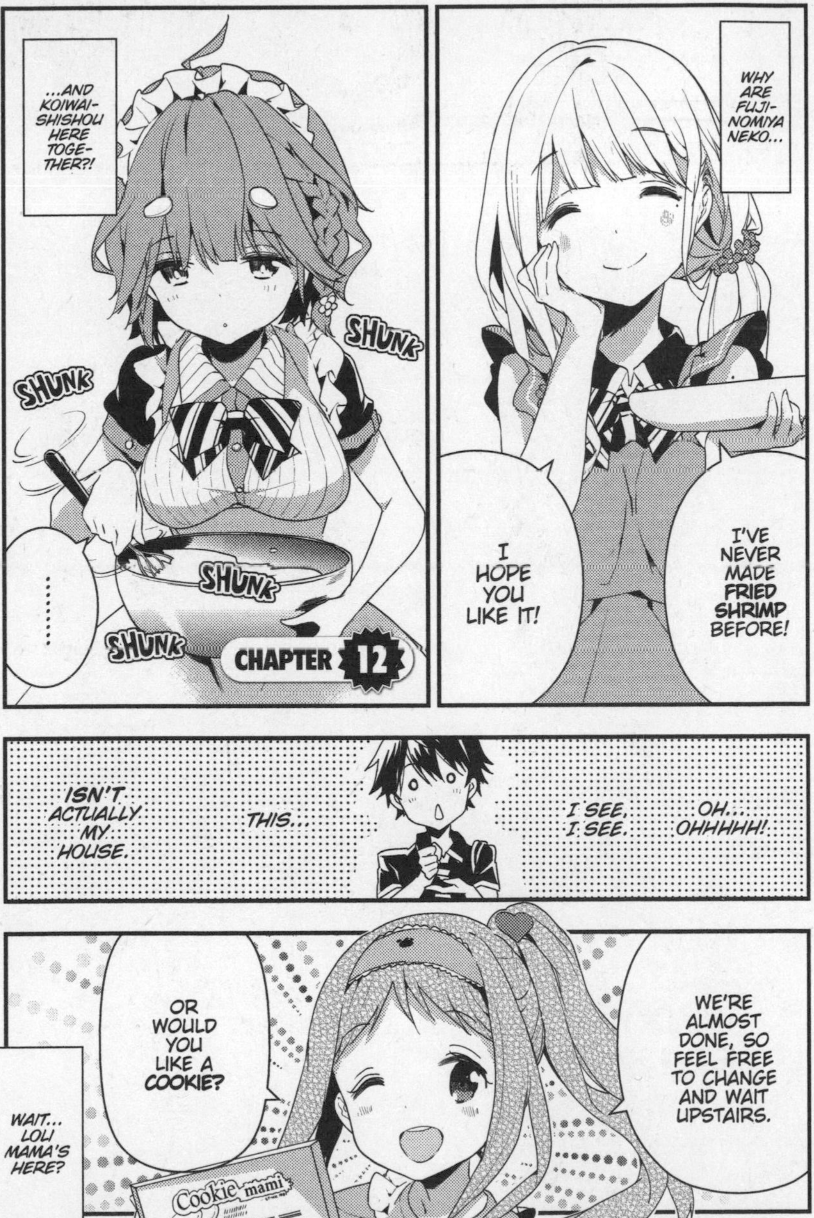
WHY ARE FUJI-NOMIYA NEKO...
I'VE NEVER MADE FRIED SHRIMP BEFORE!
I HOPE YOU LIKE IT!
...AND KOIWAI-SHISHOU HERE TOGE-THER?!
SHUNK
SHUNK
SHUNK
SHUNK
......
CHAPTER 12
OH... OHHHHH!
I SEE, I SEE.
THIS...
ISN'T ACTUALLY MY HOUSE.
WE'RE ALMOST DONE, SO FEEL FREE TO CHANGE AND WAIT UPSTAIRS.
OR WOULD YOU LIKE A COOKIE?
WAIT... LOLI MAMA'S HERE?
Cookie mami

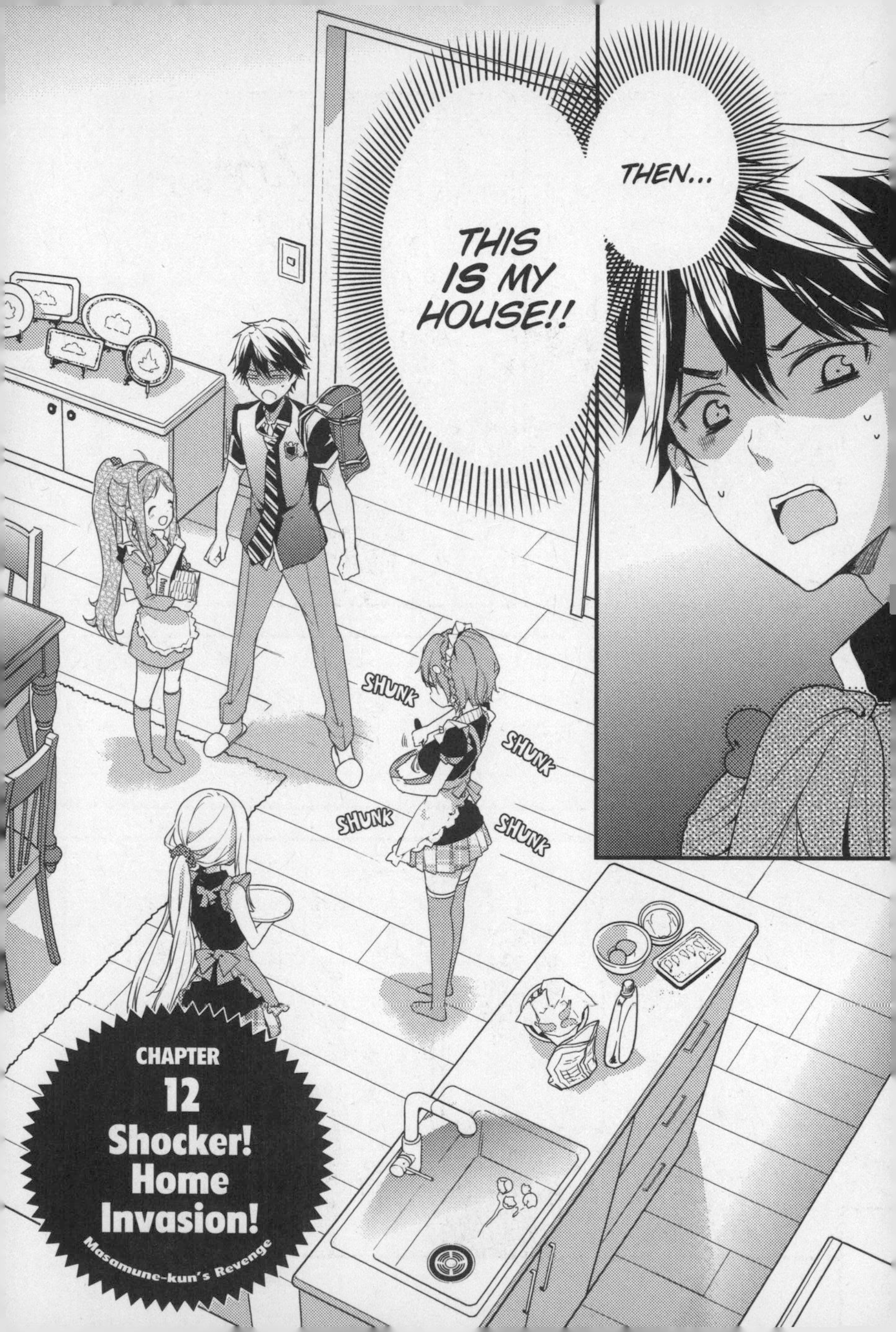
THEN...
THIS IS MY HOUSE!!
SHUNK
SHUNK
SHUNK
SHUNK
CHAPTER 12 Shocker! Home Invasion!
Masamune-kun's Revenge

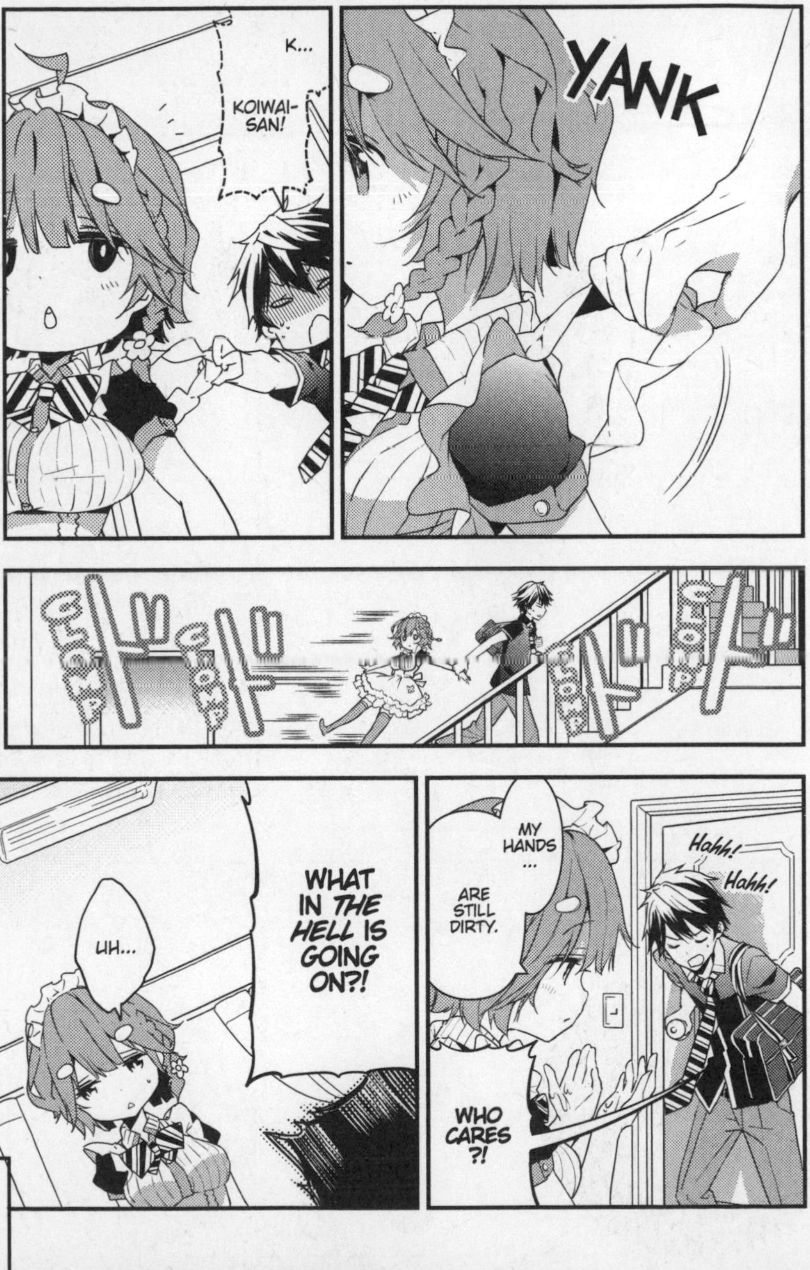
YANK
K...
KOIWAI-SAN!
CLOMP
CLOMP
CLOMP
CLOMP
Hahh!
Hahh!
MY HANDS...
ARE STILL DIRTY.
WHO CARES?!
WHAT IN THE HELL IS GOING ON?!
UH...

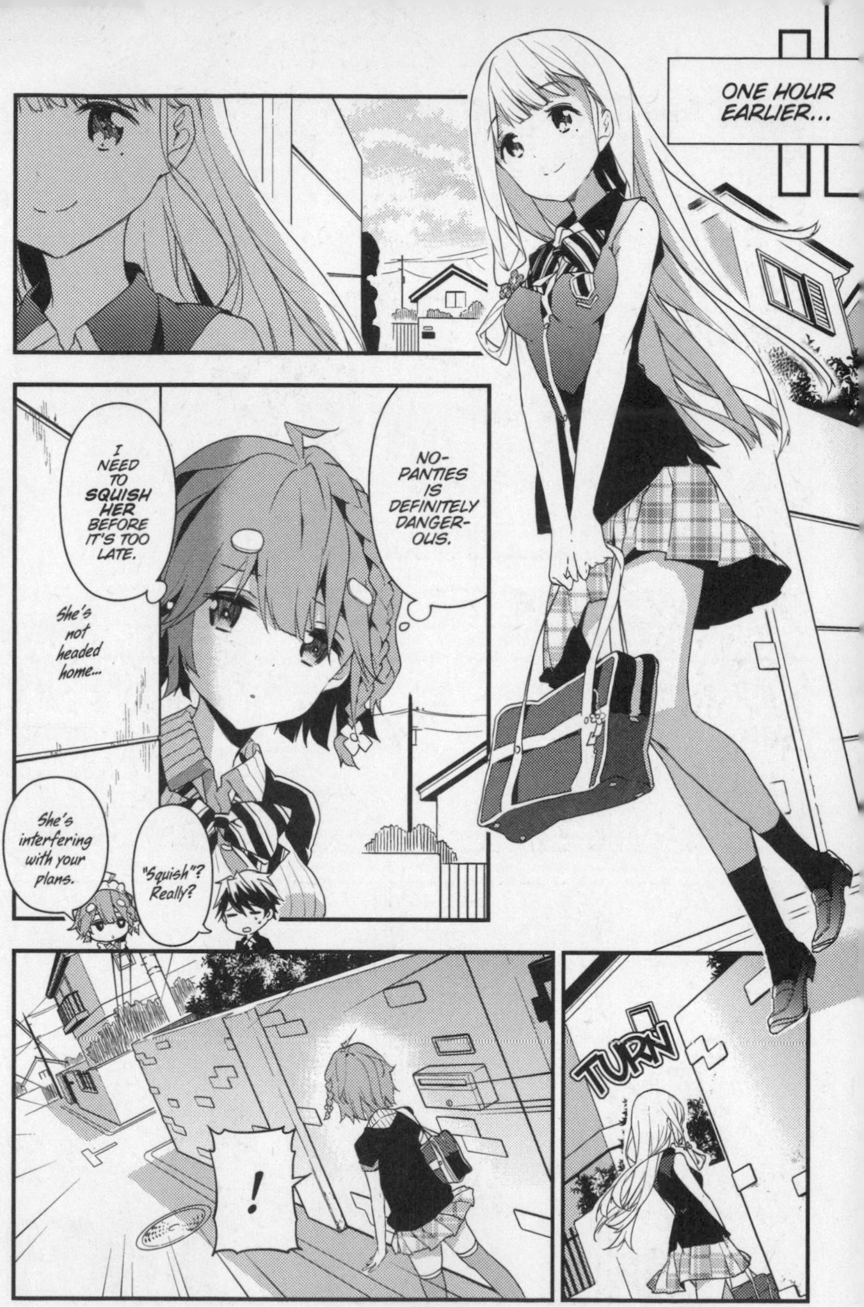
ONE HOUR EARLIER...
NO-PANTIES IS DEFINITELY DANGEROUS.
I NEED TO SQUISH HER BEFORE IT'S TOO LATE.
She's not headed home...
"Squish"? Really?
She's interfering with your plans.
TURN
!

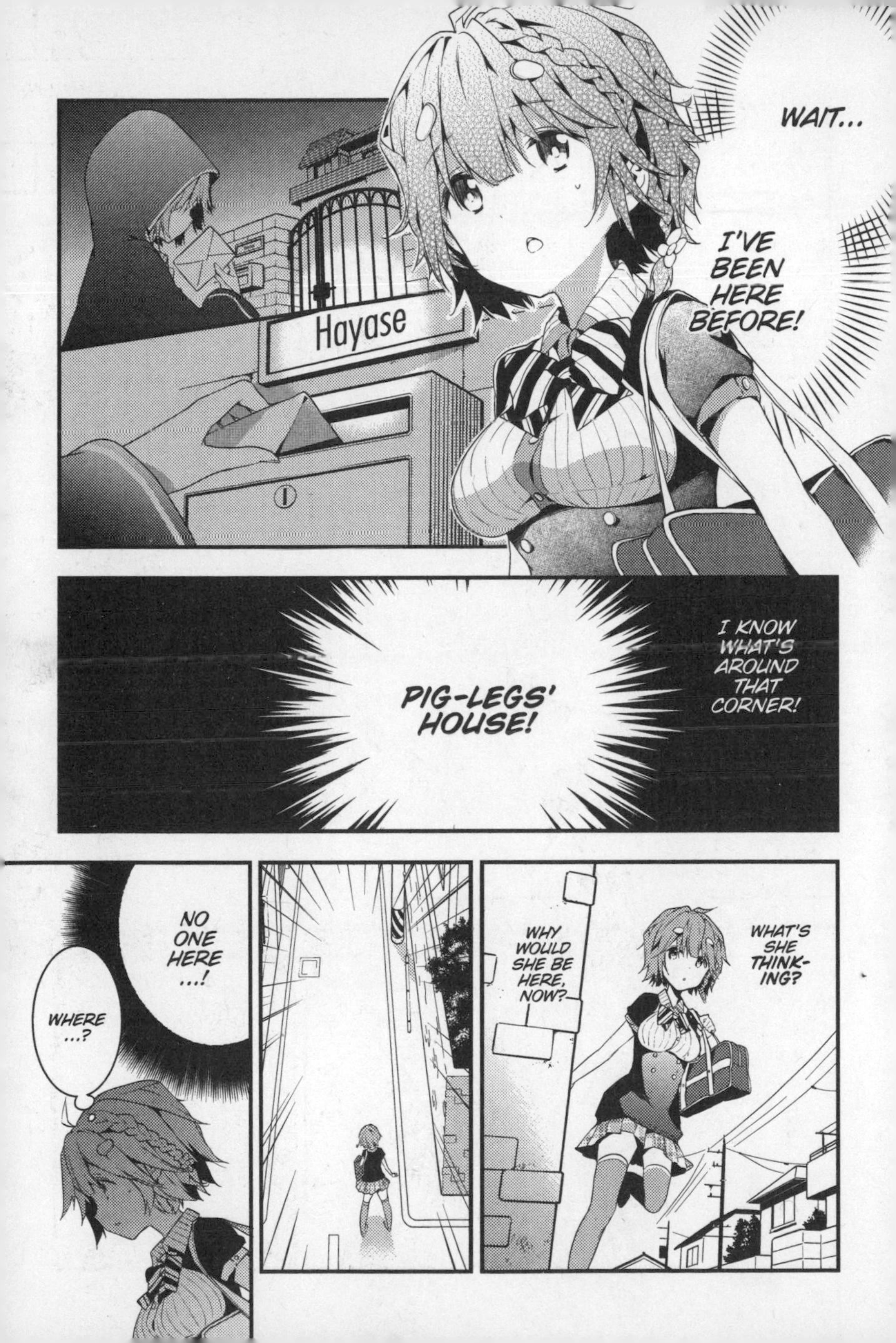
WAIT...
I'VE BEEN HERE BEFORE!
Hayase
I KNOW WHAT'S AROUND THAT CORNER!
PIG-LEGS' HOUSE!
WHAT'S SHE THINKING?
WHY WOULD SHE BE HERE, NOW?
NO ONE HERE ...!
WHERE ...?

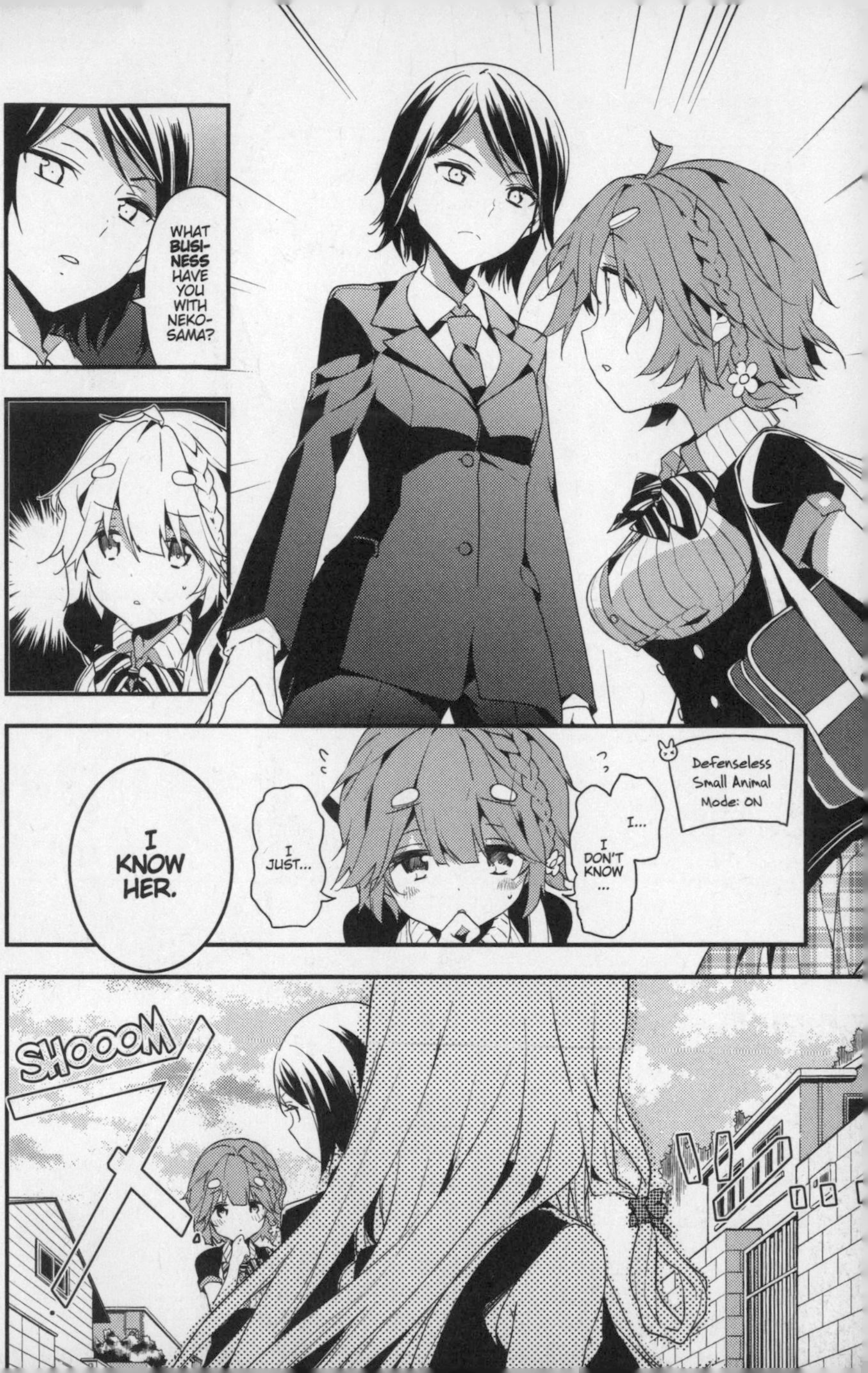
WHAT BUSINESS HAVE YOU WITH NEKO-SAMA?
Defenseless Small Animal Mode: ON
I...
I DON'T KNOW ...
I JUST...
I KNOW HER.
SHOOOM

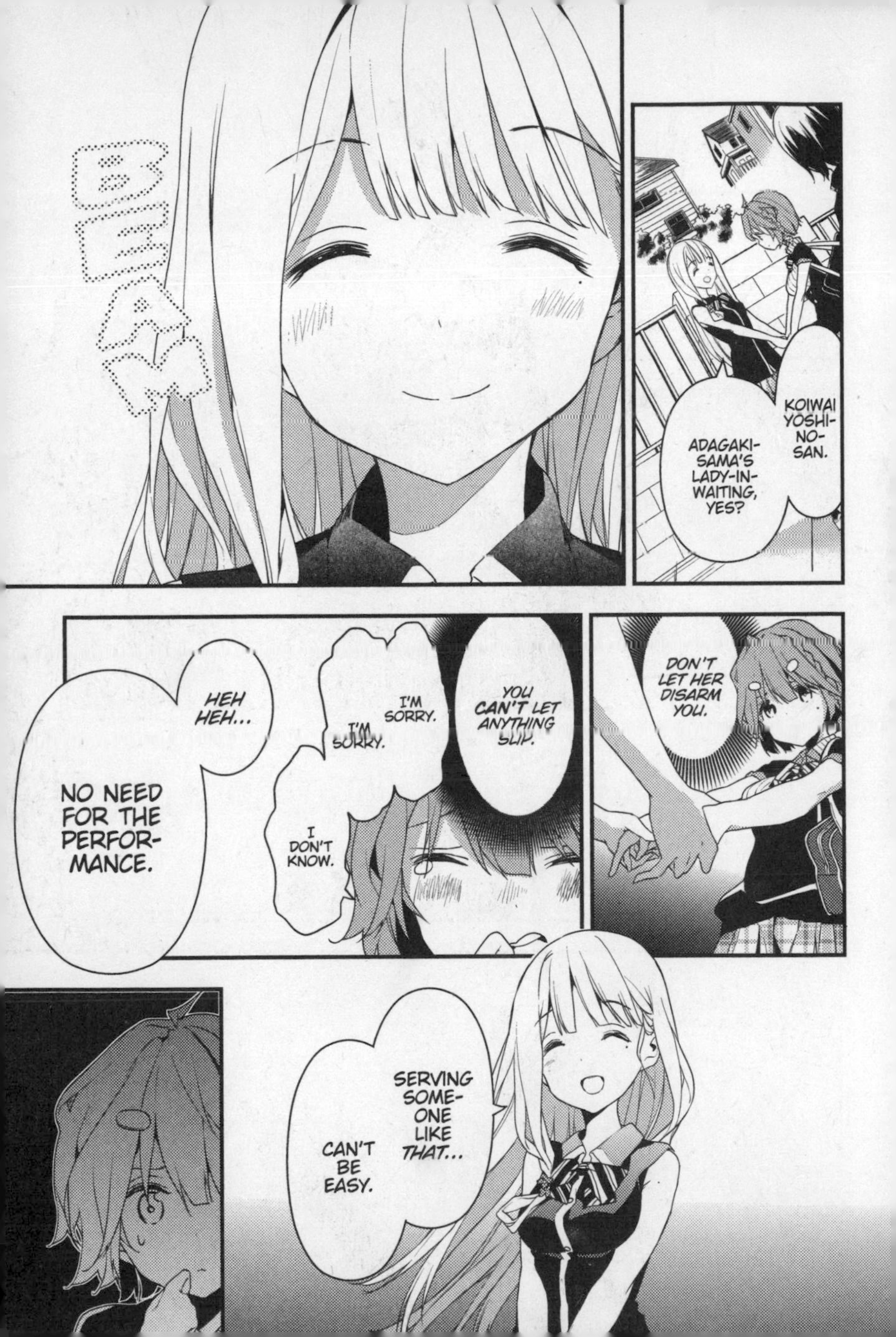
KOIWAI YOSHINO-SAN.
ADAGAKI-SAMA'S LADY-IN-WAITING, YES?
DON'T LET HER DISARM YOU.
YOU CAN'T LET ANYTHING SLIP.
I'M SORRY.
I'M SORRY.
I DON'T KNOW.
HEH HEH...
NO NEED FOR THE PERFORMANCE.
SERVING SOMEONE LIKE THAT...
CAN'T BE EASY.

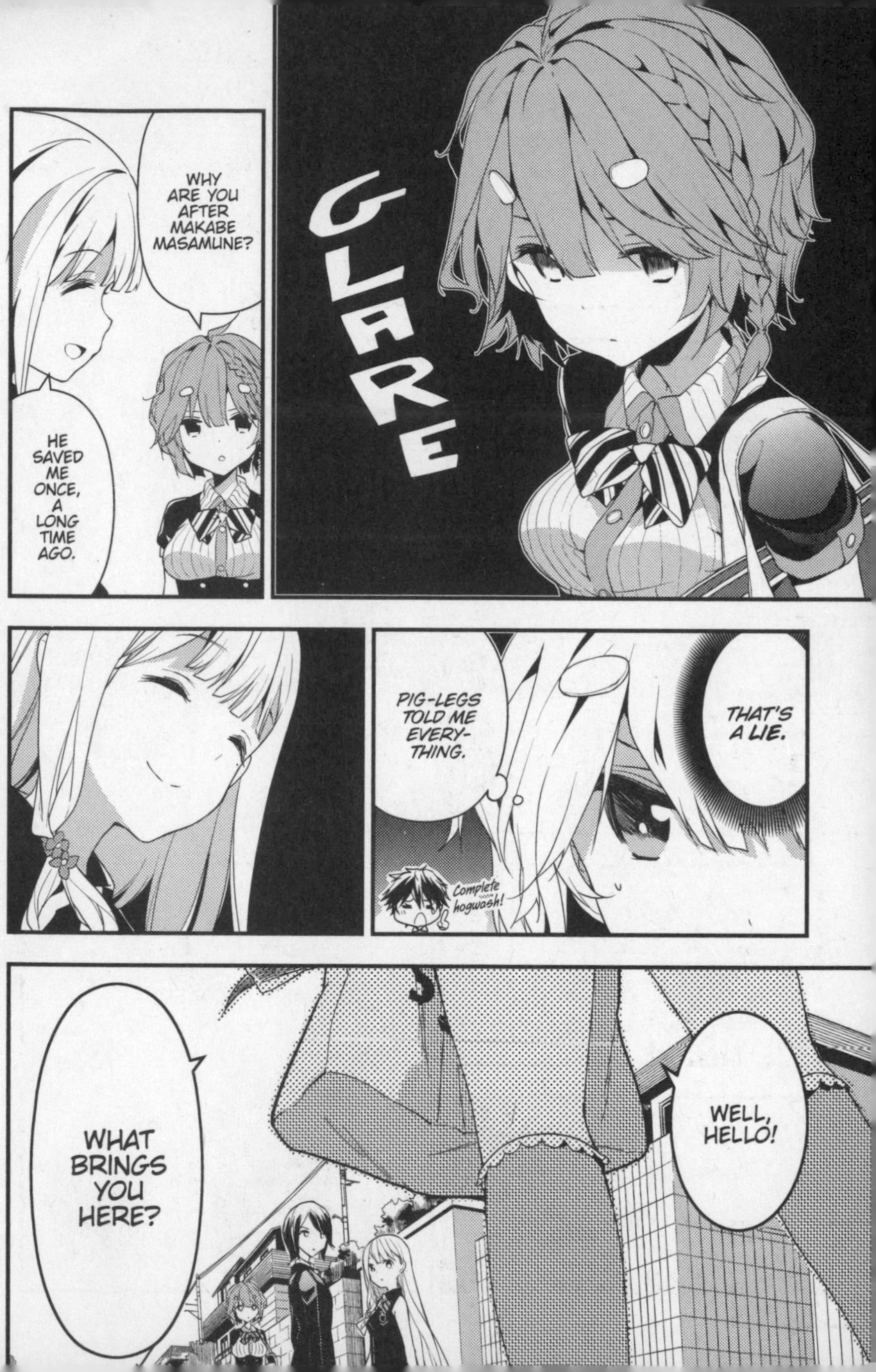
GLARE
WHY ARE YOU AFTER MAKABE MASAMUNE?
HE SAVED ME ONCE, A LONG TIME AGO.
THAT'S A LIE.
PIG-LEGS TOLD ME EVERY-THING.
Complete hogwash!
WELL, HELLO!
WHAT BRINGS YOU HERE?

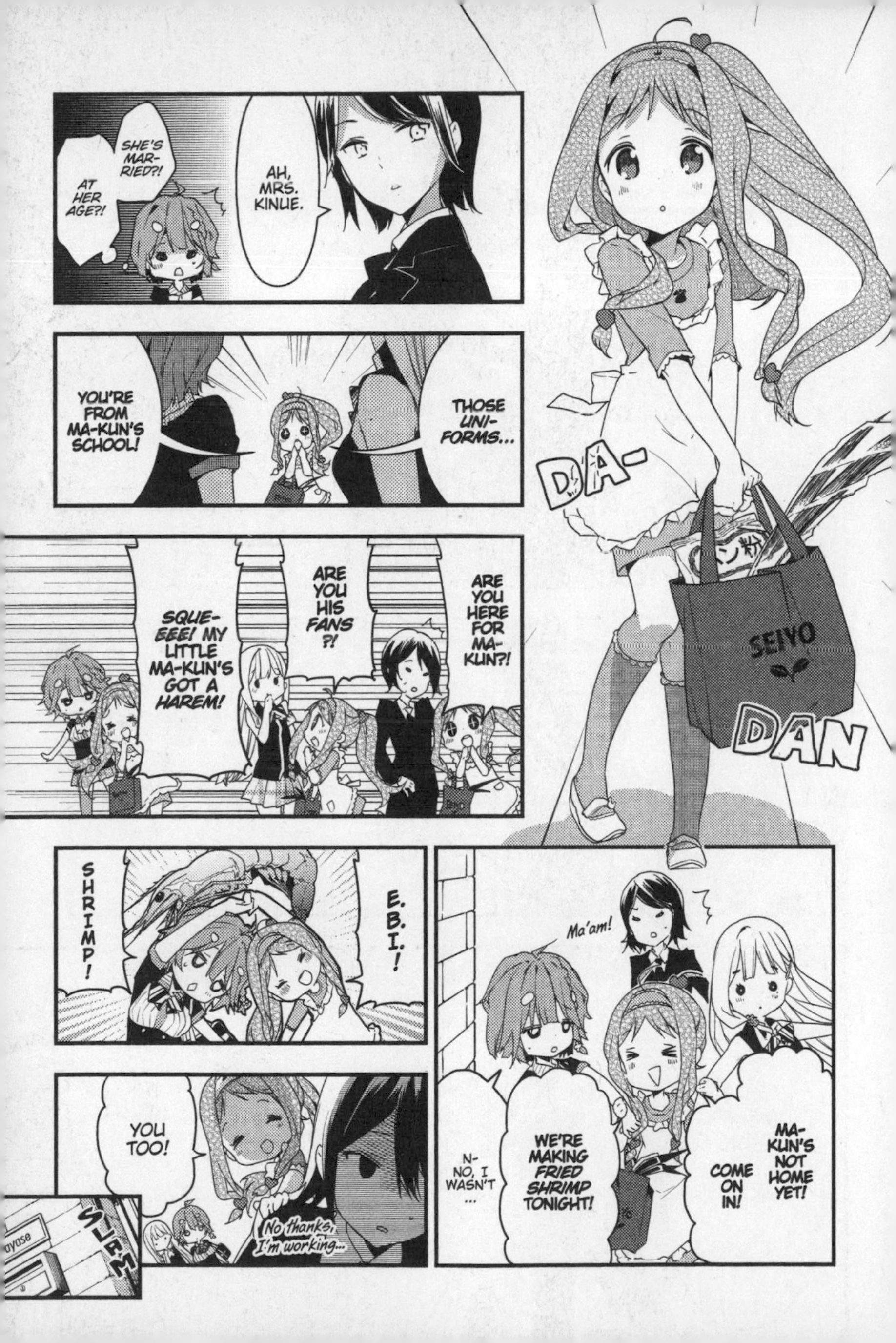
DA-
SEIYO
DAN
AH, MRS. KINUE.
SHE'S MARRIED?!
AT HER AGE?!
THOSE UNIFORMS...
YOU'RE FROM MA-KUN'S SCHOOL!
ARE YOU HERE FOR MA-KUN?!
ARE YOU HIS FANS?!
SQUEE-EEE! MY LITTLE MA-KUN'S GOT A HAREM!
Ma'am!
MA-KUN'S NOT HOME YET!
COME ON IN!
WE'RE MAKING FRIED SHRIMP TONIGHT!
N-NO, I WASN'T ...
E.B.I.!
SHRIMP!
YOU TOO!
No thanks, I'm working...
SLAM
ayase

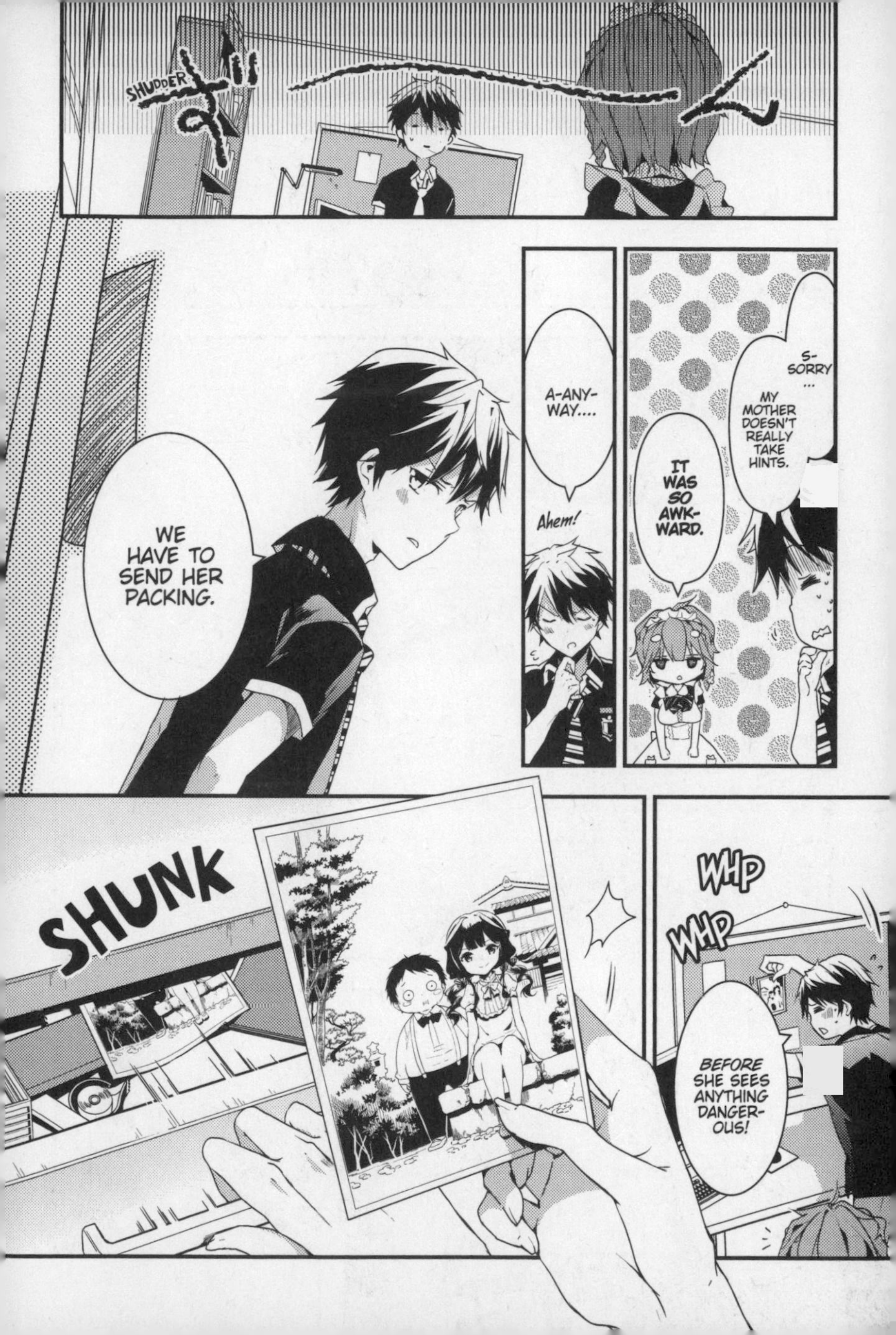
SHUDDER
S-SORRY... MY MOTHER DOESN'T REALLY TAKE HINTS.
IT WAS SO AWK-WARD.
A-ANY-WAY....
Ahem!
WE HAVE TO SEND HER PACKING.
WHP
WHP
BEFORE SHE SEES ANYTHING DANGER-OUS!
SHUNK

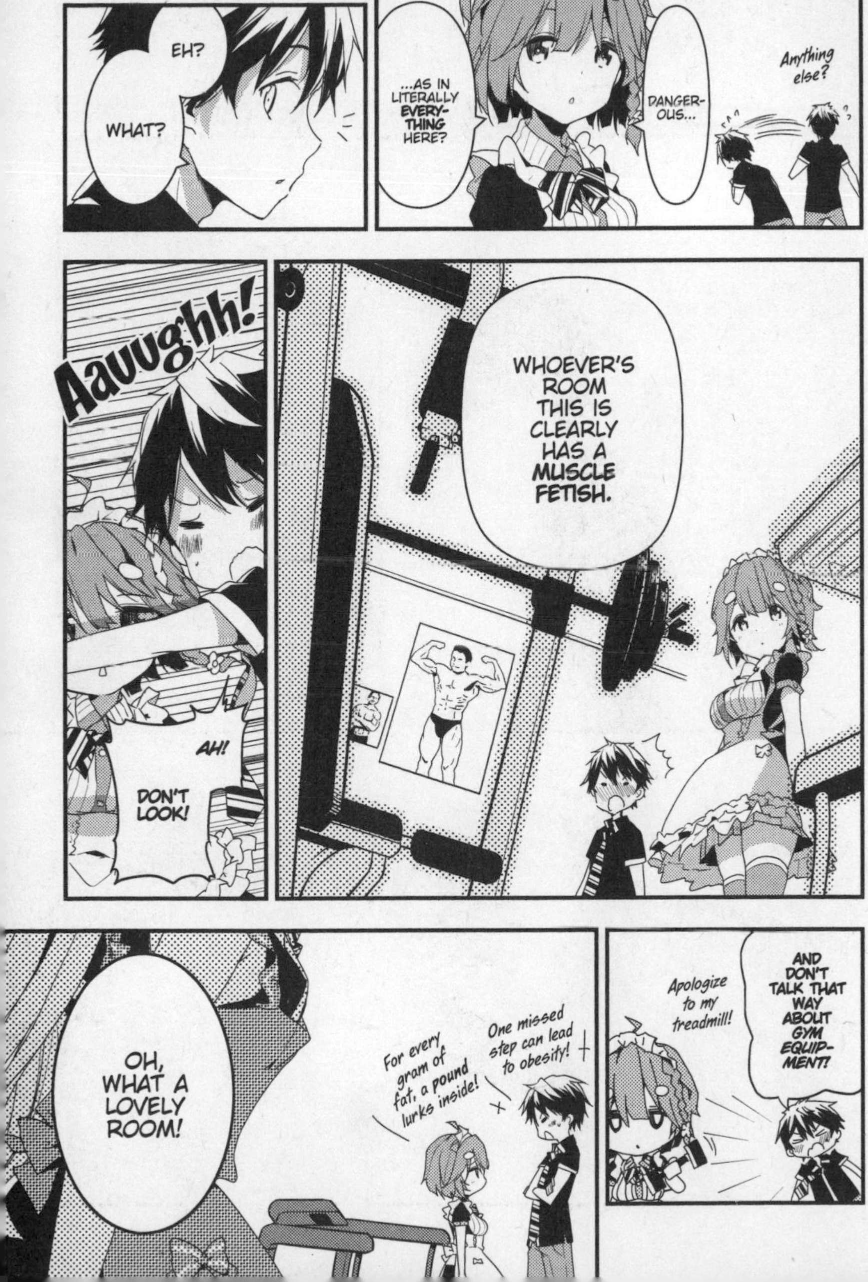
Anything else?
DANGER-OUS...
...AS IN LITERALLY EVERY-THING HERE?
EH?
WHAT?
WHOEVER'S ROOM THIS IS CLEARLY HAS A MUSCLE FETISH.
Aauughh!
AH!
DON'T LOOK!
AND DON'T TALK THAT WAY ABOUT GYM EQUIP-MENT!
Apologize to my treadmill!
One missed step can lead to obesity!
For every gram of fat, a pound lurks inside!
OH, WHAT A LOVELY ROOM!

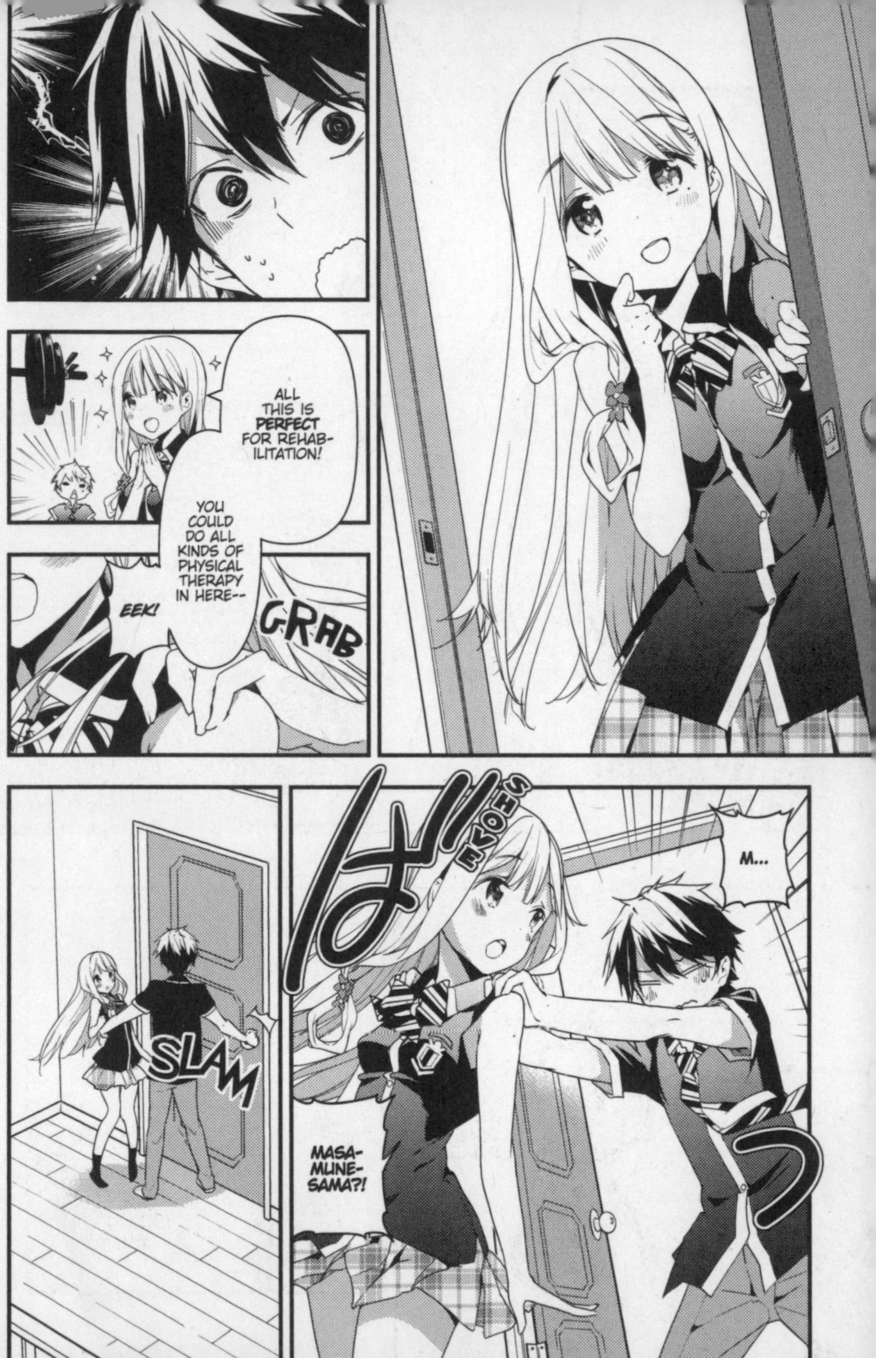
ALL THIS IS PERFECT FOR REHAB-ILITATION!
YOU COULD DO ALL KINDS OF PHYSICAL THERAPY IN HERE--
GRAB
EEK!
M...
SHOVE
MASA-MUNE-SAMA?!
SLAM

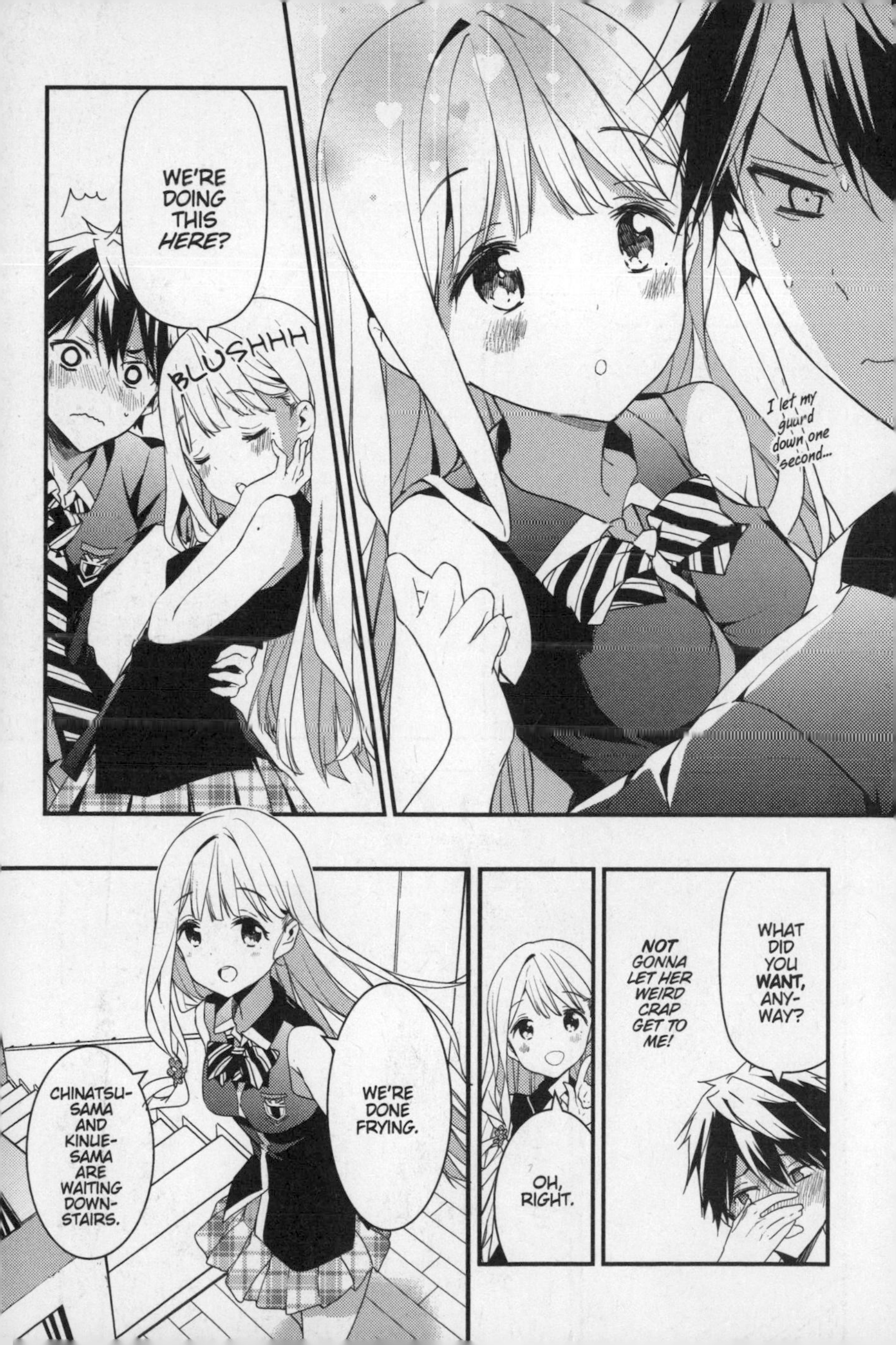
I let my guard down one second...
WE'RE DOING THIS HERE?
BLUSHHH
WHAT DID YOU WANT, ANYWAY?
NOT GONNA LET HER WEIRD CRAP GET TO ME!
OH, RIGHT.
WE'RE DONE FRYING.
CHINATSU-SAMA AND KINUE-SAMA ARE WAITING DOWNSTAIRS.

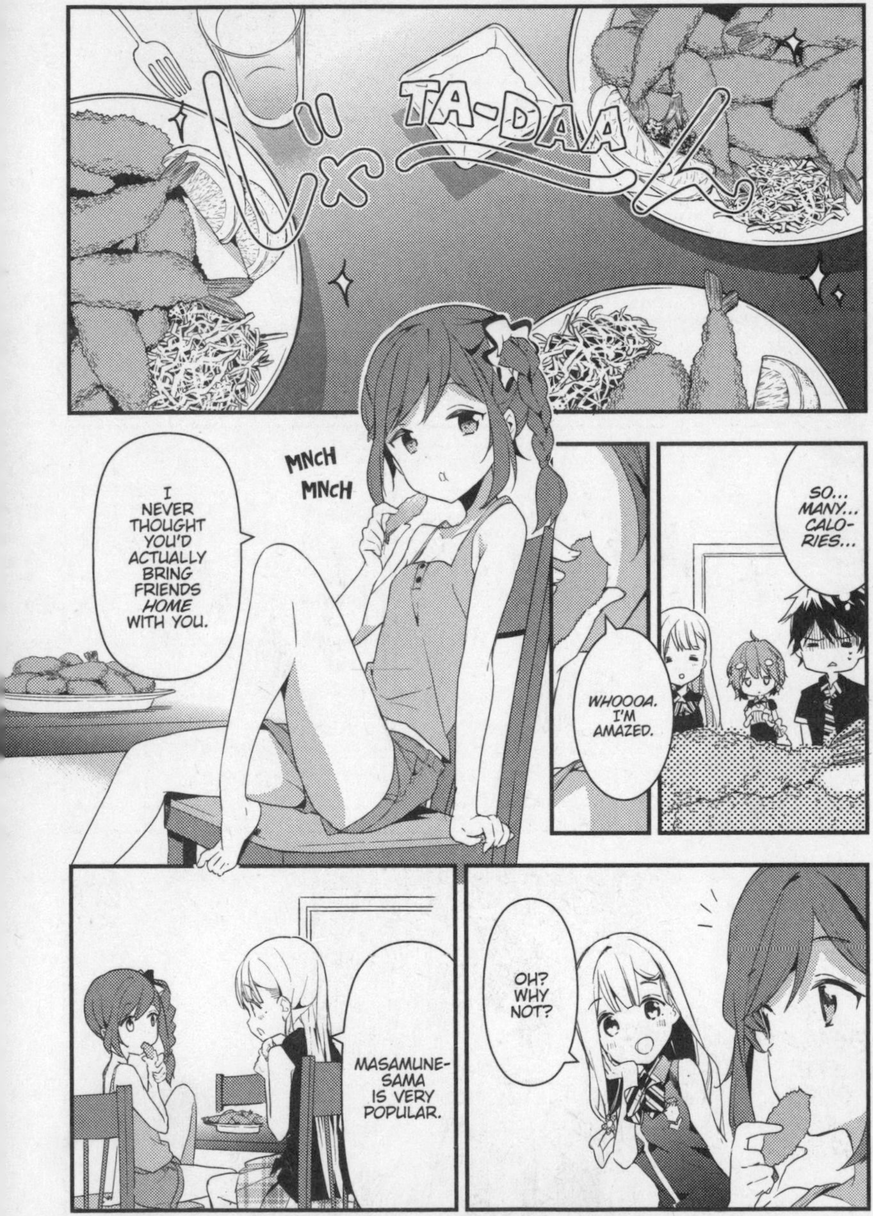
TA-DAA
SO... MANY... CALO-RIES...
WHOOOA. I'M AMAZED.
MNCH MNCH
I NEVER THOUGHT YOU'D ACTUALLY BRING FRIENDS *HOME* WITH YOU.
OH? WHY NOT?
MASAMUNE-SAMA IS VERY POPULAR.

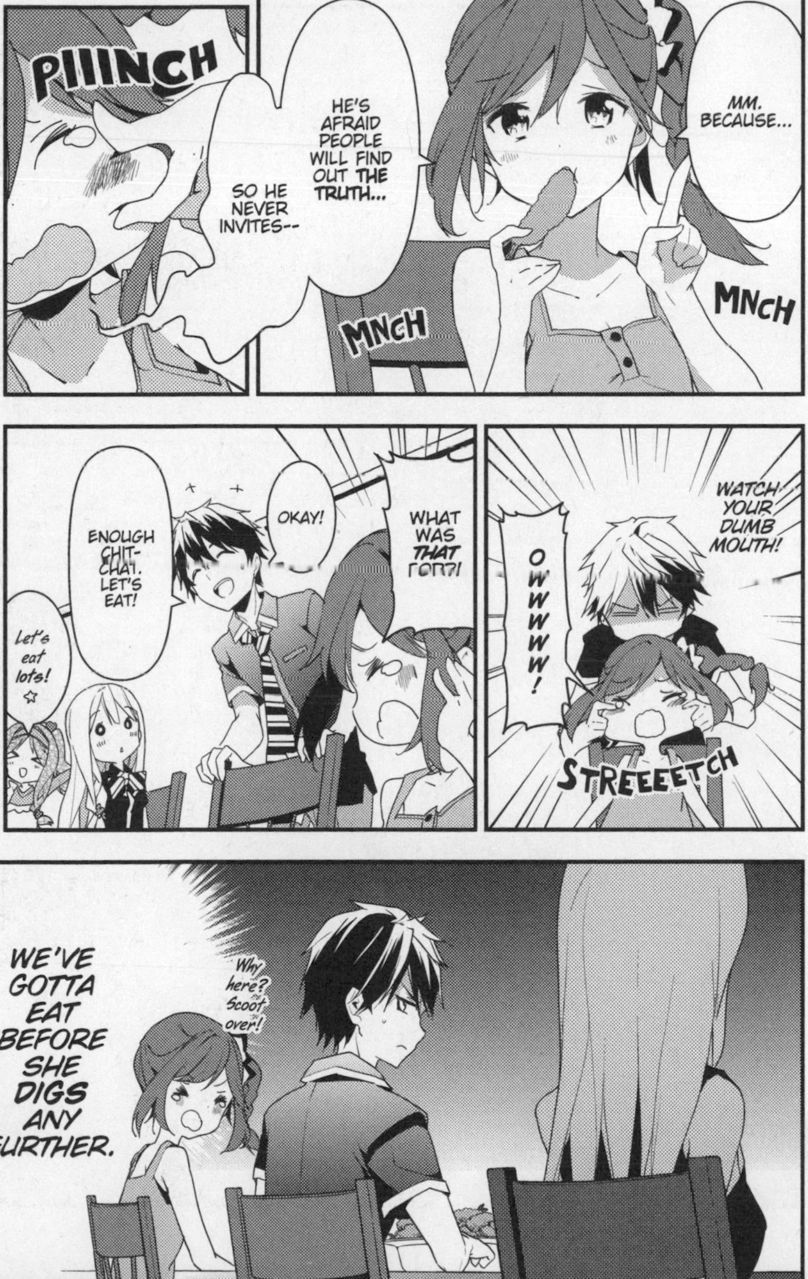
MM. BECAUSE...
MNCH
HE'S AFRAID PEOPLE WILL FIND OUT THE TRUTH...
MNCH
SO HE NEVER INVITES--
PIIINCH
WATCH YOUR DUMB MOUTH!
OWWWWWW!
STREEEETCH
WHAT WAS THAT FOR?!
OKAY!
ENOUGH CHIT-CHAT. LET'S EAT!
Let's eat lots! ☆
Why here? Scoot over!
WE'VE GOTTA EAT BEFORE SHE DIGS ANY FURTHER.

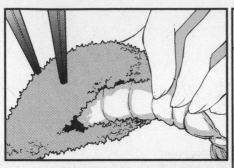

ITADAKI-
MASU!

THIS
BREAD-
ING IS
NOTHING
BUT
OIL...

Breading

POP

GULP

GLUG
GLUG
GLUG
GLUG

SCHRRRP

Omega
3

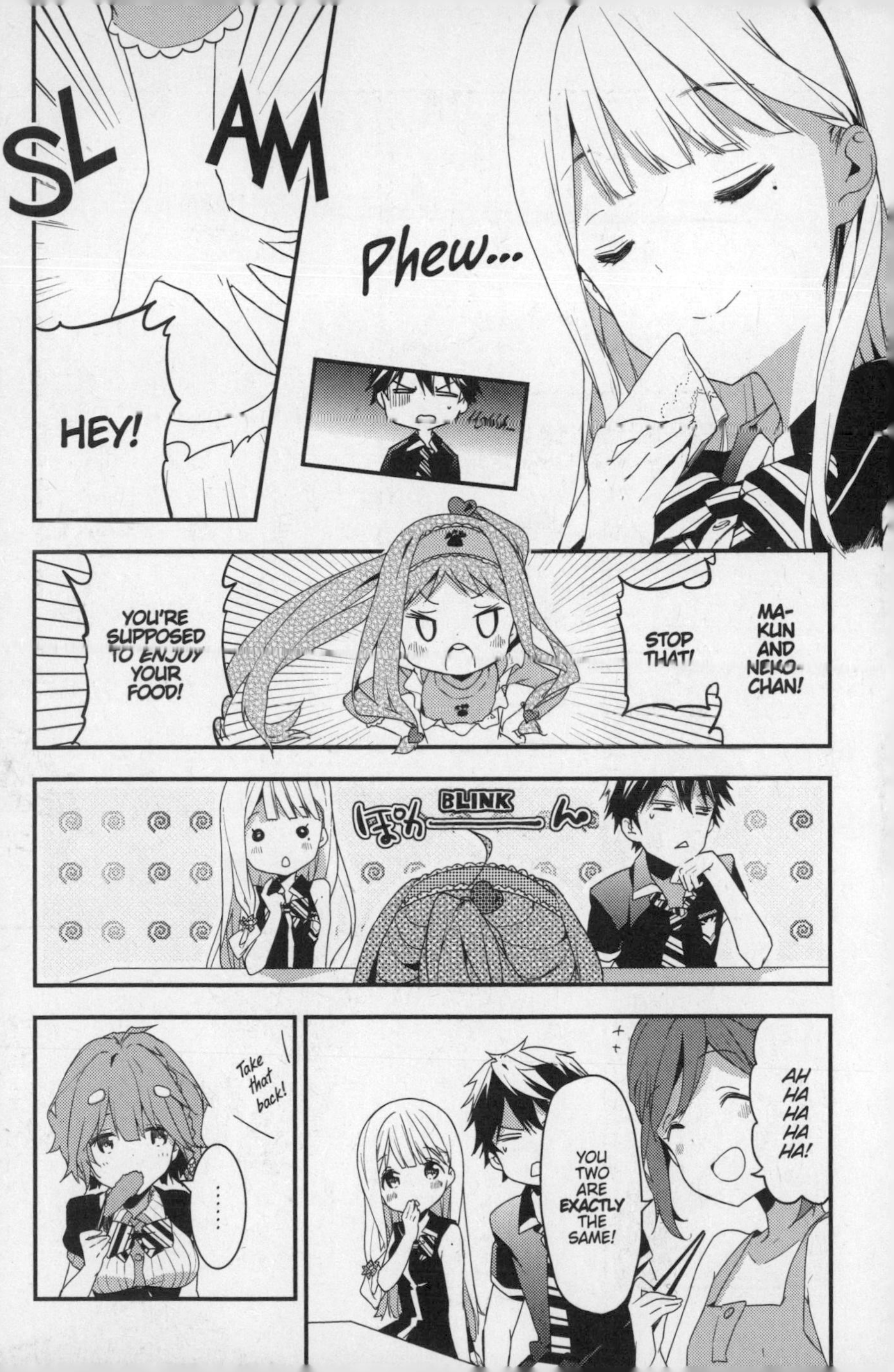

Phew...
SLAM
HEY!
MA-KUN AND NEKO-CHAN!
STOP THAT!
YOU'RE SUPPOSED TO ENJOY YOUR FOOD!
BLINK
ぽか——ん
AH HA HA HA HA!
YOU TWO ARE EXACTLY THE SAME!
Take that back!
......

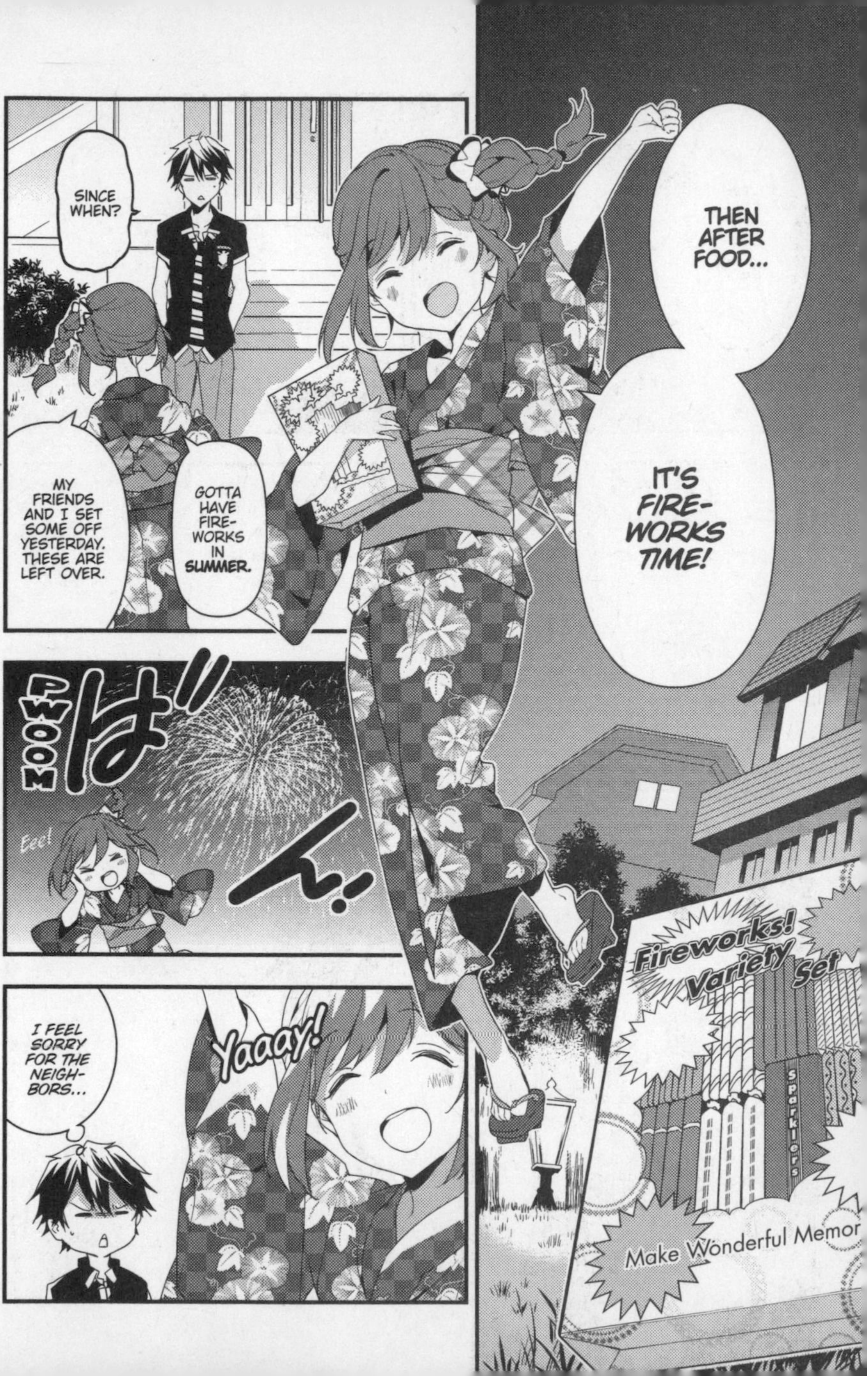
THEN AFTER FOOD...
IT'S FIRE-WORKS TIME!
Fireworks! Variety Set
Sparklers
Make Wonderful Memor
SINCE WHEN?
GOTTA HAVE FIRE-WORKS IN SUMMER.
MY FRIENDS AND I SET SOME OFF YESTERDAY. THESE ARE LEFT OVER.
PWOOM
Eee!
Yaaay!
I FEEL SORRY FOR THE NEIGH-BORS...

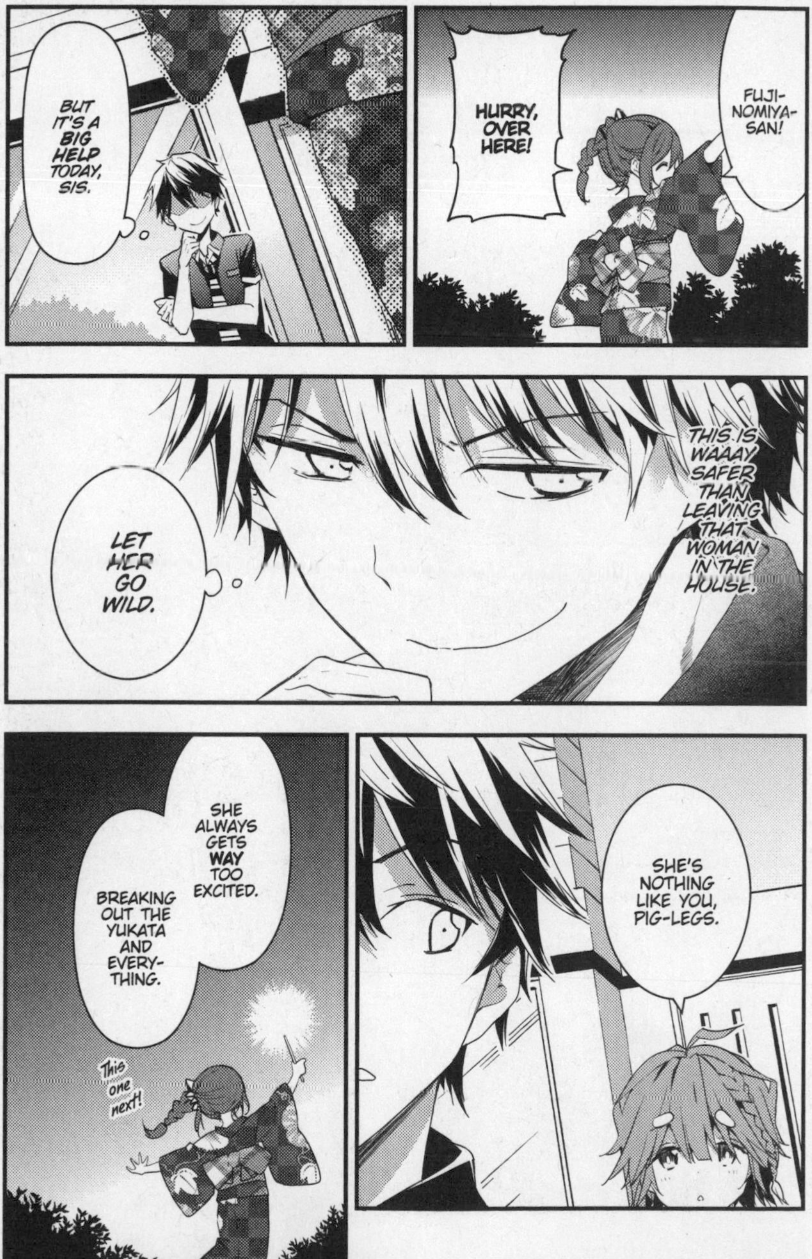
FUJI-NOMIYA-SAN!
HURRY, OVER HERE!
BUT IT'S A BIG HELP TODAY, SIS.
THIS IS WAAAY SAFER THAN LEAVING THAT WOMAN IN THE HOUSE.
LET HER GO WILD.
SHE'S NOTHING LIKE YOU, PIG-LEGS.
SHE ALWAYS GETS WAY TOO EXCITED.
BREAKING OUT THE YUKATA AND EVERYTHING.
This one next!

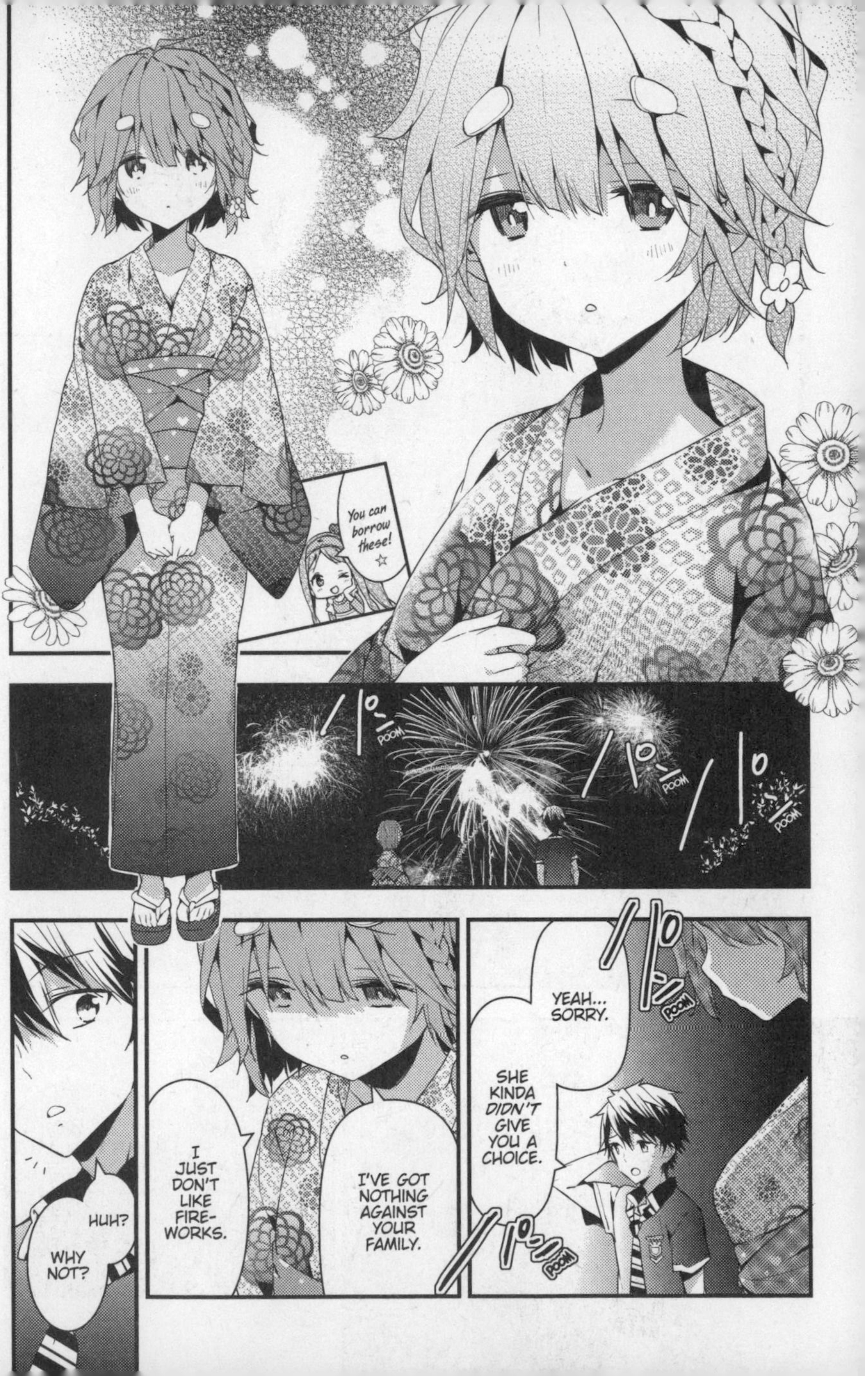
You can borrow these! ☆
POOM
POOM
POOM
POOM
YEAH... SORRY.
SHE KINDA DIDN'T GIVE YOU A CHOICE.
POOM
I'VE GOT NOTHING AGAINST YOUR FAMILY.
I JUST DON'T LIKE FIRE-WORKS.
HUH?
WHY NOT?

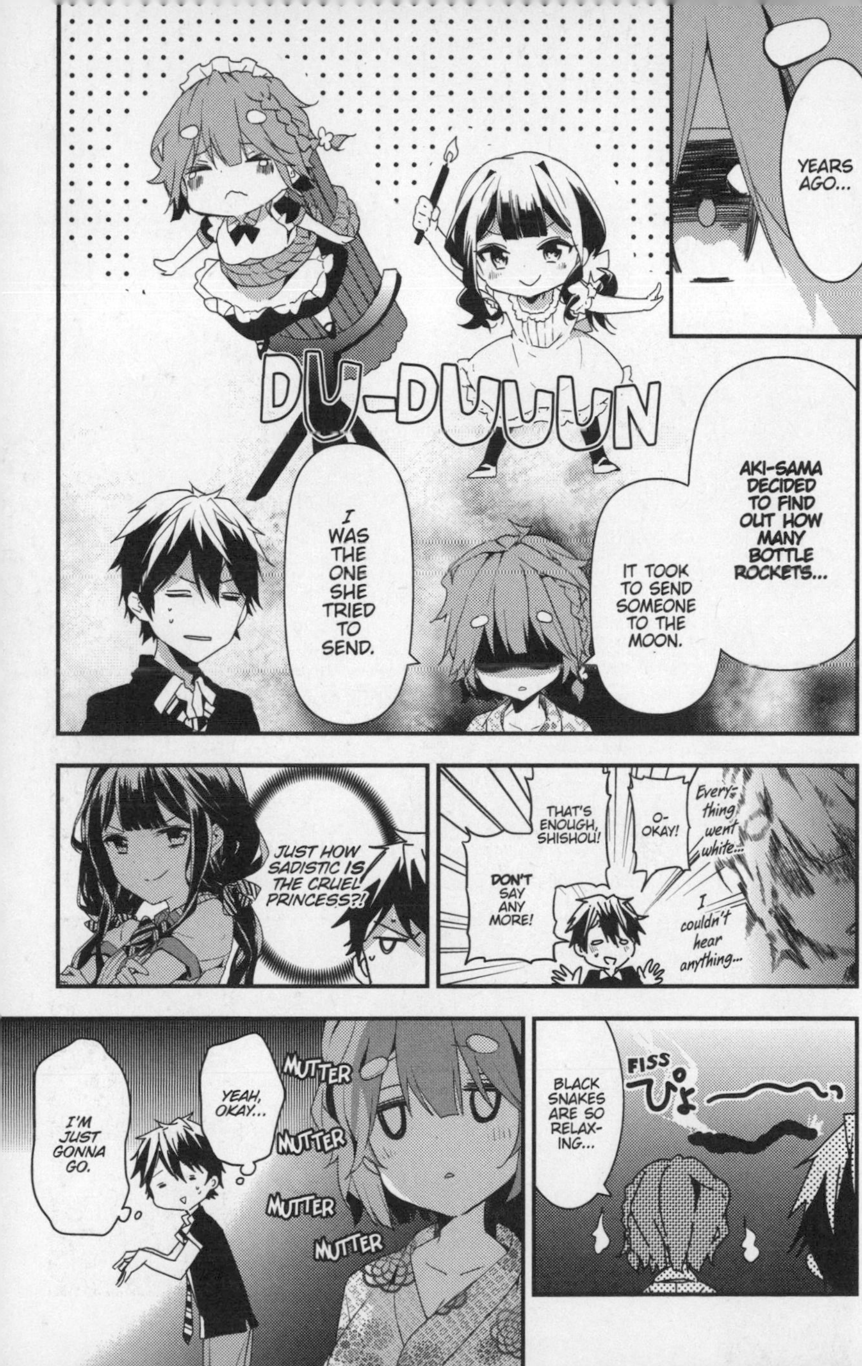
YEARS AGO...
AKI-SAMA DECIDED TO FIND OUT HOW MANY BOTTLE ROCKETS...
DU-DUUUN
IT TOOK TO SEND SOMEONE TO THE MOON.
I WAS THE ONE SHE TRIED TO SEND.
Everything went white...
O-OKAY!
THAT'S ENOUGH, SHISHOU!
I couldn't hear anything...
DON'T SAY ANY MORE!
JUST HOW SADISTIC IS THE CRUEL PRINCESS?!
FISS
ぴょ〜〜〜
BLACK SNAKES ARE SO RELAXING...
MUTTER
YEAH, OKAY...
MUTTER
MUTTER
MUTTER
I'M JUST GONNA GO.

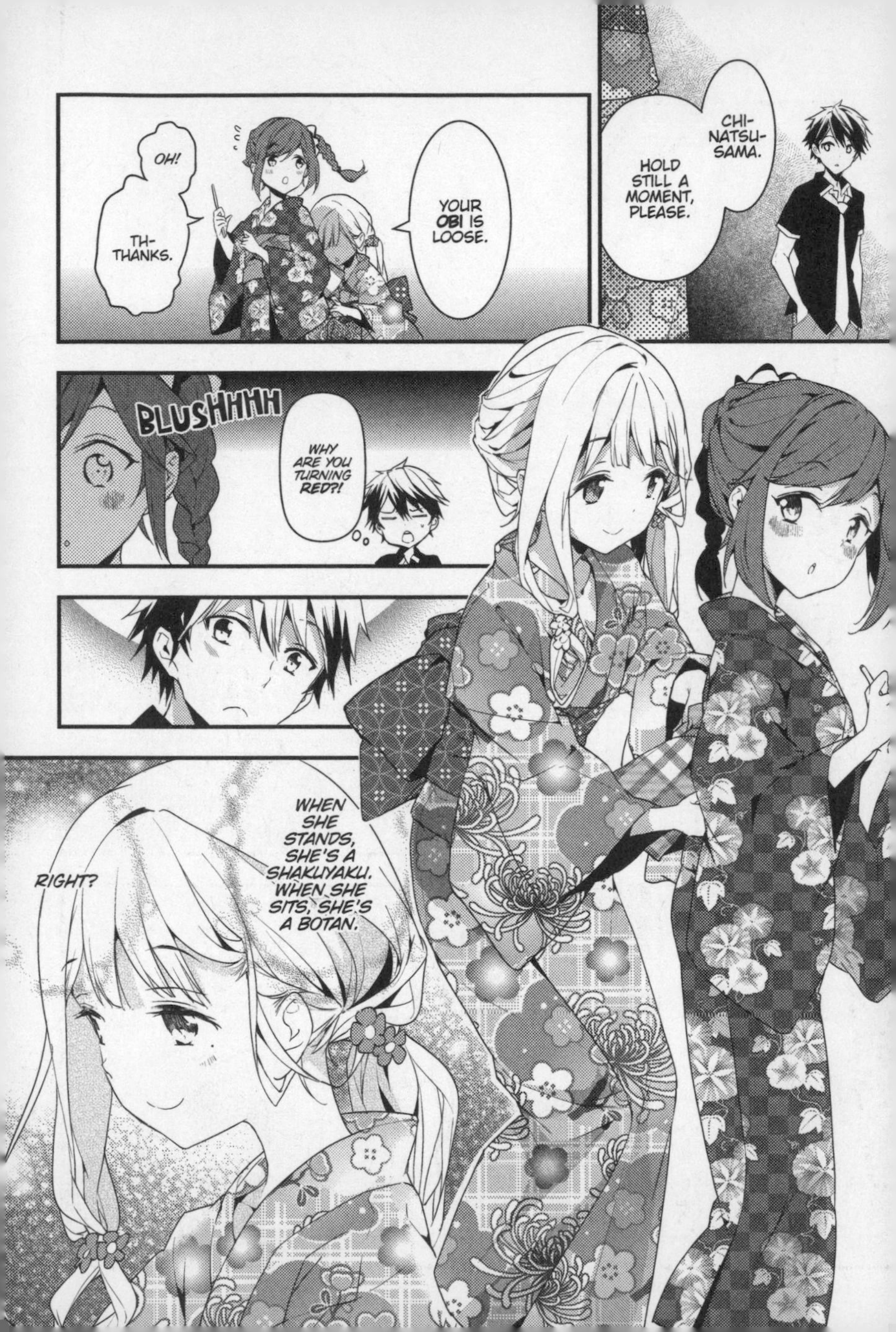
CHI-NATSU-SAMA.
HOLD STILL A MOMENT, PLEASE.
YOUR OBI IS LOOSE.
OH!
TH-THANKS.
BLUSHHHH
WHY ARE YOU TURNING RED?!
WHEN SHE STANDS, SHE'S A SHAKUYAKU. WHEN SHE SITS, SHE'S A BOTAN.
RIGHT?

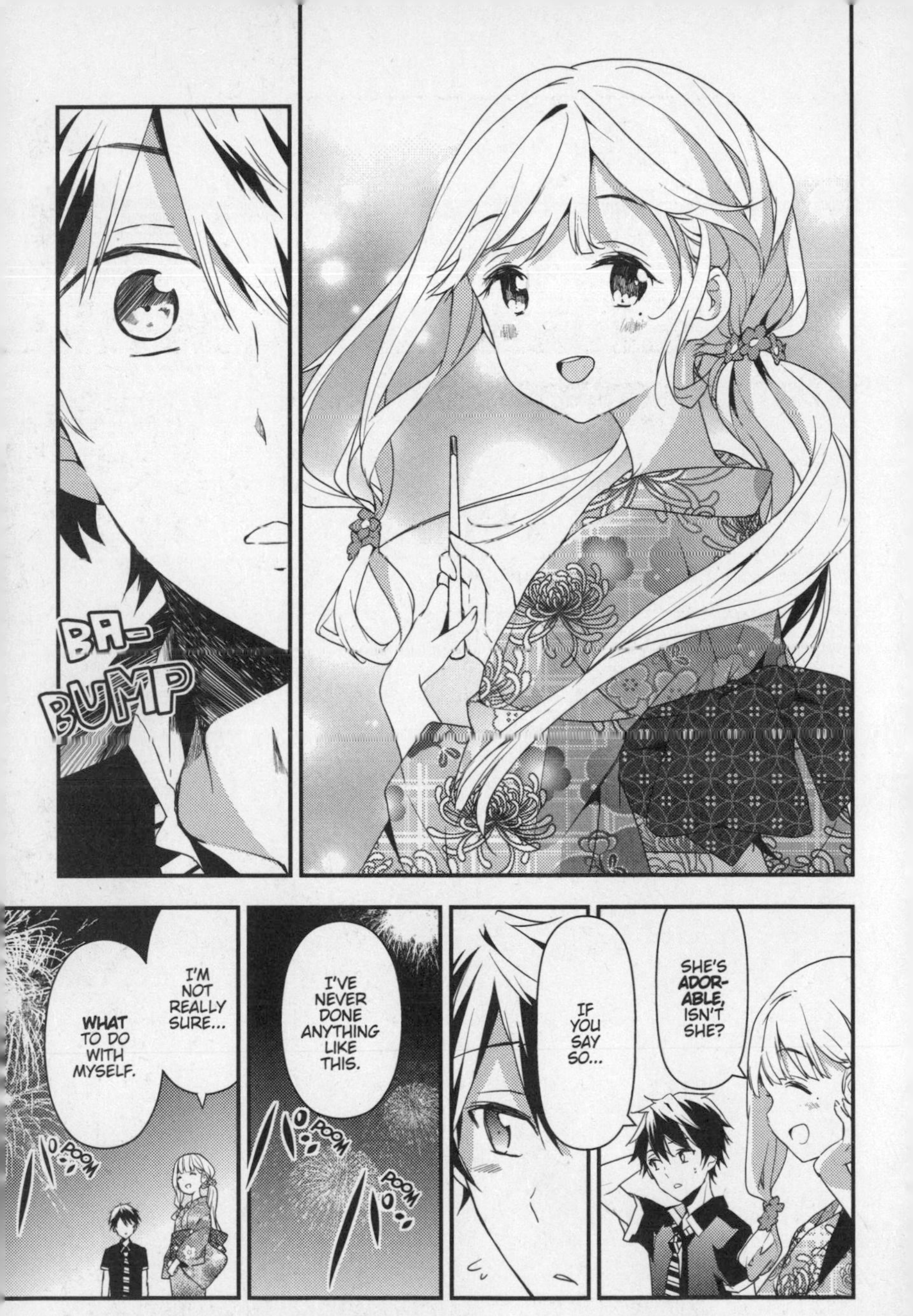
BA-BUMP
SHE'S ADORABLE, ISN'T SHE?
IF YOU SAY SO...
I'VE NEVER DONE ANYTHING LIKE THIS.
POOM
POOM
I'M NOT REALLY SURE...
WHAT TO DO WITH MYSELF.
POOM

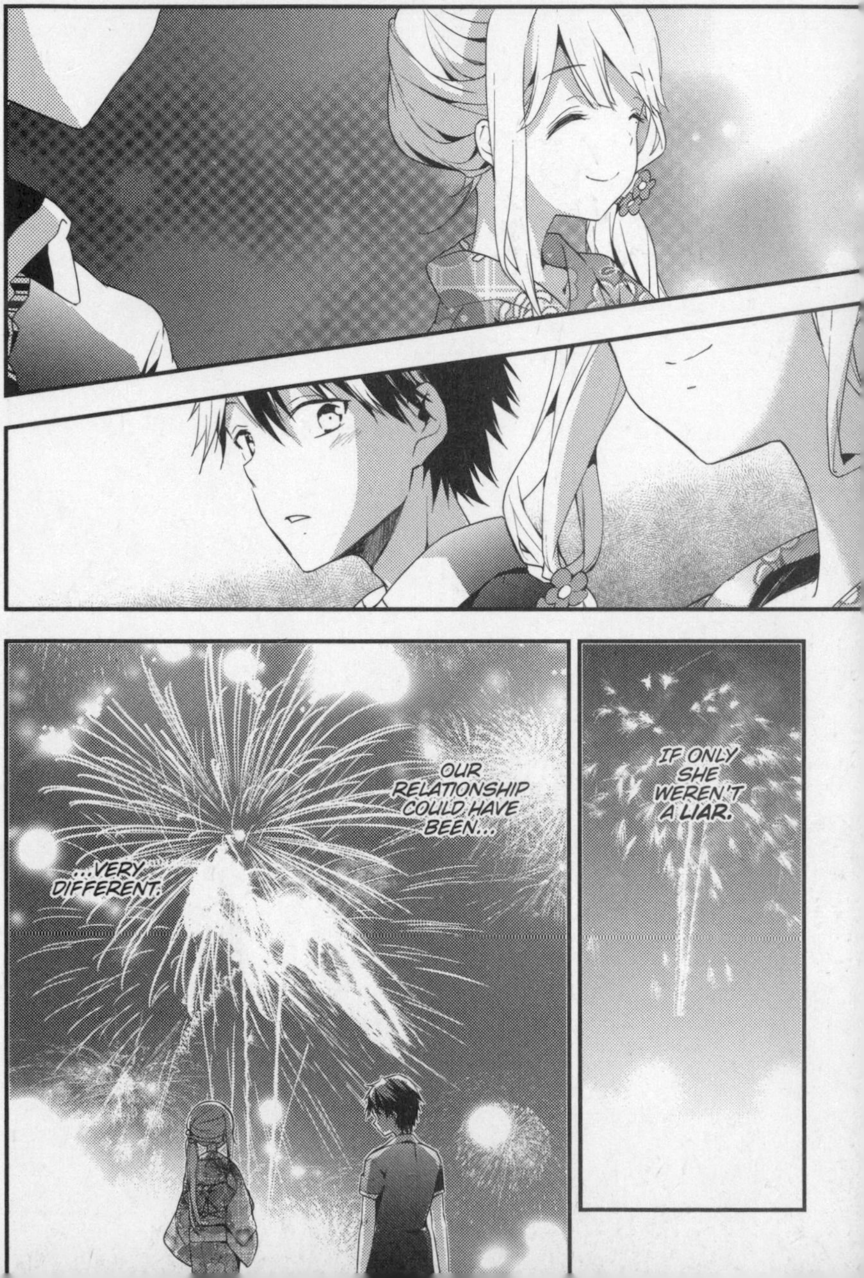
IF ONLY SHE WEREN'T A LIAR.
OUR RELATIONSHIP COULD HAVE BEEN...
...VERY DIFFERENT.

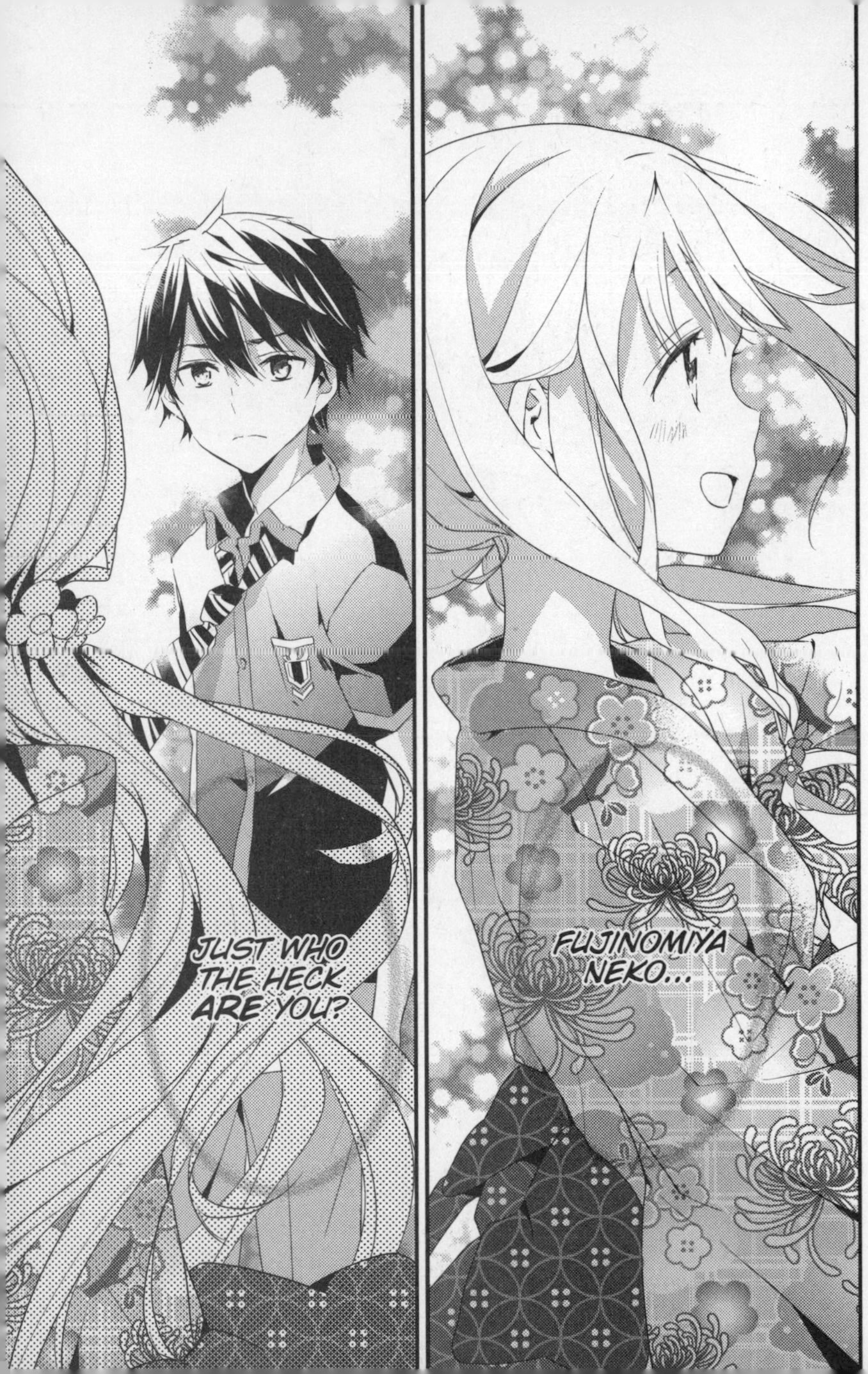
FUJINOMIYA NEKO...
JUST WHO THE HECK ARE YOU?

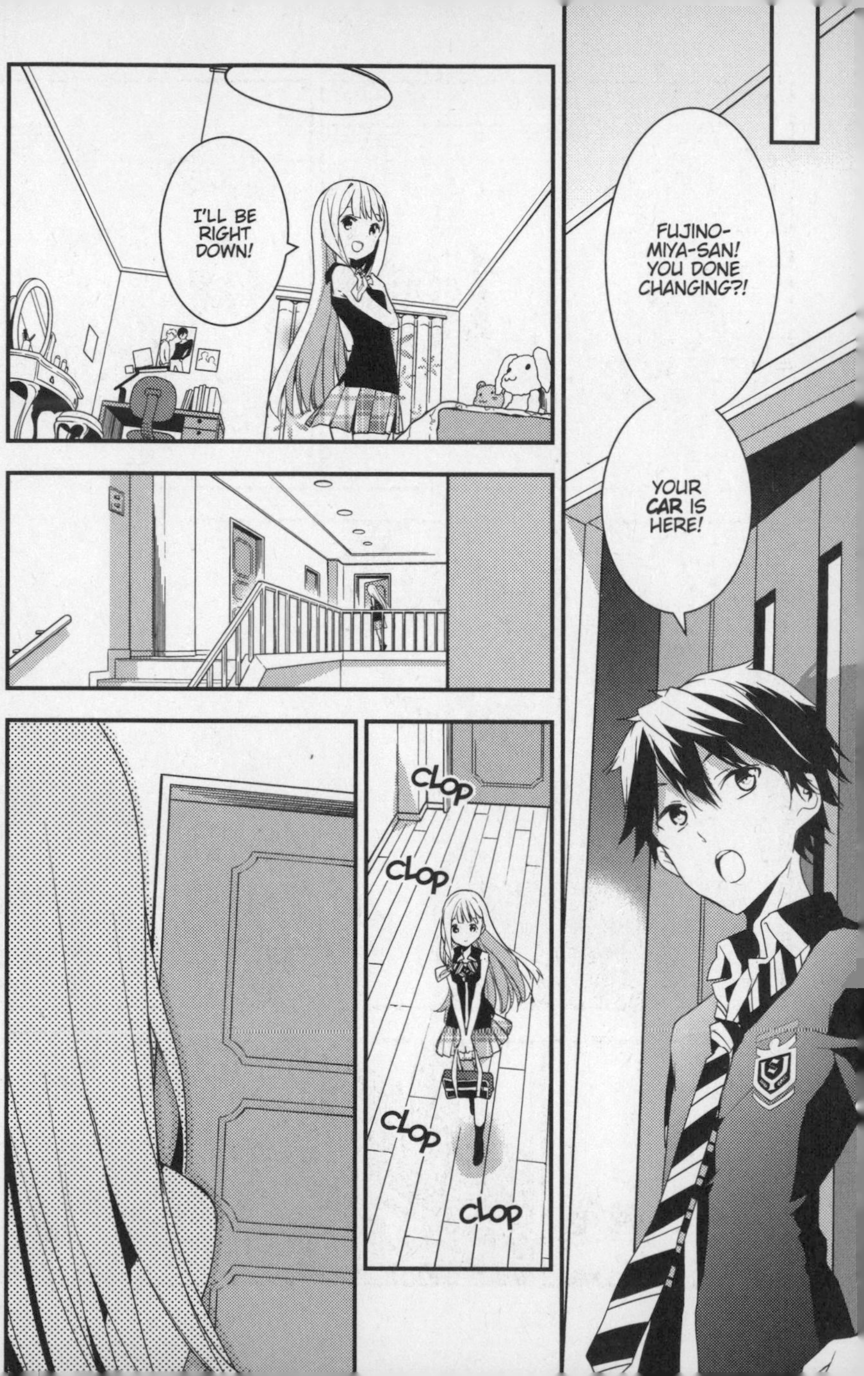
FUJINO-MIYA-SAN! YOU DONE CHANGING?!
YOUR CAR IS HERE!
I'LL BE RIGHT DOWN!
CLOP
CLOP
CLOP
CLOP

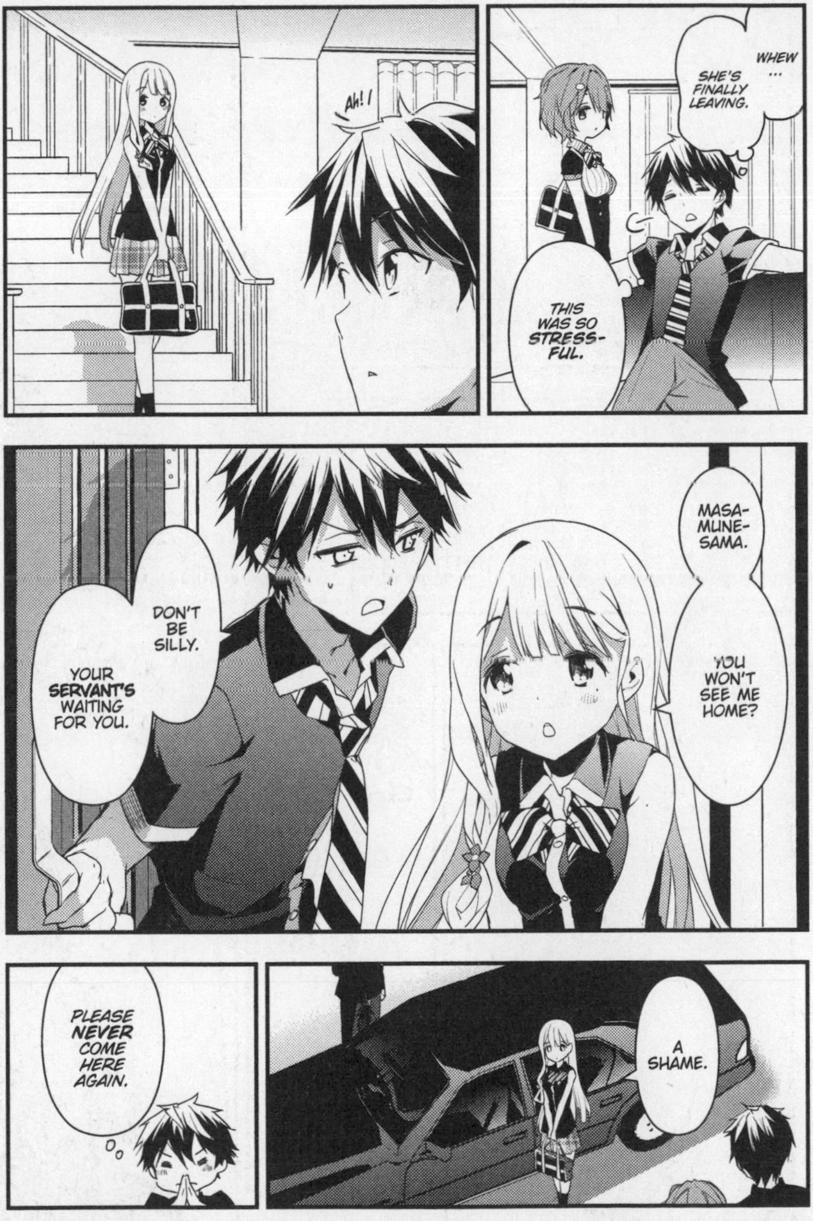
WHEW ... SHE'S FINALLY LEAVING.
THIS WAS SO STRESS-FUL.
Ah!!
MASA-MUNE-SAMA.
YOU WON'T SEE ME HOME?
DON'T BE SILLY.
YOUR **SERVANT'S** WAITING FOR YOU.
A SHAME.
PLEASE **NEVER** COME HERE AGAIN.

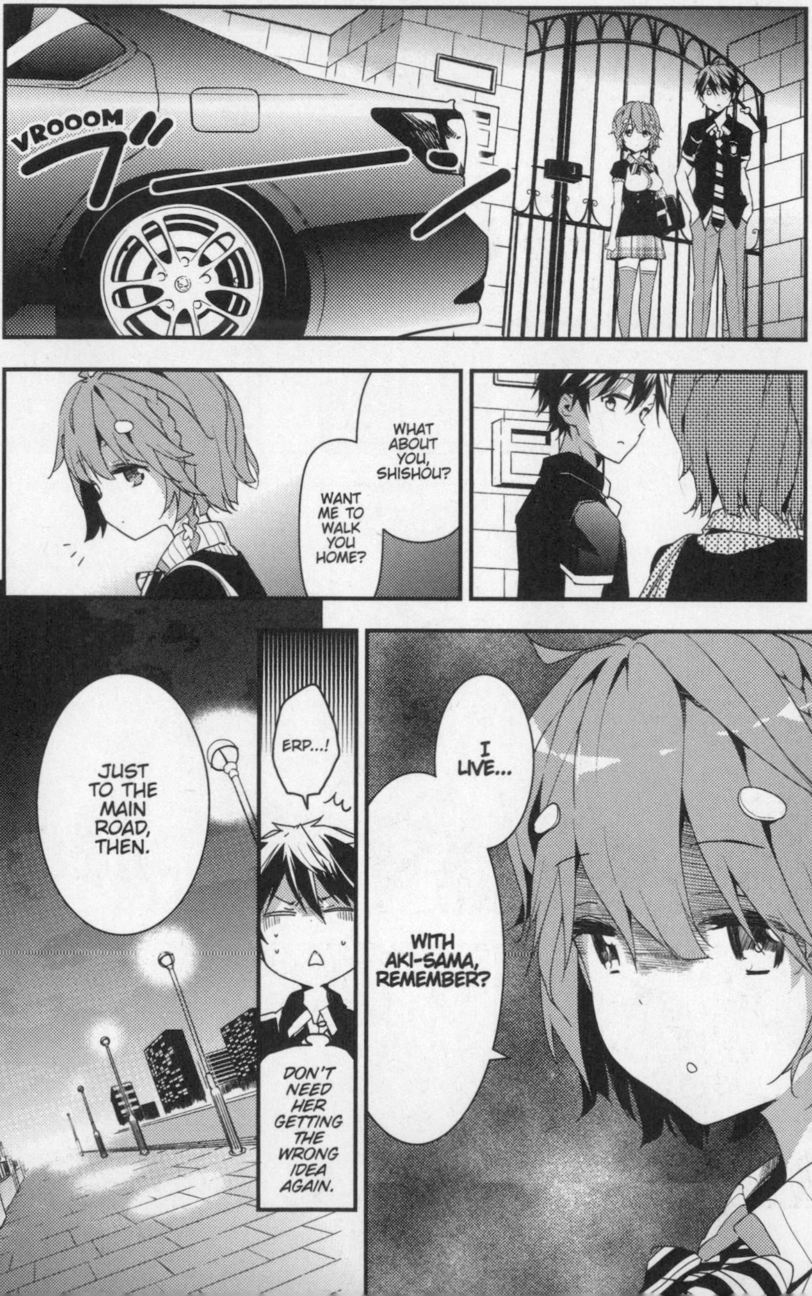
VROOOM
WHAT ABOUT YOU, SHISHOU?
WANT ME TO WALK YOU HOME?
I LIVE...
WITH AKI-SAMA, REMEMBER?
ERP...!
DON'T NEED HER GETTING THE WRONG IDEA AGAIN.
JUST TO THE MAIN ROAD, THEN.

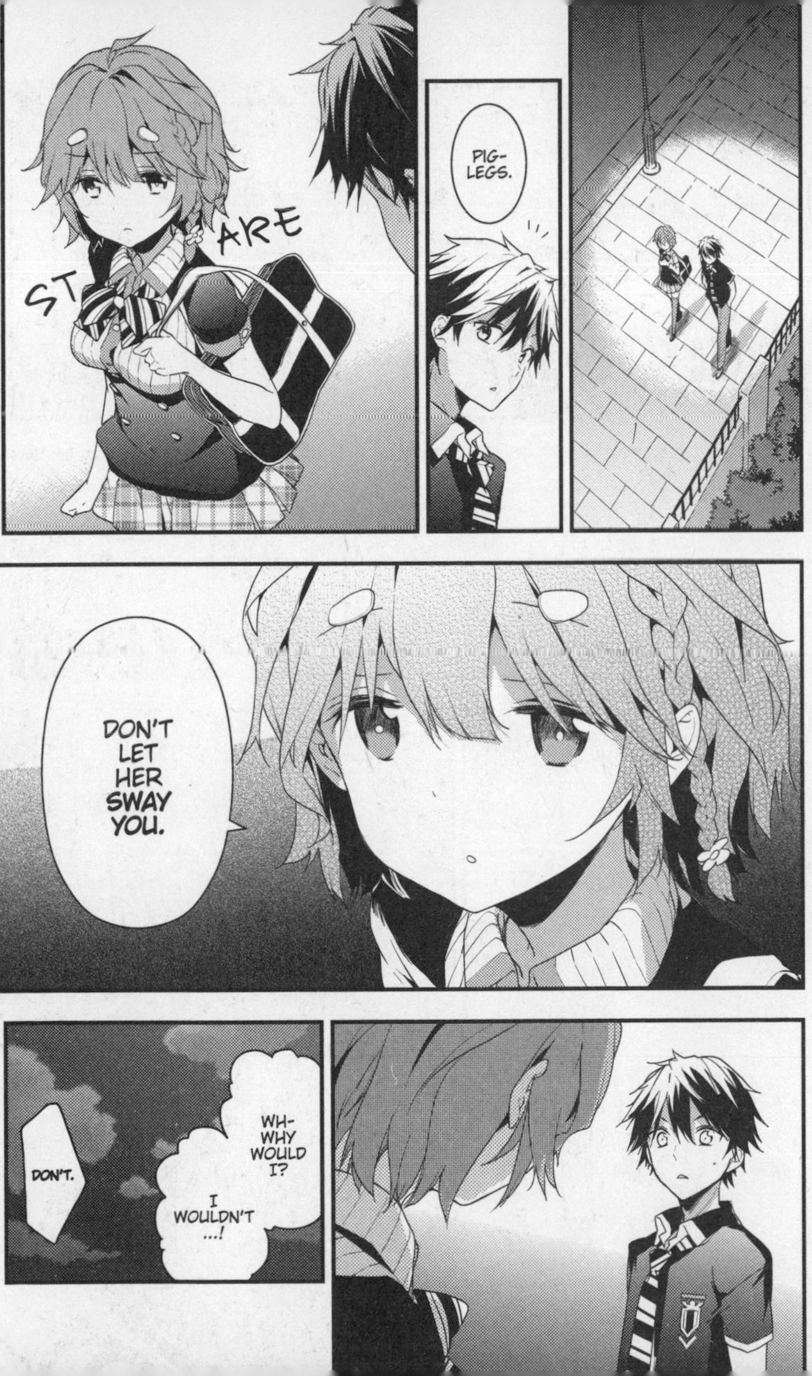
PIG-
LEGS.
ST ARE
DON'T LET HER SWAY YOU.
WH-
WHY
WOULD
I?
I
WOULDN'T
...!
DON'T.

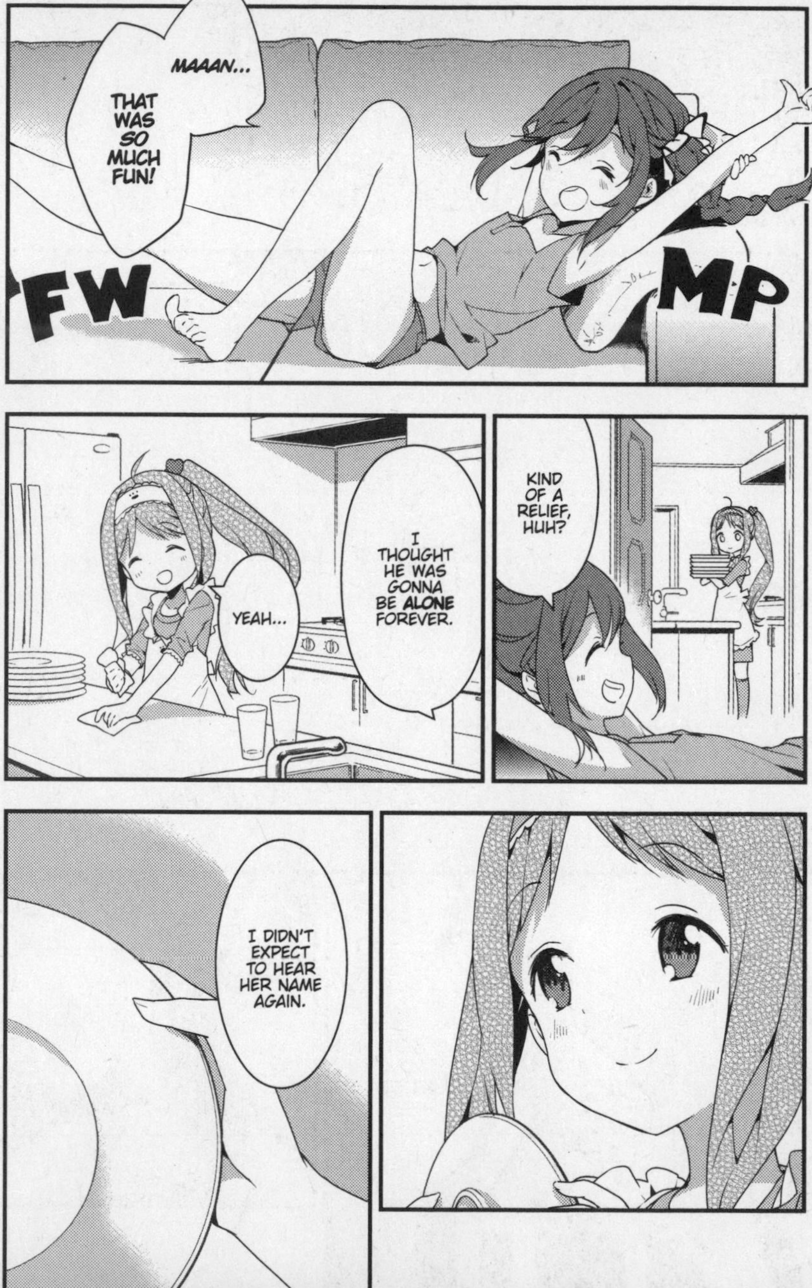
MAAAN... THAT WAS SO MUCH FUN!
FW MP
KIND OF A RELIEF, HUH?
I THOUGHT HE WAS GONNA BE **ALONE** FOREVER.
YEAH...
I DIDN'T EXPECT TO HEAR HER NAME AGAIN.

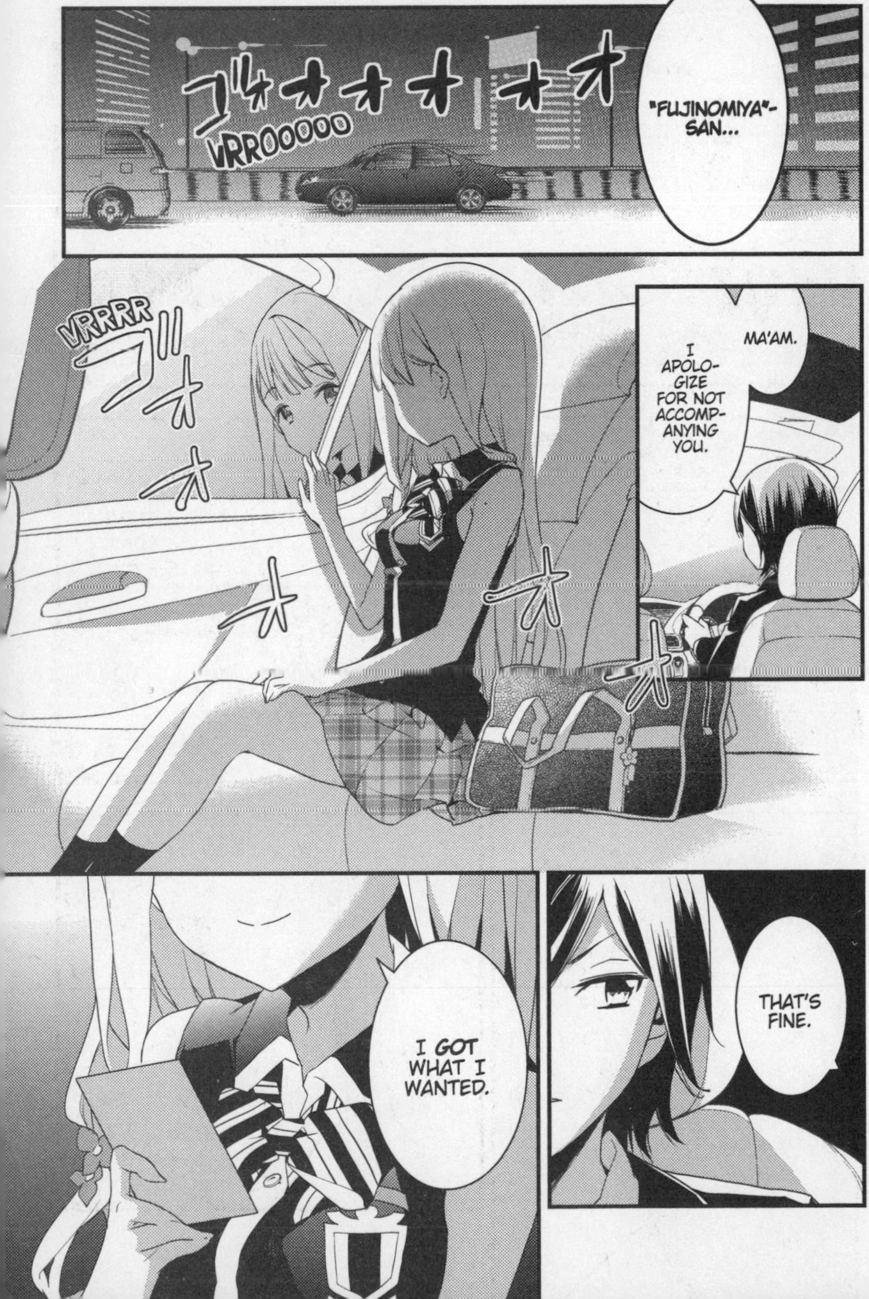
VRROOOOO
"FUJINOMIYA"-SAN...
MA'AM.
I APOLOGIZE FOR NOT ACCOMPANYING YOU.
VRRRR
THAT'S FINE.
I GOT WHAT I WANTED.

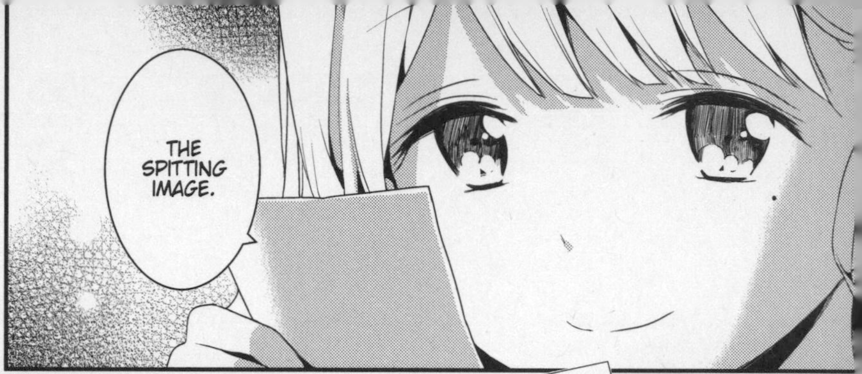
THE SPITTING IMAGE.
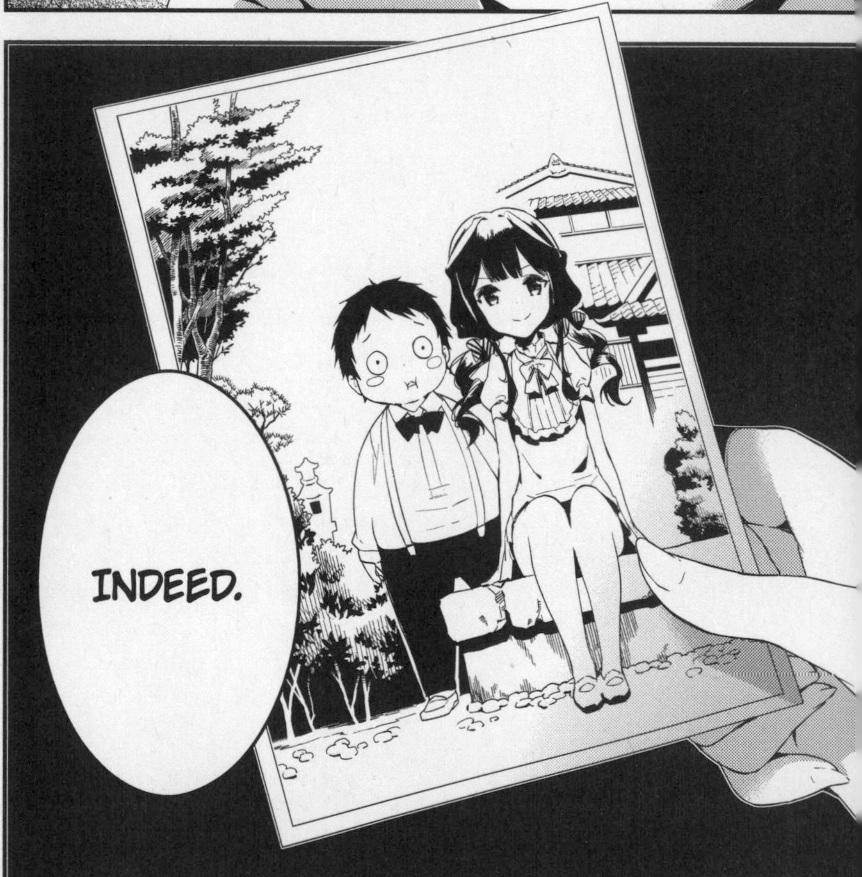
INDEED.

3

Masamune-kun's

REVENGE

Presented by Hazuki Takeoka & TIV

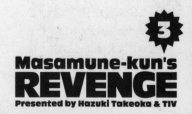

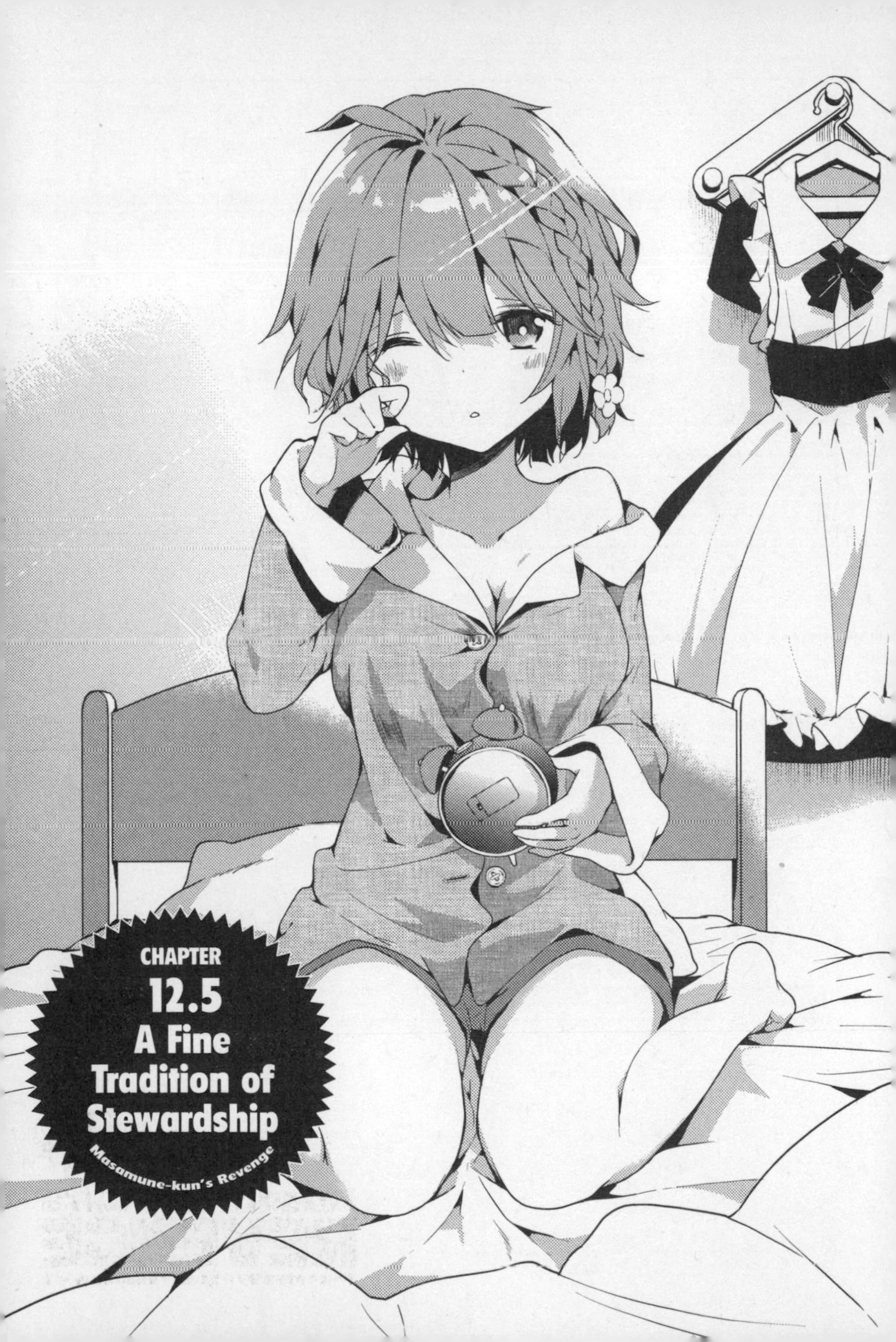
CHAPTER
12.5
A Fine
Tradition of
Stewardship
Masamune-kun's Revenge

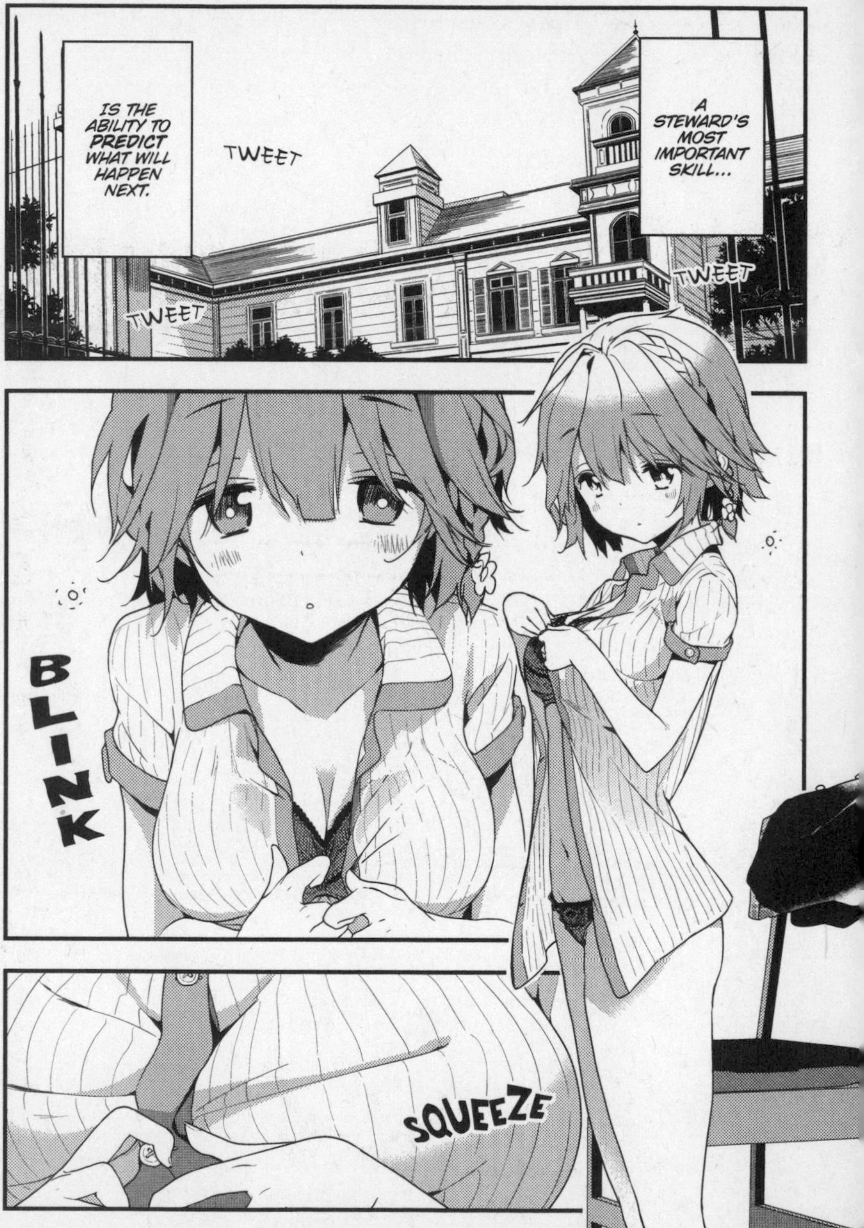
A STEWARD'S MOST IMPORTANT SKILL...
TWEET
TWEET
IS THE ABILITY TO PREDICT WHAT WILL HAPPEN NEXT.
TWEET
BLINK
SQUEEZE

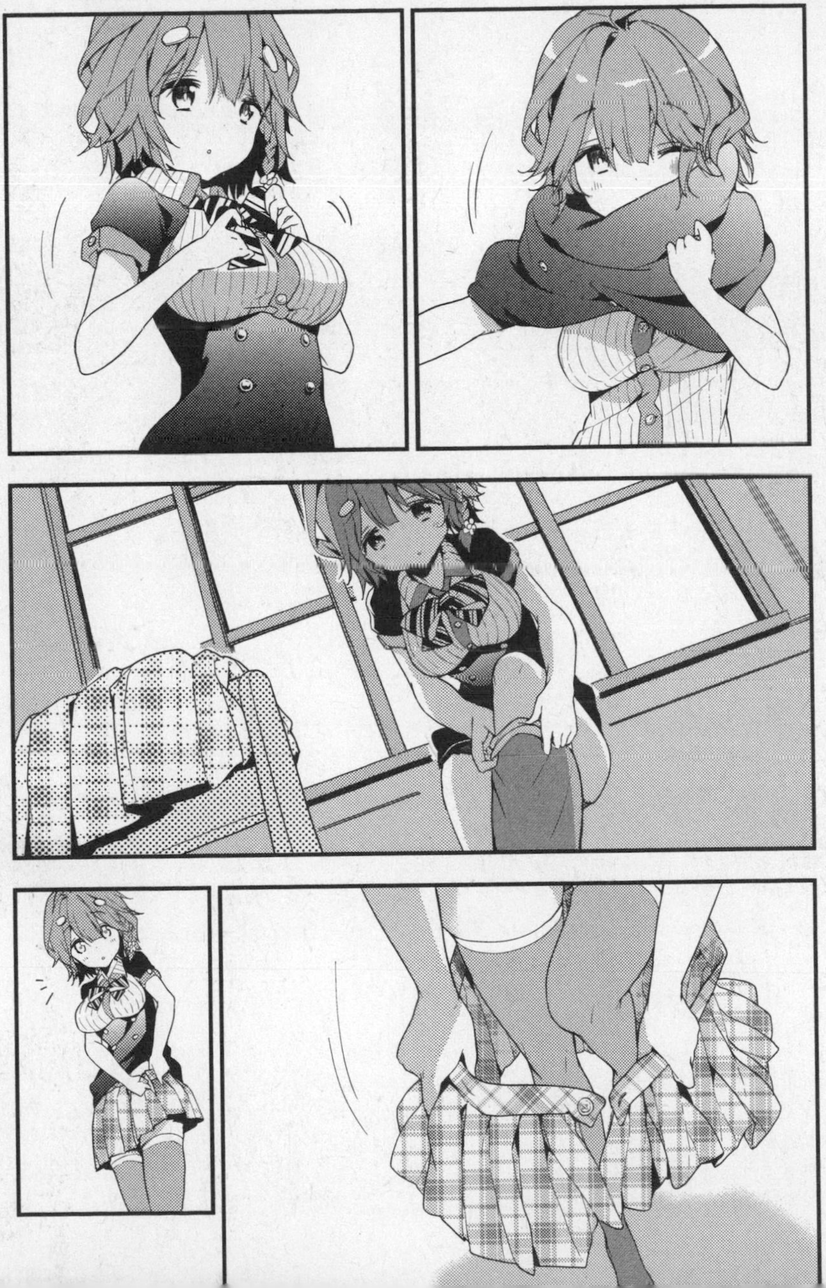

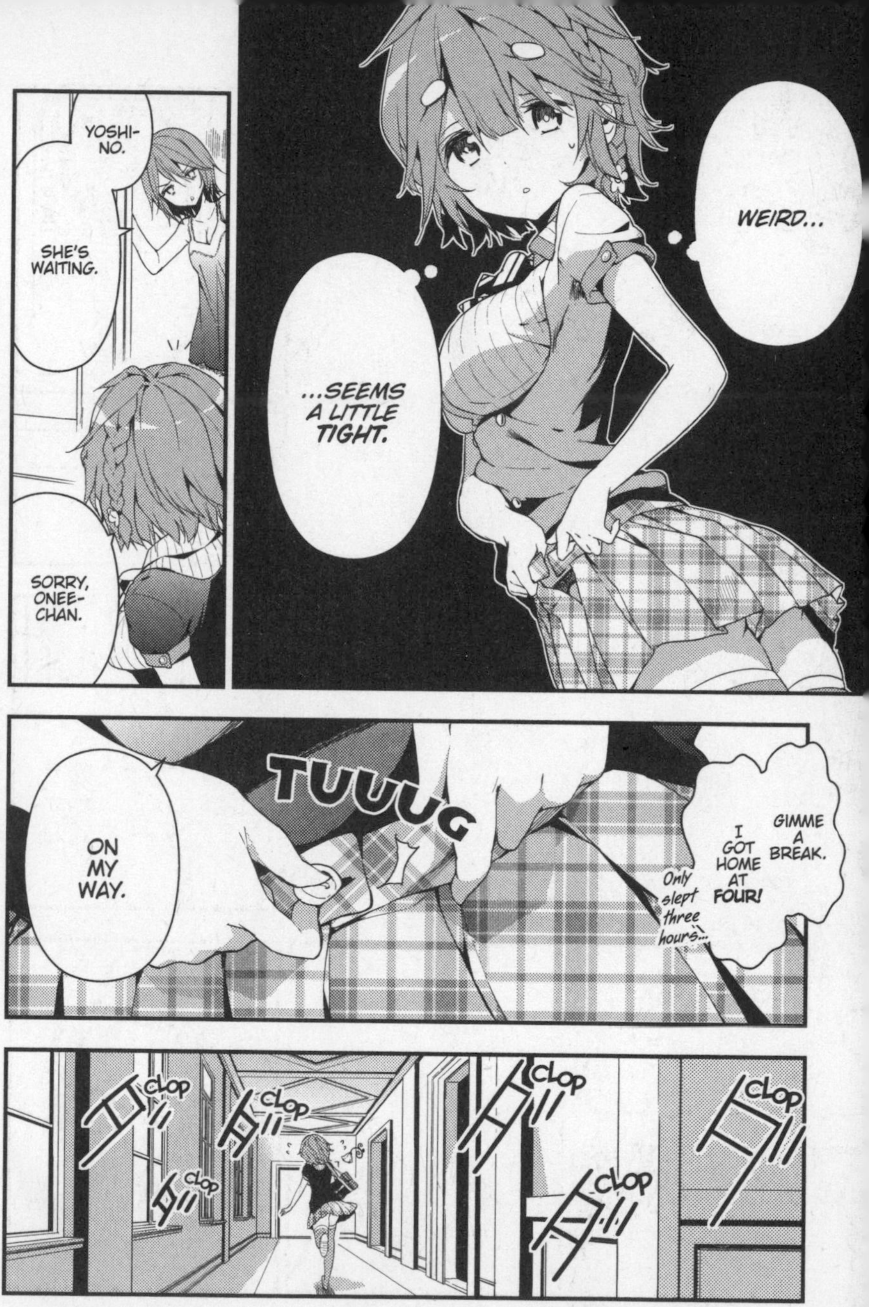
WEIRD...
...SEEMS A LITTLE TIGHT.
YOSHINO.
SHE'S WAITING.
SORRY, ONEE-CHAN.
GIMME A BREAK.
I GOT HOME AT FOUR!
Only slept three hours...
TUUUG
ON MY WAY.
CLOP
CLOP
CLOP
CLOP
CLOP
CLOP

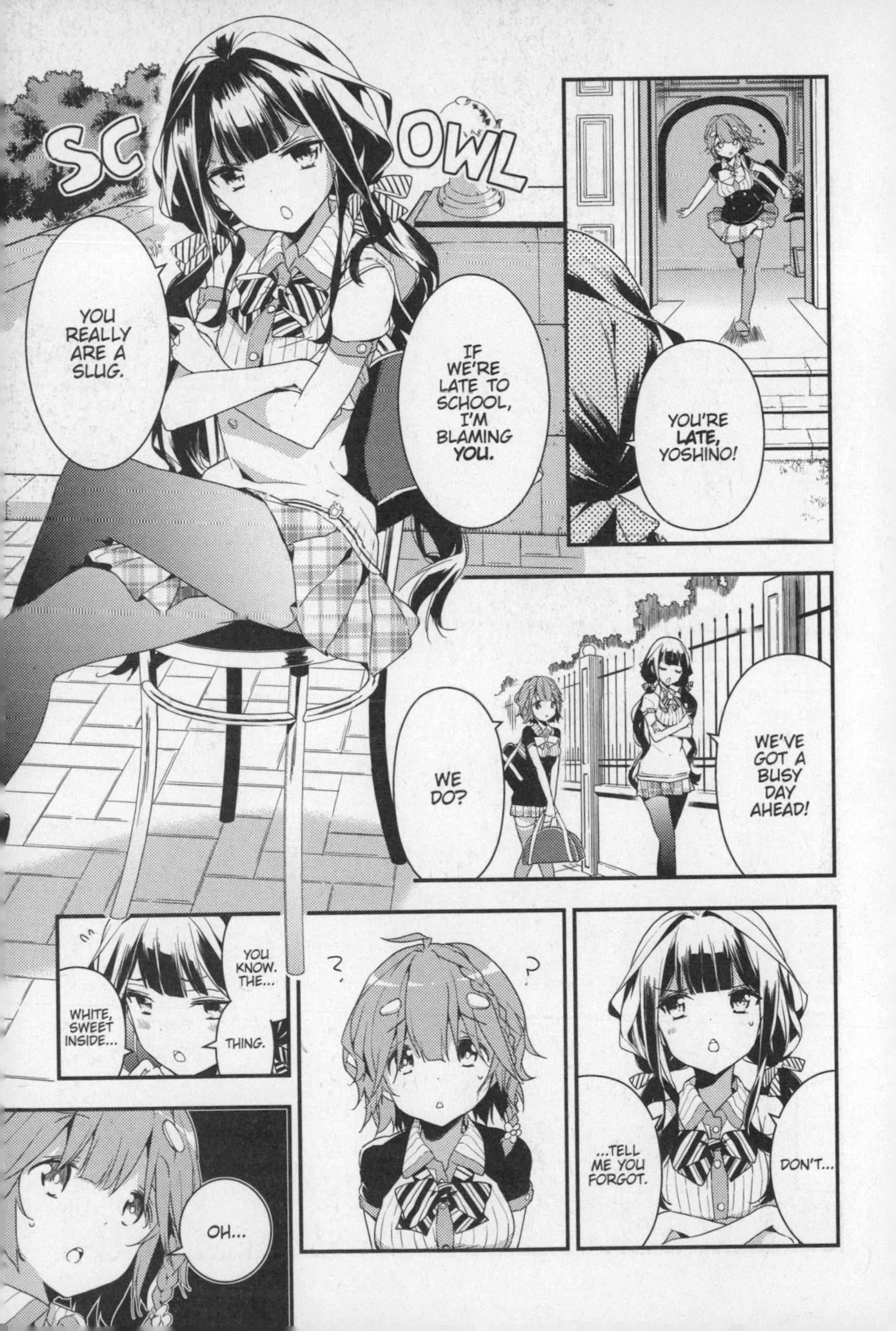
YOU'RE LATE, YOSHINO!
WE'VE GOT A BUSY DAY AHEAD!
WE DO?
SCOWL
IF WE'RE LATE TO SCHOOL, I'M BLAMING YOU.
YOU REALLY ARE A SLUG.
DON'T...
...TELL ME YOU FORGOT.
? ?
YOU KNOW. THE...
WHITE, SWEET INSIDE...
THING.
OH...

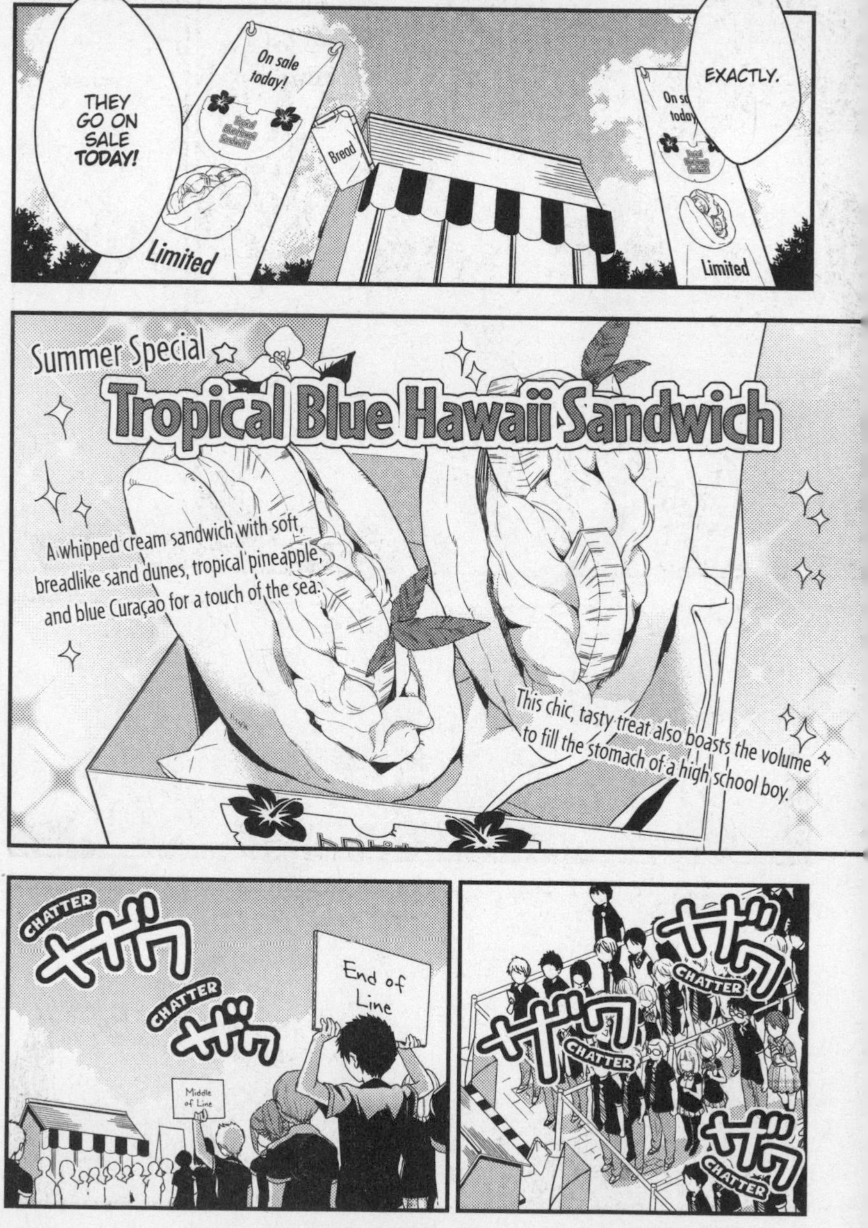
EXACTLY.
Limited
THEY GO ON SALE TODAY!
On sale today!
Bread
Limited
Summer Special
Tropical Blue Hawaii Sandwich
A whipped cream sandwich with soft, breadlike sand dunes, tropical pineapple, and blue Curaçao for a touch of the sea.
This chic, tasty treat also boasts the volume to fill the stomach of a high school boy.
ザワ CHATTER
ザワ CHATTER
ザワ CHATTER
ザワ CHATTER
ザワ ザワ CHATTER CHATTER
End of Line
Middle of Line

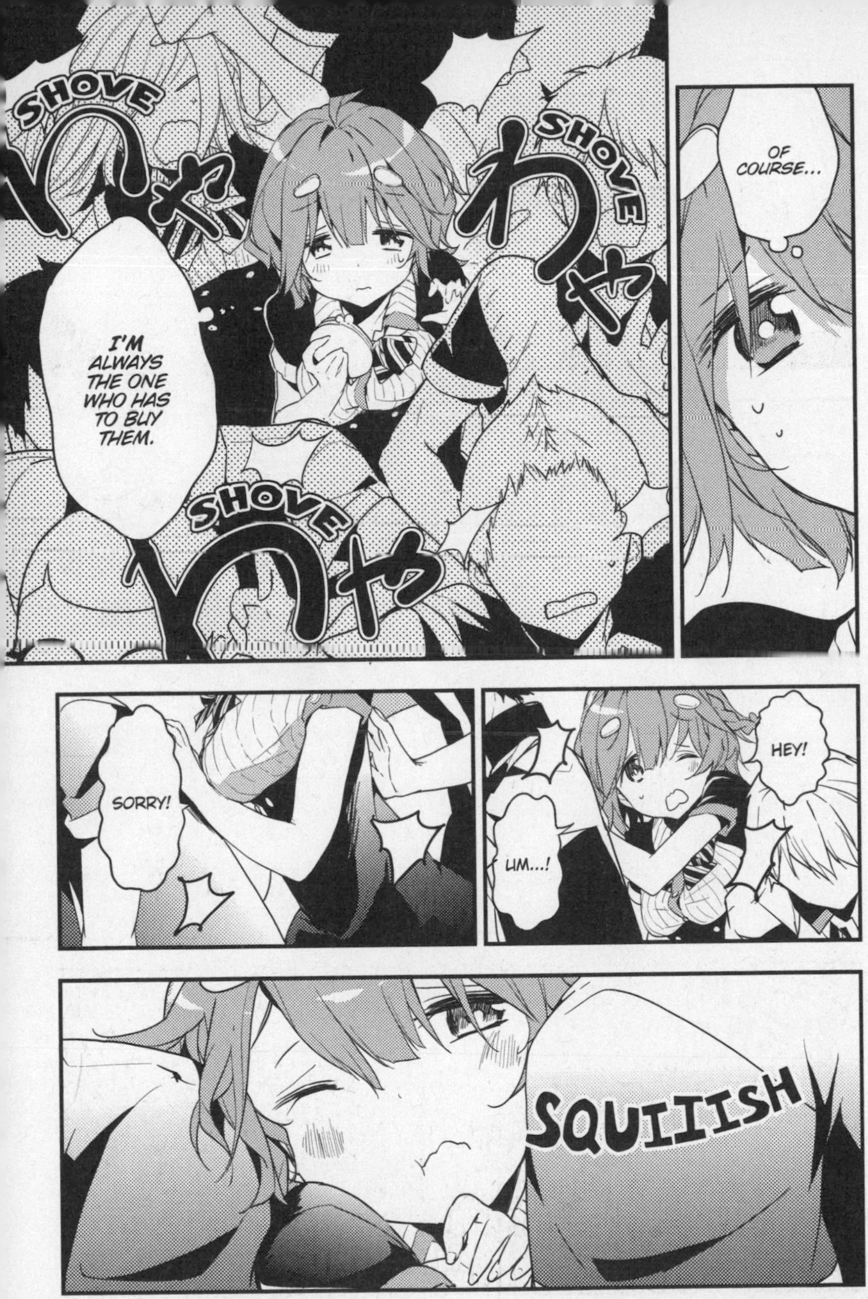
OF COURSE...
SHOVE
SHOVE
I'M ALWAYS THE ONE WHO HAS TO BUY THEM.
SHOVE
HEY!
UM...!
SORRY!
SQUIIISH

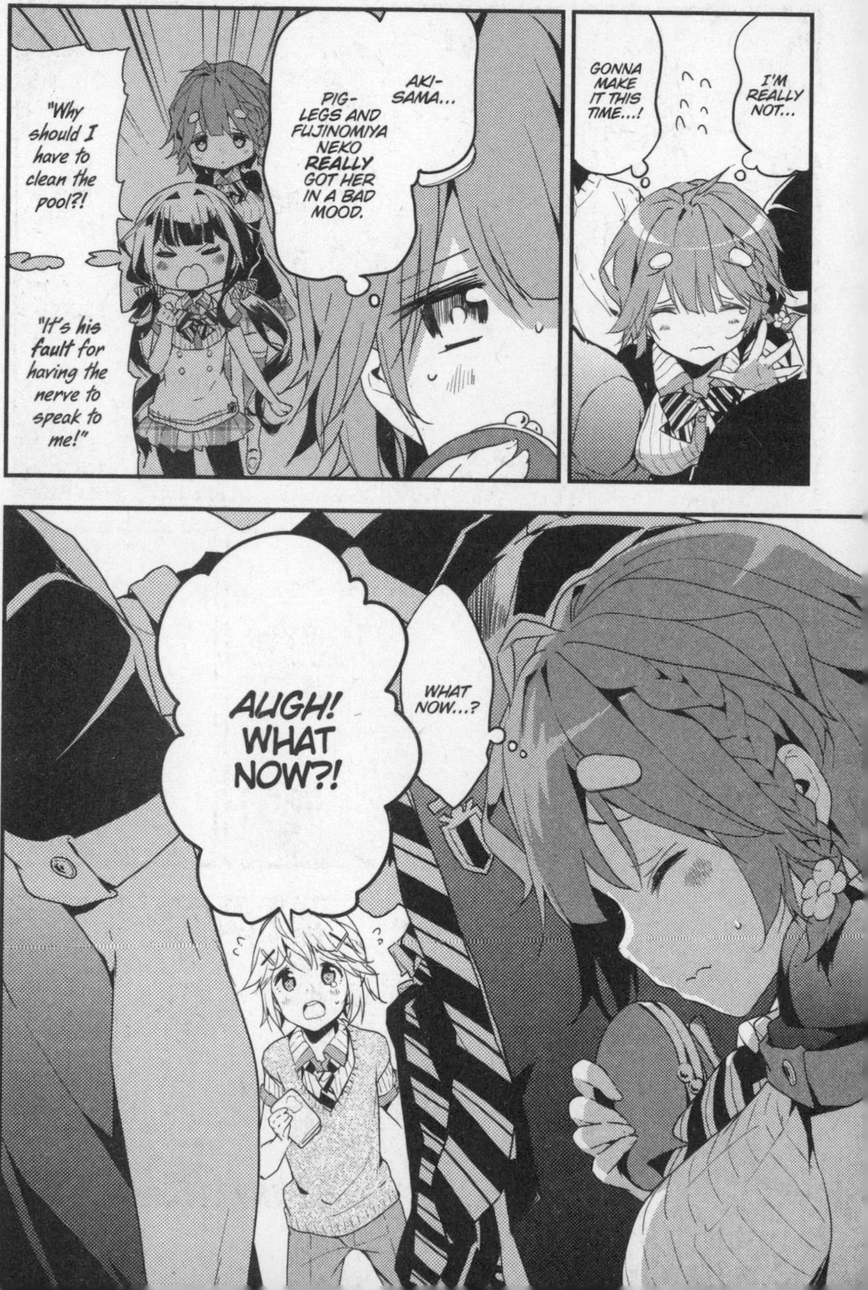
I'M REALLY NOT...
GONNA MAKE IT THIS TIME...!
AKI-SAMA... PIG-LEGS AND FUJINOMIYA NEKO REALLY GOT HER IN A BAD MOOD.
"Why should I have to clean the pool?!
"It's his fault for having the nerve to speak to me!"
WHAT NOW...?
AUGH! WHAT NOW?!

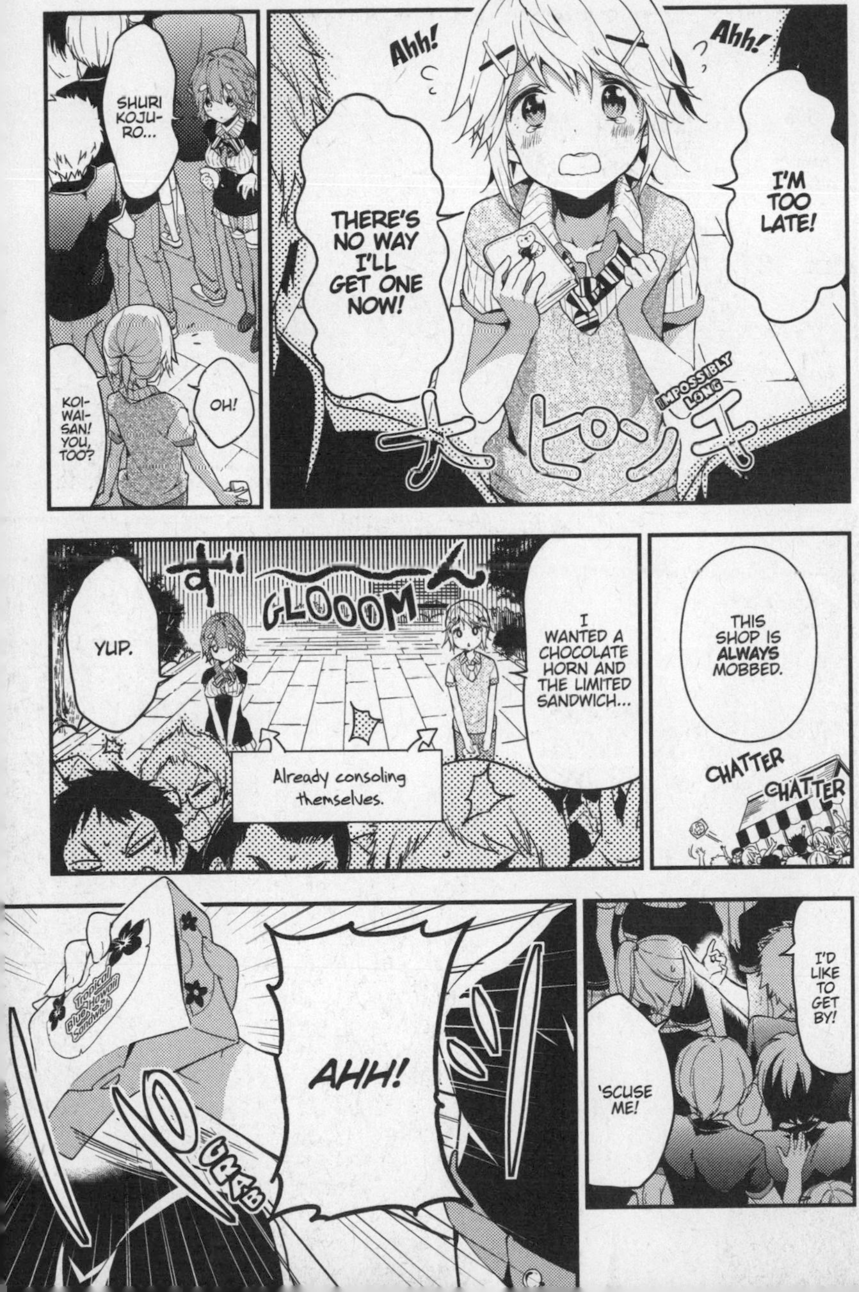
Ahh!
Ahh!
I'M TOO LATE!
THERE'S NO WAY I'LL GET ONE NOW!
IMPOSSIBLY LONG
SHURI KOJU-RO...
OH!
KOI-WAI-SAN! YOU, TOO?
THIS SHOP IS ALWAYS MOBBED.
CHATTER CHATTER
I WANTED A CHOCOLATE HORN AND THE LIMITED SANDWICH...
GLOOOM
YUP.
Already consoling themselves.
I'D LIKE TO GET BY!
'SCUSE ME!
AHH!
GRAB
Tropical Blue Hawaii Sandwich

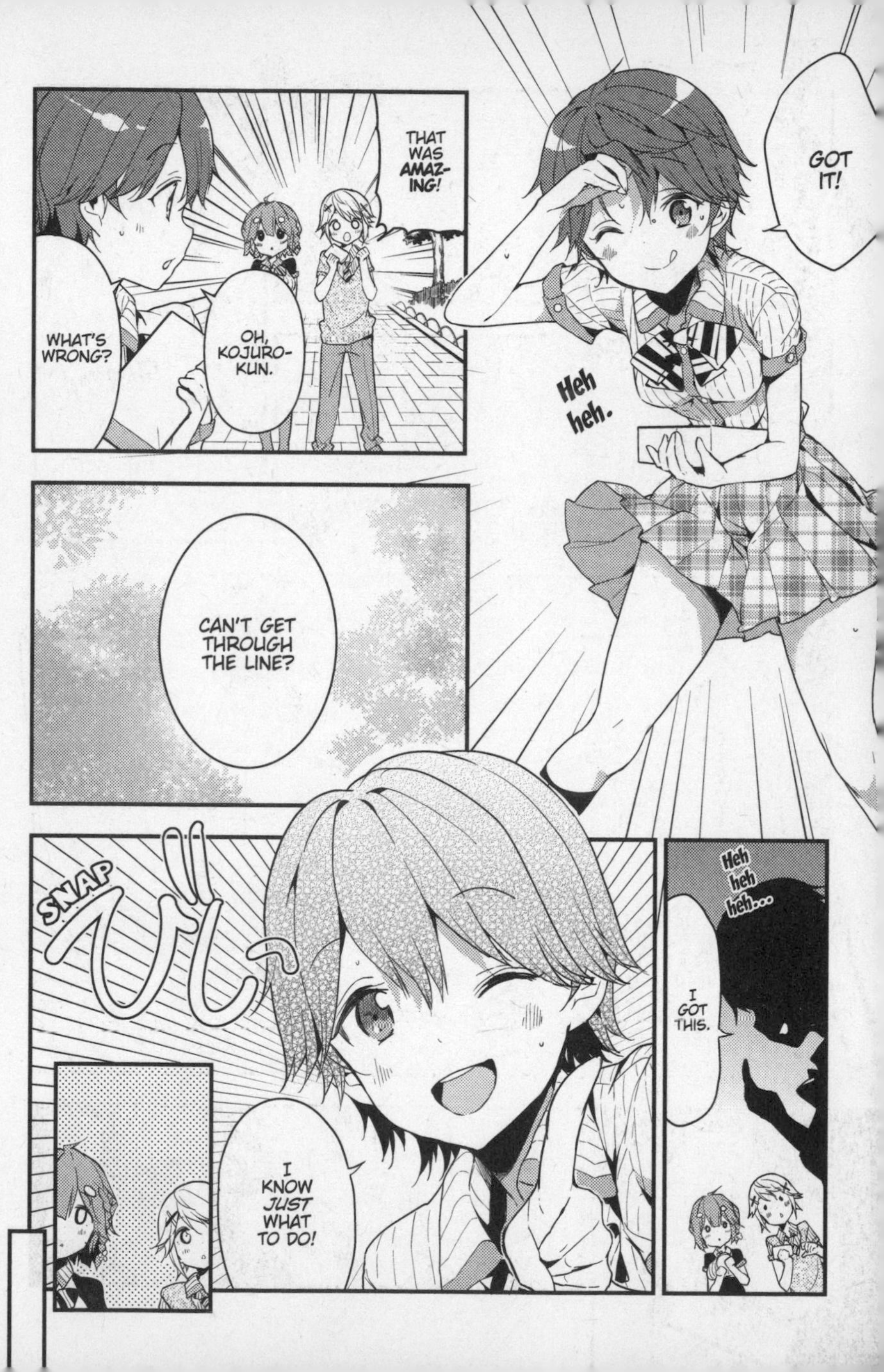
GOT IT!
Heh heh.
THAT WAS AMAZ-ING!
OH, KOJURO-KUN.
WHAT'S WRONG?
CAN'T GET THROUGH THE LINE?
Heh heh heh...
I GOT THIS.
SNAP
I KNOW JUST WHAT TO DO!

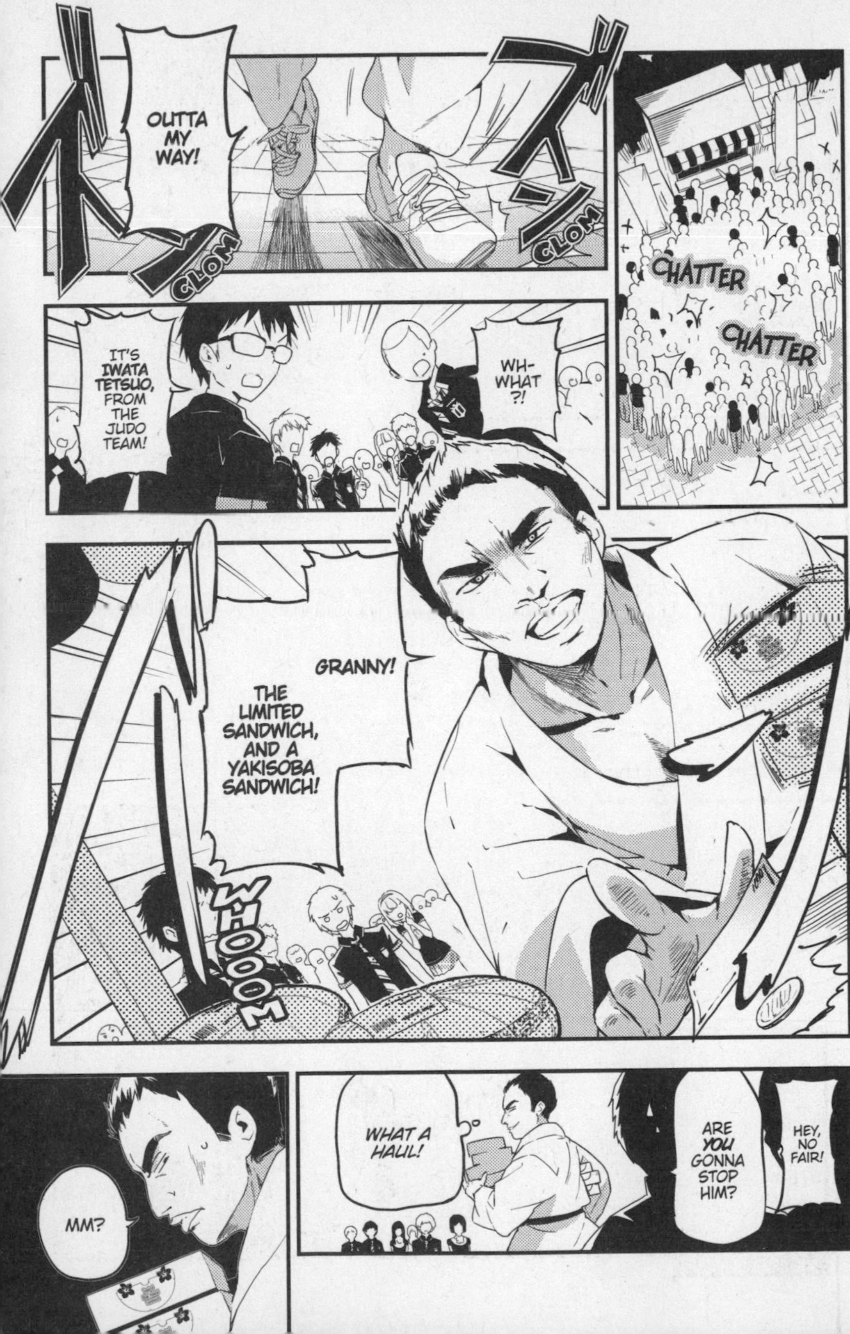
CHATTER
CHATTER
OUTTA MY WAY!
GLOM
GLOM
WH-WHAT?!
IT'S IWATA TETSUO, FROM THE JUDO TEAM!
GRANNY!
THE LIMITED SANDWICH, AND A YAKISOBA SANDWICH!
WHOOOM
HEY, NO FAIR!
ARE YOU GONNA STOP HIM?
WHAT A HAUL!
MM?

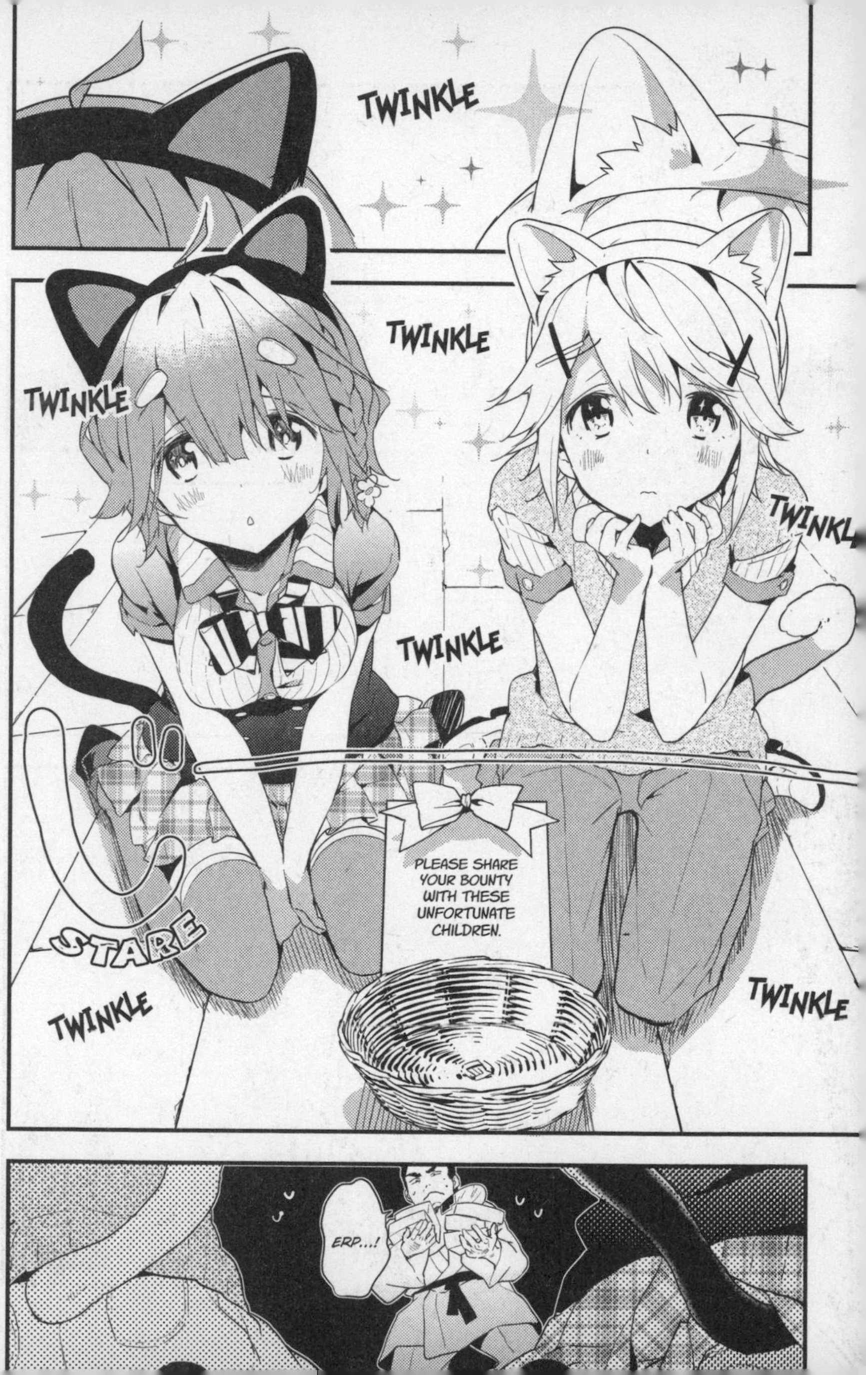
TWINKLE
TWINKLE
TWINKLE
TWINKLE
TWINKLE
PLEASE SHARE YOUR BOUNTY WITH THESE UNFORTUNATE CHILDREN.
STARE
TWINKLE
TWINKLE
ERP...!

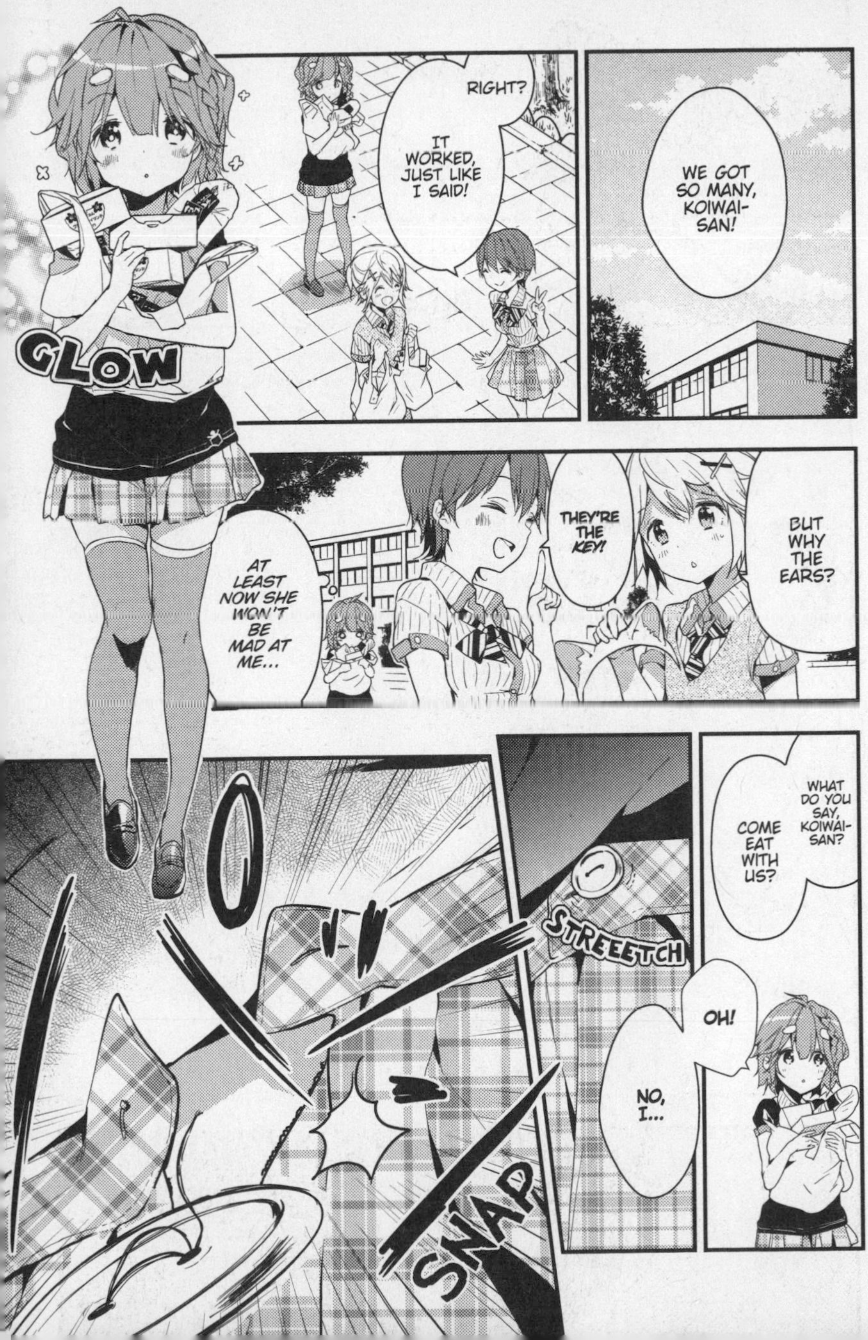
WE GOT SO MANY, KOIWAI-SAN!
IT WORKED, JUST LIKE I SAID!
RIGHT?
GLOW
BUT WHY THE EARS?
THEY'RE THE KEY!
AT LEAST NOW SHE WON'T BE MAD AT ME...
WHAT DO YOU SAY, KOIWAI-SAN?
COME EAT WITH US?
OH!
NO, I...
STREEETCH
SNAP

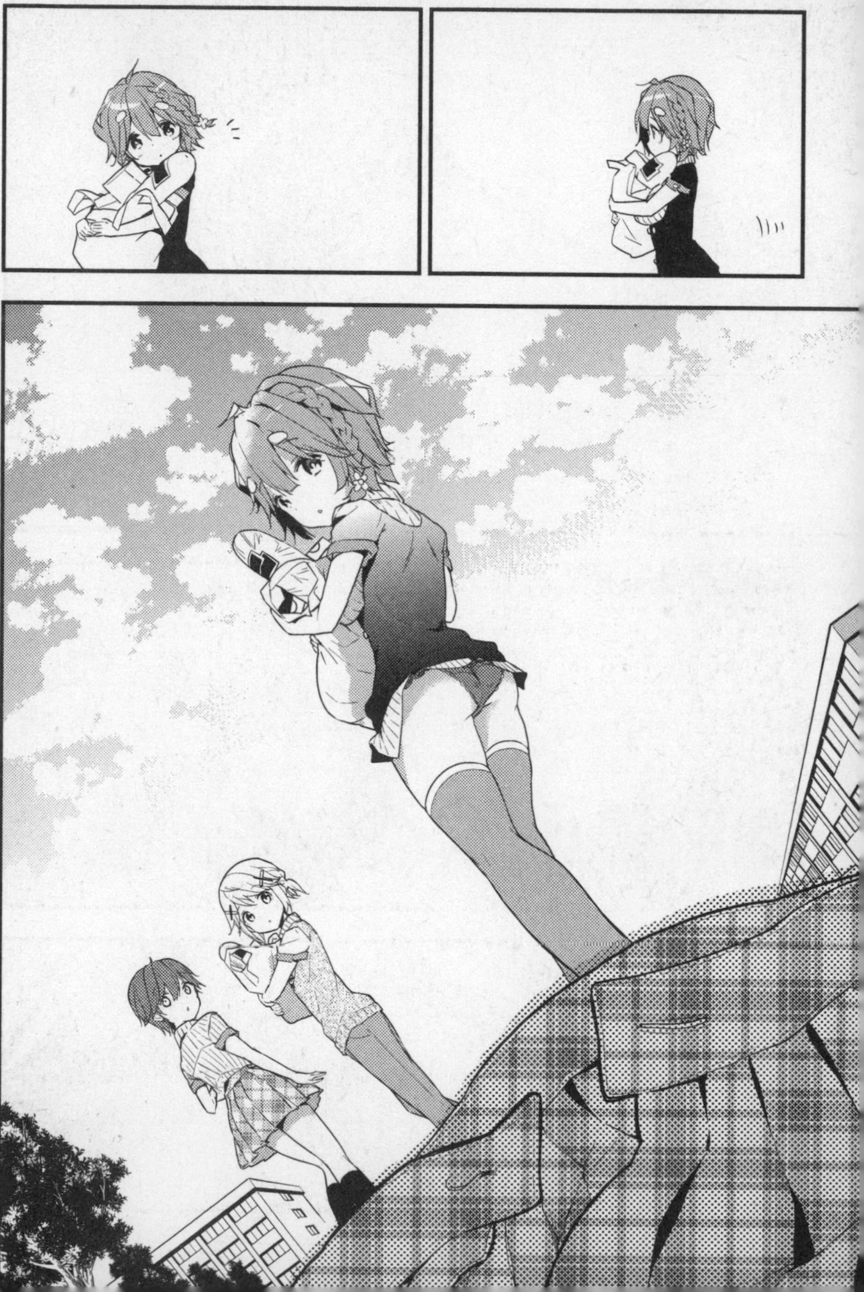

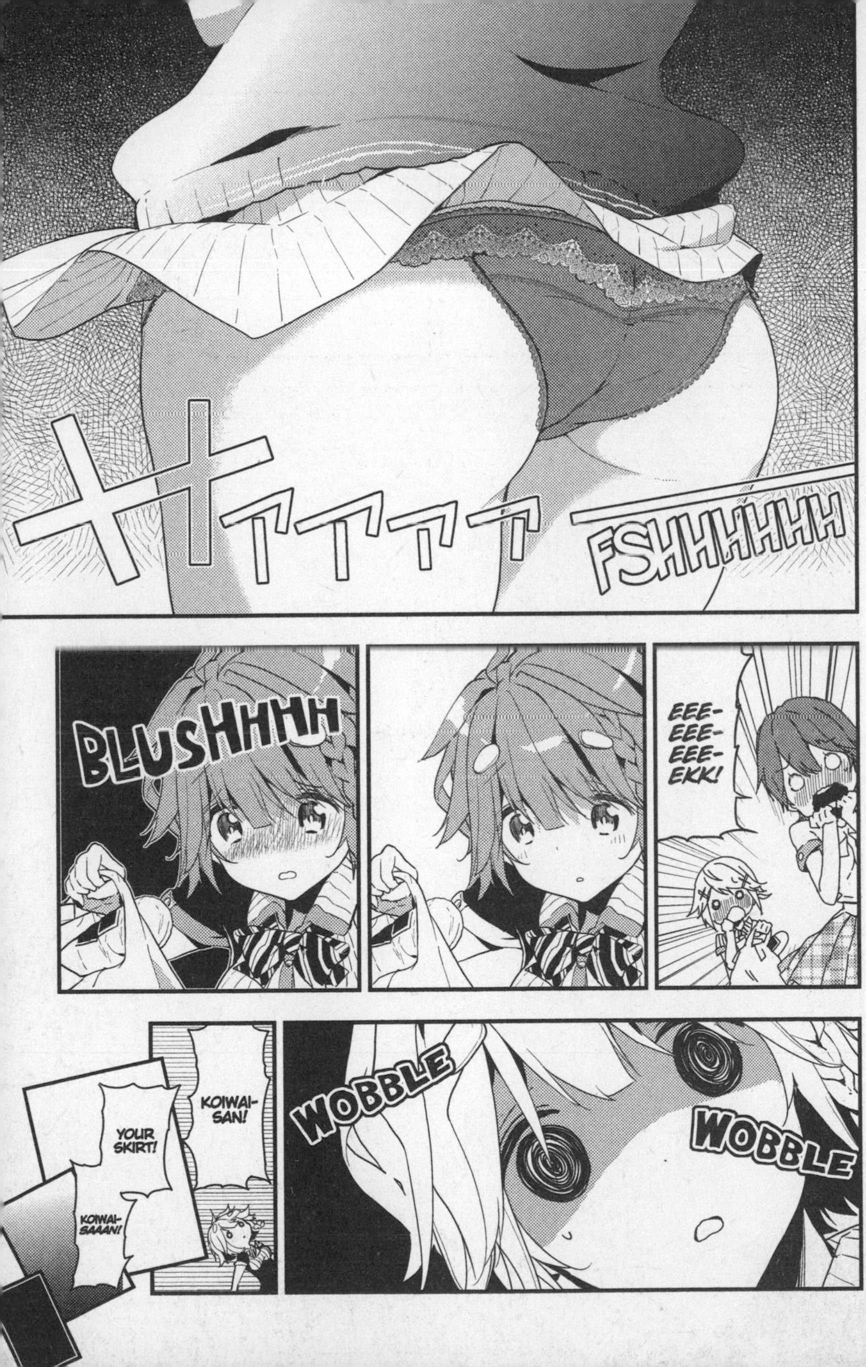
FSHHHHHH
EEE-
EEE-
EEE-
EKK!
BLUSHHHH
WOBBLE
WOBBLE
KOIWAI-SAN!
YOUR SKIRT!
KOIWAI-SAAAN!

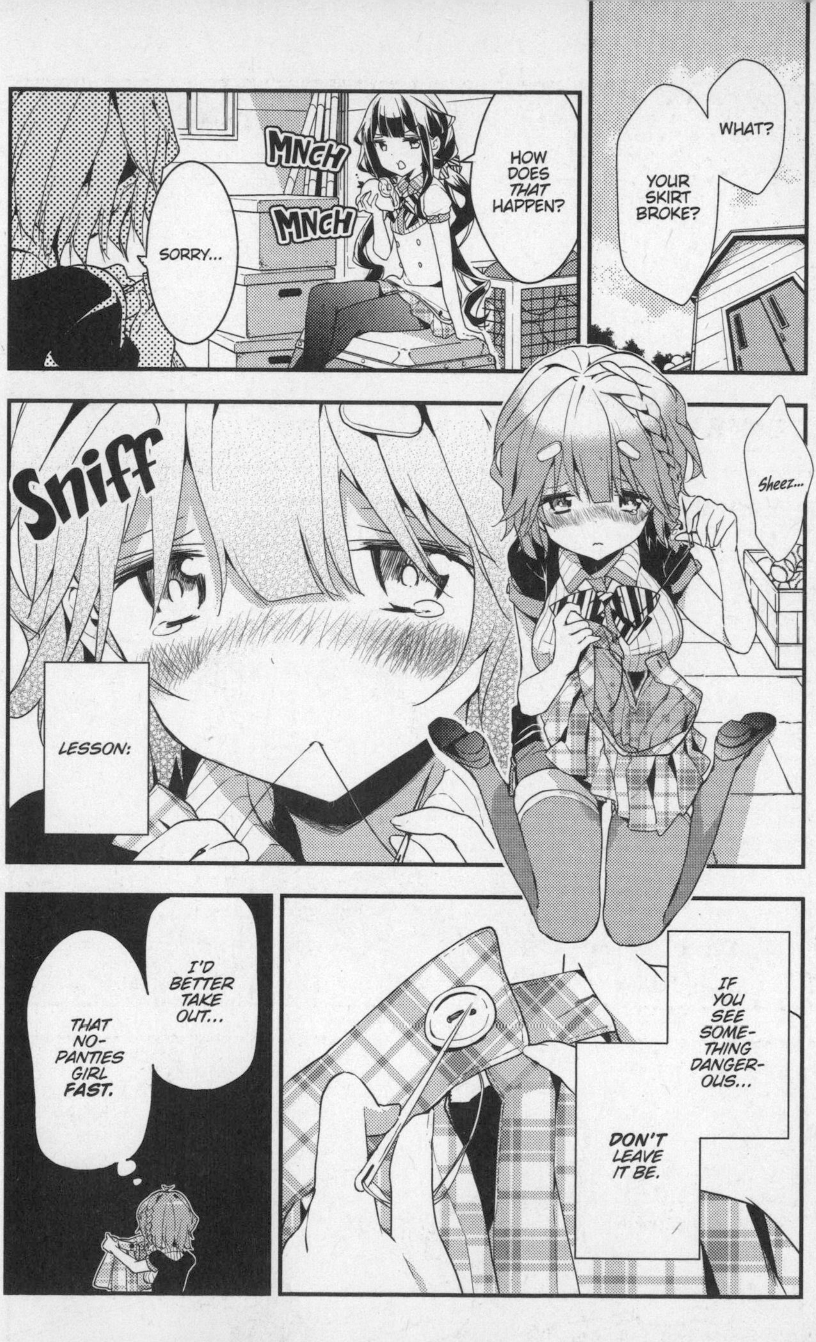
WHAT?
YOUR SKIRT BROKE?
HOW DOES THAT HAPPEN?
MNCH
MNCH
SORRY...
Sheez...
Sniff
LESSON:
IF YOU SEE SOME-THING DANGER-OUS...
DON'T LEAVE IT BE.
I'D BETTER TAKE OUT...
THAT NO-PANTIES GIRL FAST.

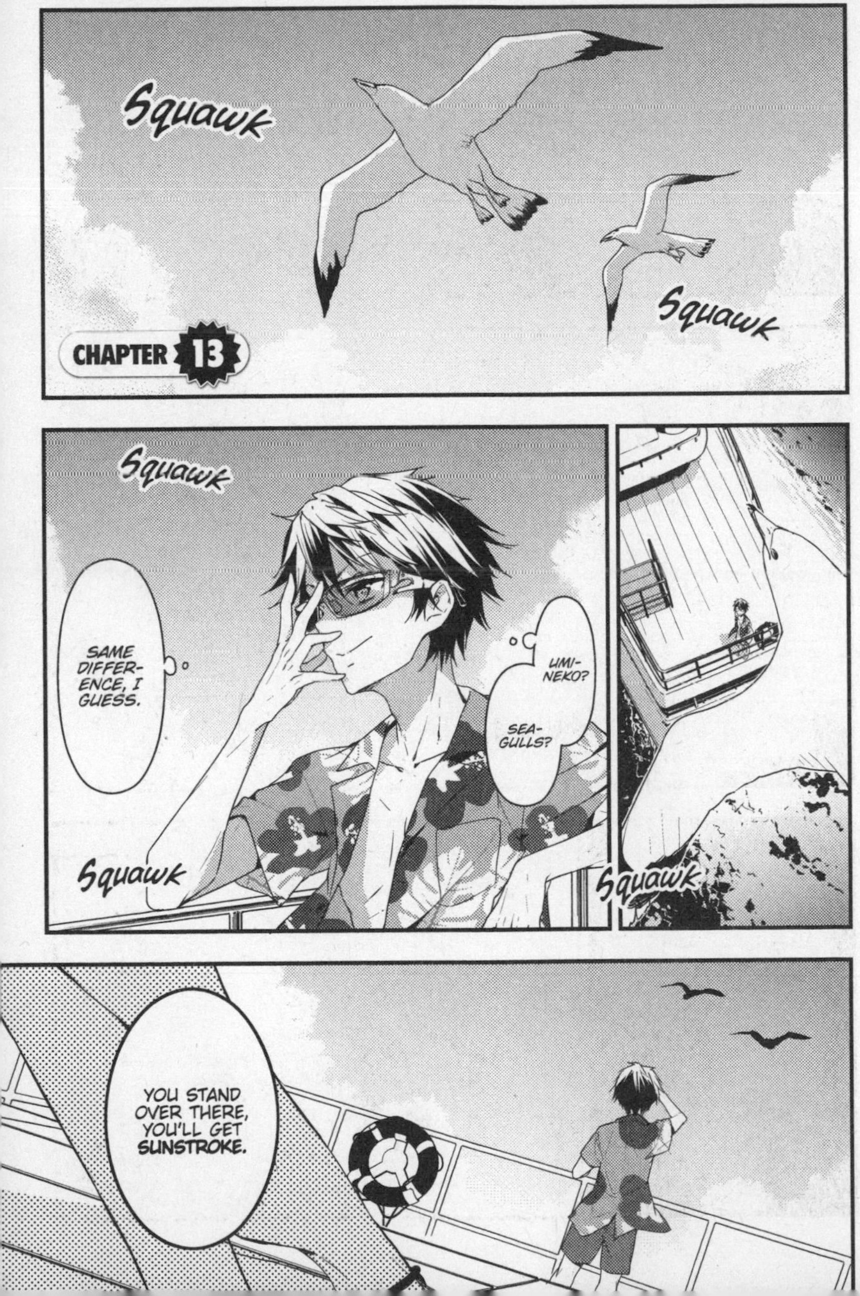
Squawk
Squawk
CHAPTER 13
Squawk
Squawk
UMI-NEKO?
SEA-GULLS?
SAME DIFFERENCE, I GUESS.
Squawk
YOU STAND OVER THERE, YOU'LL GET SUNSTROKE.

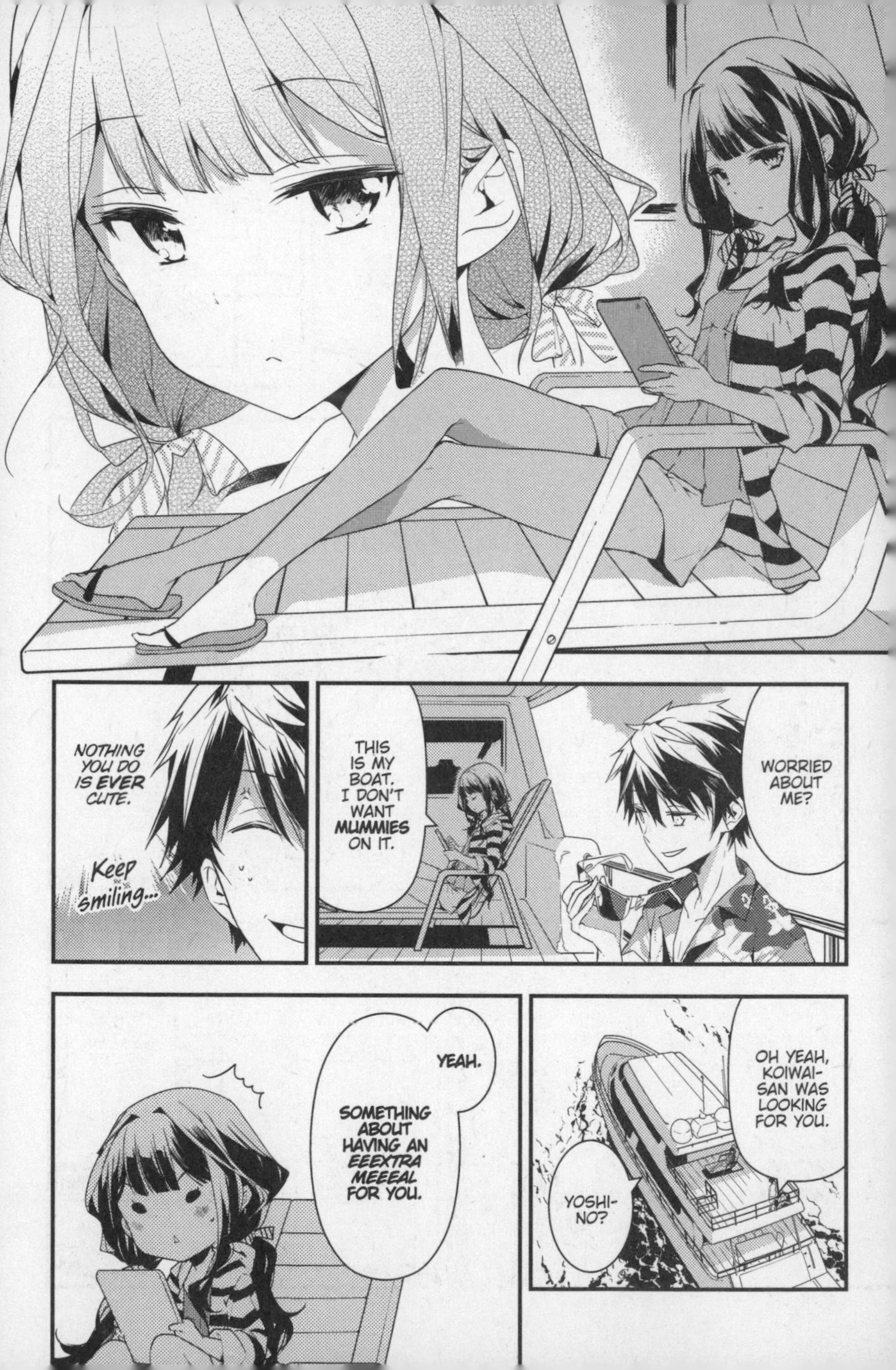
WORRIED ABOUT ME?
THIS IS MY BOAT. I DON'T WANT MUMMIES ON IT.
NOTHING YOU DO IS EVER CUTE.
Keep smiling...
OH YEAH, KOIWAI-SAN WAS LOOKING FOR YOU.
YOSHINO?
YEAH.
SOMETHING ABOUT HAVING AN EEEXTRA MEEEAL FOR YOU.

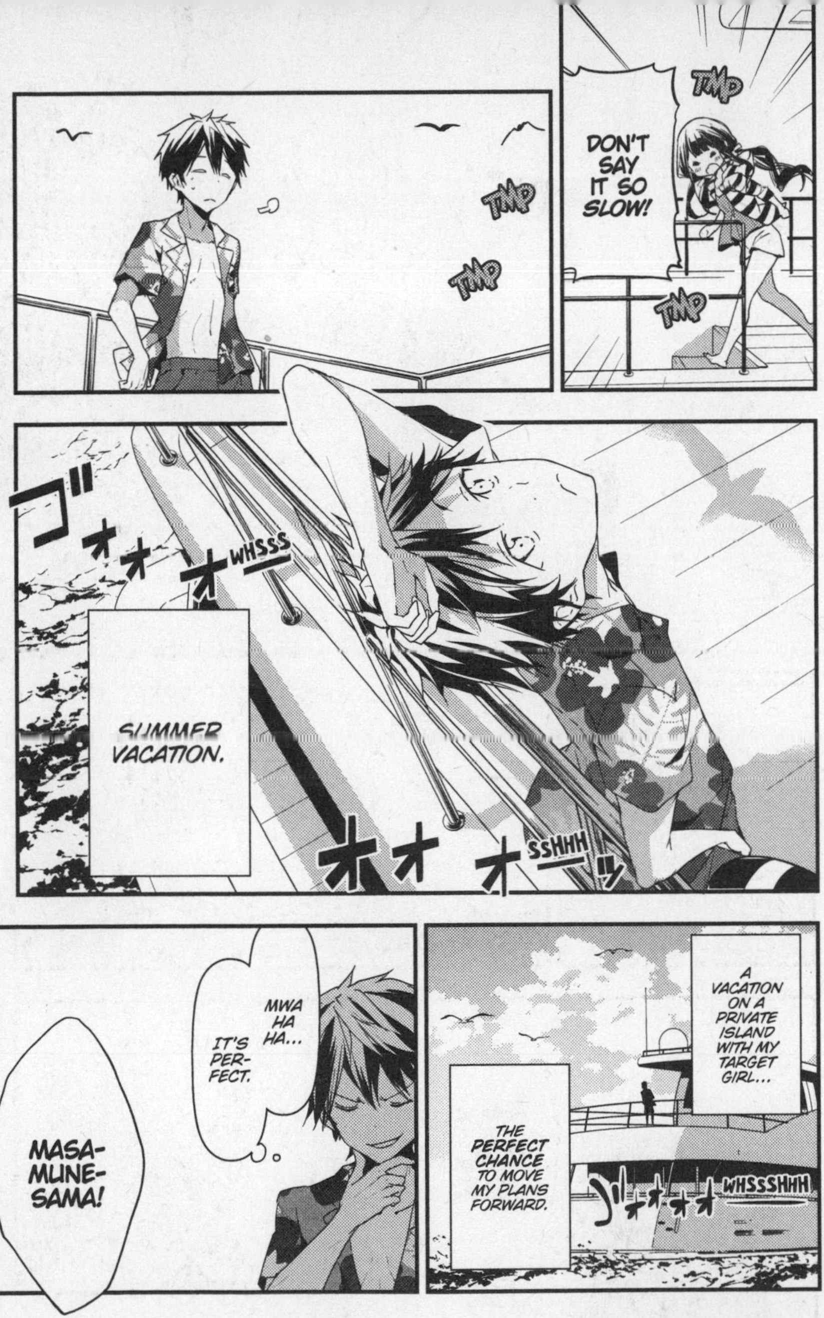
TMP
DON'T SAY IT SO SLOW!
TMP
TMP
TMP
ゴオオオー
WHSSS
SUMMER VACATION.
オオオー
SSHHH
A VACATION ON A PRIVATE ISLAND WITH MY TARGET GIRL...
THE PERFECT CHANCE TO MOVE MY PLANS FORWARD.
WHSSSHHH
MWA HA HA...
IT'S PERFECT.
MASAMUNE-SAMA!

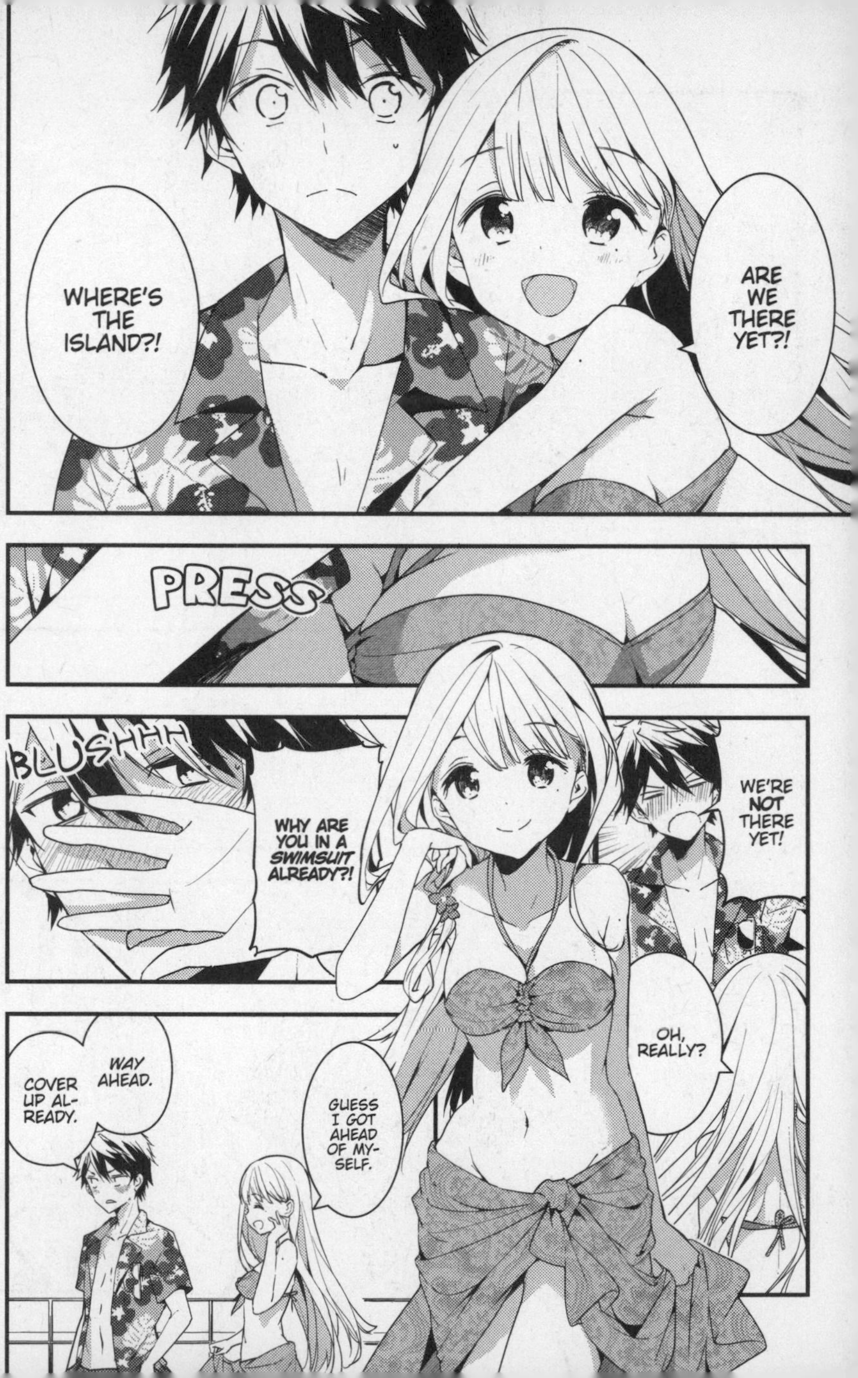
ARE WE THERE YET?!
WHERE'S THE ISLAND?!
PRESS
WE'RE NOT THERE YET!
BLUSHHH
WHY ARE YOU IN A SWIMSUIT ALREADY?!
OH, REALLY?
GUESS I GOT AHEAD OF MY-SELF.
WAY AHEAD.
COVER UP AL-READY.

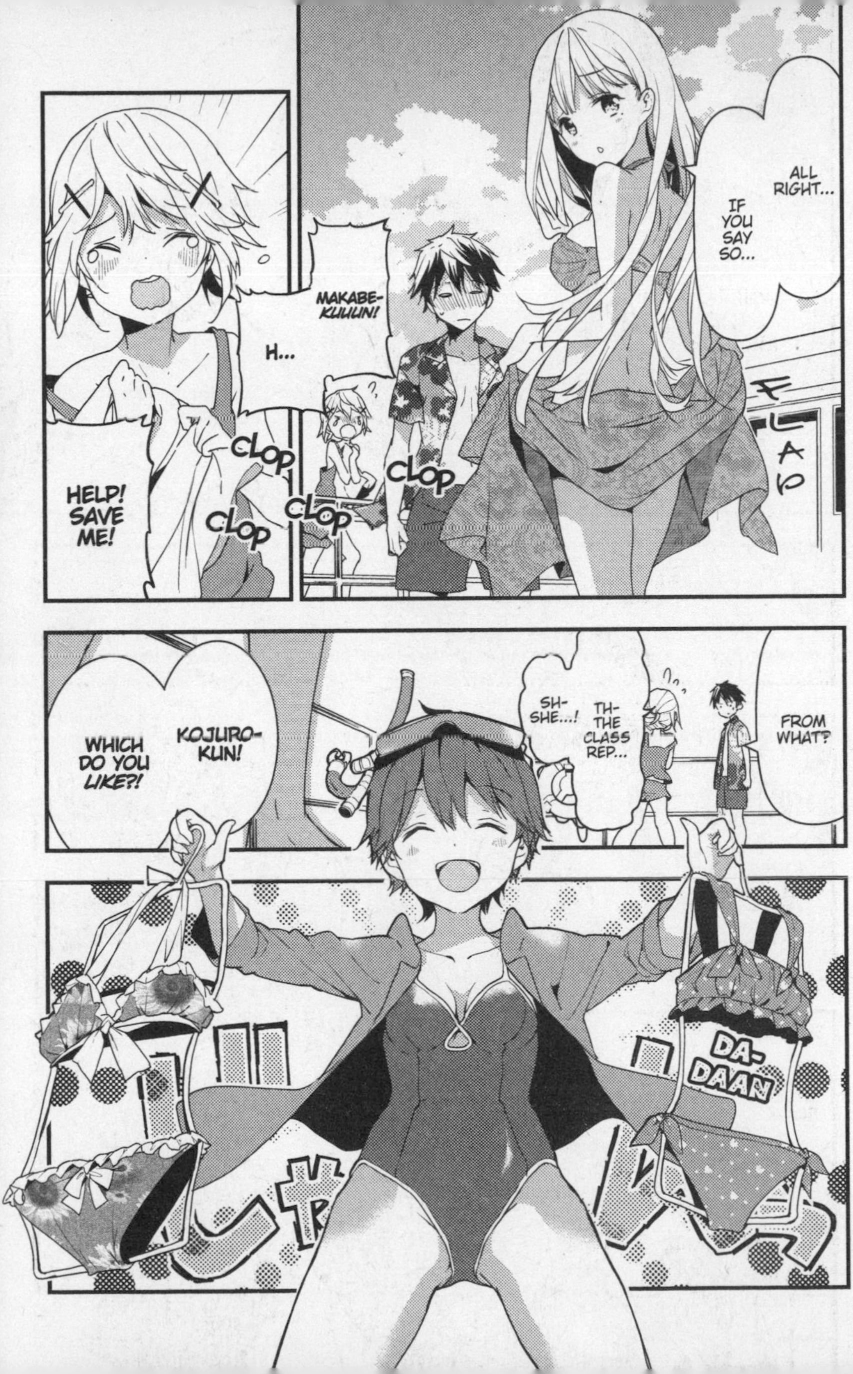
ALL RIGHT... IF YOU SAY SO...
MAKABE-KUUUN!
CLOP
CLOP
H...
CLOP
CLOP
HELP! SAVE ME!
FROM WHAT?
TH-THE CLASS REP...
SH-SHE...!
KOJURO-KUN!
WHICH DO YOU LIKE?!
DA-DAAN

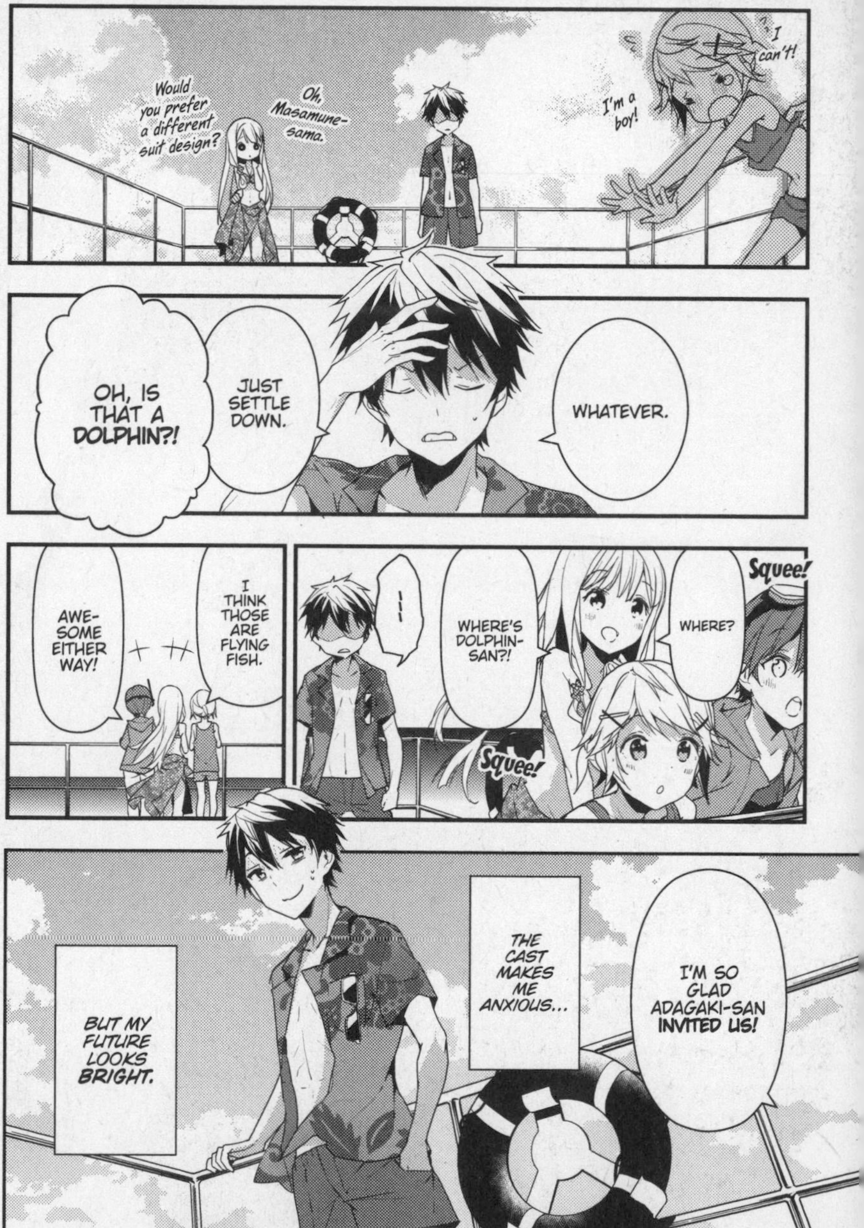
I can't!
I'm a boy!
Oh, Masamune-sama.
Would you prefer a different suit design?
WHATEVER.
JUST SETTLE DOWN.
OH, IS THAT A DOLPHIN?!
Squee!
WHERE?
WHERE'S DOLPHIN-SAN?!
Squee!
I THINK THOSE ARE FLYING FISH.
AWE-SOME EITHER WAY!
I'M SO GLAD ADAGAKI-SAN INVITED US!
THE CAST MAKES ME ANXIOUS...
BUT MY FUTURE LOOKS BRIGHT.

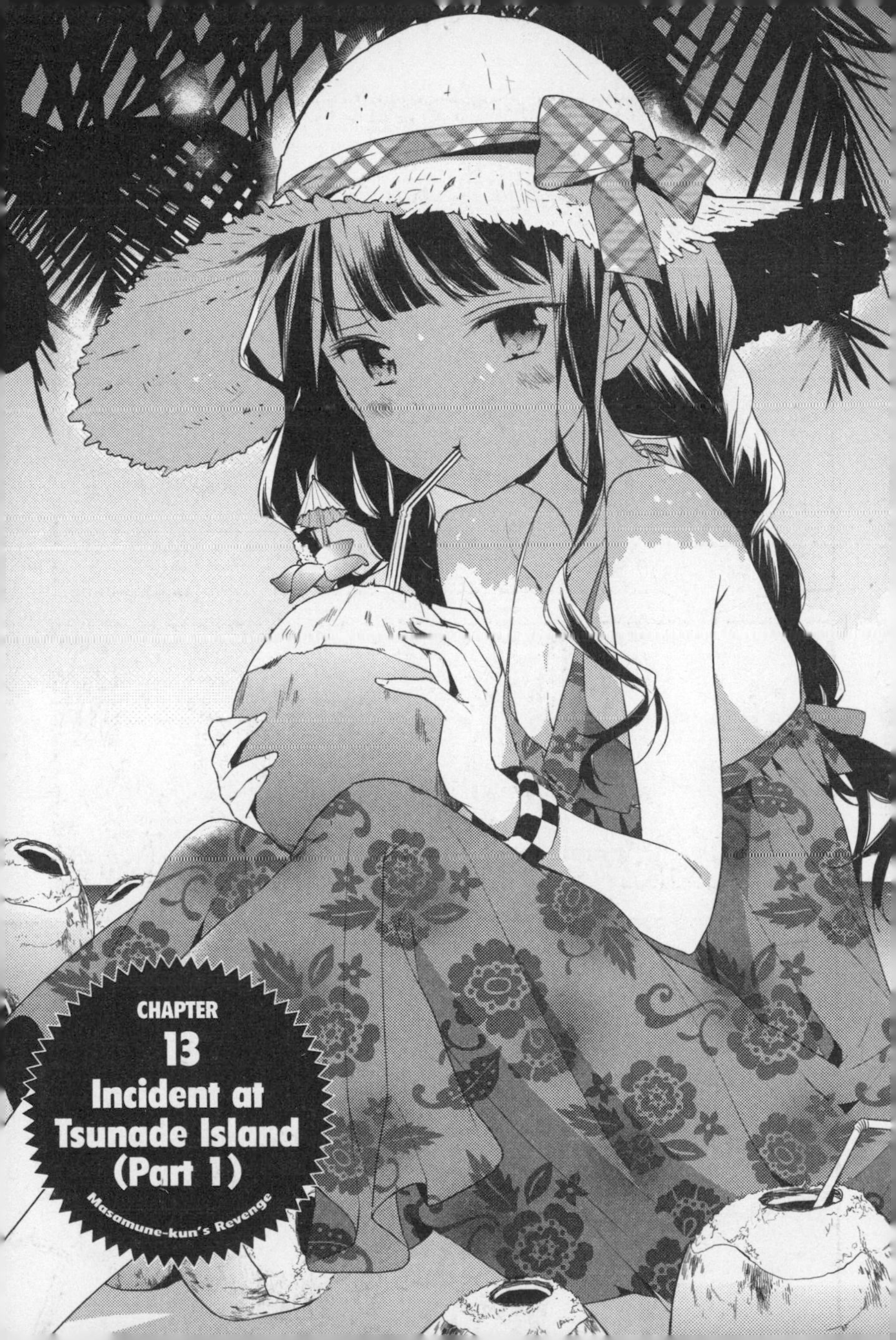
CHAPTER
13
Incident at Tsunade Island (Part 1)
Masamune-kun's Revenge

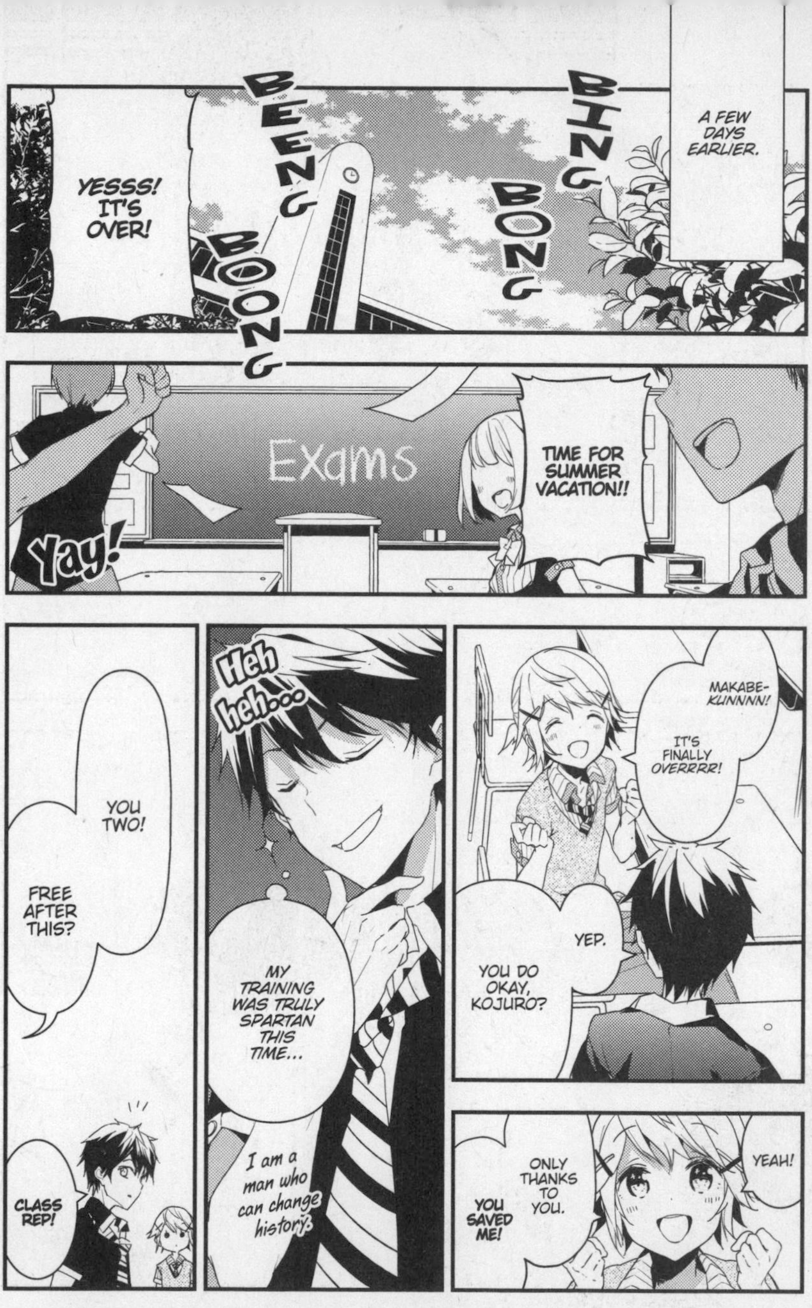
A FEW DAYS EARLIER.
BING BONG
BEENG BOONG
YESSS! IT'S OVER!
TIME FOR SUMMER VACATION!!
Exams
Yay!
MAKABE-KUNNNN!
IT'S FINALLY OVERRRR!
YEP.
YOU DO OKAY, KOJURO?
YEAH!
ONLY THANKS TO YOU.
YOU SAVED ME!
Heh heh...
MY TRAINING WAS TRULY SPARTAN THIS TIME...
I am a man who can change history.
YOU TWO!
FREE AFTER THIS?
CLASS REP!

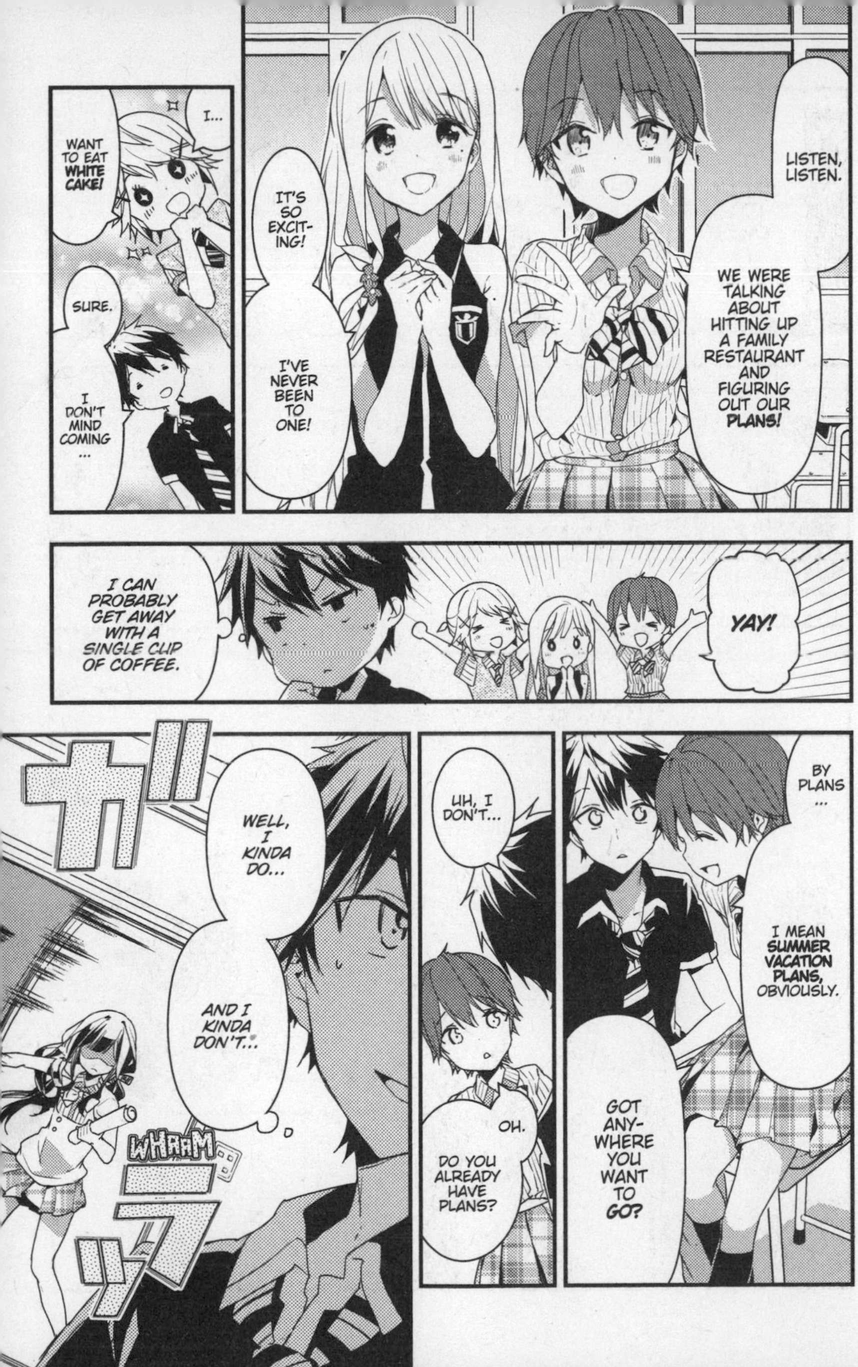
LISTEN, LISTEN.
WE WERE TALKING ABOUT HITTING UP A FAMILY RESTAURANT AND FIGURING OUT OUR PLANS!
IT'S SO EXCITING!
I'VE NEVER BEEN TO ONE!
I...
WANT TO EAT WHITE CAKE!
SURE.
I DON'T MIND COMING...
YAY!
I CAN PROBABLY GET AWAY WITH A SINGLE CUP OF COFFEE.
BY PLANS...
I MEAN SUMMER VACATION PLANS, OBVIOUSLY.
GOT ANYWHERE YOU WANT TO GO?
UH, I DON'T...
OH.
DO YOU ALREADY HAVE PLANS?
WELL, I KINDA DO...
AND I KINDA DON'T...
ガラッ
WHRAM

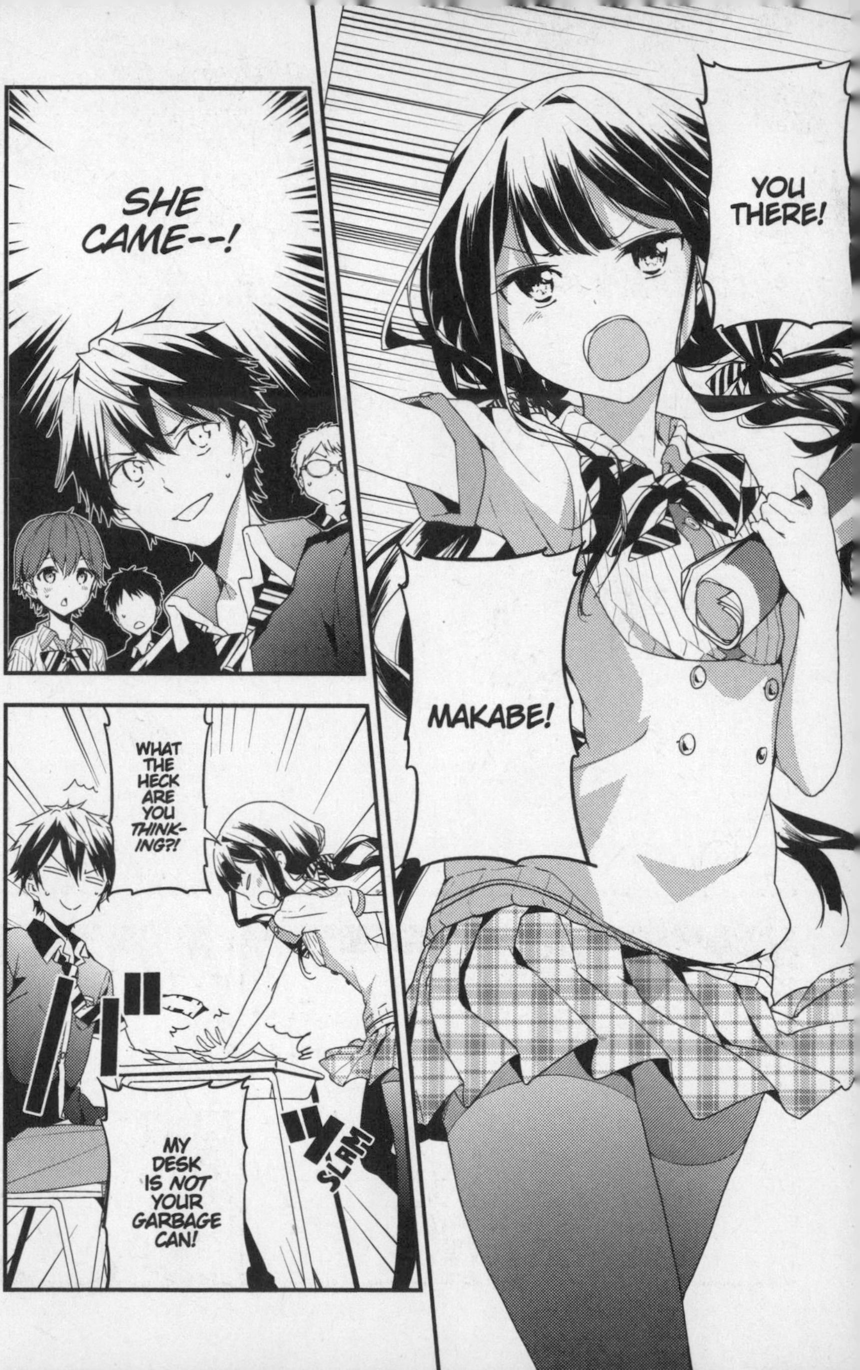
YOU THERE!
MAKABE!
SHE CAME--!
WHAT THE HECK ARE YOU THINKING?!
SLAM
MY DESK IS NOT YOUR GARBAGE CAN!

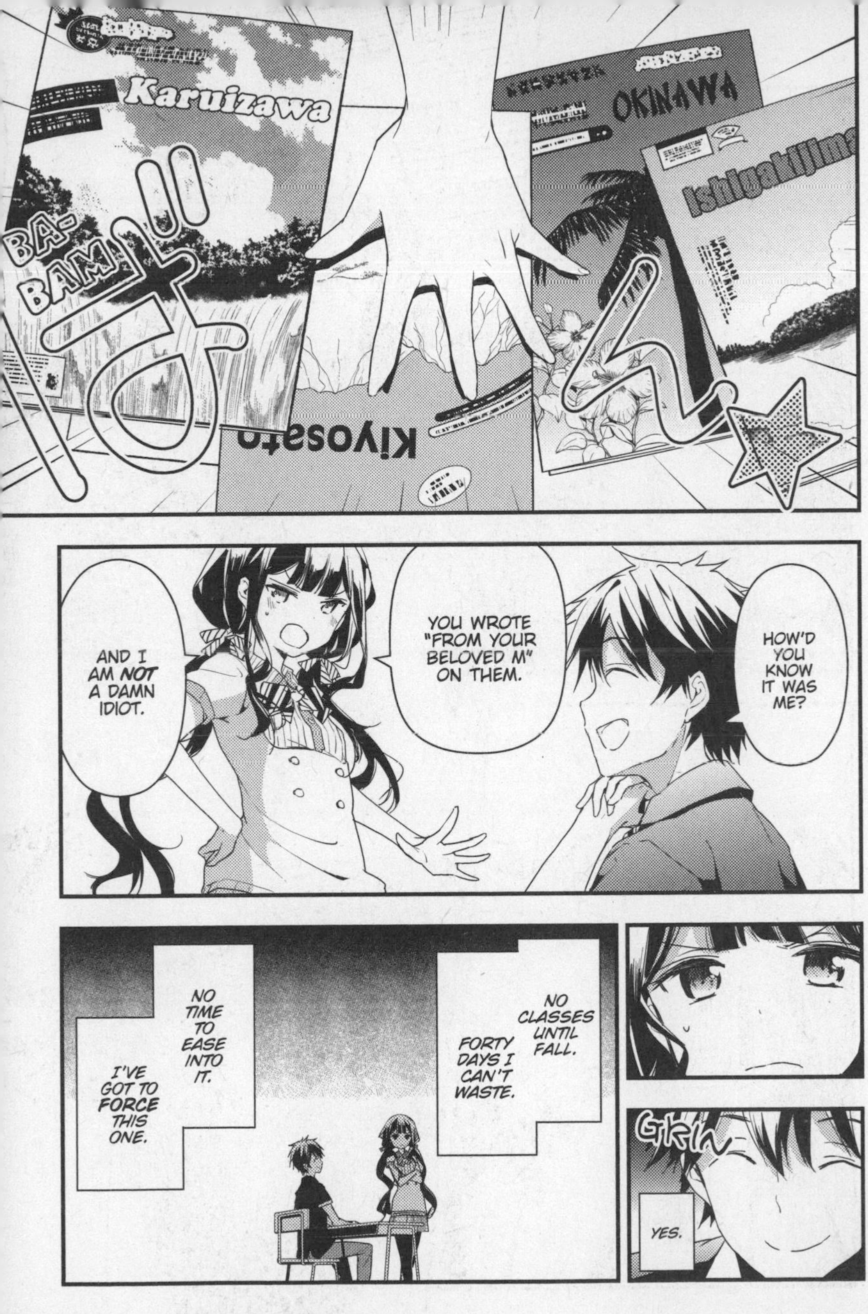
OKINAWA
Ishigakijima
Karuizawa
BA-BAM!!
Kiyosato
HOW'D YOU KNOW IT WAS ME?
YOU WROTE "FROM YOUR BELOVED M" ON THEM.
AND I AM *NOT* A DAMN IDIOT.
GRIN
YES.
NO CLASSES UNTIL FALL.
FORTY DAYS I CAN'T WASTE.
NO TIME TO EASE INTO IT.
I'VE GOT TO FORCE THIS ONE.

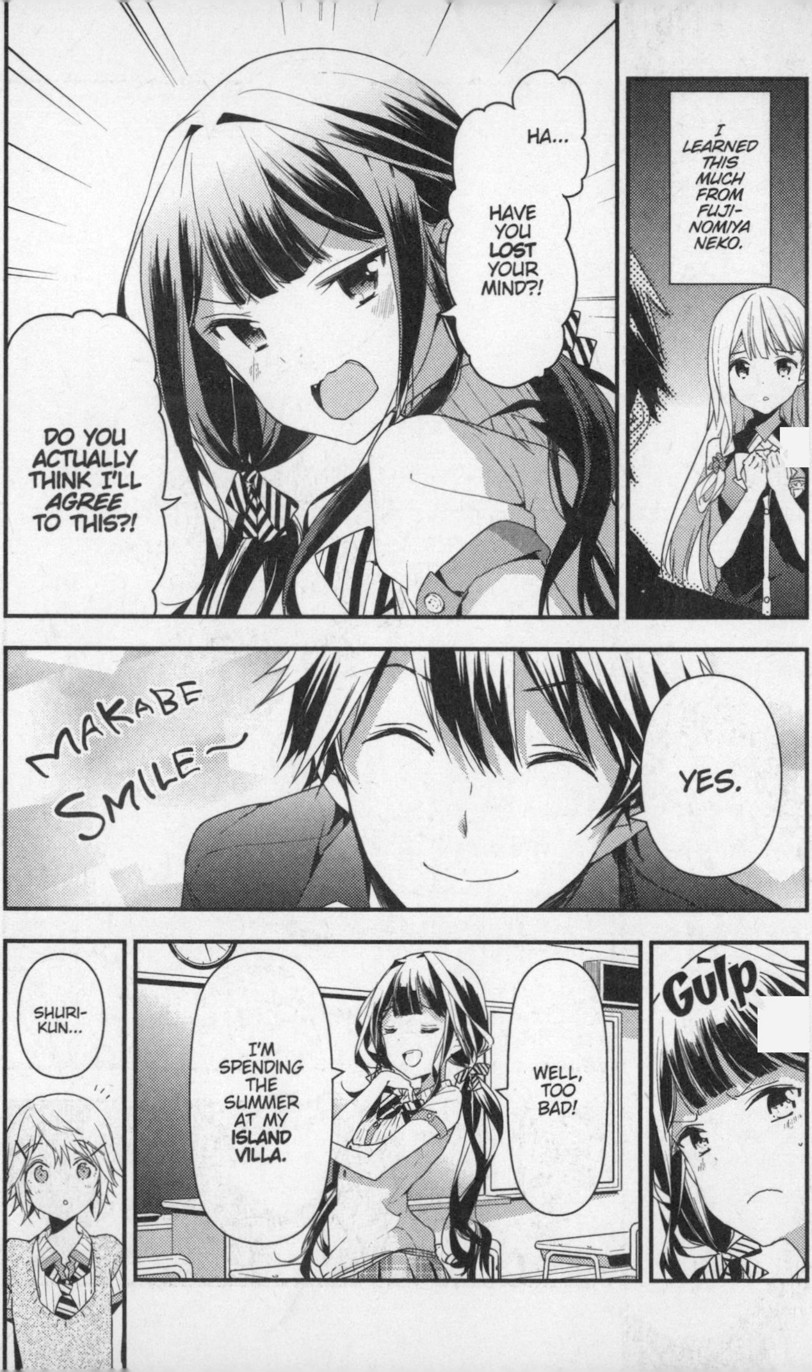
I LEARNED THIS MUCH FROM FUJI-NOMIYA NEKO.
HA...
HAVE YOU LOST YOUR MIND?!
DO YOU ACTUALLY THINK I'LL AGREE TO THIS?!
YES.
MAKABE SMILE~
Gulp
WELL, TOO BAD!
I'M SPENDING THE SUMMER AT MY ISLAND VILLA.
SHURI-KUN...

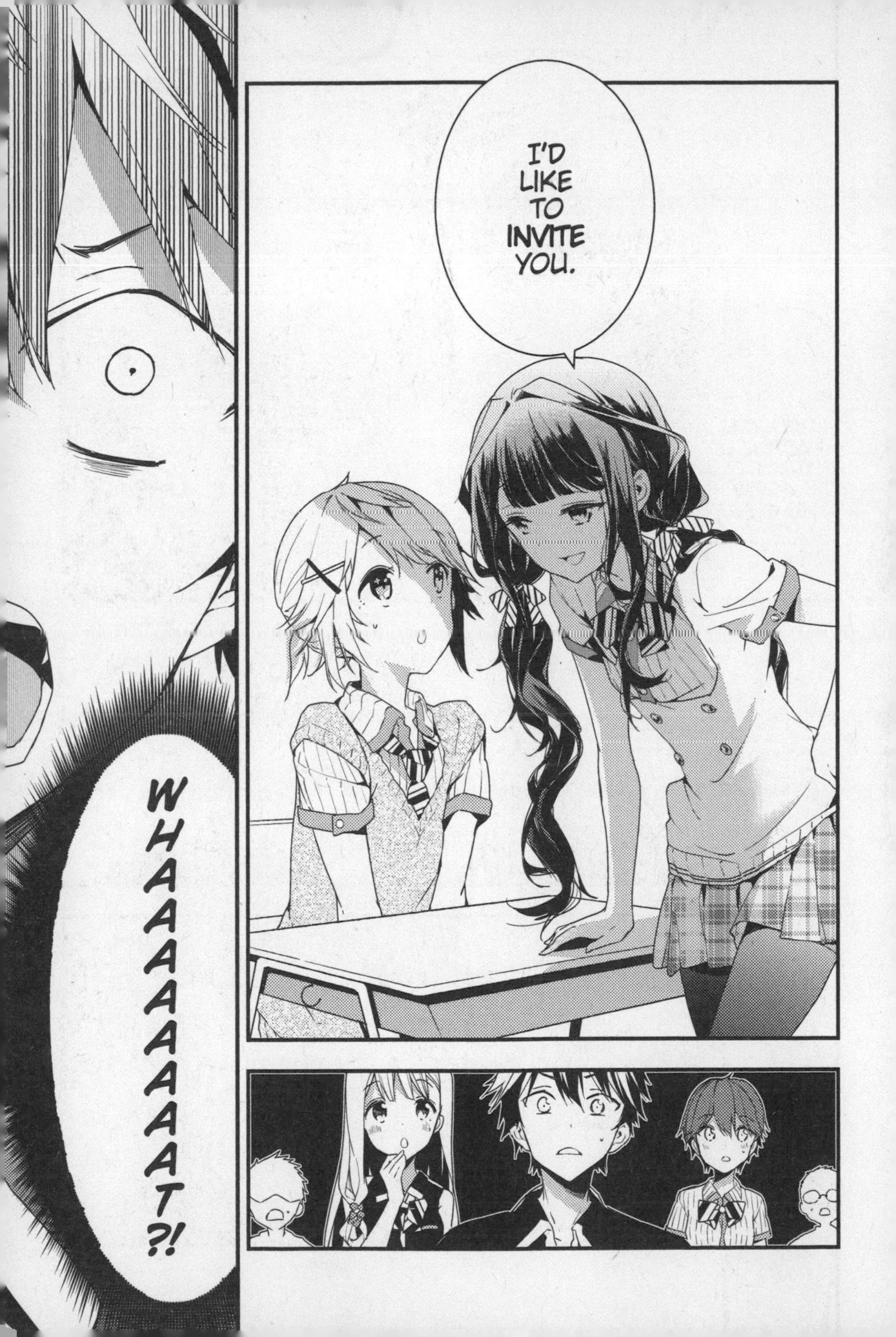
I'D LIKE TO INVITE YOU.
WHAAAAAAAAT?!

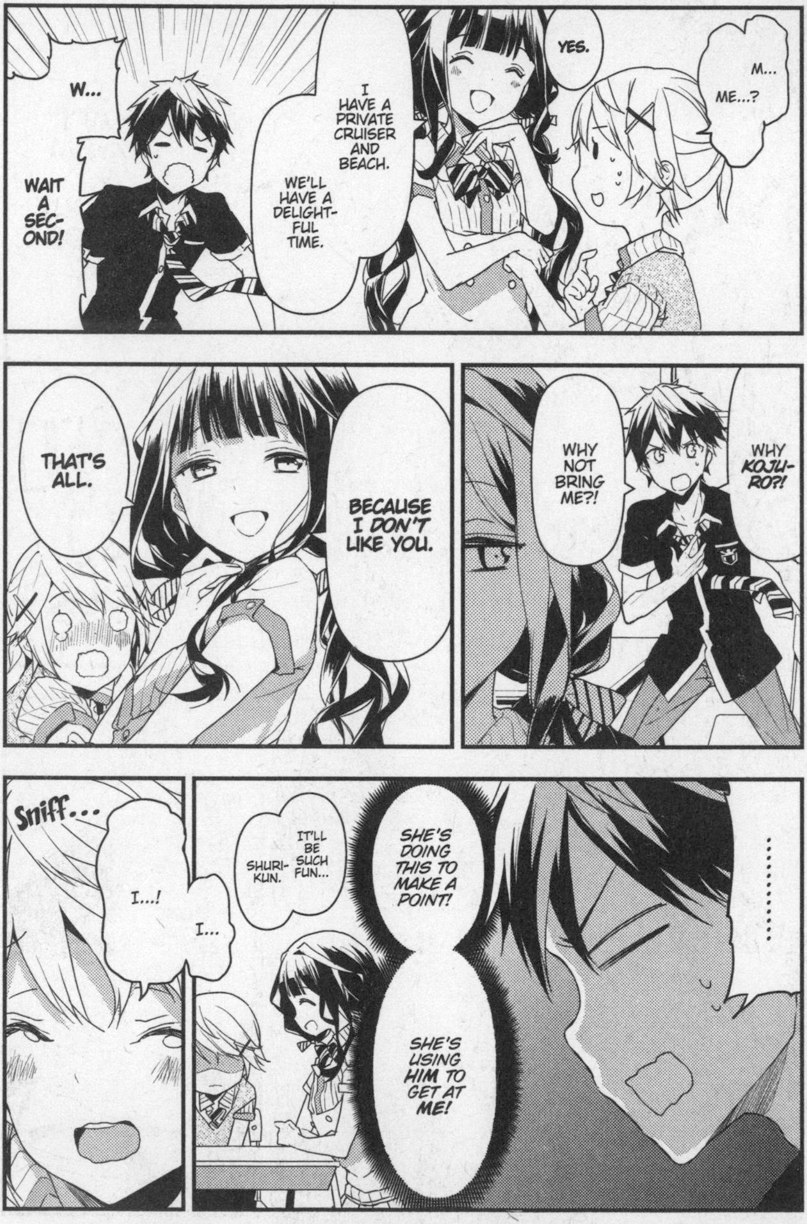
M... ME...?
YES.
I HAVE A PRIVATE CRUISER AND BEACH.
WE'LL HAVE A DELIGHTFUL TIME.
W...
WAIT A SECOND!
WHY KOJURO?!
WHY NOT BRING ME?!
BECAUSE I DON'T LIKE YOU.
THAT'S ALL.
......
SHE'S DOING THIS TO MAKE A POINT!
SHE'S USING HIM TO GET AT ME!
IT'LL BE SUCH FUN...
SHURI-KUN.
Sniff...
I...!
I...

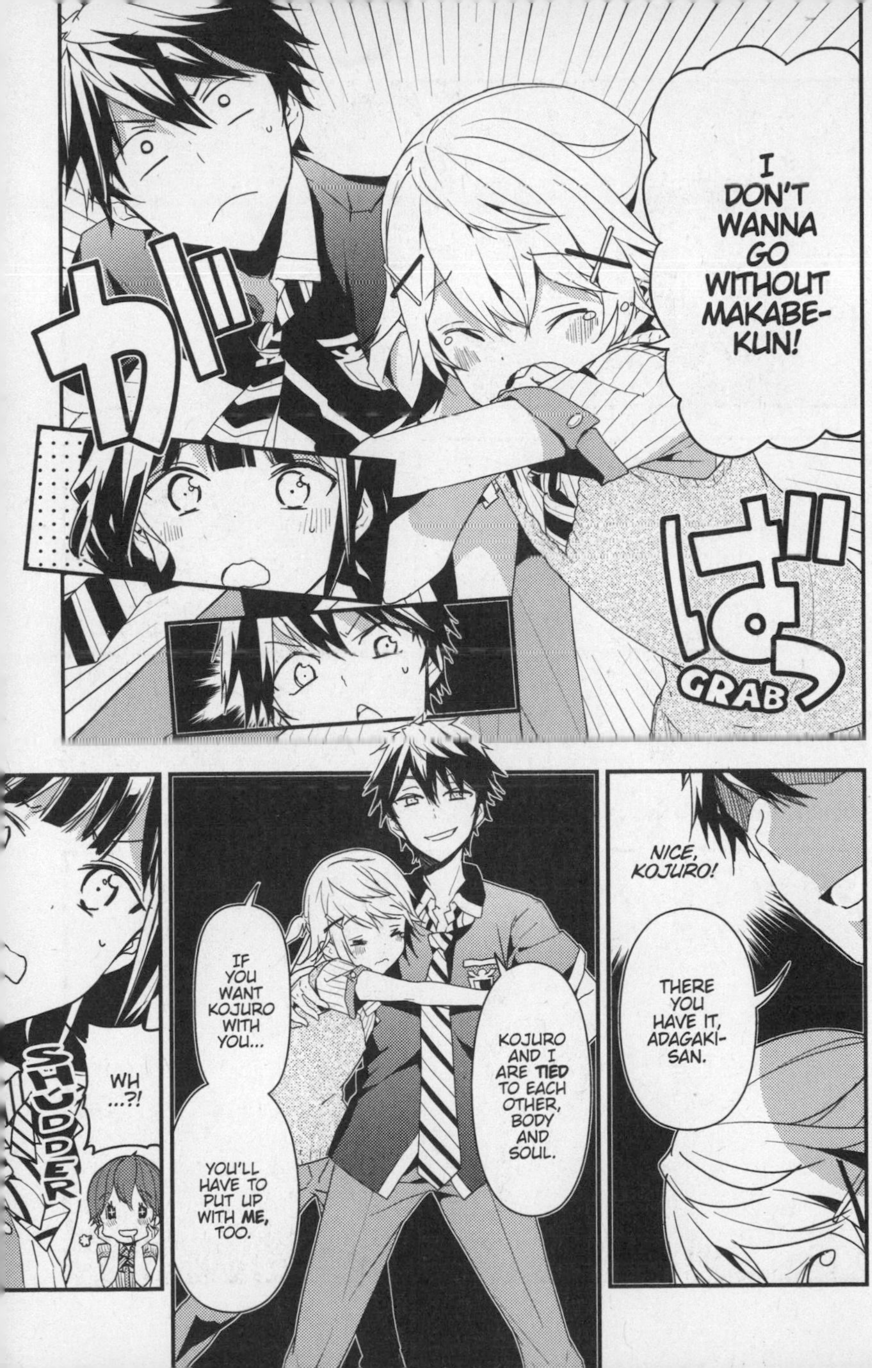
I DON'T WANNA GO WITHOUT MAKABE-KUN!
GRAB
NICE, KOJURO!
THERE YOU HAVE IT, ADAGAKI-SAN.
KOJURO AND I ARE **TIED** TO EACH OTHER, BODY AND SOUL.
IF YOU WANT KOJURO WITH YOU...
YOU'LL HAVE TO PUT UP WITH **ME**, TOO.
SHUDDER
WH...?!

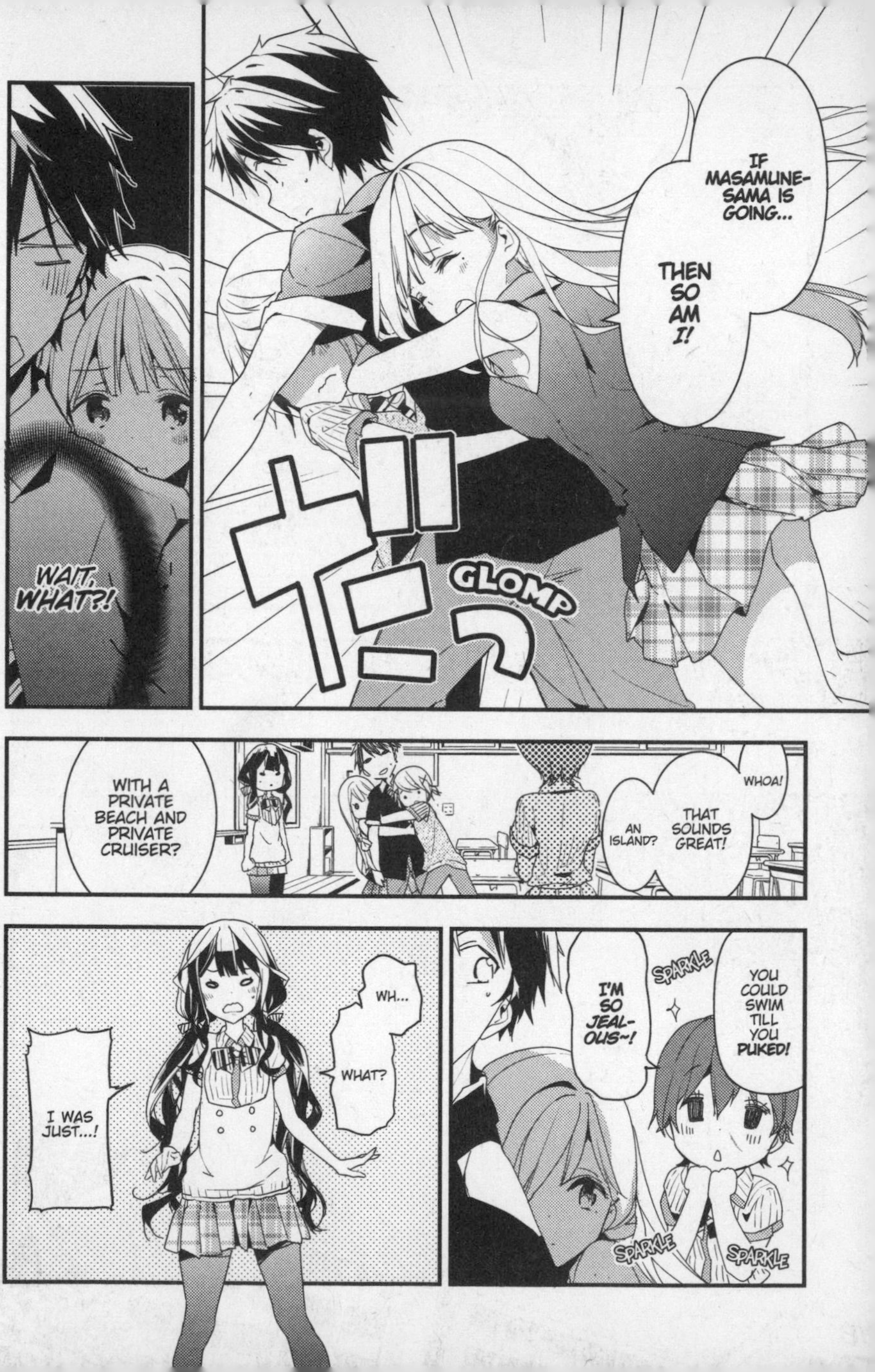
IF MASAMUNE-SAMA IS GOING...
THEN SO AM I!
GLOMP
WAIT, WHAT?!
WHOA!
THAT SOUNDS GREAT!
AN ISLAND?
WITH A PRIVATE BEACH AND PRIVATE CRUISER?
YOU COULD SWIM TILL YOU PUKED!
SPARKLE
I'M SO JEAL-OUS~!
SPARKLE
SPARKLE
WH...
WHAT?
I WAS JUST...!

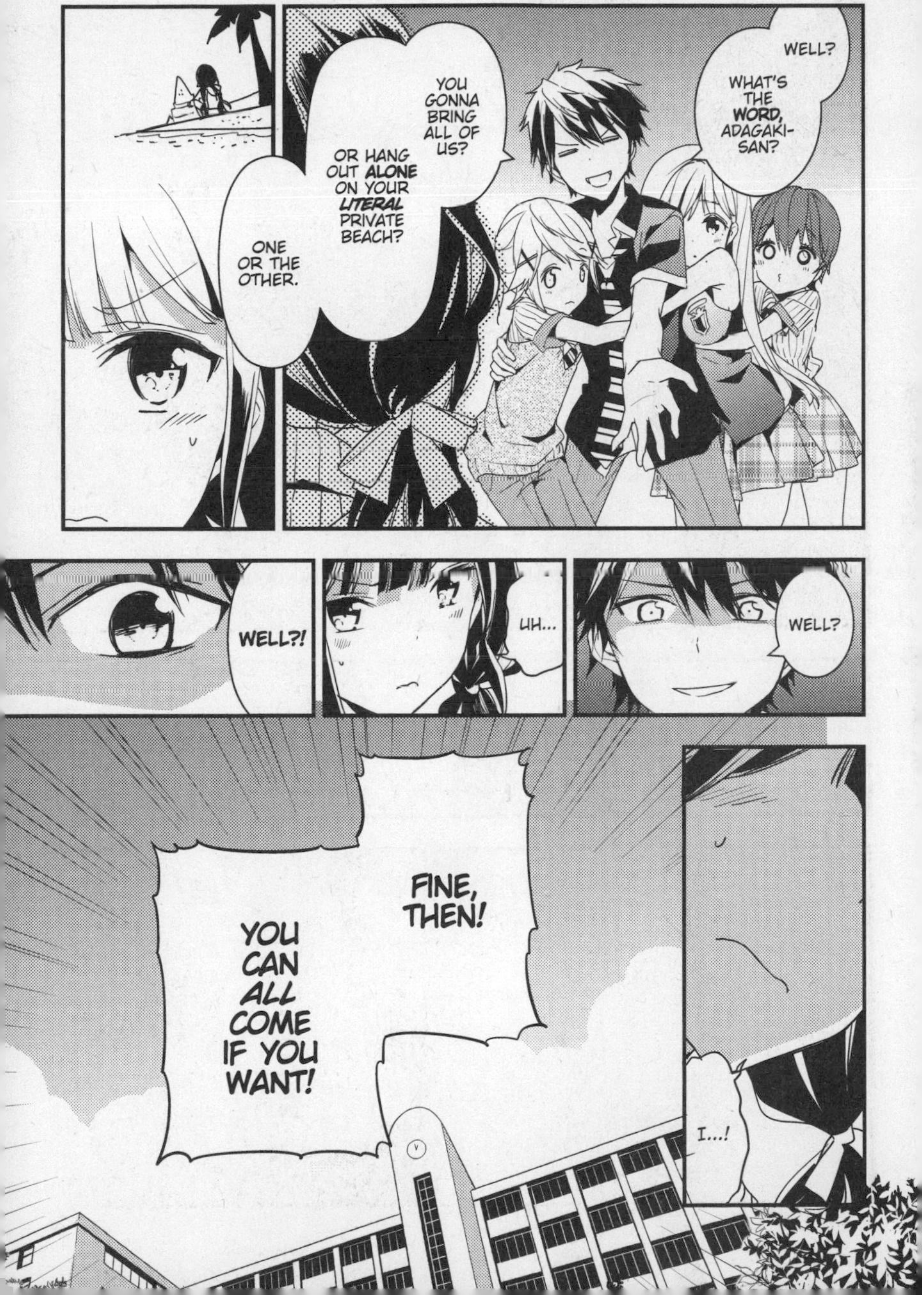
WELL?
WHAT'S THE WORD, ADAGAKI-SAN?
YOU GONNA BRING ALL OF US?
OR HANG OUT ALONE ON YOUR LITERAL PRIVATE BEACH?
ONE OR THE OTHER.
WELL?
UH...
WELL?!
I...!
FINE, THEN!
YOU CAN ALL COME IF YOU WANT!

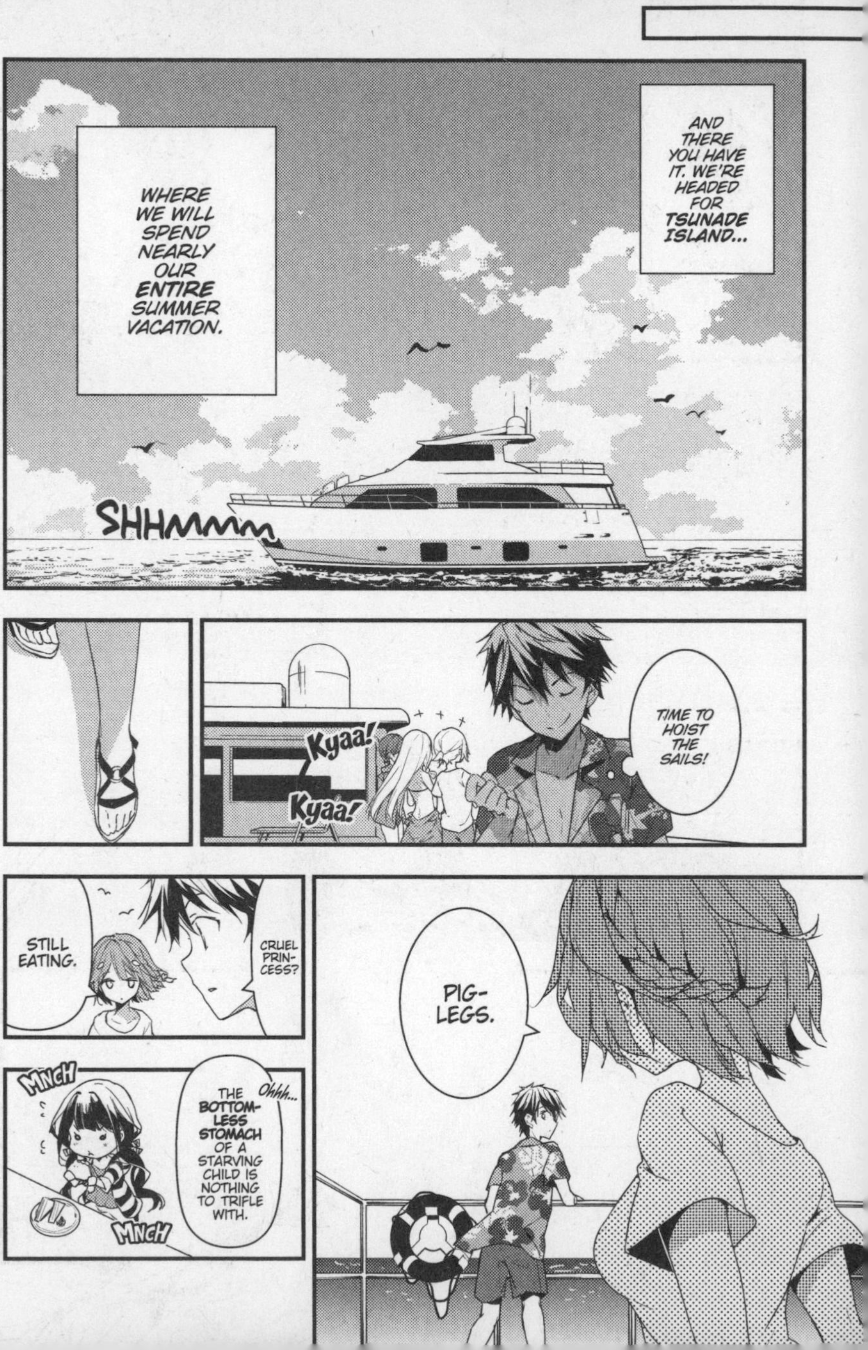
AND THERE YOU HAVE IT. WE'RE HEADED FOR TSUNADE ISLAND...
WHERE WE WILL SPEND NEARLY OUR ENTIRE SUMMER VACATION.
SHHMMM
TIME TO HOIST THE SAILS!
Kyaa!
Kyaa!
PIG-LEGS.
CRUEL PRIN-CESS?
STILL EATING.
Ohhh...
THE BOTTOM-LESS STOMACH OF A STARVING CHILD IS NOTHING TO TRIFLE WITH.
MNCH
MNCH

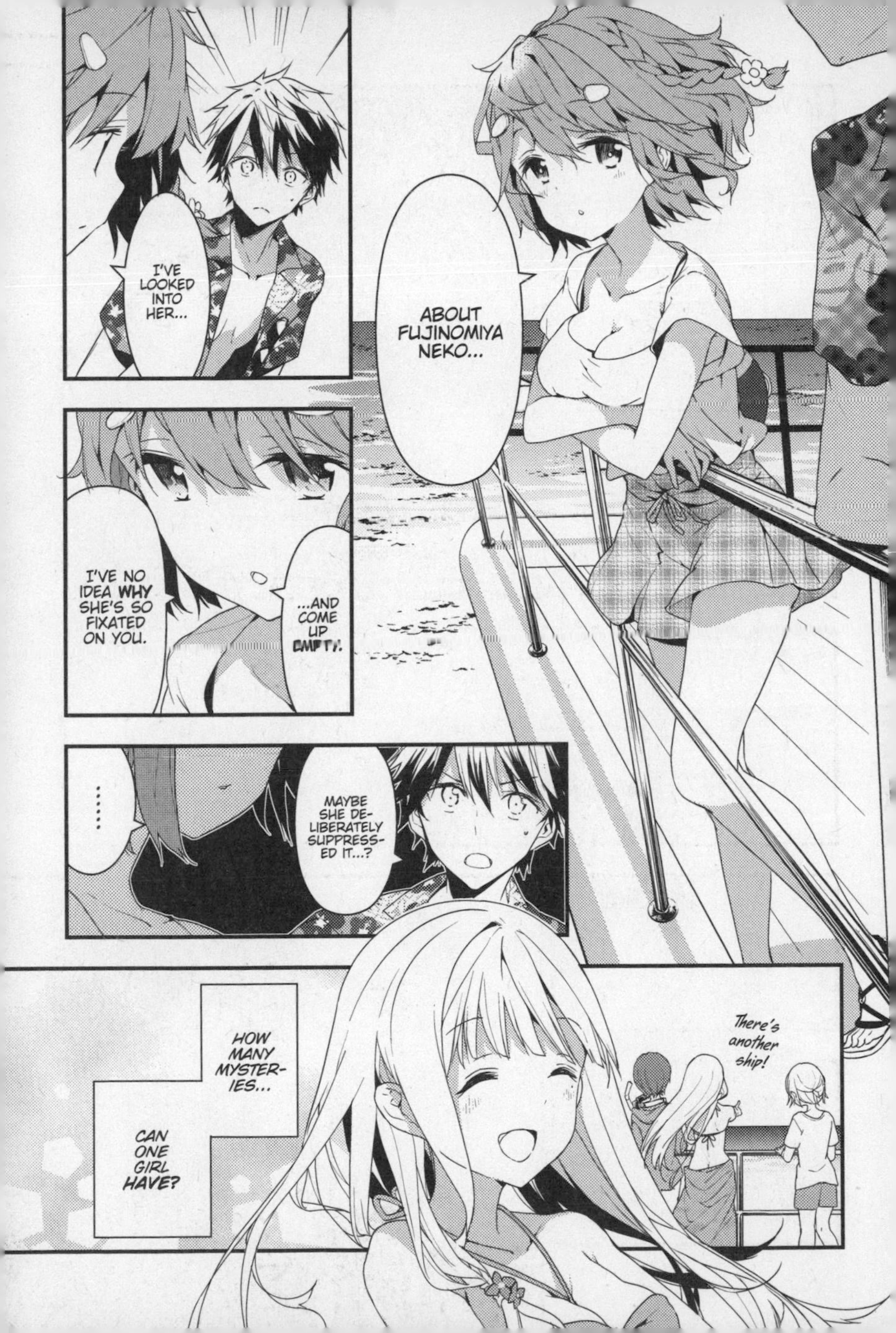
ABOUT FUJINOMIYA NEKO...
I'VE LOOKED INTO HER...
...AND COME UP EMPTY.
I'VE NO IDEA WHY SHE'S SO FIXATED ON YOU.
MAYBE SHE DE-LIBERATELY SUPPRESS-ED IT...?
......
There's another ship!
HOW MANY MYSTER-IES...
CAN ONE GIRL HAVE?

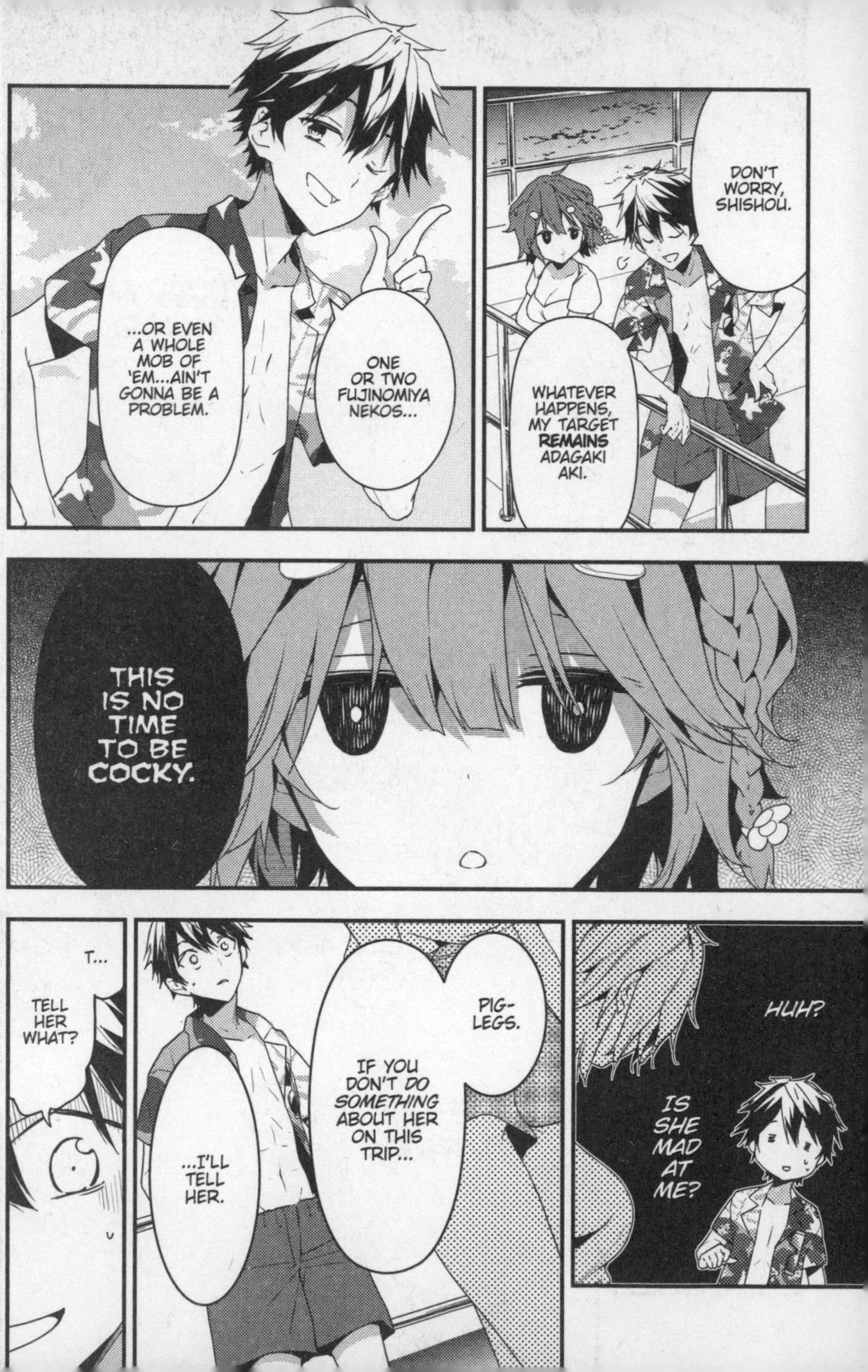
DON'T WORRY, SHISHOU.
WHATEVER HAPPENS, MY TARGET **REMAINS** ADAGAKI AKI.
ONE OR TWO FUJINOMIYA NEKOS...
...OR EVEN A WHOLE MOB OF 'EM...AIN'T GONNA BE A PROBLEM.
THIS IS NO TIME TO BE COCKY.
HUH?
IS SHE MAD AT ME?
PIG-LEGS.
IF YOU DON'T *DO SOMETHING* ABOUT HER ON THIS TRIP...
...I'LL TELL HER.
T...
TELL HER WHAT?

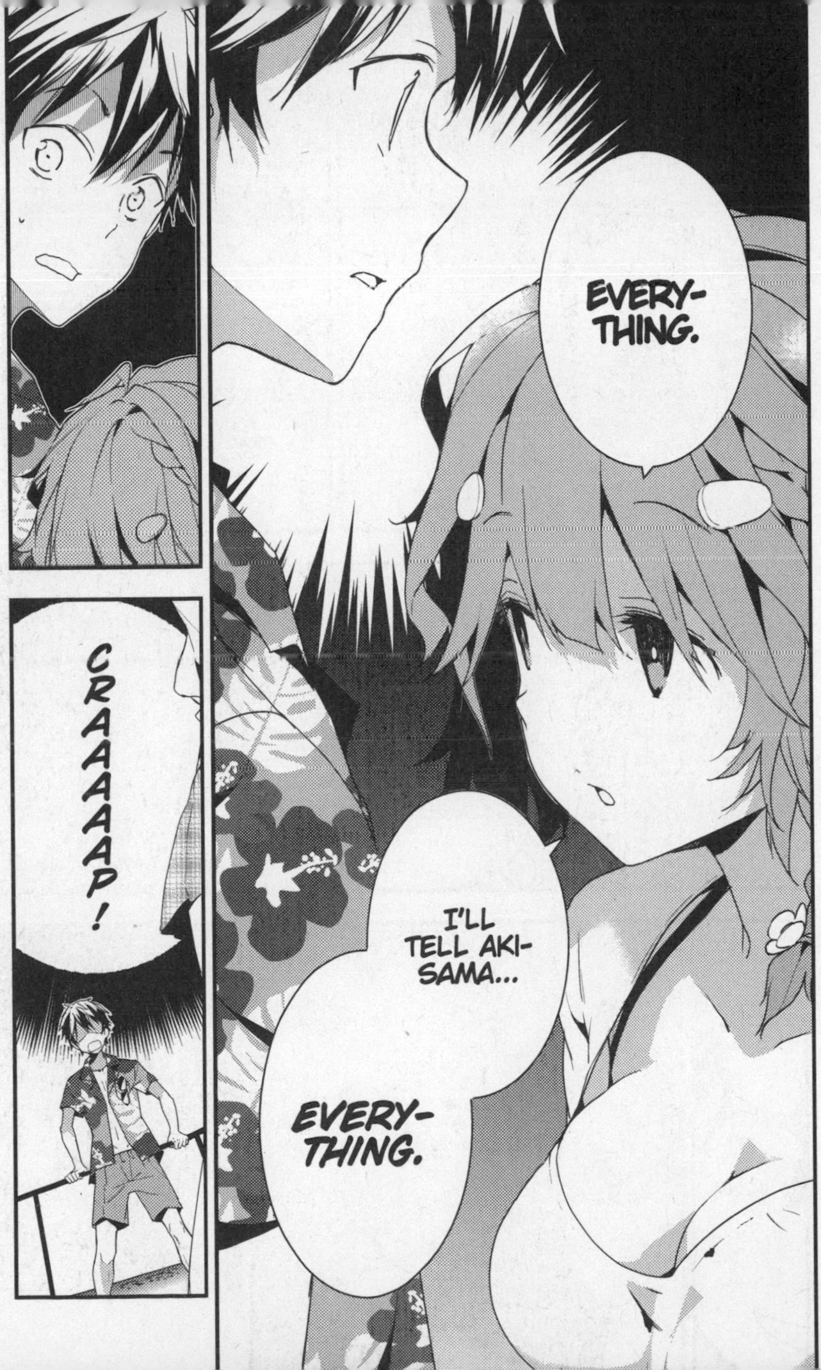
EVERY-THING.
I'LL TELL AKI-SAMA...
EVERY-THING.
CRAAAAAP!

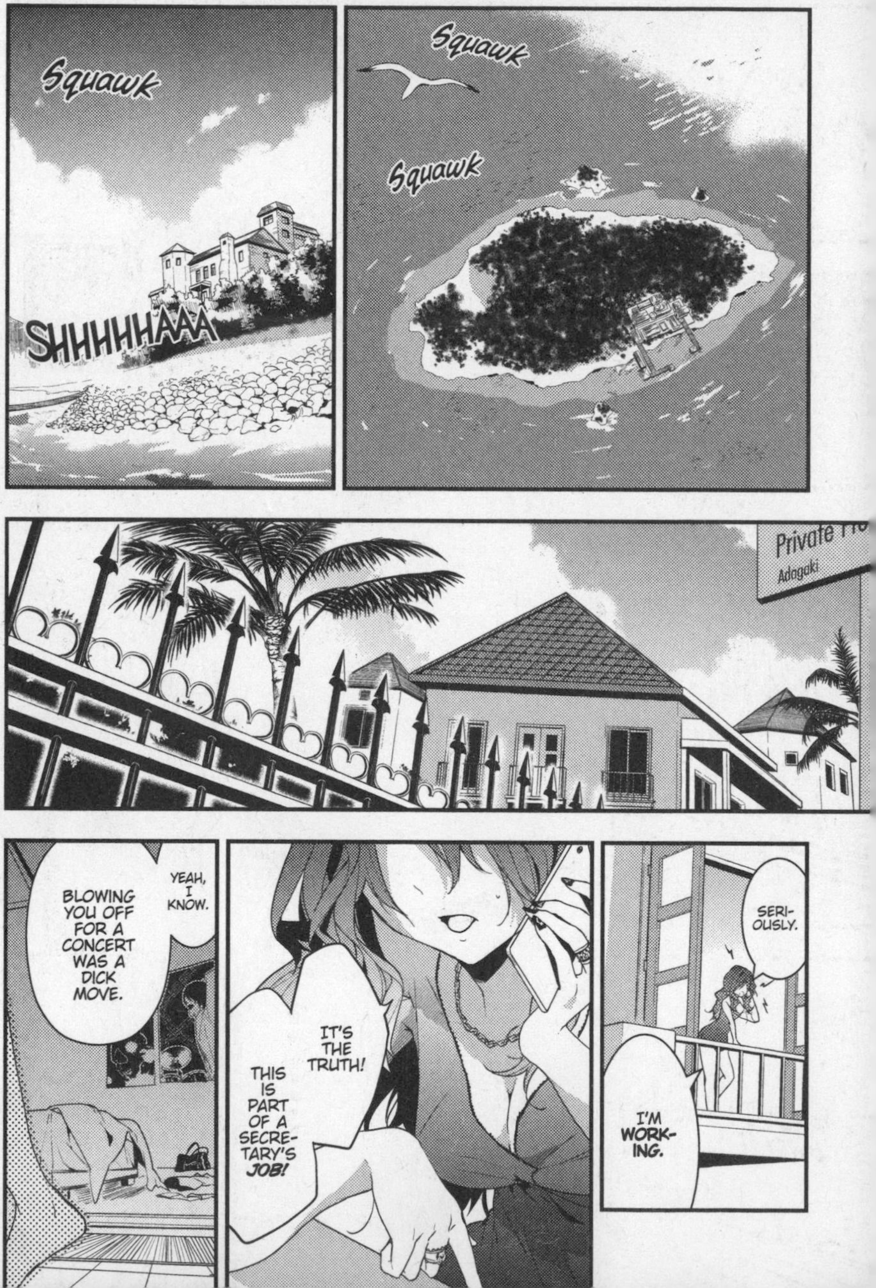
Squawk
Squawk
Squawk
SHHHHHAAA
Private
Adagaki
SERIOUSLY.
I'M WORKING.
IT'S THE TRUTH!
THIS IS PART OF A SECRETARY'S **JOB!**
YEAH, I KNOW.
BLOWING YOU OFF FOR A CONCERT WAS A DICK MOVE.

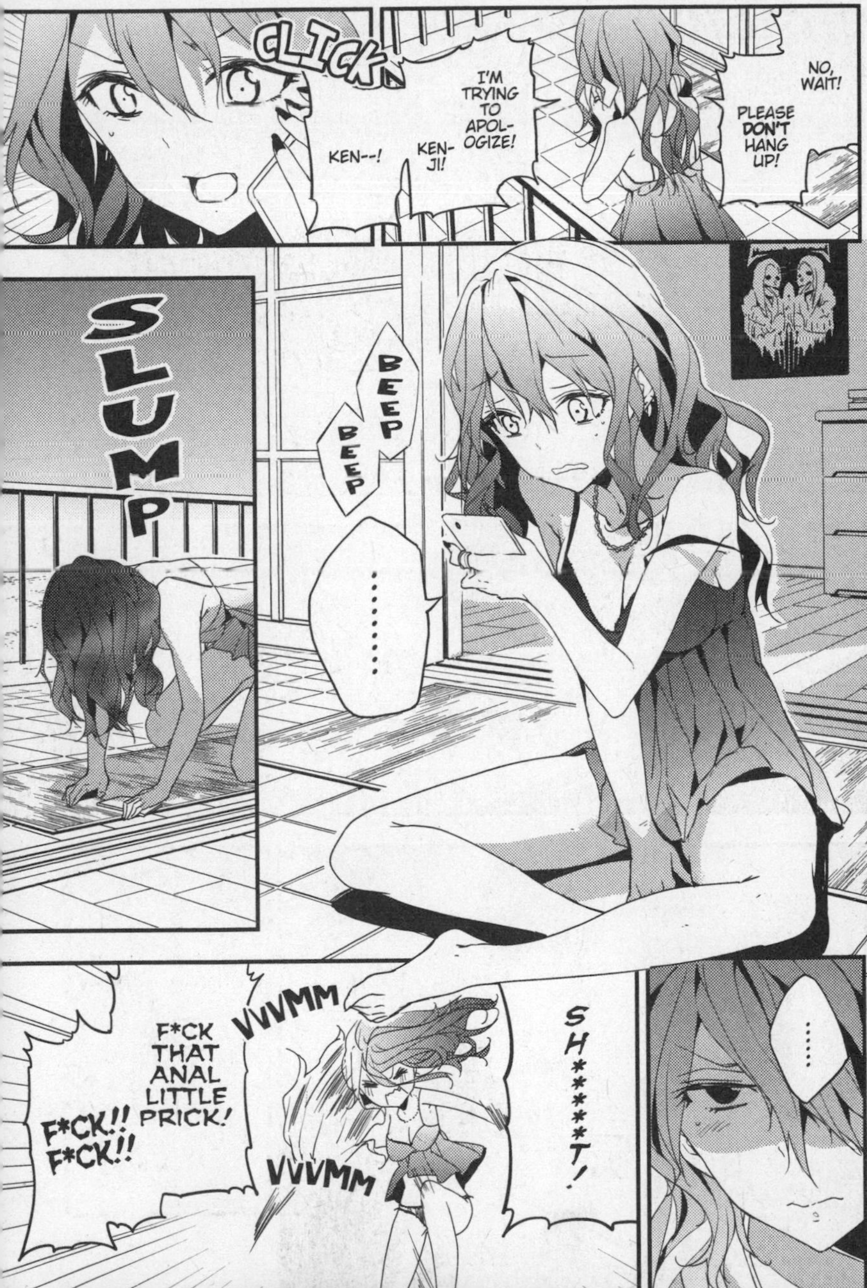
NO, WAIT!
PLEASE DON'T HANG UP!
I'M TRYING TO APOLOGIZE!
KEN-JI!
CLICK
KEN--!
BEEP BEEP
......
SLUMP
......
SH*****T!
VVVMM
F*CK THAT ANAL LITTLE PRICK!
VVVMM
F*CK!! F*CK!!

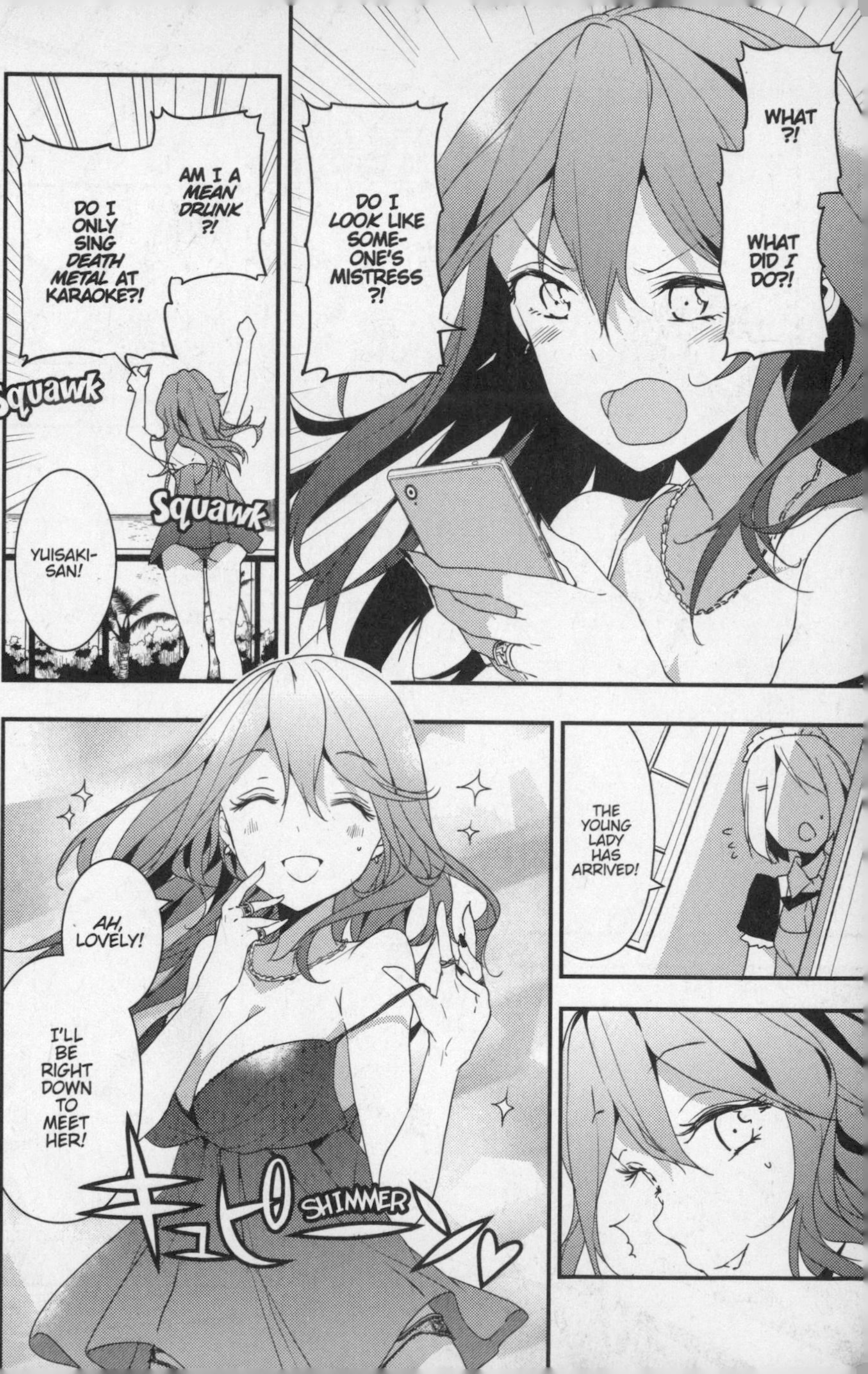
WHAT?!
WHAT DID I DO?!
DO I LOOK LIKE SOME-ONE'S MISTRESS?!
AM I A MEAN DRUNK?!
DO I ONLY SING DEATH METAL AT KARAOKE?!
Squawk
Squawk
YUISAKI-SAN!
THE YOUNG LADY HAS ARRIVED!
AH, LOVELY!
I'LL BE RIGHT DOWN TO MEET HER!
SHIMMER

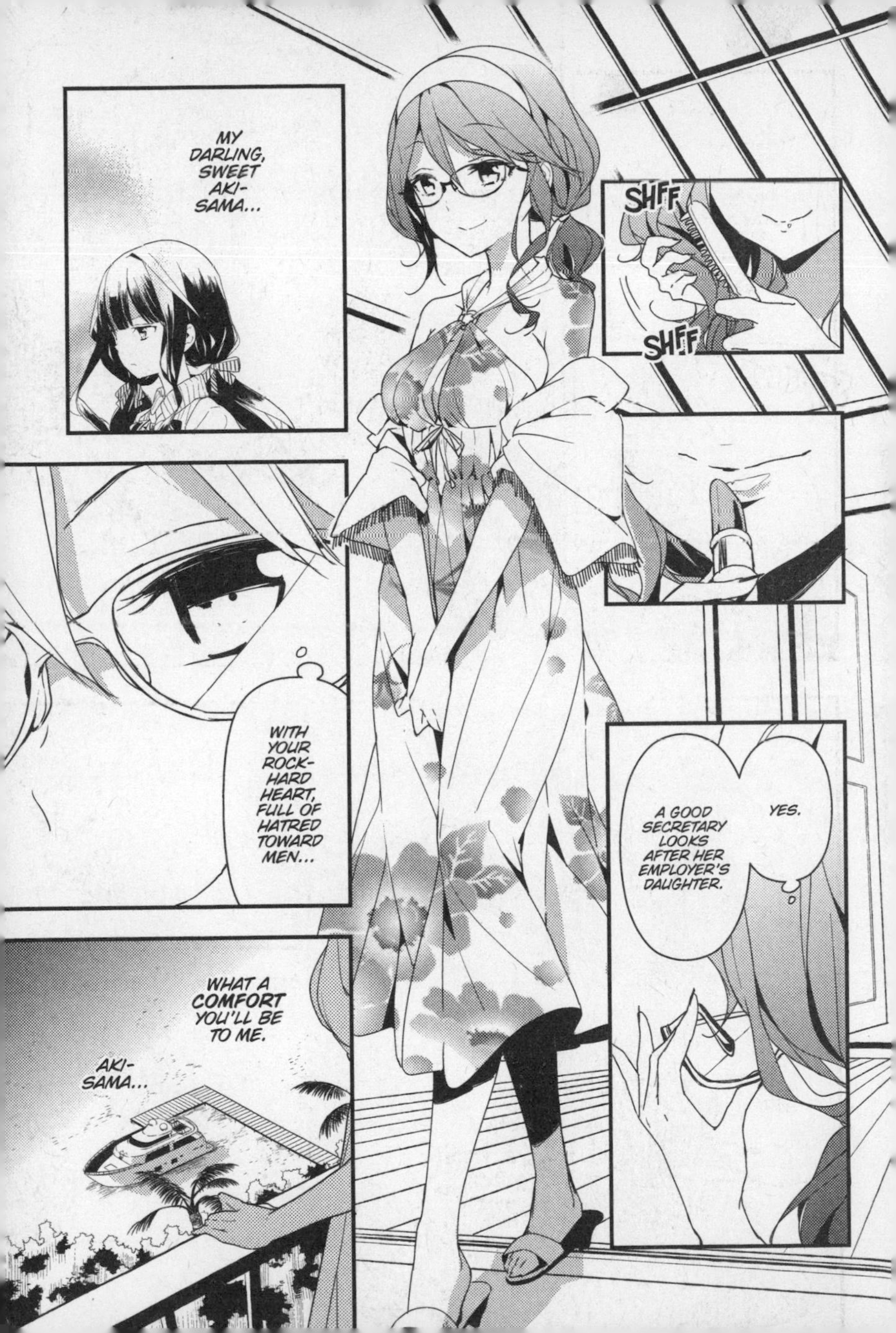
SHFF
SHFF
YES.
A GOOD SECRETARY LOOKS AFTER HER EMPLOYER'S DAUGHTER.
MY DARLING, SWEET AKI-SAMA...
WITH YOUR ROCK-HARD HEART, FULL OF HATRED TOWARD MEN...
WHAT A COMFORT YOU'LL BE TO ME.
AKI-SAMA...

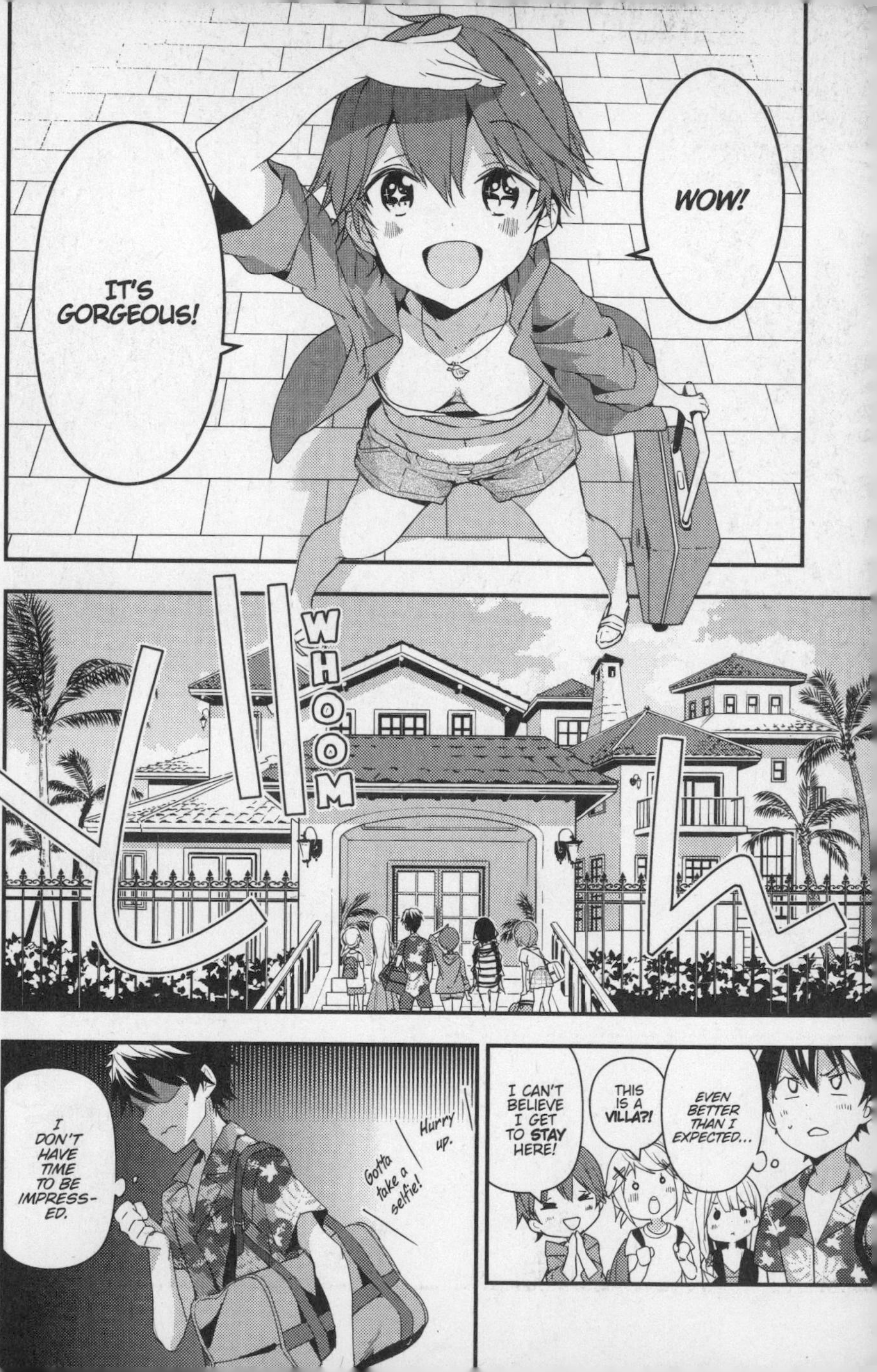
WOW!
IT'S GORGEOUS!
WHOOM
EVEN BETTER THAN I EXPECTED...
THIS IS A VILLA?!
I CAN'T BELIEVE I GET TO STAY HERE!
Hurry up.
Gotta take a selfie!
I DON'T HAVE TIME TO BE IMPRESSED.

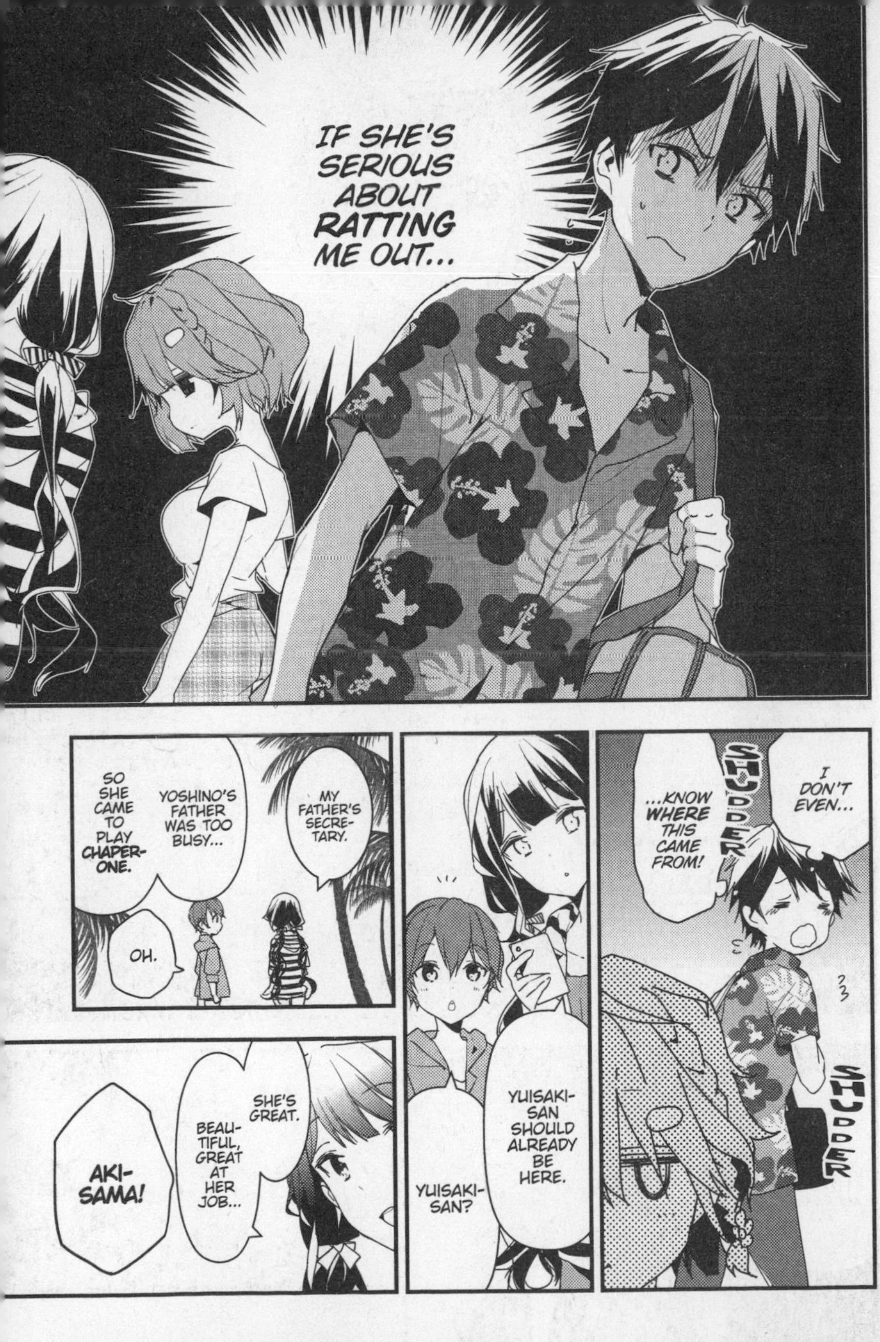
IF SHE'S SERIOUS ABOUT RATTING ME OUT...
I DON'T EVEN...
SHUDDER
...KNOW WHERE THIS CAME FROM!
SHUDDER
YUISAKI-SAN SHOULD ALREADY BE HERE.
YUISAKI-SAN?
MY FATHER'S SECRE-TARY.
YOSHINO'S FATHER WAS TOO BUSY...
SO SHE CAME TO PLAY CHAPER-ONE.
OH.
SHE'S GREAT.
BEAU-TIFUL, GREAT AT HER JOB...
AKI-SAMA!

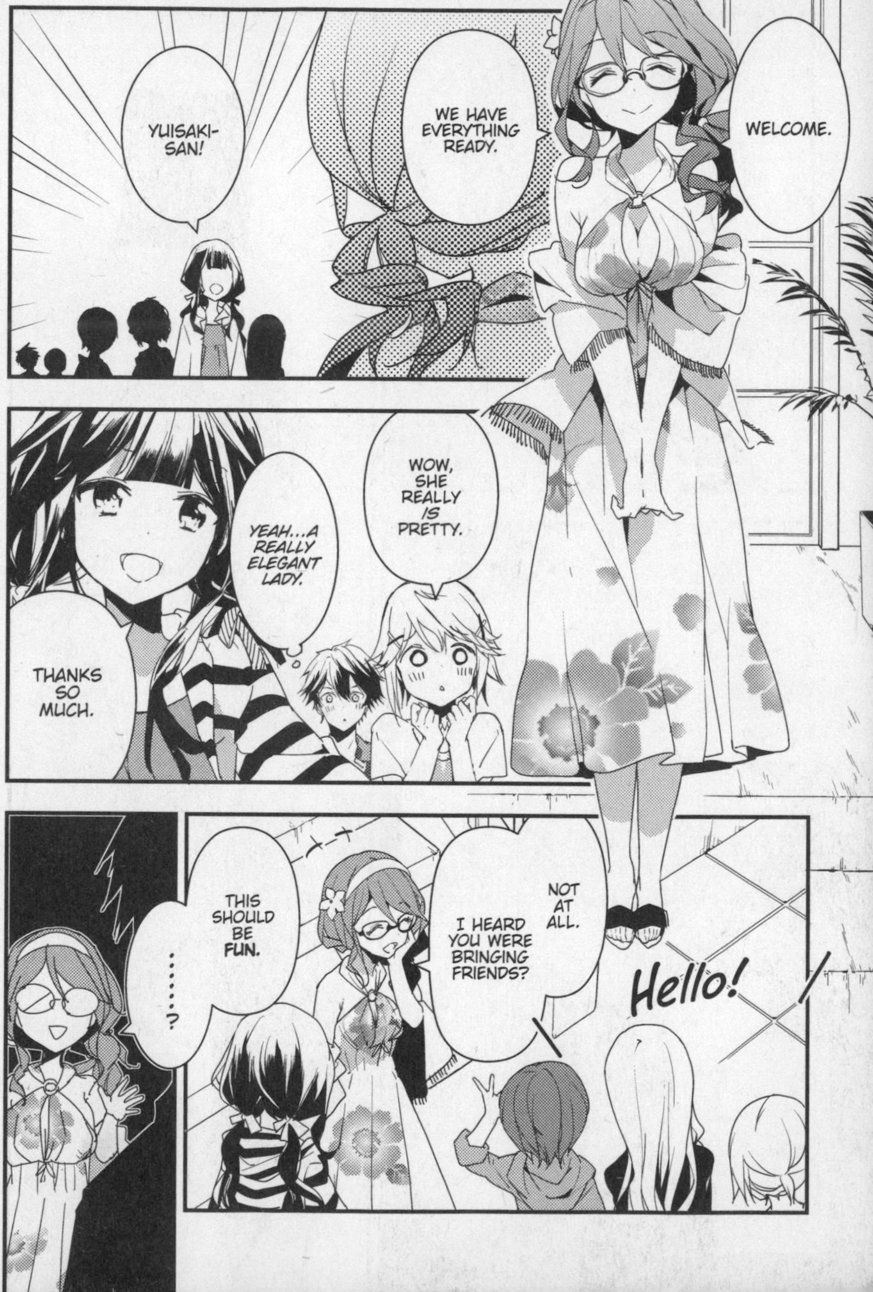
WELCOME.
WE HAVE EVERYTHING READY.
YUISAKI-SAN!
WOW, SHE REALLY IS PRETTY.
YEAH...A REALLY ELEGANT LADY.
THANKS SO MUCH.
Hello!
NOT AT ALL.
I HEARD YOU WERE BRINGING FRIENDS?
THIS SHOULD BE FUN.
......?

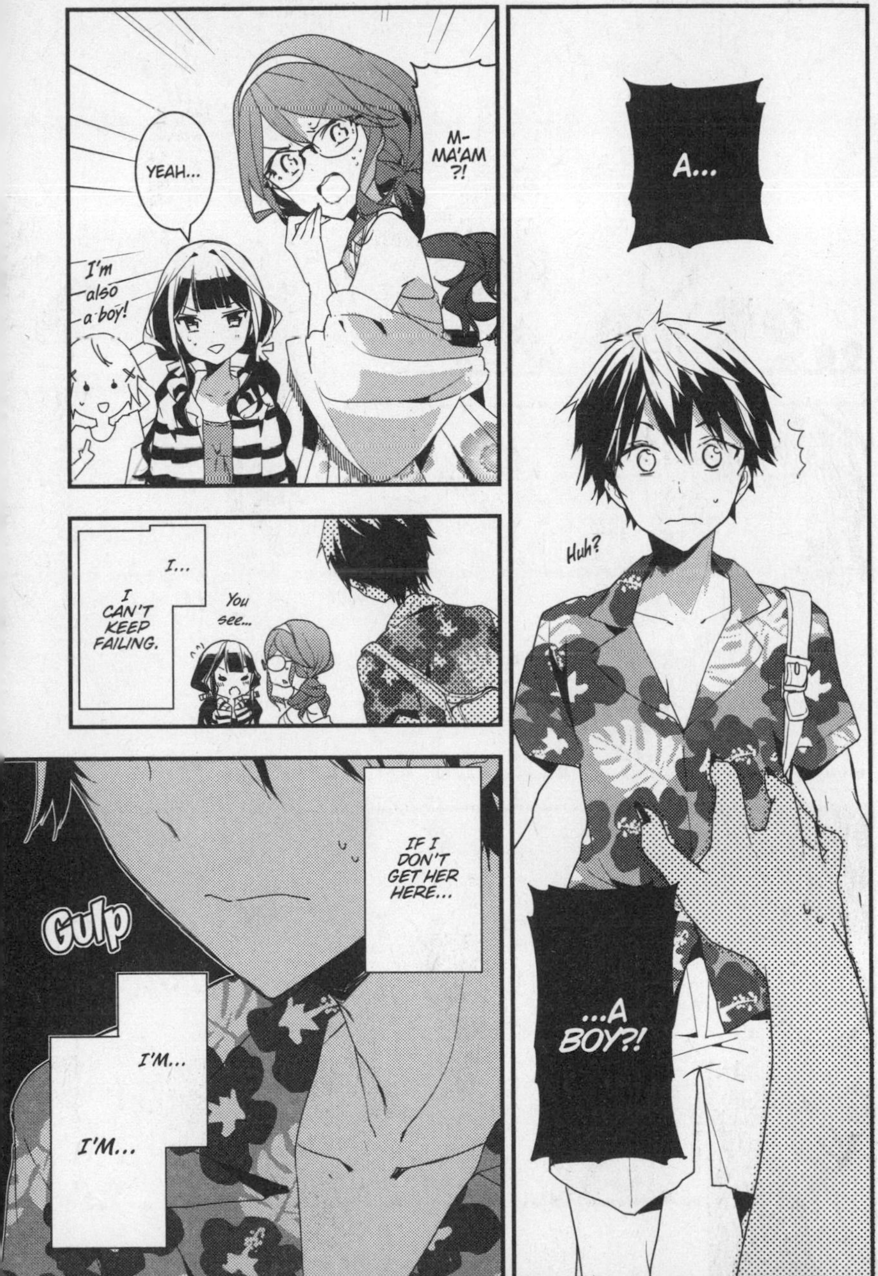
A...
Huh?
...A BOY?!
M-MA'AM?!
YEAH...
I'm also a boy!
You see...
I...
I CAN'T KEEP FAILING.
IF I DON'T GET HER HERE...
Gulp
I'M...
I'M...

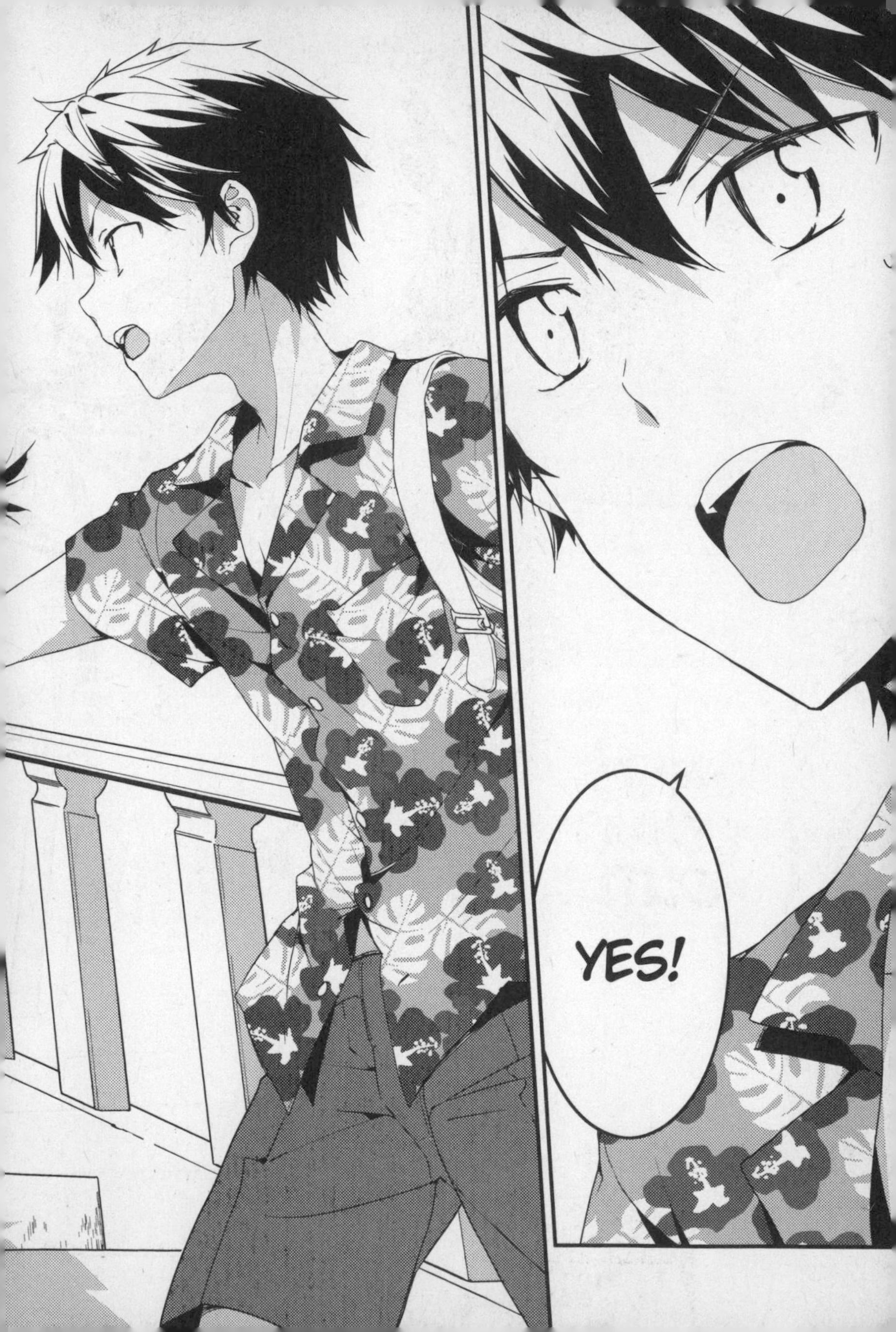
YES!

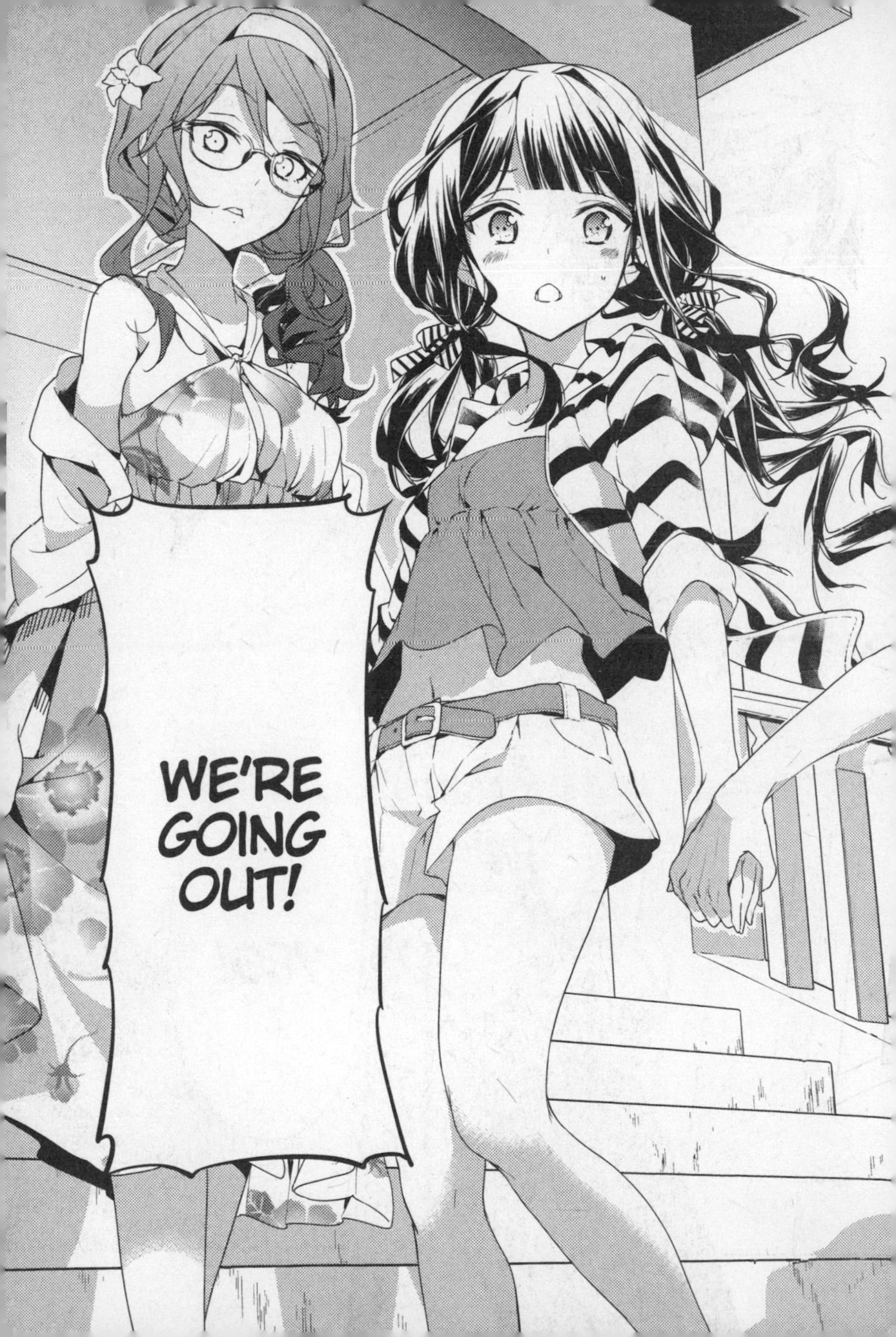
WE'RE GOING OUT!

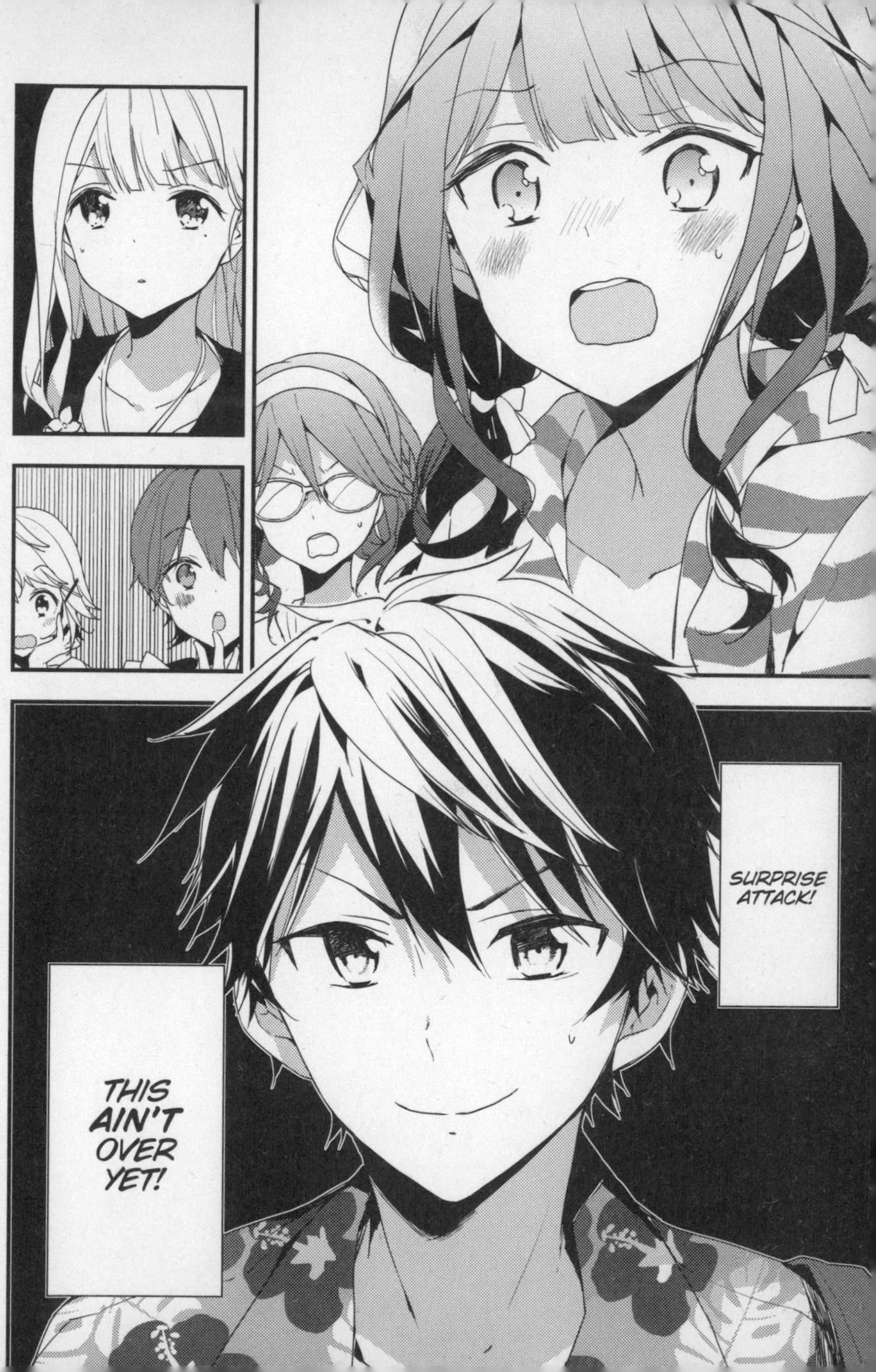
SURPRISE ATTACK!
THIS AIN'T OVER YET!